Empty Figure on an Empty Stage

Drama and Performance Studies
Timothy Wiles, general editor
Volume 13 in series

EMPTY FIGURE

on an

EMPTY STAGE

The Theatre of Samuel Beckett and His Generation

Les Essif

INDIANA UNIVERSITY PRESS   BLOOMINGTON & INDIANAPOLIS

This book is a publication of

Indiana University Press
601 North Morton Street
Bloomington, IN 47404-3797 USA

HTTP://IUPRESS.INDIANA.EDU

Telephone orders   800-842-6796
Fax orders   812-855-7931
Orders by e-mail   IUORDER@INDIANA.EDU

The paper used in this publication meets the minimum
requirements of American National Standard for Information
Sciences—Permanence of Paper for Printed Library
Materials, ANSI Z39.48-1984.

Manufactured in the United States of America

Library of Congress Cataloging-in-Publication Data
Essif, Les.
Empty figure on an empty stage : the theatre of Samuel Beckett
and his generation / Les Essif.
p.   cm. — (Drama and performance studies ; v. 13)
Includes bibliographical references and index.
ISBN 0-253-33847-6 (cl : alk. paper)
1. European drama—20th century—History and criticism. 2. Beckett, Samuel,
1906—Criticism and interpretation.   I. Title.   II. Series.

PN1861 .E77 2001
809.2'911—DC21   00-063211

1   2   3   4   5   06   05   04   03   02   01

FOR MOM, DOROTHY MARIE.

A devoted dreamer, a mother with a mission,
you always knew your five sons would go to college.
Thanks to you, we knew it too.

CONTENTS

ACKNOWLEDGMENTS

Many colleagues and friends have contributed in various ways to the production of this book. I thank the following colleagues for offering valuable advice on portions of the manuscript: Charles Stivale of Wayne State University, Judith Miller of New York University, Alan Leidner of the University of Louisville, Stanton Garner Jr., John Romeiser, and Sal DiMaria of the University of Tennessee.

I would also like to thank my former teachers. At the University of Paris (Institut d'Etudes Théâtrales), Michel Corvin's seminar on the "theatricality" of the dramatic text planted the seed for this project. The contributions of my other teachers at the Institute, especially Patrice Pavis, speak for themselves throughout the following pages. My thanks to Kirsten Nigro, formerly of the University of Arizona, for introducing me to the beauty of the practice of theatre, and to John Gesell at the University of Arizona, my Paris theatre partner.

A special thanks to my longtime friend, Mick Cerra. His feel for the oneness of the universe and his thoughtful gifts of books on oriental philosophies have impacted my world view.

Thanks to Ellen T. M. Craig and Marie Taylor of the Edward Gordon Craig Estate for their kind permission to reproduce the illustration of Craig's Übermarionette, and to Paul Draper and Michael Daniel for generously providing photos from the Draper productions. I thank Paule Tourniac (the Bibliothèque nationale de France, Dept. des Arts du Spectacle), Jonathan Kalb, and William E. Gruber for help in locating sources for several of the photo illustrations.

Given her multifaceted support and companionship, and her unique intellectual abilities, my wife Debbie deserves much credit. The precious bonds of endearment and intimacy we share with our daughter, Davenne, and our son, Amien, help place this book and my life into perspective.

Portions of chapters 1 and 2 have previously appeared in "Twentieth-Century Surrealism and the Theatrical Psychic Space of French Nouveau Théâtre," *Essays in Theatre* 12.2 (May 1994): 157–68, and in "Introducing the 'Hyper' Theatrical Subject: The *Mise en Abyme* of Empty Space," *Journal of Dramatic Theory and Criticism* 9.1 (Fall 1994): 67–87. A preliminary version of chapter 3 has appeared in *Essays in Theatre* 17.1 (November 1998): 15–32. Portions of the fifth section of chapter 4 have previously appeared in "Antisocial Empty Space and the Message of Death in French Nouveau Théâtre," *Cincinnati Romance Review* 12 (1993): 85–92.

An important part of the research for this book was made possible thanks to the Professional Development Award program at the University of Tennessee, Knoxville. Financial assistance was also provided by the University's SARIF Fund.

Empty Figure on an Empty Stage

Imagine a lone individual on a stage in any circumstance—a play, a keynote speaker addressing an audience. Remove the podium and any other furniture from the space and imagine that the stage is empty but for the human figure. Focus the light and dilute the stage into darkness in order to increase the volume of emptiness into which the human figure is set. Focus the light progressively on the head of the lone figure. The result is a highly meaningful, metaphysical image. It is readily apparent that the body of the individual figure gains significance because of the clarity of focus; it is perhaps less apparent that the empty space surrounding the figure becomes more significant, more meaningful. We tend to overlook the reawakening of our consciousness with respect to emptiness. Samuel Beckett, however, devoted the latter part of his artistic career to exploring and refining the material meaningfulness of the human figure set in emptiness.

Artists working in all types of media have been aware of the use of empty space as a strategy for meaningful expression, or, more precisely, a strategy to resensitize and complexify artistic reception. Emptiness shows up in every artform conceivable; it is always a major force to contend with, one which never can be fully hidden or disguised—or understood. Painters and sculptors have produced works in which emptiness and darkness dominate, often highlighting an individual who is isolated within an empty frame. We find the musical equivalent of the lone figure in a field of emptiness in the single note backgrounded by and emerging out of silence. Poets, painters, and composers are frequently sensitive enough to acknowledge the metaphysical background for our existence. Empty, dark areas in painting as well as protracted silences in musical compositions relate analogically and iconically to essential emptiness, whether in the form of the infinite universe or the state of non-life, two introspective reflections which engulf the temporary, delimited fullness of life. We tend to miss the point that the emptiness surrounding the figure—and our lives—determines our perception of the figure itself.

Emptiness and isolation are important to the history of Western drama. Tragic monologues of Oedipus, Hamlet, Phaedre, and Lorenzaccio have taken place on relatively empty stages. Both the classical stages of Antiquity and the neoclassical stages of the seventeenth, eighteenth, and nineteenth centuries were rather unfurnished compared to most of the post-romantic and naturalistic spaces of the nineteenth and early twentieth centuries. With the movements of romanticism, symbolism, expressionism, and futurism, the inner world of a single human consciousness tends to open up to the imaginations of dramatists and the isolated individual becomes a predominant form in these types of theatre, an approach to meaning and to in-sight. Present already in the written text, it becomes the focal point of the scenic tableau.

Not until the postwar theatre of France, however, do we have examples of theatrical art in which the lone figure in empty space becomes the primary end of the work. Unlike the bulk of their predecessors, the protagonists of Beckett's dramatic corpus are more solitary and, like the stage space they occupy, more empty. They represent extreme, reductive cases of the dramatic figure as a metaphysical, metatheatrical, human icon; they convey a sense of personal emptiness that reflects and coincides with the emptiness of the stage space, becoming an empty space in their own right, a metatheatrical space within a theatrical space, which is arguably the most disturbing and theatrically effective stage image of all time. To date, busy with the psychological and psychoanalytic nature of the theatrical space and character, scholars have paid little attention to the aesthetic force and the implications of this complex image of emptiness. They know, of course, that Beckett's plays will survive the test of time and become the classics of the new century. Since the voided, unconsummated arrival of Godot in the early 1950s, they have praised the timely, absurd originality of Beckett's works in terms of their radical rejection of naturalism in all its guises, whether on the level of character, place, action, situation, or language.

Scholars have written about the subversion of the formulaic and structural dimensions of Beckett's text, such as the illogic of the language, the story, and the action. Critics and scholars have written extensively on the "new" dramatic characters and the "new," unconventional or unnatural settings and situations in which they are placed. Nevertheless, in some part due to a general inability to depart wholly from an historical dependency on written text, they have paid vastly more attention to the "new" language, variously exposed as anti-language, metalanguage, or metatheatrical language. After all, the language of the characters is largely responsible for the construction of who they are and what they are about, i.e., their "new" situations. But, in the theatre, especially in Beckett's theatre, we must increase our attention to the contrasting view that the image and situation could be responsible for our reception of the language. In fact, due to the perhaps overly focused attention on the more or less narrative functions of language (or lack thereof), critics have not sufficiently pursued one particular aspect of the dramatic character, namely, the textual design of the character as a corporeal presence and visual image on the stage. A focused study of stage directions as well as spoken text tells us that there is something about the material image of the character, its *formal* presentation as corporeal spectacle, which theatre scholars have not adequately broached from either a theatrical, formal, or spatial point of view.

Dramatists had always been inspired to find scenic solutions to express the sentiments of the spiritual world; but Beckett and other dramatists of the nouveau théâtre[1] of the fifties, sixties, and seventies truly awakened to the importance of emptiness at the background of everyday reality as well as its link to theatrical art by way of the human icon. The material, physical presentation of theatre was at the crossroads of the inner world and the outer illusion, the visible and the invisible, reality and surreality, the physical and the metaphysical, human spirit and social convention. To be sure, the theatrical forms of Shakespeare and Racine opened to an invisible, inner depth of reality; but inner emptiness was expressed more for psychological than for metaphysical and metatheatrical purposes. This is, of course, why Artaud's formula for the revival of theatre included "no more masterpieces." Racine and Shakespeare were primarily interested in a primitive, archetypal psychology of man. In matters of structuring a human image of emptiness that duplicates the stage space, Beckett does it better. He goes directly to the source without the distraction of psychological or narrative coloring. Like Shakespeare's Hamlet, Beckett's Hamm (*Endgame*) represents more than an empty, solitary visual stage image. However, Beckett discovered a fascinating way to articulate the power of that image alone. Hamm is more metadramatic than Hamlet because Beckett introduced a dramaturgical process to align his stage presence with the power of the emptiness of the stage.

In this book I intend to show how we can view Beckett's dramatic corpus as a quest to render the complexity of the solitary human figure set in empty space. *Godot* goes a long way toward showing the power of the empty stage. The work differs from naturalist stage presentations primarily because it forces us to view the characters as figures that move around and within emptiness. In *Endgame,* we begin to see in Hamm's centrality the ostension, the showing, of an "empty" human icon set in empty space. By the end of his career, Beckett produced *Rockaby*, a play in which, to quote Enoch Brater, "Much is made out of almost nothing." For an intense fifteen minutes, spectators view an aging woman entrenched in a rocking chair on an otherwise empty stage. They hear fragmented utterances from a recorded voice. The visual economy is so radically reduced and acutely structured, and the structure is so visible, that the spectator is induced to include the body of the woman in the design of the stage. The woman, her clothing, and her chair are seemingly carved out of an unbounded emptiness that necessarily includes the audience. It is not surprising that this play inspired Charles Lyons to rethink the problem of the character–space relationship in theatre, remarking that "the dramatic image of character within space and time is irreducible and that it is impossible to separate the image of theatrical space from the image of character" ("Character and Theatrical Space" 28).

How does Beckett provoke in us an affective and intellectual response to the work in fifteen minutes? William E. Gruber argues that we cannot continue to judge Beckett's characters by the same standards we apply to more representational works and to more conventionally drawn characters. Yet, Gruber insists, in *Rockaby* "one feels the presence of character so keenly that it is harrowing" (*Missing Persons* 92). We do not "identify" with the character in any Aristotelian sense of the term. The words of the recorded voice and the action of the solitary character do not produce any clear story or plot; W's action, her outer experience—her experiences with world—do not relate comfortably to our own. To be sure, the words we hear do provide a rare outline for the metaphysical anguish of everyman even as the voice concludes the piece with the words "Fuck life." This metaphysical connection, however, is still representational to the extent that we associate it with what Camus described as the absurd rupture between the illusive-illusionary reality of the outer world and the non-mimetic, non-representational, convincingly irrelevant inner world. Yet the point of this book is to show that we identify something on the stage and in the character that profoundly affects our artistic sensibility by pushing beyond the envelope of the representational. The new poetics of space for the nouveau théâtre text does not merely defamiliarize the character; it also defamiliarizes the defamiliarizing process—and this means something to the spectator of the image. Something in the magnified status of emptiness, silence, immobility, and focus results in the magnified status of the figural image of character. Emptiness is foregrounded as character is foregrounded.

Therefore, scholars like Gruber caution that we should think of Beckett's characters and their situations not psychologically but figurally. I want to take this point of view in a new direction, focusing on the structuring of the theatrical image as it appears in the text and eventually in the performance. In so doing I emphasize what Gruber refers to as the "presentationalism" of the image over the detail of the portraiture. Realizing that my argument that

4

language is often subordinate to the visual image will raise a few eyebrows, I examine the ways in which the text works, not to compose a story told or, in Enoch Brater's words a "story half told," but to denarrativize simultaneously the voices we hear and the imagery we see. Beckett provides for us a close-up shot of the mind of his protagonist, a mind whose emptiness and silence are duplicated by the stage space. Beckett's figures provide an envelope through which we imaginatively pass into the empty psyche.

The concept and aura of emptiness become phenomenologically important to artists who challenge the conceptual and material fullness of postwar reality and life. Beckett is not the only "nouveau" dramatist to take an interest in the ostension—the showing and telling—of the empty space of the mind. In chapter 4, I show the pervasiveness of the empty space–empty mind connection through the examples of works by other dramatists of the period whom I will now introduce briefly.

In a number of other works belonging to nouveau théâtre, at the outset of the action, the theatrical space is abundantly furnished and populated, so one cannot readily detect a precisely focused protagonist equal to Beckett's W. Yet the spaces become emptier as the action progresses, and the works conclude with the image of an isolated and radically introspective character embedded in empty space. In Ionesco's *Exit the King* the plot centers around the King's death, a death that is clearly the spatial rendering of a well-structured inward turn. Outer space equals inner space. To accomplish death, the King must blind himself to the exterior world; as thought effaces (empties) itself from the King's mind, the furnishings of the theatrical space, including the other characters, literally disappear, until all that remains is the King on his framelike throne. Significantly, the play ends as king and throne embed themselves within deep theatrical space and "sink into a sort of fog." To say that this or any other nouveau théâtre work is introspective is by no means original, but when we realize that the inward turn develops a correlation with the empty space of the stage, we begin to understand the work in a new way. Figural emptiness provides the common bond between the inner psychic space and the outer stage.

A similar process takes place in Boris Vian's *Empire Builders* (*Bâtisseurs d'empire*), a play about a family subjected to a progressive restriction of living space. The work clearly elaborates an impression of spatial embedding as, from one act to the next, the family executes a vertically ascendant retreat within an apartment building, occupying quarters that are successively more squalid, empty, and compact. The individual family members themselves virtually disappear with the space until all that remains is the Father whose entire attention turns to the *huis clos* of his personal consciousness, the final spatial field of retreat. "I've always felt I was alone," he says, as he comments on his existence *as* space *in* space: "The world has no reason to extend itself much beyond the walls that surround me. One thing's for sure: I am its center." Only in this third and final act does the Father attain the kind of solitary, figural centering into which Beckett's protagonists seem to be born. Significantly, as the stage goes black, the Father's final act is to leap out the window into the metaphorical abyss of his introspective consciousness, a "death" not unlike that of the King. The final tableau—in one play, the enthroned king sinking into a fog, in the other, the father's vertical plunge into empty space—retrospectively reveals a dynamic character–space core that carries the play to an open and paradoxical conclusion: the inward focus of the subject reflects not only inwardly but also outwardly and away from its empty psyche to the exterior emptiness of the stage. This sheds more light on the import of Charles Lyons's remarks about the fused relationship between character and space.

The connection between empty stage and empty mind is important to an understanding of a new-age protagonist in many ways, not the least of which would be our perception of the protagonist as a new-age marionette. Thus I examine the protagonist of another play whose marionette likeness derives not so much from its automaton quality—the conventional way of discussing these characters—as from its quality as an organless, empty human icon. In René de Obaldia's *Senior Class* (*Classe terminale*) the role of the protagonist cannot be described as "marionette-like"—as have been the majority of Beckett's and Ionesco's protagonists —since the role has been written for a real marionette. The play is about a group of rebel students who rally around the fantastic symbol of their freedom, the class dunce (*le Cancre*), who, after seven years of detention, is brought back as "an immense clown, represented by a marionette." Once again, we have the example of a dramatic work that concludes with the close-up of a human icon on an empty stage. In this case, after enchanting the students with his "blind gaze," the dunce puts them to death with the point of a finger. Consequently, the play closes in much the same way as *Rockaby* and *Exit the King* in that it calls for a momentary intense illumination of the "Clown-God-Marionette . . . in all his tragic solitude" followed by a blackout.

Rolland Dubillard is another French dramatist belonging to the nouveau théâtre generation. Though he produced works that differed in a variety of ways from those discussed above, empty space provides a common model through which we can compare a work like his *House of Bone* (*Maison d'os*) with the others. In this play, the metaphorical empty space conveniently fits into the same paradigmatic grouping as that of the other plays (the throne room, the apartment, the classroom), for it is a house, or, as the stage directions more precisely describe it, "the interior of a house." Ultimately, like the king, the father, and the class dunce, the protagonist of this play, the Master, is highly conscious of his isolation within the bedroom of his house. In yet another work, the protagonist illustrates to the spectator-reader not so much that he is lonely, but that he is formally, figurally in touch with the emptiness of his inner psyche.

Outside of France, I examine a work by the Austrian playwright Thomas Bernhard and his *Force of Habit*. Since 1985, scholars such as Martin Esslin and William Gruber have compared the drama of Beckett with that of Bernhard. Comparisons focus on the introspective, monologic, and repetitious aspects of their dramaturgical and narrative techniques. I extend the comparison to include these authors' design and use of empty space, the ways in which they make the connection between empty theatrical space and the "empty" psyche of their "mad" protagonists. Though written in the early 1970s, more than a decade after the tidal wave of absurdist drama, *Force* presents a very absurd dramatic situation: for the last twenty years, Caribaldi, the circus master, has been trying to get his small circus troupe to perform Schubert's *Trout Quintet*. But the visual focus on Caribaldi as an isolated human icon is intense. What other critics describe in terms of the theme of fascism in Bernhard, I will discuss in terms of *hypertheatrical hypersubjectivity*.

The theory, artistry, and architectonics of emptiness behind the hypersubjective plays make important contributions to literary and theatrical concepts such as subjectivity and metadrama. In all the works we have an example of a figural, metadramatic subjectivity, a subjectivity created out of spatial construction and spatial consciousness: a visual image of the depth and intensity of the individual consciousness, an image accompanied by a verbal text that cues the spectator to the visual construction provided by the stage directions. These dramatic works are primarily about the spatial circumstance of drama and its relationship to the metaphorical inner space. Anne Ubersfeld has described theatrical space as a "space carved out of space" (*Ecole* 239).[2] She says, moreover, that to have the kind of metatheatre we refer to as "theatre within theatre" we need spectators and the observed (111). The self-sufficient protagonists of my study are, more clearly than ever before in the history of theatre, spectators of their own inner space, a space that is more clearly than ever presented as a space carved out of a space that is carved out of space. The development of a new poetics of empty space for postwar theatre is largely based on the connection between the visible empty stage space and the invisible empty space of the mind. Dramatists have effectively produced a theatrical close-up of the human icons, one that focuses our attention on their head and ultimately on their mind-space. The scenic illusions of naturalistic theatre could never serve as a metaphor of the non-representational mind-space, because the worldly outside could never equal the *extralinguistic* inside. Nouveau théâtre dramatists made a clear break from the detailed illusion of outer reality by moving toward the ephemeral extension that backgrounds and suspends the symbolic material we perceive in our dreams—and beyond our dreams, in the inner cosmos.

Empty space is first and foremost a non-representational, non-referential space. However, as the phenomenologist Henri Bergson has argued, the only way we can conceive of the extralinguistic, invisible world is through a unique, creative manipulation of language and the apparently "real" world.

The only way we can begin to truly apprehend emptiness not simply as absence but as some super signifier of presence is through the creative manipulation of the signifieds at our disposal. Thus, I demonstrate that, by effectively "entertaining" our awareness of the void, Beckett et al. have transcended the category of space in order to attain some realm of hyperspace. Likewise, by relating the emptiness of the stage to the character, they have established contact with a plane of human consciousness situated beyond the sclerosis of the referential and above the chaos of the non-referential, one that transcends familiar categories of subjectivity to attain the supra-referential[3] realm of hypersubjectivity. These authors "point toward" non-referentiality in a profound way.

This aesthetic of focused emptiness was a powerful new wave in drama. However, given the wide-ranging complexities of avant-garde art, needless to say that not all the works of the dramatists discussed above present a strong hyper-subjective focus and not all avant-garde dramatists associated with various forms of nouveau, absurdist theatre from the 1950s through the 1980s have produced works with a clear hypersubjective focus. As with surrealist art in all its guises, French and Francophile dramatists produced the clearest, most powerful examples of the empty space–empty character connection. Perhaps this is due to the freedom they enjoyed to explore the metaphysical and phenomenological dimensions of their art. Perhaps it is because there was such a hotbed of activity in absurdist, non-conventional theatrical art that they were simply forced into taking metadrama in a new direction. With this in mind, in order to situate better the truly hypersubjective works, in chapter 5 I examine works by other well-known "absurdist" dramatists, which, despite the showcasing of empty space, the extreme forms of metadrama, the rejection of conventional language, and the interest in interior, mental processes, cannot be called either theatre of the empty mind or hypersubjective. The bridge between empty space and empty mind is never clearly transparent, and the space of these plays remains largely referential.[4]

I write this book because I do not believe that the last word is in on the meanings of "absurdist" forms of theatre. The trend away from realism and toward metadiscourse is more complex than scholars have hitherto suggested, because we have failed to achieve any more than a token understanding of the dramatist's use of empty space and the spectator's perception of it in theatre. We need in particular to take a closer look at unrealistic empty space with the aim of re-evaluating theatrical concepts conventionally linked to rationalist illusion—concepts such as the subjective status of the dramatic character. Nouveau théâtre dramatists offered more emptiness on their stages and more imaginative uses of it. They were not, as prevailing scholarship contends, filling the emptiness. On the contrary, they were valorizing it as some fundamental, non-representational mana by creating visual images that accentuate the connection between the essential emptiness of the universe and the conceptual image we have today of our own psyche. This parallels our century's critical rejection of the "fullness" of rational, dialectical, mechanical theories. This book, with its "inward" approach to empty space *qua* empty space, will impact theories of the dramatic subject, the concept of the marionette-like dramatic character, and the theme of death for this theatre. I hope to foster a more focused interest and thorough study of how space, body, and mind come into their own in this century.

An adjunct purpose of this book is to provide evidence for the abiding interest of the French in the metaphysical side of theatre, of death, and of emptiness. Despite the reputation of French rationalism and formalism, these are only tools the French use to sometimes control sometimes pursue their lust for the supernatural, surreal, non-representational, irrational frame of our existence.

A METAPHYSICAL-PHENOMENOLOGICAL APPROACH TO EMPTY THEATRICAL SPACE AND CHARACTER

From *Godot* on, theatre scholars have paid some attention to the void, but not as the fundamental dramaturgical principle of the work. More often than not, they interest themselves in emptiness from an ontological point of view as a metaphor for existential nihilism, the ultimate meaninglessness of our lives. Likewise, while psychoanalysis recognizes the primordial void underlying our consciousness, it focuses on an empirical, representational, linguistic template—a psychological network inscribed within this void, one which obscures or ultimately ignores the force of psychic emptiness. I want to talk about one way in which emptiness signifies in its own right on the theatrical stage, not simply as a background for the fullness of the stage, for the objects and figures that inhabit the stage and the action that animates it, but as a background–foreground that both orients and actuates the meaning of an image. Scholars have noted the attention to form and figure in the drama of nouveau théâtre, but they have not yet seriously explored the importance of emptiness to form—not from a psychological or narrative point of view, but from a metaphysical-phenomenological one.[5]

Theatre semiotics can take us to the threshold of a metaphysical-phenomenological grasp of the empty space-empty character connection. It helps us to understand how the individual sign systems, such as lighting, movement, language, and objects (systems that the dramatist often prepares before they are constructed by the *metteur en scène*) can influence our perception of the stage. A semiotic eye toward the texts and performances of nouveau théâtre plays helps to discover the design of empty space. However, traditional semiotics have proved too objective, representational, mimetic—in sum, too physical to allow me to make the metaphysical argument to which my study has led. A recourse to phenomenology, on the other hand, helps us to avoid what Bert O. States sees as the representational imperative of semiotics.

9

In the West, the methodological conflict between the representational and the non-representational begins, of course, with the opposition of Aristotle's realism to Plato's idealism. This conflict is perhaps the first time in history where we are able to detect the pendulum swing in critical theory, and it establishes a pattern that reoccurs until this very day. Today we have phenomenology and a new (more phenomenological) semiotics intending to replace a rigidly representational version of semiotics.[6] Since my interest lies in emptiness—psychic as well as theatrical—and the extralinguistic, my approach necessarily supercedes representational semiotics. The openness and subjective license of phenomenology allows us to cross the threshold of space as we typically expect to perceive it. Phenomenology provides a meta-physical approach to theatre, to the phenomenal relationship between theatrical space and the human form, to the phenomenal-corporeal awareness of the human mind.

Elsewhere, in an essay titled "Beyond the Structuralistic Language-space of the Mind: French Theorists Detecting *Signals* from the Psychic Underworld," I wrote about how, despite the predominance of dialectics, structuralist linguistics, and Aristotelian representationalism (including systematized post-structuralist theories such as *architext*) in the twentieth century, thinkers from Breton and Artaud to Bachelard and Cixous have manifested a belief in a supra-intellectual category of extralinguistic awareness. I highlighted the expression of a theoretical belief in meaning beyond language with reference to 1) a psychic (spatial) continuum that pre-exists and encompasses any linguistic realm, and 2) the recognition of pre-linguistic particles of meaning in the form of what I call "signals" which, unlike signs, are located outside of language-space proper. In chapter 3 I expand on how this extralinguistic space of the mind constitutes an image of empty psyche that eventually translates to the stage; but for now, let me say that Beckett's human icons are more signals than signs and that signal-awareness and signal-watching are more the domain of phenomenology than semiotics. Signals are essentially signifiers that signify extra-referentially, and by so doing they point to non-referentiality.[7]

In recent studies, Bert O. States and Stanton B. Garner provide an impressive endorsement of a phenomenological approach to theatre, especially to the theatre in question. They argue the shortcomings of a purely semiotic approach to theatre and the need to take into account the phenomenal existence of the theatrical image. While semiotics primarily accounts for signs and for how they fit into a coded representational system, phenomenology brings out the extra-rational, the extralinguistic, the subjective, and especially the corporeal, including the embodied aspect of mind and thought processes. While semiotics trusts in the indivisibility of the signifier from the signified, and it prioritizes the signified and the code that produces it, phenomenology allows us to dwell on the signifier—the isolated human icon on the stage, for example—in a way that is different from the one suggested by postmodern theory (i.e., the signified as a process or system of deferral from one signifier to another). Empty theatrical space and its imaginary equivalent, empty psychic space, are signifiers whose signified is at once *the absence of a signified,* the illusion of the non-representational, and the participation in the suspension of cognition.

Roland Barthes was obliquely arguing that theatre is essentially phenomenological when he said that theatricality is "the theatre minus the text, it is a density of signs and sensations that are constructed on the stage from the written argument" ("Le Théâtre de Baudelaire" 41). He did not mean that theatre texts do not possess something unique and theatrical, for he quickly states his belief in the theatricality of the dramatic text: "Naturally, the theatricality must be present from the first written germ of the work, it is a fact of creation, not of realization" (42). On the contrary, he meant that to understand the theatricality of the dramatic text one must consider it from an authentically theatrical perspective and envision its corporeality, its performance, which has a signifying density more complex than the written or spoken word. We must avoid the logical temptation to view theatre simply as a corporeal act that produces a conceptual statement. Instead, we should pay more attention to the sensational aspect of the corporeal act and to the possibility that its phenomenological signal can be greater than its semiotic message. To put it another way, instead of a reader one must become an active spectator who corporealizes the text, realizing that the image is a real body with its own subjective existence and that even the words and ideas have the potential to stem from (and to point toward) the extralinguistic body-mind, from the extra-conceptual, non-propositional dimension of mind. We must, moreover, remain actively conscious of the phenomenological connection between the body on stage and our own. In theatre, more than any other art form, the body is both the key to the spoken language and the link to the speaking subject's mind; it is the catalyst for an awareness of the protagonist's mind-space and, simultaneously, our own.

Paradoxically, the 'corporeal' of phenomenology is distinct from the physical. Mark Johnson assails the fact that "the gap is thought to exist between our cognitive, conceptual, formal, or rational side in contrast with our bodily, perceptual, material, and emotional side" (*The Body in the Mind* xxv). On the contrary, he refers to just such a phenomenological connection between mind and body, explaining the body's relation to the mind in terms of "putting the body back into the mind":

> Imaginative projection is a principle [*sic*] means by which the body (i.e., physical experience and its structures) works its way up into the mind (i.e., mental operations). By using the term 'body' I want to stress the nonpropositional, experiential, and figurative dimensions of meaning and rationality. (xxxvii)

He calls for an acceptance of "embodied understanding," beyond the bounds of the physical: "we are never separated from our bodies and from forces and energies acting upon us to give rise to our understanding (as our 'being-in-the-world')" (205). The phenomena of corporeal awareness and corporeal participation in our thought processes come together with the equally extra-rational, extra-conceptual awareness of the empty space of our mind, especially in the theory of Artaud, as we shall see in chapter 2. They come together in the (empty) human icon on an empty stage.[8]

Consequently, theatre phenomenologists like States and Garner decry the disembodied objectivity of theatre semiotics. From a theatrical angle, phenomenology is about the "body" (embodied aspect) of theatre, or, as Garner puts it, the theatre as a "bodied space." According to Bert States, a phenomenological approach to theatre "focuses on the activity of theater *making itself* out of its essential materials: speech, sound, movement, scenery, text, etc." (*Great Reckonings* 1; States's emphasis). He suggests that a purely semiotic approach to theatre would, in the end, render little more than a literary, hermeneutic reading of the text's verbal language, a reader-response that views the text solely as a communicative vehicle. States argues that theatre is so much more than a "communicative vehicle":

> What the text loses in significative power in the theatre it gains in corporeal presence, in which there is extraordinary perceptual satisfaction. Hence the need for rounding out a semiotics of the theater with a phenomenology of its imagery—or, if you will, a phenomenology of its semiology. (29)

Leveling a similarly deferential broadside at semiotics, Stanton B. Garner says that "semiotics has shifted 'meaning' from the intending consciousness to signifying systems, relocating the perceptual object within the codified boundaries of the sign and abandoning a dialogue with phenomenology that characterized both traditions at an earlier time" (*Bodied Spaces* 20). Garner wants to exceed an interpretation of the theatrical sign in a way that will capture an awareness of the stage and the bodies that occupy it as "body-as-lived." His recent work on the spatial phenomenology of the theatrical image fleshes out the important perspective that Merleau-Ponty's phenomenological theory contributes to understanding the reception of the theatrical space-human body dialectic so fundamental to Beckett's theatre. His study begins with a succinct explanation of Merleau-Ponty's theory of basic human perception:

> we might say that Merleau-Ponty replaced *Korper* (the body as it is given to external observation, the "thing body") by *Leib* (the body as it is experienced, the "lived body"), and that he turned the attention of phenomenology to *Leiblichkeit,* or "lived bodiliness" (28).

While Garner agrees with other scholars that Beckett's theatre is a theatre "of the body," he cautions Beckett's audience not to ignore "the radical complications of corporeal self-presence that characterize Beckett's staging of the body" (28–29). The problem lies in the embodied duality present on the stage: body-as-lived versus body-as-object. Neither dramatist nor director can simplify matters by eliminating the body-as-object since, in the conventional stage arena, spectators, who are themselves subjects as well as objects (victims) of this duality, consciously or unconsciously expect in some way to sense the embodied duality. Particularly relevant to my study is the rub that the hypersubjective, marionette-like character tips the scales toward the body-as-object in a way that does not share the same sympathetic relationship that the humanized dramatic character shares with the spectator. Consequently, we see not so much a "full" object as we do an empty human frame, a paradoxical presentation of a non-living body-as-lived. According to Garner, as is the case with all "modes of materialist analysis," semiotics results in a "depersonalized" approach to theatre in general (semiotics shifts meaning from intending consciousness to signifying system), an approach that results in the "'depersonalizing' of experience by proposing that subjectivity is discursively constituted" (21). When we apply semiotics to the artistic form of the hypersubjective figure, we are all the more inclined to construe it as "depersonalized" and marionette-like. Yet, as an artistic form, the hypersubjective dramatic character is neither person nor impersonal; just so deep and profound—so far beyond the referential—that the "personal" loses relevance. In chapter 3 I return to Garner's phenomenological approach to the visual field in Beckett's theatre; and in my final chapter, the one on the marionette-like dramatic character, I refashion the notion of "depersonalized" for this theatre.

One essential distinction to make is what I will call, after Barthes, the semiotic *studium* of communication versus the phenomenological *punctum* of awareness (see note 8, p. 199). For some critics, it helps to understand this awareness in terms of the sensual. Craig Stewart Walker notes that States argues for an understanding of "theatre's capacity to give shape to our emotional or sensual energies in a manner which arouses our interest, or, . . . its capacity to fulfill a certain need by providing a 'thing' for the exchange of certain energies" ("Reckoning with States" 76). Walker emphasizes that States does not intend to undercut semiotics, but that he only wants to bring our attention to the "sensuous" aspect of performance: "I think we must, with Dufrenne, understand the phenomenology of aesthetic experience to comprise both the significant and the sensuous" (79). Like States, Walker believes that the linguistic origin and orientation of semiotics[9] has rendered the method objective, mimetic, and systematic to the extent that it falls short in accounting for many important elements of the work, namely, the sensuousness as opposed to that which the work signifies. The sensuousness of the work derives from the opportunity to dwell on the phenomenon, to suspend the fitting of the phenomenon into a system. It reveals a dynamic state of "beyond meaning," a pre-referential and—in many ways— pure form of expression. The phenomenon is a corporeal signifier—the body-as-lived rather than the body-as-expressed (or, world-as-expressed; or body-expressed-as-world).[10] The phenomenology proposed by States and Garner is neither anti-semiotic, nor a-semiotic, but extra-semiotic. Similarly, it is not anti-social, nor a-social, but "extra-socially social," a topic I will consider in chapter 2 and in the conclusion.

Phenomenology can account for the unconventional, unconnectable, "presence" or the "body" of the theatre, the "bodied space" of theatre. Defined more broadly, it encompasses a metaphysical awareness of the empty mind-space in Beckett's work. States takes up the topic of "the strain of impressionistic plays from Maeterlinck to Beckett where the characters seem to be enacting a drama of pure consciousness under a naturalistic shell of language" (*Great Reckonings* 81). He observes that the language in Beckett's works, in particular, is to some extent "concerned with a real out there; but we also have the feeling that speech is referring to another landscape that can be seen only with the metaphysical eye" (82). This accounts for the metaphysical dimension of States's phenomenology, though the metaphysical here is perhaps too psychoanalytically referential, since States subsumes Beckett's theatre under the category of the "dream play, or the drama of the interior of the human mind" (82). He seems interested more in the dream imagery, and perhaps the psychoanalytical implications of it, than in the empty environment in which the imagery materializes.

To the "scientific" scholar, "metaphysics" has a particularly harrowing ring to it. However, it is absolutely unprincipled for a scientist to become so "scientific" as to exclude either the possibility of some "scientifically exact" system other than the conventional one, or, more radically, to exclude the possibility that science has it all wrong, or, more simply, to forget that the system currently in place is fallible to the extent that its tools are not versatile enough to account for some hidden, deep, hard-to-reach "truths," like the common cold.[11] Rationalism is a sophisticated tool, which, as the British philosopher David Hume pointed out, merely allows science to discover hidden effects, never the original cause (not a virus!). The greatest of scientists and scholars respect the essential mystery of life. Einstein succeeded to the extent that he believed in meta-science and metaphysics, i.e., a science beyond the science in which he was forced to *begin* his work, and which provided no more than a point of departure for his extracurricular venture into quantum science. Likewise, Artaud's approach to theatre was a metaphysical-phenomenological one. He is no less important to theatre analysis because his theories, and especially his visions, allow us to exceed the simply semiotic or linguistic. When he describes for us the primordial response to the hieroglyphical sign system of the Asian dancer, he means to challenge our faith in conventional language and offer proof of its unfathomable complexity. If we truly peer beyond the language space of the mind, including the space of the dream language, we add one more metaphysical "eye" to our view of theatre: our mind's eye. Our vision becomes triocular rather than "binocular" (States's term for adding the phenomenological view to the semiotic). I will return to my argument for a more metaphysical phenomenological approach to theatre in chapter 3.[12]

[1]

EMPTINESS: ONTOLOGICAL,
THEATRICAL, THEATRO-PSYCHIC

> We do not think in a continuous manner any more than we feel in a
> continuous manner or live continuously. There are breaks, there is the
> intervention of nothingness. . . . it is impossible to render an exact
> image of the aspect of thought if we do not take into account what is
> blank and what is intermittent.
>
> —PAUL CLAUDEL

THE EXTENDED EMPTY SPACE OF LIFE

Scientists, philosophers, and even the unphilosophical have mused that the primitive wilderness is our home, that our earliest ancestors must have felt as much at home with the animals and plants as with other human beings. Why not take a giant step backward and deeper into the thought that emptiness is our most primordial home within and beyond the space of wilderness?

It is not easy to either conceptualize or articulate nothingness. Yet it is impossible to ignore it. As paradoxical, tautological, or banal as this may sound, emptiness is the essential ingredient of our material world. Consequently, it is also an essential component of our ontological consciousness of the outer world and of our spiritual awareness of our inner world. But we usually do not think about it, busy as we are with the fullness of life, content to dedicate our physical and mental energies, our activities and consciousness, to "filling the glass." The vessel of our existence is emptiness. We are concerned with the contents of the vessel and not the vessel itself. One marvels at the reminder that two-thirds of the earth's surface is covered by water, because we usually travel over water, sometimes play in it, or contemplate its vastness from the solid ground of the shore. But we do not feel we live in it or on it. On an even larger scale, we are almost totally inattentive to the "mass" of the universe, of which all but an infinitesimal part is not essentially empty, neither form nor matter. We ignore it because it is, well, "empty." However, as the vast oceans orient the land on which we live, creating continents and civilizations, it is the celestial, universal void that contains the water and earth that is our planet. Empty space orients our very consciousness: It not only creates the ultimate perspective of meaninglessness, but it also provides a psychic space within which our concrete ideas are suspended.

Thus we sporadically continue to make spiritual, aesthetic, and even cognitive "connections" with the emptiness that is all around us and deep within us. The great symbols of Western civilization operate through an appeal to this primordial connection. When we view the open, expansive ocean from the referential, oriented shore, we are seduced into empty chaos. Like the Gothic cathedral pointing to the heavens, the vertical majesty of our skyscrapers points even beyond the celestial ether. With each new generation of scientific discovery, we learn that the empty sky surrounding our world is merely a threshold to the void surrounding our galaxy. Trees and stars, which we do not readily perceive as particularly empty or ethereal in themselves, become more significant and pathetic when they are set in an empty universe or on an empty stage. What more fascinating vision in the forest than the barely visible empty sky seen through the foliage of the trees? If, that is, we take the time to look upwards. The other most mesmerizing sensation in the forest is our awareness of the infinite silence from which emerge the discrete murmurings of nature. Those sounds that proceed from total silence are especially stirring. Visual and sonoral vacuity are essential to all perceptual practices, especially to the arts with its mission to transcend the reality of the half-empty vessel we call life. The void is always there and it is always on and in our minds. It represents, first of all, the primordial chaos—not the slime—from which the universe and life forms appeared, a history that goes back to the dawn of psychic life.[1]

"Space" and "empty" are oxymoronic terms for some philosophers and at some point of the ontological cogito argument. The idea of the void fascinates because of its unique ability to, in a sense, void the category of space and convey a sense of spatial extension, an image that perplexes the dialectical logic of the Western mindset. Foucault has observed that

> The space of emplacement was opened up by Galileo. For the real scandal of Galileo's work lay not so much in his constitution of an infinite, and infinitely open space. In such a space the place of the Middle Ages turned out to be dissolved, as it were; a thing's place was no longer anything but a point in its movement, just as the stability of a thing was only its movement indefinitely slowed down. In other words, starting with Galileo and the seventeenth century, extension was substituted for localization. (23)

Foucault implies here ("starting with Galileo") that an ontological awareness of extension begins with Galileo. More likely, however, he is merely referring to the rupture operated by Galileo's work with respect to the medieval spiritual culture, where celestial extension was separate from worldly reality.[2]

Galileo's science jolted Western civilization back into metaphysical contact with the universe in the place of a god, and from that point to the present, science and its humanistic avatars have refashioned the screen that obscures our awareness of essentialist empty space. For example, Foucault believed that "the anxiety of our era has to do fundamentally with space" and that today "site" has been substituted for extension as a template (or form of "software"?) for our mindset: "Our epoch is one in which space takes for us the form of relations among sites. . . . we live inside a set of relations that delineates sites which are irreducible to one another" (23). Perhaps "site" could have displaced extension, but it could not have replaced it, for extension is an obviously more primary, primordial, existential *prise de conscience*. "Site" is merely a representational-operational modem for our psychic hardware.[3]

We are still entranced by creative illusions of extension. Ontologically, the awareness of extension (the continuous) can only assume metaphysical proportions and so it has stood in binary opposition to the more limited and rationalizable concept of space (the discontinuous). The philosophical semiotician A. J. Greimas argues that "all knowledge of the world begins with a projection of the discontinuous onto the continuous" (11), that is, a projection of space onto extension (*étendue*). While the mundane, functional variety of space offers up a discontinuous image, one constructed by a rational human being's necessarily limited point of view, the concept of extension evokes the idea of an all-encompassing, unbroken and formless, perhaps chaotic, *whole*, an idea that, alienating itself from language, boggles the rational mind. The concept of "infinity" stifles expression. As we ordinarily perceive it and refer to it, space is little more than a construction which, for Greimas, is an "impoverishment . . . the emergence of space erases the greater part of the richness of extension" (12). In order to signify, to elaborate the world into a signifying system, the rich continuity of extension is "impoverished" because one must necessarily and selectively dismantle its absoluteness, reconstructing it to fit into some kind of conventional scheme, into a "discontinuous" ordering of space.

From the beginning of this century, phenomenologist thinkers have struggled to retain an awareness of extended emptiness by either totally rejecting or carefully qualifying our perceptual and cognitive grasp of space. Once again the idea of deep, essential awareness confronts not only representational communication, but also cognition and perception. Deep down, we are *aware* of more than we perceive, know, or are able to communicate. We perceive the trees in the forest and consequently we know that they are there; but the perception and the cognition do not preclude the awareness of the emptiness that the trees—as well as the forest—inhabit. Henri Bergson saw the light through the trees. For him, the absolute void stood as a background for the *élan vital* of human life. He rejected rationalistic and mechanistic explorations of the life force, emphasizing the categories of time and action over space. In fact, he was hostile to the ontological category of space, believing that, historically, dialectical thinkers had wrongly privileged space over time and action. Before Greimas, he had articulated a dichotomy of the continuous and the discontinuous; but unlike Greimas, he associated space with the discontinuous and only time with the continuous. Consequently, he believed our awareness of space is always form-ulated, structured, and never extended; extension is so difficult to imagine from a spatial point of view that it requires the abstractness of time. Only the category of time could truly convey to us the unformulated extension, the "emptiness" of life, of universe, and of our psyche. Connecting world to psyche, Bergson derogatorily insisted that "the representation of emptiness is always a full representation" (*L'Evolution créatrice* 306) and that "We spend our lives thus filling in the voids, which our intelligence conceives under the extra-intellectual influence of desire and regret, under the pressure of vital necessities" (322).

For another phenomenologist thinker, Edmund Husserl, space and time were simultaneously extensive. He was well aware of the backdrop of extension within which we function as perceptive organisms:

> I am aware of a world, spread out in space endlessly, and in time becoming and become, without end. I am aware of it, that means, first of all, I discover it immediately, intuitively, I experience it. Through sight, touch, hearing, etc., in the different ways of sensory perception, corporeal things somehow spatially distributed are for me simply there, in verbal or figurative sense "present" . . . (91)

Merleau-Ponty too perceived the light through the trees. He was content to deal with life and consciousness in terms of space alone: "We have said that space is existential, we might just as well have said that existence is spatial, that is, that through an inner necessity it opens to an outside, so that we can speak of a mental space" (293). In his description of the effects of mescaline, we observe extension, or "empty vastness" quite clearly as the container of conscious life:

> Under mescaline . . . [t]he walls of the room are 150 yards apart, and beyond the walls is merely an empty vastness. . . . The subject is alone and forlorn in empty space, "he complains that all he can see clearly is the space between things, and that this space is empty." (Cited in Garner 34–35)

This hyper-awareness of emptiness could easily apply to most of the protagonists of Beckett's late plays.

Contemporary artists and scholars have continued to hold the rational order of our civilization up to the light of extension. David Grossvogel, for example, speaks of a book as a kind of rational space that opposes metaphysical extension: "A book is an ordering. . . . its very being denies . . . the structureless and unpronounceable chaos, the infinity of space and formlessness that extends beyond man's ability to measure and to shape" (*Mystery and Its Fictions* 129). Artists, not content to be ontologically aware of the void, create fictions and images that will aesthetically disclose it. At the beginning of his writing career, Beckett's prose was dedicated to this type of disclosure. Livio Dobrez, examining the "Irreducible" in Beckett's prose works, writes of the novelist's quest to get beyond the *cogito* and beyond the "voice of consciousness" to "that obscure origin of things which is also the operative presence *beneath* the *cogito*." Dobrez describes Beckett's desire "to touch the void, to be able to point to the intersection of silence and speech, nothingness and existence."[4] Beckett began his career as a phenomenological artist by sketching and embedding primordial emptiness in his narrative "stories," creating characters like Malone who would both say and mean "Nothing is more real than nothing" (*Malone Dies* 16). But his interest soon turned toward the scenic display of emptiness available through theatrical art. As we see in chapter 3, from the empty background of *Godot* his theatrical work evolved into the multidimensional void of short pieces like *Rockaby* and *Not I*. To be sure, Beckett knew that, like an absolute vacuum, absolute emptiness is impossible; but, because of the conflict it presents with respect to our desire to comprehend and establish reality, he also knew that the impossibility of its representation renders it more artistically effective for the truly avant-garde dramatist. Finally, Beckett knew that it is no more impossible or unrepresentable than absolute fullness.[5]

THEATRICAL EMPTY SPACE, THE (EMPTY) HUMAN FIGURE, AND SYMBOLISM

Perhaps the greatest contribution of twentieth-century dramatists to the historical evolution of theatre art has been the development of a new poetics of space for the text, one based on emptiness. In their determination to rid themselves of the straightjackets of naturalism and bourgeois psychology, dramatists from Chekhov to Beckett realized that they would have to create a new "spatial language" for the text, and that to accomplish this they faced two major challenges. The first was the emptying of stage space. The distinguished French theatre semiologist Anne Ubersfeld even believes that "A history of contemporary theatrical space would characterize this period as a sort of march toward the void" (*L'Ecole* 116). Since the revolution of realism and naturalism at the end of the nineteenth century, and despite the continuing influence of these movements throughout our own period, emptiness in theatrical space, whether evidenced by the dramatic text or witnessed on the stage, has literally come into its own. Stage sets, as well as the objects and characters occupying the sets, were no longer supposed to recreate exterior reality, but to suggest the possibility of an alternative, truly fictional, realm where the naturalistic concern for detail would be of little consequence.[6] Symbolist-surrealist visionaries, such as Alfred Jarry in France and Gordon Craig in England, express in their theories the need to remove the veil of ideological rhetoric from the aesthetic base of theatre and let the theatre speak *for itself* and *as itself*—as a more pristine signifier rather than a dictatorial signified. Clearing away the naturalist clutter, they believed, would help to redirect all referential force inward to the theatrical medium itself and to reestablish theatre as an imaginary fiction rather than a materialist illusion. Thus the symbolic substance of the stage comes to depend on the theatre's unique potential for emptiness.[7]

The second major challenge for dramatists of this century was the portrayal of inner life on the stage. As even a performance-oriented theorist like Richard Schechner has admitted, since the advent of modern psychology, dramatists such as Chekhov, Pirandello, Genet, Ionesco, and Beckett actually set the pace for theatre practitioners by meeting the challenge "to exteriorize the inner life transforming it into a mode of action" (194). One cannot deny that this century has seen a shift toward a new interest in the mind as a space. Thanks to Freud and the surrealists at the beginning of the century, we have begun to think of our mental space as an independent spatial field. Today, after all, when we speak of inner space we do not refer to our stomach or even to our chest cavity; the only valid reference for inner space is the subject's mind, a mind located in the head, the "container" of a space whose inner emptiness is no more fathomable than that of the twentieth-century conception of the outer cosmos. Emptiness has taken on a new meaning in this century, primarily because we equate it with both epistemological and ontological openness.

Thus it is that, in the postwar avant-garde theatre of France, two revolutionary concepts—one concerning empty space, the other, inner space—became inextricably connected, as the written text focused on the mind of the dramatic character and on how best to represent it on the three-dimensional stage. The one great virtue of theatre is that ostension can replace language. To be sure, the visual, aural, and physical display of emptiness can function linguistically as part of a semantic and syntactical code. It can also function extralinguistically to the extent that it connects "immediately"—in the full sense of the word—with the open space of our imagination, which produces an image of empty psyche that far exceeds language's ability to express it. Dramatists and directors like Beckett work from the complete emptiness of the stage toward a visual image that points to the idea of emptiness as the common denominator between the inside and the outside.

The visual image that provides the link between empty stage and empty mind is the human body on the stage.

Besides the comment about this century's "progression toward the void," Ubersfeld makes other observations about twentieth-century theatre that help us understand that dramatists did not blindly progress toward emptiness, but they used its signifying power to explore more elaborate ways to put it into play with other elements of the stage. She points out, for example, that the *tréteau* (stage boards) saw increased usage in this century. Because of its emptiness it was the place where signifiers (instead of signifieds) and the connotative (instead of denotative) values of character and object would be emphasized (*L'Ecole* 115). In empty space "signs become more valuable in themselves" (118), as opposed to the naturalistic spaces of the Théâtre de Boulevard, for example, where the emphasis is on the signifier and on denotative value. On the empty boards, there is not just a focus on the object and the character, but on them as a theatrical object and a theatrical character. She also observes, as others have done, that in this century there is a renewed interest in the body: "The return to the body in contemporary civilization is connected to a new definition of stage space: no longer merely a playing area, the space of the performance, but a mobile architecture of human bodies" (118). Placing this exploration of emptiness together with the focus on the functional, self-conscious role of the theatrical sign, and with the new interest in the body, we understand that the emptiness could have greater effect on our perception of the body. Empty theatrical space means a display of the human body as a human icon. It is not simply that the body stands out when surrounded by emptiness, but also that the quality of emptiness begins to transfer to our perception of the body. Finally, Ubersfeld observes that the stage can serve not merely as a textual or a theatrical space, but as the icon of a psychic space as well (*L'Ecole* 69). I would add that the increased focus on the body went a long way toward transforming the body into the icon of psychic space.

Dramatic theory, dramatic fiction, and performance practice were all penetrated by the renewed interest in both the volume of emptiness on the stage and the network of signifiers that cooperated or coordinated with emptiness, especially the human icon. The interest intensifies with the symbolist aesthetic sensibility that intruded on the tendency of late nineteenth century naturalism to fill the stage with environmental realism and psychological portraiture. Whether one examines symbolist theatrical art from a literary-dramatic point of view or from a material-production point of view, simplicity, emptiness, and silence begin to reimpose themselves on the artistic mind. Stage directors, who began to assume the status of independent artists only at the close of the nineteenth century, cleared the naturalist clutter from their stages as dramatists created texts that sacrificed psychological portraiture for figural imagery. The truly revolutionary discoveries of the symbolist-leaning dramatists have to do with 1) a desire to use empty space for its evocative, symbolic value; 2) the dramatist's view toward the character as a spatial form; and 3) the desire to create a "theatre of the mind," as Jean-Pierre Sarrazac puts it, a move from *"theatrum mundi to theatrum mentis"* (71). The symbolist penchant for form and figure caused a shift away from fullness and toward emptiness as well as a highly elaborate search for ways to present this emptiness on the stage and to connect it with the "space" of the character as well as the extrascenic space and the space of the audience.[8]

Notwithstanding the aesthetic labels attached to their works, symbolist dramatists like Maurice Maeterlinck chose a supercharged language that depended decreasingly upon the detail of scenic realism—with the object of conveying a psychological portrait of the character—and increasingly upon non-discursive otherworldly symbolic icons—with the object of conveying a deeper, more universal truth. To be sure, symbolist theatre was first and foremost a textual theatre; but symbolist thinkers and artists had a very definite vision of what kind of poetic medium the stage should provide for their verbal poetry. In an article on the theatrical in-sight of Mallarmé and Maeterlinck, Patrick McGuinness explains how these artists came to provide a very strong dramaturgical theory for posterity:

> The Symbolists' preference for bare stages, rudimentary sets, stylized acting and monotonous declamation, must be seen as an attempt to control the non-textual input that goes into a performance. . . . ("From Page to Stage and Back" 35)
>
> Despite all this experimentation with non-verbal media the Symbolists attempted to preserve the primacy of the word in theatre. But by the time they had finished they had left behind them, ironically enough, an almost complete theory of production and performance, coupled with at least a partial account of how non-textual elements generate meaning on the stage. Their legacy is a theory governing the entire range of media in use in performance which, in its attempts to safeguard "le Verbe," inadvertently reveals the potential of the non-verbal. What they create, in their attempts to bend the stage to the page, is a power-vacuum which only the director, the *modern* director, is able to fill. (37)

Maeterlinck had, in particular, a precise vision of the human medium on the stage that would render his text. He also had a strong feeling about the personal, sensuous, idiosyncratic semblance of the medium that could interfere with the universal, poetic expression of the text: "A masterpiece is a symbol and the symbol can never tolerate the active presence of man" ("Menus propos" 334). He therefore sought to de-naturalize, de-psychologize, and de-familiarize the stage space, primarily in order to reemphasize at once the text (through the isolation of the word and the separation of message from medium) and the empty environment in which the word is uttered. But he also took an interest in the dramaturgical value of the actor and the

22

dramatic character, i.e., in the symbolic-iconic significance of the isolated human form. The depersonalized human element on stage, in the form of the character as well as the actor, sacrifices its expressive personal psychology to become a center-stage icon. McGuinness refers to "the Symbolist passion for taking the specific human form, converting it into something non-human, depersonalized, and then reconverting it into an abstract, universal conception, a 'sign' of humanity at large rather than any one human being" ("From Page to Stage" 31). More important, however, is the connection between the symbolist interest in the human icon and its importance to a "theatre of the mind." This concept of the "theatre of the mind" is even more complex than McGuinness and other scholars have realized, at least with respect to the parallel between the mind and the theatre as an extended empty space.[9]

The image of the isolated human icon was largely responsible for driving Maeterlinck to provide a dramaturgical response to the psychological theatre that was prominent at his time, primarily because the human icon, albeit a dehumanized human icon, was the means by which Maeterlinck could induce the spectator into the mind of the psychologically empty, metaphysical form of the character. In his essay "Menus propos: Le théâtre," Maeterlinck's discussion of Shakespeare is enlightening in this respect. He says, "the majority of the great poems of humanity are not for the stage. Lear, Hamlet, Othello, Macbeth, Antoine et Cléopâtre cannot be represented, and it is dangerous to see them on the stage" (331–32). Maeterlinck was struck by Shakespeare's ability to draw the spectator's attention to the mind of his characters; so he cites at length British author Charles Lamb's extreme frustration at seeing Shakespeare's characters represented by real human beings on stage: "Lear's greatness does not reside in his corporal dimensions, but his intellectual dimensions. The explosions of his passion are terrific like a volcano; they are tempests turning over and laying open the depths of the sea of his mind. . . . When we read, we don't see Lear, we are Lear. We are in his mind" (332). It is as much to say that the action of Shakespeare's plays only counts through its connection to thought, whether as a catalyst for thought, or as a consequence of it. The primary aesthetic principle is the connection between their thoughts and ours, their minds and ours. In effect, there is tremendous depth in the chaotic minds of these characters, and to this extent there is emptiness. Consequently, Lamb emphasizes that Shakespeare's characters are "objects of meditation" (333). With respect to Shakespeare, Maeterlinck's modern symbolist sensibility drew him farther from realist illusion and historical relevance and nearer still to the idea of the character's body as evocative of a mental space. Shakespeare's characters are prototypes of Maeterlinck's symbolist theatre as they are of Beckett's hypersubjective characters. But, as history runs its course, the dramatic character's function as stage image evolves for dramatists and spectators alike, a point I discuss in some detail in chapter 6 on the marionette-like dramatic character. For now, let us say that Maeterlinck comes close to a clearer understanding of the mind as empty space; but not as close as the surrealists, a topic I address in chapter 2.

At this point, it would help to take a look at the symbolist practices of stage design that began to appear at the end of the nineteenth century and which continue to evolve today. With an examination of the illustrations and repro-ductions of Denis Bablet's excellent study, *The Revolutions of Stage Design in the 20th Century*, we remark the dramatic shift from the detailed decor of "fourth wall" naturalism to the apparent simplicity of symbolism, or, as Bablet has described it, the shift from a pictorial-paintorial approach to an architectural one in matters of set design. The architectural approach, to be sure, is "simplified" in the sense that the detailed, functional, three-dimen-sional "painting" of the naturalist set yields to the "simplified" geometry of architecture. Simplicity was a move away from the detailed complexity of verbal language, especially narrative language, not only in the text, but also in the stage design. This trend was part of the symbolist "package." The simplicity was, of course, illusory.[10] Within the symbolist setting, the character's body would no longer be "painted" into the scenery of the stage, but instead would be *figured* into the architecture of the stage.[11]

Before symbolism, scenic design was a rather independent and gratuitous project that more often addressed practical concerns instead of aesthetic concerns of the production; or it simply followed the tenets of illusionist realism, often independent of the individual text. With symbolism, the de-sign of the stage not only closely resembled the symbolic resonances of the text, but it also sought to affect and effect the mood of the spectator. Michael Kirby tells us how, in 1876, Richard Wagner's Festspielhaus was

> one of the single most important moments in the history of theatre—not because, as some say, it introduced the fan-shaped auditorium that has been so prevalent in the last century but because Wagner had created a "dream machine." This was the first theatre designed not for practical (usually economic) concerns but to induce in the spectator a particular perceptual state—a state modeled on the dream." (56)

Bablet explains that, practically a century after Wagner, in Jerzy Grotowski's work, "the scenographer's function was no longer to create a scenic place, but a specific physical rapport, which along with psycho-spiritual relation-ships, were meant to give the production its special dynamic power" (357). "The task of the scenographer here is to organize the spectator's perspec-tive" (359).[12] As a theorist-dramatist, Maeterlinck, too, sought to organize the spectator's perspective, and this, with respect to a "theatre of the mind." From the beginning of symbolism, many dramatists and practitioners—some wittingly, some unwittingly—worked to build a focus on the personal psyche of the spectator, to catalyze for the spectator the common bond between the psyche and the stage. The stage's task was decreasingly to create the illusion of some physiological and environmental reality affecting and reflecting some deeper personal reality (personality), and increasingly to create an image that would allude to a deeper, hyper-personal, psychic awareness. Eventually, with the theatre of Beckett et al., the "reality" depicted by the stage images was even deeper than psychoanalytical models and dream states. We can, of course, analyze nouveau théâtre quite satisfactorily from a psychoanalytical point of view; but this approach, with its emphasis on a complex chain of signifiers and signifieds, does not account for the nouveau dramatists' profound interest in emptiness, the substance from which dreams are made and in which they are suspended.

The most important writers and directors from the late nineteenth century on—symbolists, expressionists, futurists, surrealists—all acquired a new respect for the primordial simplicity of emptiness. On the one hand, Gordon Craig in England was indeed interested in working with the schematics of a relatively empty space, and he echoed Maeterlinck's scorn of the all-too-human actor in proposing his theory of the *Übermarionette* to replace the live body on stage (see fig. 5). On the other hand, Jacques Copeau at the Vieux-Colombier in France begins with an almost uncanny respect for the "naked stage": "Let the other charms fade away and for the new work leave us with the naked boards!"[13] Many critics claim that Copeau's fondness for empty space was a way of emphasizing the text. As Surel-Tupin puts it, with Copeau "The *Tréteau* is not added on to the play." She cites Copeau as follows: "Only the text counts, there is only the text" (77). But we cannot interpret this emphasis on text solely as an emphasis on language. I believe this represents a great error of contemporary dramatic critics. Like Maeterlinck, Copeau was beginning to articulate a highly problematic and controversial process that only Beckett could bring to terms: the rejection of the signified of language for the signifier of space. Copeau's sense of text was not limited to words on a page or even to the scenic articulation of those words.

Following other scholars, Surel-Tupin points to Copeau's empty stage as a place where the actor stands out: "In the naked theatrical space, with its juxtaposed volumes, the actor plays with a few props that are rigorously selected" (79). To be sure, Copeau implores the theatre industry of his time to

> Give up the idea of scenery.
> The more naked the stage, the more the action can give birth to wonders. The more it is austere and rigid, the more freely the imagination comes into play.
> On this arid stage the actor is obliged to achieve everything, to bring everything out of himself. ("Registres 1" 257)[14]

In addition, like other scholars, Surel-Tupin points to Copeau's theatre as "theatre in its purest state" (85). Thus, scholars are primarily impressed with

Copeau's vision to unite the audience to the stage by means of the hypnotic invitation of focused emptiness, on the one hand, and, on the other, the elimination of a network of signifying systems that become, in effect, barriers to the pure and primitive theatrical principle of display, of ostension (as opposed to ostentation). It is important that Copeau sees the solution to the theatrical boredom of his time to be architectural and no longer decorative: "It did not seem to me that there could be a decorative solution to the problem of the stage, only an architectural one" ("Registres 1" 257). Equally important is his view that the body (form and volume) of the actor completes the architecture of the stage space, and more than that, the stage is not a substitute for man but completes him, extends him: "On this stage all means must be linked to man, begin with him, remain within his grasp and his scale. This includes the machinery. It should not replace man, but should extend him, help him, complete him" ("Registres 1" 258).

Copeau's writings exemplify the twentieth century's avant-garde calculus for an empty, extended space in terms of stage, body, mind, audience. There is something about the emptiness *qua* emptiness—not the signifying potential implied by absence, but instead the dynamic, nonrepresentational and suprareferential dynamism of its extension—that Copeau and others of his generation did not miss. This is evident in Copeau's remark that the stage "is never so beautiful as in its natural state, primitive and vacant, when nothing is happening there and when it rests, silent, dimly lit by the half-light of day" ("La Scène et l'acteur" 734). To a large degree we are expected to see in the imaginary potential of the empty stage what the contemporary novelist sees in the blank page; but the material space of the stage—as envisioned first by the dramatist—has the unique capacity to concretize self-representation through spatialization. Gazing upon the kind of stage space that Copeau and others (like Schlemmer, Craig, and Piscator) sought to create, we would somehow remain conscious that what we see has been created out of nothing, that this space is essentially and ultimately backgrounded by its potential for vacuity. Like other modernists and postmodernists, Copeau understood that you cannot empty the theatrical stage of meaning, that the more empty you make it, the more essential, concrete, and primitively self-conscious it becomes—the more it is *about* itself. Correspondingly, on the modern stage, the limited materials—decor, objects, and especially human bodies—that would fill the void would surely gain in aesthetic value if they were carefully selected for their ability to enhance or reflect the void. The void of the stage as well as the human icon are received by the spectator as psychic phenomena that evoke the power of meaninglessness. There is great meaning in meaninglessness, especially when an artist aesthetically draws our attention to it. In this respect, the history of the stage runs parallel with theories of surrealism, wherein the "emptier" the mind, the more it can resist the contamination of psychological realism and concentrate on itself. In chapter 2 I examine theories of surrealism—Artaud, in particular—which foster the possibility to go beyond the exterior human form to the empty space beneath and beyond it: the human form is not comprehensively related to psychic empty space; but, when the corporal form is perceived as empty, this leads to a focus on the head and to a perception of the head as empty.

CREATIVE MIMESIS: METADRAMA AND THE SUBJECTIVE IMAGINATION

Before examining the move from symbolism to surrealism with respect to the interest in inner psychic space, I would like to discuss the concept of mimesis. If drama is a mimetic act, what object does symbolist drama imitate? The symbolist shift from fullness to emptiness was indeed a mimetic crisis, one connected to a shift from a rhetorical purpose of art to a more absolutely aesthetic one, and one which is not without its connection to cultural politics. Symbolism responded to the challenge to the poet-dramatist to "represent" the unrepresentability of emptiness, its non-mimetic quality. How does one *present or re-present* nothingness? The answer, of course, is: directly, through presence. Bergson knew that the only way to represent absence was through some kind of presence, in the sense that one does not so much represent it as point toward its ineluctable presence. Here, I depart from Bergson by reasserting the opposition of (a priori) emptiness to (a posteriori) absence. The category of absence implies referentiality and representability in a way that the category of emptiness does not. Emptiness is a primary presence; only its absence, one found in realist forms of theatre, could set the stage for a perception of a presence. As regards artistic production, the conveyance of a sense of absence is one process (a referential one) whereas the recognition of emptiness is quite another. Emptiness requires a redoubled form of creativity that can turn the referentiality and representability of presence back against itself, so that the fifth dimension of emptiness and meaninglessness provides the primary context for the meaning of the text. The controverted "referentiality" of empty space is a priori self-referential. In the absence of a code in or through which to refer, emptiness turns back on itself. This explains the difference between the empty stage in classical theatre and the empty stage in Beckett's theatre. Classical theatre attempted to induce narratively in the spectator a mytho-psychological sensation of a full psychological state, whereas the non-narrative images of Beckett's theatre creatively induce a primordial awareness of emptiness. In other words, Beckett presents emptiness instead of representing it. Oedipus's blindness constitutes a psychologically and mythically motivated tragic event, while in Beckett's *Endgame,* Hamm's blindness is a theatrical condition that points directly toward inner emptiness.

The great question for the idealist, non-realist aesthetic movements—from romanticism forward—was how to subvert *representation* (mimesis) through *presentation* (theatricality). With symbolism came the self-consciousness of theatrical art as opposed to the illusion of an outside reality. Maeterlinck shows a radically new concern for form of space and form of character and for a linkage between the two. In the beginning of the twentieth century, Gordon Craig, a practitioner and theorist noted for his work with theatre space, followed up on Maeterlinck's ideas about the need for the dramatic character to have a more spatial and theatrical stage presence. Craig charged that "Imitation is a form of mockery ... [it] is distasteful to everything in Nature; it irritates, it angers, or it bores" (*The Theatre Advancing* 157). Instead of presenting the narrative detail called for with imitation, theatre artists should focus the spectator's attention on the artistic object, on the artistic medium, a process that would bring the spectator onto the stage within the same perspective and atmosphere. What does this have to do with the mimetic representation of life?

It all begins with Plato and Aristotle—of course. For Plato, imitation or mimesis was a mere copy of a copy, the latter copy being no more than the idea that is ultimately inaccessible to the artist. Because of his critical skepticism, Plato gives future scholars less food for thought than his most celebrated disciple, Aristotle. With his more "positive" concept of reality as well as the imitation of it, Aristotle is more important for modern aesthetic theory and is a great deal more cited in connection with the notion of mimesis. His pragmatic conceptualization of mimesis (the imitation of an action), applied to works of art, has been more useful to theorists of theatre.

In his comments on mimesis Patrice Pavis reaffirms the fact that in Aristotle's theory, "Imitation does not apply to an ideal world, but to human action (and not to characters)" (*Dictionnaire* 207). Aristotle had a particular interest in the mimesis conveyed through and by theatrical space, theatrical mimesis, which has always been regarded as a special kind of imitation. As pointed out by Pavis, it is important to note that for Aristotle, the artistic imitation of the theatre should not concern itself with either idealized reality or the assessment of human character. This is one reason why Aristotle, whose conception of "creative" imitation is fundamentally different from that of Plato, is not as concerned with the moral aspects, with the practical, political dangers of artistic mimesis. Taking into account the fundamental philosophical distinctions between Plato and his disciple, it is quite possible that they could have come to a basic agreement on mimetic theory, at least on the grounds that it closely links aesthetic theory with ideology and that its moral danger is proportionate to its purported relationship to perceived reality. Nevertheless, since the very beginning, the dialectic of mimesis as it relates to some authentic reality has an unsteady history. Mimesis, our perception and our conception of it, has indeed evolved with ideology. Since the Romantic period of the eighteenth century, the scholars of the West have place it at the center of the debate on literary as well as dramatic art.[15]

To consider the mimetic "crisis" of the Romantic period we would do well to get a closer look at a more contemporary viewpoint on Aristotelian mimetic theory. Two exemplary commentators are Roselyne Dupont-Roc and Jean Lallot. In the introduction to their edition of Aristotle's *Poetics,* they address the question of the productive-creative potential of mimesis by explaining their selection of the French verb *représenter* as much closer—than *imiter*—to Aristotle's intentions to define the mimetic operation:

> Now we see why, against all tradition, we have chosen to translate *mimesthai,* not by "to imitate," but by "to represent": the theatrical connotations of this verb require it, especially because, as in the case of *mimeisthai,* it suggests the idea of both the object-"model" and the object-product, whereas "to imitate" excluded the use of the latter term, the most important. (20)[16]

Like other contemporary interpreters of Aristotle, they believe that the emphasis should be shifted to the mimetic product or so-called "copy," to the extent that it would take on a certain aesthetic independence. In a later note on Aristotle's text, they further comment that the mimetic operation "establishes between two objects, model and copy, a complex relation; implying at the same time resemblance and difference, identification and transformation, in a single sweep" (157). Finally, in accord with this insistence that, due to his profound respect for mimetico-aesthetic distance in representation,[17] Aristotle was not concerned with mimetic *duplication,* they comment on his fundamental precept of man's tendency to experience and to seek pleasure in representation:

> The pleasure wrought by the representation as such is one of recognition, the intellectual pleasure of the putting together of the represented form (created by the representation) with the already familiar natural object. The pleasure deriving from recognition depends on the fact that the painting *is not* the exact replica of the object. (165)

The pleasure of mimetic recognition is one of "the pleasure of discovery that is simultaneously pleasure of surprise (*thaumazein*) and pleasure of learning (*manthanein*): 'Look, it's him' and 'So that's its particular form!'" (165).[18]

It is clear, therefore, that this contemporary reevaluation of mimesis is a hearty response to naturalism's passion for the illusive (and elusive) authenticity of duplication. Contemporary scholars aggressively attack naturalistic conceptions of theatre. On the one hand, Ubersfeld adamantly proclaims that what artists set out to copy is not reality or any "real" object, but already some kind of conventional, conditioned image or illusion of reality:

What is "presented" [donné] in the theatrical space, is never an image of the world,
but the image of an image. What is "imitated" is not the world, but the world
refigured according to fiction and within the framework of a culture and
a code. We find here the presence of the anterior geno-text: the concrete
scenic space imitates an imaginary space within a specific cultural framework. One can define the truth of a scenic image, or if you prefer, its
realism, not by its conformity to an elusive reality, but to this imaginary
space." (*L'Ecole* 67–68; author's emphasis)

Other theorists are concerned with the mimetic quality of aesthetic self-consciousness or *self-re*-presentation. Robert Abirached is particularly sensitive to
the resulting polemic and is, in this respect, somewhat of a spokesperson for
contemporary French theory of the theatre. He believes that the new bourgeois
culture of the mid-eighteenth century produced a profound mimetic crisis,
which had a profound effect on the subsequent production, theory, and practice of theatre. This ever-advancing culture affirmed individual rights by placing
the economy at the center of all human relationships; and in so doing it undermined the art patron's sensitivity to the sacred and the imaginary in order to
promote the imperialism of the rational order (92–93). According to
Abirached, this new dominant ideology subsequently deformed the dynamic
classical concept of mimesis:

> Entering the bourgeois era, theatre moves progressively to dissimulate its
> theatrical nature, to which the history of all the modes of performance had
> attested, from the ancient mask to the declamatory style of seventeenth-
> century tragedians. (108)

Here we begin to appreciate Abirached's understanding of the Aristotelian
dynamics of mimesis, which he evidently perceives as reflecting a concept of
self-consciousness in the theatre arts:[19] the mask and the declamation, for
example, are in a more *direct* mimetic relationship to the essence of the theatre arts than they are to the physical appearance or voice quality of the
spectator. They are signifiers that refer back to a theatrical code. The pleasure of the theatrical mimesis operates through the mask at the level of self-
revelation or the display of the theatre's "creative" wares, so to speak. This is
all in keeping with the tenets of the complex relationship between model
and copy, simultaneously implying resemblance and difference, identification and transformation.[20] In the theatre, self-representation is part of
the concept of dynamic representation based on aesthetic distanciation as
elaborated by Dupont-Roc and Lallot. However, Abirached seems to suggest that the dynamics of theatrical representation are generated around
three objects and not just two. Between the object-model and the object-
product/"copy," there lies the object-theatre (a mask-like object), the latter
becoming the legitimate focus of theatrical mimesis. Theatrical art *presents*
itself through the work as much as the other way around. It is not that the

object-model is either simply or complexly reproduced in the theatre, but that it becomes—it is simultaneously transformed *by* as it is transformed *into*—a theatrical model both before becoming and *in order to become* an object-product. Consequently, the representation, which is a self-presentation, is necessarily a *self-re*-presentation of the theatrical sign.

This imposition of the theatrical sign in the mimetic operation is special precisely because of the profound relationship between theatre and life. Our perception of and our response to theatre, where humans are confronted by humans,[21] is not the same as it is in other mimetic arts. Perhaps it would be more appropriate to say that the "representation" carried out in the theatre acquires a *displaced* quality that uniquely and completely reflects the spectators' perception of their self-image as having a theatrical quality; this is insofar as they participate in an imaginative reality in some way similar to that targeted by the stage (either directly or indirectly). There is a universalized theatrical identity at work here where emphasis is placed on the dramatization of perceived reality as a means of broadening one's understanding of this reality (or hoax).[22] This implies not only a *prise de conscience* of its artificiality but also certain insight into its imaginative potential and into its capacity to participate in a creative life process.

Agosto Boal has explored the bond of theatre to life for his socially committed Forum Theatre. He has explained that theatre is unique among the arts for the forum it provides for self-observation, an activity that is socially therapeutic. "Theatre is born," Boal says, "when the human being discovers that it can observe itself; when it discovers that, in this act of seeing, it can see *itself*— see itself *in situ;* see itself seeing. . . . The human being alone possesses this faculty for self-observation in an imaginary mirror. . . . Therein resides the essence of theatre: in the human being observing itself. *The human being not only 'makes' theatre: it 'is' theatre.* And some human beings, besides being theatre, also make theatre" (*Rainbow* 13; author's emphasis).[23] This doubling of the actor into the role of spectator has led to Boal's concept of the "spect-actor" (13). Boal has also emphasized that theatre means change: "Theatre is conflict, struggle, movement, transformation, and not simple exhibition of frames of mind. It is verb and not simply adjective" (*Jeux pour acteurs et non acteurs* 69). He believes very deeply in creative mimesis, since he has translated Aristotle's dictum "Art imitates nature" as "Art re-creates the creative principle of things created" (*Theater of the Oppressed* 1; trans. modified).[24]

New interpretations of mimetic theory take into account theatre's participation in the life process, theatre as cultural process, and its use of the faculty of the imagination to affect this process.[25] Abirached reminds us of how, in direct contradiction to this perspective, the commercialism of bourgeois culture had undermined notions of Aristotelian mimesis in order to exploit a politics of illusion for purely ideological reasons. Instead of respecting the historical evolution of an *aesthetic of displacement,* the artistic creation—or, technical precision—of an *illusion scénique* would effectively and practically modify reality.[26] The new bourgeois, naturalistic theatre avoided "the traces of dramatic stylization" (108) in order to create a false but amenable illusion of social and domestic harmony and of individual liberty. The developing new theatre aesthetic ignored what Abirached calls the "acquiescence to imagination" [*acquiescement à l'imaginaire*] (158) deduced by Aristotelian mimesis. Bourgeois propaganda theatre took interest only in the production of a certain false, but harmonic imagery that counterpoised the paradoxes of the newly acquired, but all too profitable[27] tenets of individual liberty.

To appreciate Abirached's harsh criticism we must recognize the important status of the fictional universe in the classical theatre, that is, in the theatre of ancient Greece as well as of Europe of the classical period. Beyond the representation of the "exterior" world, and beyond the interior, psychological portrait of an individual hero, these theatres evidently placed much of the mimetic emphasis on the "interior" world of the theatre itself which was seen to be in direct correspondence with the imagination of a collective consciousness; or we might say, with the imaginative reception of a collective.[28] This aspect is made clearer by distinguishing between the terms "fiction" and "illusion." The representation in the classical sense was meant to be perceived as a fiction, without "degenerating" into an illusion of some idealized exterior world. In this sense, all theatrical representation was, to a lesser or greater extent, metatheatrical.[29] Thus Abirached's warning concerns the fictional quality of the representation being deformed into illusion: the essentially aesthetic becomes fundamentally political, creative truth becomes technical propaganda.

Finally, Abirached's history of the dramatic character suggests that it is not really until the symbolist movement of the late nineteenth century, and in particular the theatre of Alfred Jarry, that theatre again begins to emphasize the imaginative faculty in order to rediscover the true sources of mimesis:

> By demanding the preservation of the stage's radical strangeness, [Jarry] treats the character as an *autonomous mask*, relieved of all immediately figurative pretension. . . .
>
> Jarry, who defines the character as "a walking abstraction," rediscovers *the essential paradox of mimesis*, which fabricates the real with the fictional and life through *an action generated by its own logic*. This brings mimesis back to the elemental forces that govern its functioning and it rids the signs that it traces of all reference to some understood object, which would be nature. . . . Mimesis is called upon *to turn against itself*, and to produce, not a release induced by tears or by laughter, but an effect of derision and pained expression which, from the stage, is passed along to men, things, and events. (188–89)[30]

We see that, for the new symbolist sensibility of the late nineteenth century, "reality" is supposed to be produced by an action that generates its own logic thereby demonstrating a creative mimesis that turns against itself, transforming the sense of passive mimetic imitation into active representation, as Dupont-Roc and Lallot would have it. The theatre looks increasingly to its own aesthetic resources, to the creative presentation of its art. It converts the dramatic character into a theatrical sign ("an autonomous mask") whose autonomous nature makes it possible to speak of the inception of a new theatricality based on a concept of *aesthetic subjectivity*. When we speak of the "self-consciousness" of an art form we are, no doubt, in an anthropomorphic mode that personifies the art form as having consciousness. Creative theatre has more of a "consciousness"—a self-awareness, an awareness of its liminal, subjunctive purpose—than illusionist theatre.[31] If we continue in this mode we may view the theatre form itself as a subject, one which is questioning the principles of its extension, the principles of exterior and interior, past and present, as they relate to its form. For Jarry, Maeterlinck, and post-symbolist dramatists, human subjectivity was out of place in the context of the self-conscious *theatrical subjectivity* of their theatrical art. It was much later in the twentieth century that nouveau dramatists were able to co-relate hypertheatricality and hypersubjectivity to the dramatic character. The "acquiescence to imagination," so crucial to contemporary mimetic theory, was transformed by the surrealist inward turn into an image of a human psyche that was empty and therefore, like Jarry's characters, "relieved of all immediately figurative pretension." The idea of representing the "unrepresentable" on stage shifts from the universal-mystical toward the personal-psychic. Representation in terms of the pure presentation of experience is necessarily the presentation of an inner experience. So the metatheatrical shift to the "medium" of theatrical art, is likewise a shift to the inside: the creative potential of the stage is at once limited to and unlimited by the creative mind. Thus the confrontation between theatricality and mimesis, the concept of mimesis and the artistic practice of theatre. This is how Beckett helped to put art back on track.

[2]

SURREALIST INNER SPACE:
THEATRE OF THE (EMPTY) MIND

In the end, one experiences only oneself.

—FRIEDRICH NIETZSCHE

SURREALIST THEORY AND THEATRICALITY

We have seen that the *prise de conscience* with respect to the empty container of human existence provided fertile ontological terrain for the growth of a less representational symbolism in art. Moreover, the artist who sought to rise above the perceptual barriers provided by ideological world and doctrinal, mythical heaven assumed a critical-creative attitude toward the illusion of reality. Symbolist dramatists and directors, from Maeterlinck to Chekhov to Craig to Copeau, fostered a creative approach to mimesis, one which rejected the illusion of realism, while bringing to light the authenticity of theatrical imagery. The more theatre focused on itself, on its form and structure, the more the human individual on stage transfigured into the image of a human icon, one which dramatists increasingly exploited for its ability to duplicate simultaneously the aura of the stage and the frontier of the "inside and outside" dialectic. Symbolist dramatists and directors increasingly regarded the stage as an empty psyche at the same time they envisioned the protagonist's form as a material representation of an inner empty space. The psychic space envisioned by the dramatist for the protagonist was doubly self-conscious to the extent that it duplicated the empty space of the stage as a representation of itself. The perspectival move from the outer theatrical space (which doubles as a psychic space), through the frame of the center-stage human icon into the psychic space (which doubles as a theatrical space) would provoke a hypertheatrical condition. Inside and outside would coordinate through emptiness.[1]

Contemporary scholarship balks at the idea of inside and outside—not so much the outside as the inside. In his seminal essay on postmodernism, for his part, Fredric Jameson criticizes the postmodernist rejection of the hermeneutic model of inside-outside, one which, for most scholars, presupposes a Romantic-modernist belief in subjective interiority. Jameson questions the "new depthlessness, which finds its prolongation both in contemporary 'theory' and in a whole new culture of the image or the simulacrum" (6). In postmodernism "depth is replaced by surface, or by multiple surfaces" (12). Jameson uses Edvard Munch's painting "The Scream" as an example of a form of art that develops the important hermeneutic "depth model" of inside and outside. The new-age protagonist, born of a non-representational aesthetic shift at the turn of the century, a protagonist I will call "hypersubjective," is in many ways a return to the depth model, but to a whole new metaphysics of inside *as* outside and outside *as* inside. As a self-sustaining signifier whose signified materializes in its referral to the "meaning" of emptiness, the hypersubjective dramatic character overreaches conventional dialectics. Munch's human figure in "The Scream" could have taken pause on Maeterlinck's stage on his way to Beckett's. The mask-like human image represents not so much a "crying out" as a "calling in" of the spectator's attention. Scholarship has missed this *mise en abyme* aspect of the cry opening to the headspace. In the hypersubjective theatre of Beckett et al., suggestions of the "calling in," and of the speechless, soundless scream, form a part of a subtle and thoroughly comprehensive theatricality.

One of the most important questions to ask, however, is if there is subjectivity beyond language—an extralinguistic inside. The interest of symbolist visionaries like Maeterlinck turned from psychological narrative to figural and musical poetry. An important component of this shift was the artist's conception of his own human mind, the inner world. Behind the rejection of narrative lurked a rejection of the mind as a language space. The idea of a thought became more material and eventful and less systematic or instrumental. Albert Camus would remind us at the beginning of the existentialist movement in the 1940s that "[reason] is an instrument of thought and not thought itself" (*Le mythe de Sisyphe* 71). The instrument does not produce the same representation at all times and with all its individual users. Within an empty mind, as within an empty stage, artists could free themselves from the web of signification and search for "thought itself," thought without a code, without writing or text. The emphasis would shift from a collective, communicative *understanding* of thought-as-system to an individualized communicative *awareness* of thought-as-event. Artists envisioned a freer, more open, pre-conceptual communication of a psychic event. The new interest in empty space as empty space, with the focus on the individual as a figural icon, and a deemphasis on the text as narrative, provided the impetus for the surrealists' interest in the theatre of the empty mind.

To understand Beckett's particular, "psycho-theatrical" use of inner emptiness, we must, I think, return to the writings of the surrealists, who, more deliberately than the symbolists, turned their observation inwards. In this chapter I will trace the psychic reference of the image of the human figure isolated on a dark, empty stage to the theoretical writings of early twentieth-century surrealist thinkers. A fresh look at some rather well-established surrealist theory will help me to explicate the aesthetic level on which this image works. Certainly, one would not have to go far to find existentialist or psychoanalytical readings of the dramatic texts I examine in the following chapter. In fact, there is probably no serious intellectual movement that critics have not advanced as either a pretext of these works or as the proper hermeneutic tool to decipher their codes. I have already explained the importance of an integrated semiotic-phenomenological approach to the design of empty space in this kind of theatre. In this chapter, I will focus on the connection to surrealism, albeit a phenomenological dimension of surrealism. Antonin Artaud is the quintessential model for an integrated semiotic-phenomenological-surrealist theatro-metaphysical vision of the world, one that culminates in "the dead void of space" located in a human psyche at the dead center of the stage. But other surrealist thinkers, not usually associated with theatre, are also important to a broad understanding of Artaud's vision. Surrealist writings will help articulate concepts of hypertheatricality, hypersubjectivity, and the *mise en abyme* of empty theatrical space for the "hypersubjective" plays.

Nouveau théâtre's connection to surrealism has not seemed to move beyond what the distinguished Beckett scholar Ruby Cohn has described as "the surrealist liberation of the imagination" and the "turn inwards" ("Surrealism" 165). Indeed, most studies of the influence of surrealist theory on French nouveau théâtre actually downplay the theatrical potential of surrealism's central concepts, focusing instead on the surrealist quest for a new non-rational form of language, one capable of revealing authentic, primitive thought processes. One would sense that the processes revealed by automatic writing about the faculty of language—its origins or its production, rational or non-rational—were not seen in a theatrical light, i.e., as a dimension of human awareness that supports and completes a visual image.[2] In his search for a surrealist aesthetic, however, David G. Zinder offers a new perspective on the connection between automatic writing, psychoanalysis, and untheatrical aesthetic verbosity. On the one hand, Zinder reiterates the fascination of the surrealists for the "inexhaustible intellectual, spiritual, and artistic sustenance in the psychological mechanisms of man, particularly dreams and the irrational . . . " (36), and, more particularly, for the "uncensored expressions of the unconscious" (38). On the other hand, however, he recognizes at least one surrealist's reluctance to pledge allegiance to psychoanalysis. Zinder points out that Salvador Dali was wary of the organizational and in many ways rationalizing capacity of psychoanalytic systems, their capacity to undercut the essential mystery of surrealist reality:

> The starting point for Dali's new method was the Surrealist preoccupation with images wrested from the human consciousness. . . .
>   The problem with the images produced by the technique of automatism was their "virtuality," their unobjectifiable potential which rendered them, in Dali's term, "non-evolutive." What is more, Dali felt that this order of images fell too easily into the realm of psychoanalysis. Consequently, while remaining residually enigmatic, they were easily reduced to "current and logical speech," and for the most part lost their mystery. (43)

In addition, though Zinder is more implicit than explicit in this regard, he relates Dali's skepticism at the usefulness of psychoanalytic theory within a surrealist aesthetic to the more authentically theatrical quality of Dali's vision. Thus he praises Dali for having brought "a distinctly theatrical cast to the hitherto literary passivity of the Surrealist movement" (42). We should, I believe, construe "theatrical cast" as relating to the visual, spatial dimension of theatre.[3]

Zinder's remarks shed new light on the surrealist connection to nouveau théâtre where the poetic language of the early surrealists becomes subordinate to the visual-spatial dimension of the stage. Beckett and his contemporaries can be credited for having understood that before language there was space—inner, mental space as well as outer space; they recognized the capacity of the stage to represent inner as well as outer space and to suggest a connection between the two.[4] Existentially speaking, an awareness of extension precedes space, and an awareness of space precedes and backgrounds language, or, in other words, the most fundamental systems of human language were a posteriori constructed and inscribed within a primordial awareness of inner space. Theatrically speaking, behind every utterance lies a visual image which in turn is backgrounded by the space out of which the stage is carved. Paradoxically, the theatre that exploits this message to its fullest must shun the rigor and structure of psychoanalysis and construct its essential mystery around a concept of empty space: empty stage equals empty mind.

This connection between inner-mental-psychic space[5] and outer-aesthetic-stage space, if not apparent in the creative drama of the early surrealist movement, was present in the form of a precise concept that originates in the theoretical writings of the surrealists: the paradigm of the empty psyche. Celebrated surrealist theorists such as André Breton, Roger Caillois, and Antonin Artaud depict the human psyche as a particular form of space whose ability to create meaning transcends complex psychoanalytic structures by signifying, more simply, in terms of vacuity.[6] Moreover, it is largely from its status as an unstructured empty space that the theatricality of this psychic space derives. This connection will be made clear in the following chapters where I examine the effects of the concept of psychic empty space in works of French nouveau théâtre.

Maurice Valency has recognized the late nineteenth-century symbolist effort "to achieve a more significant experience than the material world afforded" (422). He also recognized that the most fundamental divergence of surrealism from symbolism lies "in the translation of reality from the outer to the inner world" (425). The symbol was no longer perceived as an authentically conventional figure born of the outside world, but an almost self-generating entity produced in the mind of a solitary individual. The symbol is no longer reliable as a reflection of nature because the thinking subject makes a conscious effort to move in an opposite direction toward an opposite pole, that is, to turn his psychic activity inward on itself. But what attracts the surrealists to this inner world? Simply stated, the attraction lies more in its metaphorical, figural emptiness than in its psychoanalytical fullness, more in its potential to signify non-representational vacuity than to organize psychological substructures.[7] At the core of surrealism's aversion for traditional artforms and its desire to liberate the imagination by inverting and subverting established artistic convention, lurks a very specific and in many ways theatrical conception of the individual psyche, the locus of surreality.

At the same time that theatre theoreticians, dramatists, and practitioners are trying to reach beyond the naturalist-materialist illusion of the stage, surrealist theoreticians attempt to look beyond the material illusion of the intellectual mechanisms of the mind, a part of our being that we all tend to spatialize in our more introspective moments. Like empty theatrical space, the surrealist psyche will redirect its referential force inward, so to speak, to the spatial medium itself. Begun as an alternative to the straightjacket of conventional language, which evokes an impression of organized intelligence within the mind, the surrealist method betrays a fascination for the communicative potential of a vacuous mental space. André Breton, for example, explicitly acknowledged his enormous debt to the psychoanalytical theories of Freud, especially as they relate to the irrational intelligence of dreams.[8] Yet, considering Freud's contribution to the spatialization of the psyche, a closer look at Breton's references to psychic space demonstrates at once a particularly "extensive" rendering of Freud's dreamland and a significant divergence from both the classical and psychoanalytical metaphors of mental inner space. Breton transforms Plato's cave into a wholly interior psychic phenomenon, perceiving the mind less as a potentially fillable stage than as a stage backgrounded by its essential emptiness:

[L]et us not lose sight of the fact that the idea of surrealism aims quite simply at the total recovery of our psychic force by a means which is nothing other than the [vertiginous][9] descent into ourselves, the systematic illumination of hidden places and the progressive darkening of other places, the perpetual excursion into the midst of forbidden territory. (*Manifestoes* 36–37)

This perpetual, vertiginous descent was to take place, not in the crammed space of an overly intellectualized mind, not even in some primordial (but still mechanical) Id organized according to psychoanalytic theories, but in the *abyss* of the inner psyche.[10] I employ this term "abyss" to make a more precise connection to the writing of another surrealist theorist, Roger Caillois, who explains the mental operation to gain access to what he calls the "authentic universe" wherein we can find a "secret language of the personal 'abyss'":

From forbidden dark regions, there emerges a second world (that is actually the surreality) which, by nature, only shows up on the surface as incomplete and ambiguous manifestations which have the value of signals. (237–38)

"Personal abyss" implies inner emptiness. The surrealist language discovered within this personal abyss would not belong to the same superficial psychic realm of the conventional signifying sign systems, but would exist in the form of mysterious, pre-symbolic "signals" seemingly suspended in inner space. These signals correspond rather neatly to the illuminated "hidden places" described by Breton on his perpetual inner journey. They equally evoke images of not only the celestial bodies themselves (signals) but also the interstellar medium (abyss) of an inner cosmos, which, like the outer cosmos, is characterized primarily by its vacuity.[11]

This sounding of the depths of the inner psyche resonates even in Beckett's earliest drama, and it pioneers a non-narrative, hypertheatrical form of subjectivity for the character and the artistic medium alike. Shimon Levy has observed that in *Endgame* Hamm's blindness greatly contributes to one's perception of the stage space in the work as "a self-reflective metaphor of internal or inner space" (24). But let us take this suggestion a step further by adding that Hamm's blindness evokes not just inner space, but also the imaginary emptiness of this space. Consider Hamm's recurrent and cryptic references to the drop of water in his head suggesting something on the order of a vertiginous descent into a psychic abyss. Early in the work, when Hamm entreats Clov to let him sleep—i.e., to let him turn inward into the space of his consciousness—he adds a seemingly irrelevant remark: "There's something dripping in my head . . . A heart, a heart in my head" (18). Much later in the work the reference to this dripping is reinforced: "Something dripping in my head, ever since the fontanelles. . . . Splash, splash, always on the same spot. (*Pause*). Perhaps it's a vein. (*Pause.*) A little artery" (50). This dripping within the cavity of Hamm's head (a psycho-surrealist version of Plato's cave?) stands as an aesthetic attempt to uncover and express the primitive surreality of psychic space, and a means of generating the communication of primitive signals. One can see and hear the supra-referential drops, as they penetrate below the language-space of Hamm's mind. Perhaps Hamm's psychotic obsession indicates a personality disorder. But does it really suggest a loss of subjectivity? Perhaps one could more accurately argue the contrary: that, turned inward into the empty space of his mind, his hyperconsciousness becomes a more essential and inextricable part of the work as a whole—a microcosmic empty space representing an alternative, more "hyper," form of subjectivity.

What I call "hypersubjectivity" in Beckett's theatre is a direct function of empty space, which is itself an outgrowth of the dramatist's essentialist perspective on space. Robert Langbaum has effectively argued that the "identity" of Beckett's dramatic character "approaches zero," that Beckett is haunted by the Cartesian image of a disembodied mind as the center of life and identity, of "mind surrounded by void" of "self isolated in the head" (137, 142). Yet, like many other theorists, Langbaum has not acknowledged the essentialist perspective on space that operates this image. Building on his excellent account of the aesthetic relevance of Beckett's existential world view, let us examine the hypothesis that, metatheatrically as well as existentially, the void that *surrounds* the mind is duplicated *within* the mind, producing a double referent that invokes metatheatricality in a profound way. When Beckett brings the concepts of stage and mind closer together—when he makes the connection between outside and inside—the head of the dramatic character becomes the central self-referential icon or *mise en abyme*[12] of theatrical empty space. The body of the dramatic character functions as a cerebral, acutely focused, theatrical "hyperspace," a form for the subject which allows us to draw a fresh parallel between Beckett's theatre and Artaud's theory.

ANTONIN ARTAUD ON THE METADRAMATIC UNION OF EMPTY SPACE AND EMPTY CHARACTER

Antonin Artaud shares the idea of a vertiginous psychic descent with Breton and Caillois. Monique Borie's comments on Artaud's version of surrealism make this clear:

> In this way, against rationalism and the walls which it has constructed at the heart of its language, surrealism, for Artaud, represents a call from within, a will to return to the origins of inner space. (*Antonin Artaud* 100)

Because of his theatro-metaphysical vision, however, Artaud does more than any other surrealist thinker to establish the parallel between the emptiness of theatrical space and that of the psyche. Artaud's writing represents the acute historical-critical point at which a modern ontological interest in empty space and an aesthetic interest in the empty theatrical stage come together with the concept of the dramatic character as a form whose focal point is its essentially empty psyche. The close affinity between psyche and stage forms the crux of Antonin Artaud's surrealist and metaphysical theory of theatricality, a theory in which the void becomes a nodal point of space, and in which emptiness begins in one's head. With Artaud, the space of the dramatic representation constitutes an especially "imaginary"—in the full sense of the word—kind of space closely related in form and content to the conceptualization of psychic space as a material void. Monique Borie impresses upon us both the fundamental and highly structured ("*mise en abyme*–like") nature of Artaud's conception of the void: "All this materialization of the void ad infinitum has the value of creation" and "The space of the theatre is space of creation, but it is also the space of perpetual return to the void" (249, 254). One must understand, moreover, that, with Artaud, what is fundamental for the theatre is equally fundamental for the thinking subject, so a notion of vacuity underlies all metaphysically meaningful space including that of the personal psyche: "When there is agreement in the thoughts of men, where can we say that this agreement is reached, if not within the dead void of space?" ("Le Théâtre et les dieux" 202). Artaud describes his acceptance of the Void as a kind of metaphysical leap of faith:

> When I thought I was rejecting this world, I know now that I was really rejecting the Void.
> I know that this world does not exist and I know *how* it does not exist.
> The source of my suffering until now is my rejection of the Void.
> The Void that was already in me. ("Les nouvelles révélations de l'être" 149–50)

Like Beckett, Artaud transcends the Cartesian image of mind surrounded by a void. He does this by anchoring theatrical space to a central focal point, the vacuous mind at the center of that void: "Always the void, always the point around which matter thickens" ("Le Théâtre et les dieux" 204). This dualistic concept of the void links the metatheatrical to the metaphysical by ultimately referring to an internal world, a psychic space, like that of the metaphysical Balinese central dancer so prominent in Artaud's theory. Artaud was particularly fascinated by the "highly significant" and "absolute" gesture of this central character who "always touches his head at the same place, as if wishing to indicate the position and existence of some unimaginable central eye, some intellectual egg" (*The Theatre* 63). The head becomes at the same time the central core of theatrical space in this theatre and an inner, psychic point of reference that reflects the outer theatrical space: "And always this confrontation of the head, this Cyclops eye, the inner eye of the mind which the right hand gropes for" (66). We can understand more clearly Artaud's fascination with the Balinese central dancer in the light of his constant and often paradoxical references to a mind at the center of space, to the "metaphysical idea . . . of the dead center of space through which the mind must pass" ("Le Théâtre et les dieux" 202). In a remarkable parallel to Hamm's report of dripping in his head (*Endgame*), the central dancer signals with gesture what Hamm signals with language: the "intellectual egg" or central sign of empty, non-psychological theatrical space.

Why the void? We can only understand Artaud's conceptualization of an internal, empty world in terms of a surrealist notion of empty space, which itself must be understood in terms of the concept of spatial extension, the primordial awareness outlined by Greimas that I discussed in chapter 1. "Extension" (*étendue*) becomes a synonym for space in Artaud's writings: "The language of the theatre aims then at encompassing and utilizing extension, that is to say space, and by utilizing it, to make it speak" (*The Theatre* 110–11). Thus Artaud rejects constructed space for extension. When he refers to space, he envisions an *extensive form of space,* an attribute that attaches to a twentieth-century conception of the mind. His primary dramaturgical goal was to rediscover a spatial language—image, gesture— that could resist epistemological and intellectual constraints of "construction" by signifying in terms of extension. When he speaks of "space" he is really speaking of an extensive form of space, a formless extension of "hyperspace." So the extension of empty space into the uncharted depths of the human psyche mirrors its extension outward into the cosmos, making the connection between inside and outside in the surrealist mind. This mirroring has a profound effect on the dramatist's use of metatheatricality and on the spectator's reception of the dramatic character surrounded by a void.

Through the metaphorization of an extensive inner void and the perpetual vertiginous descent into this void, Breton, Caillois, and Artaud attempt to resist rationalist construction and to preserve an impression of extension. This is the kind of surrealism that orients the theatricality of much of French nouveau théâtre, a surrealist mode that to date most scholars have overlooked. The protagonist, linked by both discourse and corporeal image to this phenomenological merger of space and character, offers a striking example of how Breton's concern for the "concentration of [one's] mind upon itself" (*Manifestoes* 29) can orient the theatricality of a play, one that further substantiates Charles Lyons's point concerning the impossibility of separating "the image of theatrical space from the image of character" (27–28).[13]

THE HYPERSUBJECTIVE *MISE EN ABYME* OF EMPTY SPACE

The extensive hyperspace of the cosmos turns inward in this century. Artaud's theory endows the concept of empty space with a new aesthetico-ontological dimension that helps to merge Copeau's outer stage with Breton's inner stage in two essential ways: not only does it "theatricalize" the representation of the inner psyche, but it also signals the psyche's function as an intermediate (meta)theatrical image that "extends" empty space by "placing it into *abyme*."

The concept of *"abyme,"* which I will reservedly translate as "abyss," is crucial to any theory of metadiscourse that intends on the one hand to explain theatrical self-consciousness in terms of space and, on the other, to establish a direct link between character and space. In the nineteenth century, the concept of "abyss" was very popular with symbolist poets, most notably Baudelaire, searching for an expression of existential nothingness (*néant*). When twentieth-century surrealism takes hold of the concept, it becomes even more prominently associated with the personal psyche, as is the case with Caillois's reference to a "personal abyss." Still more interesting, however, is that, since André Gide, the concept of *mise en abyme*, "placing into abyss," has served as a spatially oriented rendering of what the Anglo-Saxon critical tradition has referred to as aesthetic self-consciousness. Taking Lucien Dällenbach's full-scale study of *mise en abyme* into account, Mieke Bal has emphasized the iconic aspect of the reflective "fragment" or "enclave," defining it as "any *sign* having for *referent* a pertinent and continuous aspect of the text . . . which it *signifies*, by means of resemblance, once or several times" (123; author's emphasis).[14] The kind of concrete iconic resemblance identified in a "play within a play," on a textual as well as a per-formative level, is the most conventional example of theatrical *mise en abyme*. But Beckett and his contemporaries take this kind of mirror reflection several steps further by making the empty, supra-referential and extra-linguistic connection between aesthetic self-consciousness and ontological self-consciousness, be-tween theatre space and psychic space. On an aesthetic level, the "emptiness" of the outer (visible) stage requires the kind of self-referral that could resist the closure of rational, referential meaning precisely by virtue of its capacity to suggest an internal, infinite abyss or infinite extension—of self-reflection. On an ontological level, Breton's notion of the "vertiginous descent" into our own consciousness suggests a psychic *mise en abyme* where each successive "illumination of a hidden place" reveals the essential "emptiness" surrounding the preceding not-quite-rational image.

With Artaud and Beckett, then, avant-garde theatre reveals itself as a spatial abyss analogous to the metaphorical imaginary space of the psyche. Thus the spatial aspect of *mise en abyme* is emphasized and more evident. Whether we speak of a psychic, theatrical, or textual *mise en abyme*, like the surrealists, we think in terms of space. The "absolute gesture" of the Balinese central dancer points to the metaphysical and imaginary realm of a human psyche that plays a major role in the creation of theatrical space. Artaud's revolutionary "theatre of cruelty" could only realize its metaphysical and metatheatrical potential by identifying and focusing on its own "central eye" or central sign. Mind is spatialized at the dead center of theatre where it constitutes the "raison d'être" of "organic culture":

> There is in this [organic] culture an idea of space, and I say that true culture can only be learned within space, and that it is an oriented culture, oriented as is theatre.
> Culture within space means the culture of a mind which does not cease to breathe and to feel itself living within space, and which calls to itself the substance [*les corps*] of space as the very object of its thought, but which, as a mind, situates itself in the middle of space, that is, at its dead center.
> This is perhaps a metaphysical idea, this idea of the dead center of space through which the mind must pass.
> But without the metaphysical there is no culture. ("Le théâtre et les dieux" 201–202)

And we remember that without the essential void—the only kind of space that allows extension—there is no (metaphysical) space.

Where is the thinking subject in this metaphysical system? Or rather, what becomes of the subject once it is transformed into an empty mind centered in void? The idea of mind assumes a new kind of subjectivity which is at the same time based on space (located at the center of space) and unconstructed by the Cogito. Space constitutes a precondition for the very existence of mind, for which the "substance of space" is "the very object of its thought." From this spatial ontology there evolves a theatrical world-view wherein the "dead center of space through which mind must pass" is not simply the theatre, but the *mise en abyme* of theatre as represented by the psychic space of a uniquely prominent dramatic character, the hypersubject of hypersubjective theatre. As space becomes hyperspace, the inner space of mind determines the hypersubject.

In Beckett's works not only does space become more concentrated and acutely defined, but this spatial concentration indicates an intensification of subjectivity. In fact, much has been written about the "destructive" quality of Beckett's works. According to many scholars, not only do these works signal the disappearance or "weakening of the subject" and the "abandonment of place" in particular, but they also testify to an "obliteration of time and space" in general.[15] Suppositions of the rejection of space seem to coincide with the rejection of the subject. But as French theorist Michel Corvin rightly points out, unlike classical forms of theatre where one "acts *in* space and constructs dramatic action *on* space," since the advent of nouveau théâtre one "acts *with* space": "Modern [theatrical] space possesses individuality and personality, in other words, a unique and complex character" ("Contribution à l'analyse scénique" 63; my emphasis). The suggestion that modern theatrical space achieves a new "individual" and "personal" dimension could be construed as according this space a more subject-like or subjective status; and as space becomes more "personal," the "person" becomes more spatial. To date, we have taken more interest in the dehumanization of the nouveau dramatic character than in the personalization of the nouveau theatrical space. Yet, since the advent of nouveau théâtre, the inseparability of character and space has been taken to an extreme.[16]

Critics who have downplayed both space and subjectivity in nouveau théâtre are right in one sense: the dramatic character is not really "alive and well" in Beckett's theatre. But he (or she) is still more dramatically significant—and dramatically subjective—than ever before. If, as we shall see, Beckett's focus on a unique central character such as Hamm is spatially determined, then we are dealing more with a concentrative effort than with a destructive one. In terms of theatre within theatre, there is not really any internal "play" because the entire expanse of the action coincides with the meta dimension of the drama. Beckett does not inset the play as do Shakespeare or Marivaux; his characters do not overtly or covertly discuss theatrical convention in the way that Pirandello's or Genet's characters would; and they do not refer thematically to life as a stage as in so many modern plays. Hamm is more theatrical, more *"en abyme,"* in the sense that he constitutes a more densely compacted theatrical sign; his apparent loss of personality and psychology yield to the elaboration of a simultaneously personal and theatrical empty space that extends the bounds and the force of the work's theatricality. His subjectivity is the primary source of the work's theatricality—and vice versa.

Rather than any weakening of the subject or obliteration of theatrical space, we should speak of a "hyperconscious," "hyperimaginative," theatrical *hypersubject* that serves as the center of gravity of a theatrical *hyperspace* constituting a *hypersubjective* theatre, which has been justly labeled as "hyper-theatrical."[17] Hypersubjective plays are those in which one solitary and introspective dramatic character becomes the overdetermined focal point (*mise en abyme*) of a theatrical metadiscourse based on an image of empty space. The head of this hypersubject constitutes the definitive material frame for an "empty" psychic space that equals the central theatrical metaphor.

THE HYPERSUBJECTIVE HAM(M) IN BECKETT'S *ENDGAME*

At this point, like many other scholars, I feel compelled to defend a "performative" reading of a dramatic text along with the belief that the perceptive reader can discern the "theatricality" of the dramatic text, i.e., the text's strategies to suggest concrete stage images to readers as well as to practitioners. Many scholars, Patrice Pavis among the most prominent,

have downplayed the importance of the original written text in the production of the "finished" performance. We must bear in mind that Pavis's
remonstrations against any belief in the "specificity" or theatricality of the
theatre text stem from his critical focus on the performance rather than
the text. He therefore concludes that the text can be no more than one
signifying system among many others in the performance, and he cautions
that any analysis of a performance must "at all costs avoid comparing the
mise en scène to the text from which it is supposed to issue" (*L'Analyse*
188). He recommends therefore that we "think separately of the study of
written texts and the study of stage productions that contain texts" (189).
However, despite this caution, Pavis freely admits that "the writing of texts
is largely influenced by the production practices of a given historical period, by what the period knows how to do theatrically" (186). This fact
alone would indicate that the dramatic text is theatrical to the extent that
the dramatist writes it with not only a stage but also a given state of performance art in mind.[18]

Despite the skepticism regarding the specificity of the dramatic text, we
cannot ignore that one reason dramatists write drama is to avoid narrative.
Another is to instruct a stage director in the design of the stage imagery. Still
another is in order to engage and to orient what Ubersfeld has referred to
as the "holes" in the dramatic text.[19] Directors who stage written texts begin
by reading them, by reading them as texts to be staged. A successful director
can be the ideal "performative" reader of the text, or a wholly original artist,
but many directors will admit to the former.[20] If we read the dramatic text
"performatively," that is, from a spatio-material point of view, we can usually
recognize the theatrically oriented imagination of the dramatist. When
Beckett wrote *Godot*, he imagined how the solitary tree could orient the
emptiness of the stage. When *Godot*'s first director, Roger Blin, read *Godot*,
no doubt that, even before consulting with Beckett, he too imagined the
connection between the tree and emptiness, though the tree he imagined
probably differed in its barrenness and its placement. When a director like
Alkalaitis comes along and tries to stage *Godot* in a subway, it is not because
she reads this in the text, or in the 'holes" of the text, but because she
effectively "rewrites" the text, adding her own text—and her own theatricality—to it. Scholars can legitimate a performative approach to the dramatic
text by approaching it with a spectating mind that is similar to that of the
director: by attempting to understand why the author has opted to ostend
and to frame his or her work.[21] Accordingly, I agree with Erik MacDonald's
insistence that, though the text is not the only element worthy of analysis in
a given theatrical project, it does remain "the central juncture for theoretical reflection on the theater" (*Theater at the Margins* 6). What is more, the
text is especially important to the theatre I have undertaken to analyze.[22]

As a form of introduction to Beckett's late works, which I will discuss in the following chapter, at this point I would like to demonstrate the hypersubjective spatial economy of Beckett's metadramatic *Endgame*. Applying some basic methodology from recent semiotic theories of the theatre text, I examine dramatic space—space as depicted (encoded) by the dramatist and imagined (decoded) by the reader of the text with or without the intent to produce the play—as a semiotic system of a given play.[23] The kind of space emerging from the *Endgame* text has the double referent of 1) the stage itself, and 2) a personal, inner psychic space. Hamm's body, reduced to a "thinking skull," delimits two primary contiguous and contingent spatial fields, one of outer and the other of inner theatrical space (see fig. 6). Finally, to complete fully the *mise en abyme*, the text communicates an impression of focalization on the inner theatrical space of Hamm's head through the creation of a series of Chinese-box-like intermediate frames between the outermost borders of the stage frame and Hamm's head, the ultimate interior frame.

I will concentrate primarily on those spatial indications that suggest—and therefore virtually create—the image of a hypersubject by contributing to a discourse on the general concept of empty space on the one hand, or, on the other, the spatial embedding (*"emboîtement"*) or *mise en abyme* of this empty space. These two important paradigms of the dramatic space in *Endgame*, empty space and spatial embedding, have close corollaries in the forms of "blindness" and "multiple framing." While the first constitutes a preliminary, simple *mise en abyme* by reflecting an image of emptiness, the second spatially reinforces (and overdetermines) the "abyss"; the multiple framing works to focus (embed) the head of the protagonist within a spatial continuum that suggests the extension of empty space into an infinite, interior, abyss.

Both of these spatial paradigms are present in the "explicit" didascalia (what Anne Ubersfeld refers to as the stage directions proper, set apart from the dialogue) as well as the "internal" (implicit) didascalia (the references to space contained in the verbal dialogue of the dramatic characters) ("Pedagogics of Theatre" 139–40). Michael Issacharoff too has proposed a useful semiotic tool for the analysis of textual space: the dichotomy of mimetic space versus diegetic space, a dichotomy that does not directly correspond to one of explicit versus internal didascalia. According to Issacharoff, within the global semiotic system of dramatic space, the mimetic space is "that which is made visible to an audience and represented on stage" ("Space and Reference in Drama" 215). Mimetic space is "not conveyed by verbal language" (220) per se, since it is visible on stage, that is, its referent is visible. Diegetic space, on the other hand, is merely "described . . . referred to by the characters . . . mediated through the discourse of the characters, and thus communicated verbally and not visually" (215). I hasten to caution that, at the level of the theatre text, "visualization" is a very complex process.

The opposition between the visualization of mimetic space and that of diegetic space becomes a highly subjective matter of degree, since it depends on the extent to which the reader (decoder) of the text allows the diegetic references to influence his or her imaginary construction of the theatrical space. As we shall see, in the case of Beckett's theatre, the distinction between the diegetic and the mimetic tends to blur. Beckett exteriorizes inner life, he makes the "outside inside" as Schechner puts it (194), by bringing the inside outside in part by means of a spatializing discourse. So when Issacharoff tells us that diegetic space works to focus and anchor mimetic space (220), I would add that, in the case of Beckett's hypersubjective theatre, it also works to actually create a kind of mimetic space.

What is the most basic configuration of the mimetic (visible) empty space of *Endgame?* At the primary level of the explicit didascalia Beckett describes the stage space as a "bare interior" (1). At this same level of explicit didascalia, scholars have noted the resemblance of this bare stage—with its two rear windows or "high peepholes," as Hugh Kenner calls them—to the inside of an immense skull.[24] Thus the bareness of the stage transfers to the skull of the character. The didascalia also describe Hamm as wearing dark glasses, an indexical feature that serves not only to indicate his blindness,[25] but also to emphasize the depiction of his head as a framelike skull. By virtue of this iconic relationship between stage and head, Hamm's head acquires a unique status as a spatial entity/image, and the emptiness of the stage space tends to transfer analogically to the psychic space inside the skull, a space which here qualifies as a special kind of mimetic space since it is essentially a visible, iconic construct fashioned out of the didascalia. Furthermore, the paradigm of "blindness" associated with Hamm reinforces the virtual image of inner emptiness. Hamm's blindness evokes not just inner space, as Shimon Levy claims,[26] but also the imaginary emptiness of this space.[27]

Despite the importance of the material, mimetic references (like the dark sunglasses) to Hamm's blindness, only at the diegetic level (through the verbal reference of the dialogue) does the emptiness of his blindness become fully "extended" into the realm of the personal psyche. Hamm can "see" no more than the void that bolsters his own bitter consciousness, an inner world to which he often refers in terms that accentuate the spatiality of his "empty" world vision. In warning Clov of his own future blindness, Hamm portrays this malediction as some sort of ontological contagion:

> In my house. (*Pause. With prophetic relish.*) One day you'll be blind like me. You'll be sitting there, a speck in the void, in the dark, for ever, like me. (*Pause.*). . . . Infinite emptiness will be all around you. . . . (36)

Hamm's head, centered within an "infinite emptiness," recalls Artaud's "dead center of space through which mind must pass," a mind that fully reflects the emptiness in which it is embedded.[28] Hamm is not simply "centered" within the theatrical space of the stage—the "house" to which he refers in the above quote; rather, his head is the embedded core of a spatial continuum involved in a metadramatic mission. Michel Corvin makes an important, "theatrical" contribution to the notion of embedding implied by the concept of *mise en abyme*. In applying this concept to contemporary theatre, Corvin links the spatial aspect of the "embedding" of the fragment (or enclave, or frame) to the syntagmatic chain of meaning:

> the embedding [*emboîtement*] entails a hierarchical relationship and it almost automatically clears the path to the domain of signification, since the embedded thing constitutes a syntagma destined, not to become the part of a whole . . . but the raison d'être of this whole. ("Espace, temps, mise en abyme" 144–45)

In the three-dimensional, multilayered space of the theatre, where notions of "framing" or "layering" exceed the one-dimensional or purely conceptual "framing" found in the other arts, spatial embedding can have a more direct and determinant relation to meaning. The "embedded thing" constitutes a central sign, which Corvin sees as the "raison d'être" of the work, or more precisely, the "first cause" of all the other—exterior and convergent—frames or layers of meaning.[29]

How does the spectator perceive Hamm's head as embedded (the second of our primary paradigms) within the theatrical space of the stage? How has Beckett inscribed this "intellectual egg" into the dramatic space of the text? Let us first consider the mimetic (visual) embedding before discussing how this is enhanced and anchored by the diegetic spatial indications. We remember, of course, that Hamm's individual, center-stage, physical presence is at the outset visually more framelike within a "bare interior" than it would be on a more furnished stage. Considering that the centering of his body is called for in the explicit didascalia and is the recurrent subject of Hamm's verbal language (the internal didascalia),[30] the mimetic space can be schematically described as a body centered in empty space. And the delimiting aspect of the walls enclosing the stage space (Hamm's house) is greatly enhanced when Hamm has Clov take him for "a little turn. . . . Right round the world," insisting that he "hug the walls" before bringing him back to the center again (25).

Yet, between the definitive *mise en abyme* of Hamm's skull and the outermost stage frame his "little turn" has described at the borders of the stage, there is a class of intermediate frames that assist the overall effect of embedding by bringing Hamm's head into a more acute focus. To this end, Hamm's infirm and useless body is "framed" not only by the wheelchair in which he is seated upright, but also by an old sheet that provides additional cover, and again by the dressing gown he wears, constituting the most immediate of frames for his more or less inactive body. His head is, in turn, covered by a "stiff toque" and a "large blood-stained handkerchief" (1), the most immediate of frames for this active talking skull. This "Chinese-box" tableau of layers of meaning converges on a central core that, in turn, signifies a progression of "deep" metatheatrical and metaphysical meaning in the reflective empty space of his skull. Hamm has a head or a skull, but not a face. Beckett has avoided specifying facial expression in his stage directions, so Hamm's voice will carry the brunt of his emotional shifts ("yawns," "gloomily," "violently," "relieved," "anguished," etc.). Consequently, the unveiling of Hamm's head at the beginning of the play, with the outlining effect created by the glasses and the hat, and the rigidity of the head that is a common posture of a sightless person, Beckett diverts the spectator's attention from the psychological detail of a human face to the architectonic quality of head and skull, the powerful center of the stage architecture.

Thus, in a strict sense, the mimetic space stops at the physical surface of Hamm's head, a form that provides the border between two contiguous and contingent spatial fields that are simultaneously evoked from the very beginning of the play when, on awakening, Hamm removes the handkerchief serving as the "curtain" to his inner theatrical space. While Beckett scholars have not missed the metatheatrical aspect of the handkerchief, they have not considered its function as an intermediate frame between the two fields of empty space. Hamm's psychic stage lies behind the sightless facade of his blind eyes, covered by black glasses that function more as "peepholes"—reminiscent of Hugh Kenner's reference to the windows of the skull-like stage—than as "peepers." Significantly, the very last gesture of the play, described in the explicit didascalia, is for Hamm to replace the curtain-like handkerchief over his face just as the (exterior) stage curtain falls. The inner stage physically closes to the gaze of the audience, demonstrating the correspondence between the inner and the outer theatrical spaces. As a theatrical object, the handkerchief effectively transforms the image of "centered body" to one of "centered mind," where the metatheatrical mind becomes an "inner theatre" centered in space. As the dividing envelope between outer and inner extension, Hamm's skull presents the proscenium arch of hypersubjective theatre. Unlike the "fourth wall" of the eighteenth and nineteenth centuries, however, its very presence invites free movement and comparison among the various theatrical spaces.

Working in conjunction with the visual cues, the diegetic spatial references of the text reinforce the mimetic focalization on the space of the inner stage as they concretize the representation of its virtual emptiness. Here, I will diverge considerably from Issacharoff's idea of diegetic space, which he defines as more of a conventional kind of unseen space, usually referenced to offstage ("outside space"). With Beckett's "inward-turning" theatre, however, one must look inside as well as outside the stage for diegetic spatial references.[31] For the most part, Hamm verbally engenders a poetics of space that closely coincides with Artaud's theory of inner space. We remember the analogy I drew early in this chapter between the absolute gesture—the central sign—of the touching of his head by the Balinese central dancer and Hamm's recurrent references to the constant dripping in his head. The latter represents the diegetic equivalent of this mimetic confrontation with the space of the "inner eye" announced by Artaud. First, dripping implies emptiness, for water can only "drip" through space that is empty.[32] Second, the dripping gives an impression of focalization. Hamm's self-conscious "cerebral confrontation" is expressed as physical, cerebral penetration through the force of successive dripping. And third, the central core that is metaphorically engraved into the space of the head by the constant dripping becomes, in effect, the "heart" (core) of the psyche. By evoking the displacement of the heart into the head ("A heart, a heart in my head") Hamm effectively places the paradigm of focalization *"en abyme."* With a heart in his empty skull, the "dripping" Hamm senses contrasts with the cerebral "throbbing" one might expect of a fully "furnished" mind within the furnished space of what Artaud has beratedly dubbed psychological theatre. Consistent with postmodern horror of epistemological closure, the core of meaning is continuously displaced. Psychic depth, here sounded and penetrated by the metaphysical drop of water, corresponds to metatheatrical depth. Hamm's image, and the textual discourse that supports it, constitute a new-age theatro-social subject, as well as an original, displaced form of meaning.

SUBJECTIVITY-SOCIETY-MEANING: THE CHARACTER REBORN AND THE SOCIAL HYPERSUBJECT CONCEIVED

Here, I return to the topic of subjectivity for hypersubjective theatre, subjectivity in light of the concept of dramatic character, on the one hand, and the quality of sociocultural relevance of the artform, on the other. To be sure, the determination of a category of subject coincides with the assessment of a concept of character in dramatic criticism. Consequently, the so-called death of the subject-character in postmodern art and theory impacts directly and brutally our theories concerning the mimetic relations between art and society. How can we conceptualize one individual or even a community of individuals, if individuals do not truly exist independently of a "social" system, one which deals with them simply as functions? Likewise, when critics speak of the death of the character, they generally refer to the elimination of the illusion of a subjective center in a nonnaturalistic character. The drama of Beckett et al. produces a highly integrated illusion of a disintegrated social fabric. But the characters designed by nouveaux dramatists, though unconventional, are not as fragmented as scholars believe. Furthermore, the theatrical space which they inhabit—and which inhabits them—is, as Ubersfeld reminds us, a playing space or "place where the action taking place has no need of an external reference" at the same time that it "always represents a symbolization of sociocultural spaces," a symbolization derived not from some "real" world, but from a man-made image of reality (*Lire* 144). Thus, in a sense, the stage is a theatrically induced form of society as the character is a theatrically induced subject.

Yet scholars from a variety of backgrounds have claimed that subject and society disappear from avant-garde drama in this century. Bert States notes almost nonchalantly what other contemporary theorists consider a major aesthetic crisis: "In the modern era, for example, the real drama is the gradual isolation of the protagonist from any social context whatsoever. Society is quite often absent" (as in Beckett) (*Great Reckonings* 173). Theorists like Mikhail Bakhtin and Peter Szondi have traced this century's shift from social drama (including psychologically social drama) toward subjective drama, identifying this shift as a break with the social value of the drama and an alienation of the individual's social essence. Paradoxically, this shift threatened subjectivity itself because, as the drama of symbolist authors (Strindberg, Ibsen, Chekhov) became increasingly monologic, they contradicted the fundamentally dialogic nature of both drama and (for Bakhtin) the subjective identity of the individual. We will deal with Bakhtin's theories of subjectivist modernism in the final chapter on the marionette-like character, so I will focus on Szondi at this point.

Szondi has written an illuminating study on the subjective crisis in drama. He was particularly struck by the symbolist-expressionist version of subjective drama in the late nineteenth century that could be traced to

> the forces that drove people out of interpersonal relations and into isolation. The dramatic style called into question by this isolation survived nonetheless because the isolated individual, whose formal equivalent is silence or the monologue, was forced back into the dialogic of the interpersonal relation by an external agency. (*Theory of the Modern Drama* 57–58)

These subjectivist tendencies were innately contradictory for society as well as for dramatic art: "'Closure' and the incapacity to engage in any (interpersonal) 'dialectic' destroyed the possibility of the Drama that had arisen from the decision of individuals to disclose themselves to one another" (58). Having violated the *sine qua non* of drama, i.e., interpersonal activity, Maeterlinck's characters are "speechless victims of death" (47). The "death" Szondi refers to is the death of the subject. Speaking of Strindberg's "expressionist *I* dramaturgy," he explains how extreme subjectivity tends to negate subjectivity altogether:

Because its exclusive focus on the subject finally leads to the undermining of that same subject, this art, as the language of extreme subjectivity, loses its ability to say anything essential about the subject. On the other hand, the formal emptiness of the *I* precipitates as the stylistic principle of expressionism—as the "subjective distortion" of the objective. . . . it is not the isolated *I* but the alienated world confronting the individual that is expressed thematically. Only through self-alienation, by becoming congruent with alien objectivity, could the subject manage, nonetheless, to express itself. (64)

Szondi argues that the aberrant production of this self-contradictory *I* style, carried on into the "drama" of Sartre and Beckett. Thus in *Godot* the characters press toward "the abyss of silence" in an "empty metaphysical space—a space that gives importance to whatever fills it" (54).[33]

According to Szondi, from at least 1880 onward, dramatic form is in trouble primarily because of its self-contradictory denial of the interpersonal and intersubjective essence of drama—a denial of social relevance—but also because of the way in which this contradiction eventually leads to a denial of the "relevant" meaning thought to be so essential to art. Thus Theodor Adorno writes an essay on *Endgame,* claiming that "concreteness in Beckett—that shell-like, self-enclosed existence which is no longer capable of universality but rather exhausts itself in pure self-positing—is obviously the same as an abstractness which is no longer capable of experience" ("Trying to Understand Endgame" 14). He too traces the aporia of the symbolic in Beckett to Strindberg, to what he calls Strindberg's "pan-symbolism" ("a tapestry in which everything and nothing is symbolic, because everything can signify everything"). For Adorno, the crux of Beckettian absurdity is that "Not meaning anything becomes the only meaning" (27). Adorno's still modernist-structuralist evaluation of *Endgame* considers meaninglessness in a negative light.

When we move to a poststructuralist point of view, however, meaninglessness acquires new relevance. Just as postmodernist-poststructuralist theorists and critics have reconsidered the concept of realism for drama they also have revised their judgment of meaning and meaninglessness in dramatic art as well as the role played by character and subject at the "center" or "decentered" locus of meaning or meaninglessness. In a recent study of the "death of character," Elinor Fuchs explains and exemplifies "the resistance to totalizing thought that is in the very nature of postmodern art and theory" (12). In the introduction to her study she traces the deconstruction of the subject by theorists such as Debord, Baudrillard, and Barthes, for whom "The interior space known as 'the subject' was no longer an essence, an in-dwelling endowment, but flattened into a social construction or marker in language, the unoccupied occupant of the subject position" (3). Absolutely refuting the Hegelian linkage of the Absolute with subjectivity, which results in a "quasi sacralization of dramatic character" (27), she writes of the "deindividualizing impulse that appears in the final decade of the [nineteenth] century in Mallarmé, Maeterlinck, and Yeats, along with the dehumanizing attack of Jarry" and of "an allegorical modern dramatic genre that can be traced from Strindberg through Beckett and beyond." The "modern mystery/morality plays," including Beckett's drama, "typically reduce the autonomy and dramatic range of their protagonists." Instead of producing subjects (or hypersubjects), these plays develop "recognizable metaphysical patterns" (10). The symbolists gave birth to a metaphysical "mysterium" that played itself out in the pattern-generated rather than character-generated dramaturgies beyond Beckett into even the American postmodern avant-garde of the Wooster Group and Richard Foreman (48).[34]

There is, however, another perspective on the evolution of symbolism from Strindberg to Beckett, one taken by the French theorist Jean-Pierre Sarrazac. Sarrazac too sees the roots of nouveau théâtre in Strindberg's subjectivist drama; but, unlike modernist-structuralist theorists such as Szondi and Adorno who have analyzed drama and subjectivity as social constructs, and unlike postmodernist theorists like Fuchs who harshly refute modernist conceptions of subjectivity, he discerns the positive, theatrically valid aspect of this subjectivity. First, he sees it as a type of realism and not a turn from it. He speaks of "Intimate Theatre," a term he borrows from Strindberg who called his work *"Intima Theatern"* (*Théâtres intimes* 65). Like Szondi, he recognizes a *dramaturgie de la subjectivité* with respect to this theatre (66); but he draws a major distinction between the current of intimate theatre (running from Strindberg through Beckett) and what he calls a *"théâtre intimiste"*:

> [I]ntimate theatre, in the Strindbergien sense, is the opposite extreme of intimist theatre. The latter signifies a drawing in, closure, the restriction of dramatic action to the sphere or to the phantasmal barrier of "private life," while the former implies an aspiration toward the exterior—social as well as cosmic—by way of the interior, by way of the inside space. (68)
>
> Intimate theatre is no more intimist than it is individual. . . . A bold and adventurous self, the place of its adventure is the world. (71)

Unlike Fuchs, Sarrazac sees the social and aesthetic relevance of this "dramaturgy of subjectivity" in nouveau théâtre because 1) he realizes he is evaluating an artform that is meant to creatively present social reality; and 2) he perceives the connection between psyche and stage. He writes of a theatre that is, in fact, based on a model of psychic *mise en abyme:*

> To radiate and to penetrate us, theatre needs a restricted space . . . But, in the imaginary world of theatrical performance, this smallness of space is capable of an infinite expansion. It has the capacity to contain the whole world. Drama marks its path and attains its true dimensions by passing through the eye of a needle. (9)

He is particularly perceptive when it comes to identifying the importance of Beckett's revolutionary focus on the formal presentation of character. Later in his book we realize that the "eye of the needle" corresponds to the head of the hypersubjective dramatic character. With intimate theatre, the idea of theatre transitions from world to psyche: "Passing from the modernity of theatrum mundi to theatrum mentis. . . . intimate theatre engenders a dramaturgy of subjectivity only because mind, in effect, subsumes world" (70–71). Thus subject identifies with psyche, and Beckett's *théâtre intime* is concerned exclusively with "the psychic reality of the characters" (101). The locus of intimate theatre shifts from world to psyche: "intimate theatre requires a space which is as restricted as its immensity is interior . . . only the psyche, with its apparent narrowness, can rival the limitless extension of the world" (79).

In effect, Sarrazac is suggesting that Beckett's primary dramaturgical objective was to open his theatre to a universe of limitless proportions by reaching into the depths of the psyche, that Beckett's intentions were not to describe the innermost language, text, or narrative of the mind, but primarily to draw the spectator's attention to the idea of mind as extended space. This (hypersubjective) strategy is, of course, apparent in *Endgame*. First, the architectonics Beckett inscribes in the text (Hamm's costume, including the dark glasses; his placement, fixity, and movement on the stage and with respect to other elements of the setting including other characters; the relationship of objects such as the handkerchief to his body and headspace, etc.), then the denarrativized, non sequential utterances that subserve the architectonics (references to the dripping in his head, to the emptiness that surrounds him on the stage and that infuses his "vision" of the world, and to the architectonic elements of the stage themselves, such as the empty walls), demonstrate Beckett's complex strategy of drawing the spectator into the mind-space. This is the subjectivity of the hypersubject. Paradoxically, the hypersubject is not an absolute subject, but, on the contrary, it signals the absolute irrelevance and untenability of the concept of subject as, in Jameson's words, "a self-contained monad." With hypersubjective drama, the intensity of the subject-character "position" stems from its union with the subjectivity of the stage (hyper-metatheatricality) thereby ultimately subverting ontological subjectivity.[35]

Hypersubjective theatre and the empty space from which it is designed are not asocial and they are only "antisocial" insofar as they co-operate to produce a masterpiece of dramatic art.[36] The dramatists I examine in the following chapters have constructed socially relevant plays and characters, which are the more socially relevant in that they attain a hyper-social dimension of dramatic art. Philosophers, anthropologists, and critical theorists tell us how very complex art is, especially in its relation to reality. But somehow, the human mind can better handle complexity as a premise than as a process. We find it terribly difficult, if not impossible, to move from one world view to a new one, which is necessarily more complex. It is difficult to radically change our minds about a particular judgment of the world. Very few individuals, Marx, Freud, Einstein among them, have been able to thoroughly and satisfactorily pursue a reconceptualization of human understanding of reality that could stand the test of time. Perhaps the key to the success of these individuals lies in their ability to simultaneously see beyond conventional wisdom and to take account of its subtleties. We remember Orwell's celebrated novel *1984* and its positing of "Big Brother." How many of us were truly able to incorporate into our world vision the most profound message of the text, i.e., that whatever form Big Brother would take to control our lives, it would be one that we would never suspect? To have a hypothesis or suspicion of Big Brother (Stalin's communists, Hitler's fascists, the U.S. government's politicians or corporate capitalists) is to be wrong about it. "Big Brother" works in the abstract without a perceptible form. Yet we continue to hypothesize, and this is very natural.

Likewise, theorists hypothesize the social and the a-social. Modernists offer theories of the hero; new modernists offer theories of an image of society based on the socially constructed identity of a hero; postmodernists, of the untenability of the hero or subject, and of a fragmented image of social reality. Too many theorists, however, are reactionary in that with each new shift in critical history they tend to categorically clean house of formerly valid concepts such as realism and the subject. The most astute theorists, however, proceed with two inviolable principles in mind. First, all new theories, however unconventional they might be, can only enter the field in dialogue with all preceding theories. Instead of a precipitous reaction to and rejection of conventional wisdom, we should attempt to redefine it. Instead of eliminating "subjectivity" from our critical vocabulary, we "postmodernists" should first hypothesize a new form of subjectivity. (Though eventually we do reconsider concepts such as realism and subjectivity, we too often do this only after a destructive period of vengeful rejection.) Besides this principle of inclusion, astute thinkers apply a principle of antagonism and contradiction to new theories of art.

Most great art is a priori antithetical to current modes of thought, and therefore it is always immediately and on the whole unintelligible. In his contrasting of art with aesthetics ("a system of judgments and not a process of creation"), Jon Erikson explains that

> Art as a vital force, whose force depends upon a free practice, will posit itself against the standard ethos of its age, attempting to either avoid categorization, and so stand outside of judgment, or to create a new category that defies the judgments of its age, as a willful negation. Art as such can only effectively exist in protean form. . . . The so-called antiart movements are but a further extension of the desire for an art autonomous from aesthetic, thereby social, control. Antiart movements are not anti*art* at all, but anti*aesthetic*." (33–34)

We recall, of course, that too many scholars still refer to nouveau théâtre as *anti-theatre*. One of the principal points I have intended to make is that the theatre of Beckett et al., in its most nonreferential and meaningless moments, is not antitheatrical but hypertheatrical, and that its hypertheatricality renders it not antisocial, but hypersocial. Adorno tells us that

> Art, however, is not social only because it is brought about in such a way that it embodies the dialectic of forces and relations of production. Nor is art social only because it derives its material content from society. Rather, it is social primarily because it stands opposed to society. Now this opposition art can mount only when it has become autonomous. By congealing into an entity unto itself—rather than obeying existing social norms and thus proving itself to be "socially useful"—art criticizes society just by being there. . . . What [art] contributes to society is not some directly communicable content but something more mediate, i.e. resistance. Resistance reproduces social development in aesthetic terms without directly imitating it. (*Aesthetic Theory* 321)

By his own admission in the statement I quoted earlier by Adorno, the meaninglessness ("Not meaning anything becomes the only meaning") of Beckett's work could represent the highest form of art. In accord with art's objective of pushing the envelope of meaning, and similar to Erikson's contrasting of art with aesthetics, Bert States has introduced the opposition of "antisign" (theatrical anticonventions) to "sign" (theatrical conventions). He explains that antisigns become signs through "an attempt to break into the circuit [of convention], to pester the circuit with nuance, to wound it with the resistance of its presence." The sign began "as an image in which the known world was, in some sense, being recreated or revised out of its primal linguistic matter" (*Great Reckonings* 12). But what human awareness precedes the primal linguistic matter?

In response to a highly structured dramatic convention based on language (articulate expression and psychological complexity), Beckett et al. have proposed an acute primary reference even beyond the "primal linguistic matter" to the antistructure of the void. They take us to the threshold of referentiality (the potential of convention)—and beyond. They point to a realm of supra-referentiality by drawing a bold outline around the form of the protagonist transfigured into the *mise en abyme* of empty space. This is art in its truest sense, its purest form, which the anthropologist Victor Turner has referred to as the "liminoid" form of art, the art responsible for cultural growth.[37] Since it is always easier and less risky to account for and evaluate structure and order than to locate antistructure and chaos, what Erikson, Adorno, and Turner imply is that it is quite difficult, and, in extreme cases of originality, probably impossible, to accurately determine valid forms of art simply through an historical perspective. No doubt we will fail to recognize the most original of great art at first glance and far too much of it over a period of time. The greatest drama is constructed around the most profound (the most profoundly contradictory) subject positions.

57

Paradoxically, we are not witnessing the "death" of the subject in any of the hypersubjective works we will examine in the following chapters. On the contrary, the works signal the birth of a new kind of subject that forms the crux of tragedy in contemporary theatre. In his seminal work, *The Birth of Tragedy,* Nietzsche claimed that the "state of individuation," the aberrant resistance of the individual to the "oneness" of all living things, was perceived by the Greeks to be the "origin and primal cause of all suffering," and consequently, it became the very raison d'être of classical Greek theatre (73–74). The theatrical hypersubject, a modern-day Dionysus, demonstrates a new metatheatrical form for individuation in a world where art and artist give the impression that they have nowhere to turn but "in." As we have seen, the inward turn does not constitute any loss of space, but rather a radical change in the configuration and status of the emptiness of theatrical space. Theatrical space, which historically has represented a microcosmic focus of the world (*theatrum mundi*), adopts a more concrete, precisely focused, center of gravity within the virtual, imaginary psychic space of the theatrical hypersubject—the last in a series of converging spatial configurations, from world, through stage, to personal psychic space. Subject and space become more clearly and closely associated, more directly aligned, and, as Charles Lyons has pointed out, "impossible to separate."

One cannot help but think how concretely the hypersubjective work delivers this metadramatic message. What closer relationship can the character have to space than to actually become the *mise en abyme* of that space? At the beginning of this chapter I expressed the regret that because contemporary theorists have concentrated so heavily on the psychological structures of certain theatre texts, they have consequently underestimated the importance of spatial relationships. Yet, once the spatial work begins, one finds that contemporary psychoanalytical theories are not entirely incompatible with theatrical hypersubjectivity. In Jacques Lacan's theory, for instance, Nietzsche's "*state* of individuation" would translate into more of a signifying *process:* an alienated postmodern subject whose identity is characterized (and ravaged) by the perpetual yielding of the signified to a (renewable) signifier.[38] In the case of hypersubjective theatre, the hypersubject becomes a signified of pure theatricality, a given "stage" of character-space identity that must yield to subsequent, deeper levels of identity of the character with space. While observing Hamm center-stage, one imagines the course of the drop of water through the darkness of his inner world. In hypersubjective theatre, there is no actual "decentering" of the subject. Intricately tied to space, oriented and focused by the outer (visible) framework of the stage, the line of displacement of the signified is actually quite linear and centered. The body-skull of the protagonist provides an acute and privileged point of intermediary signification as the border between outer and inner emptiness.

Never before has one dramatic character been so singularly and comprehensively representative of theatrical space; never before has he (or she) been so determined by and determinant for this space. The hypersubjective protagonist carries the gene of Artaud's cycloptic hieroglyphic framework for theatrical space: its personal psychic space represents the "central eye"— or, to employ Corvin's term, the "isotopy of concentration" ("Espace, temps, mise en abyme" 144–45)—of the structured empty space it inhabits. By creatively elaborating the new-found correspondence between the depths of metatheatre and the depths of the self-conscious "mind centered in void," the hypersubjective work encourages us to rethink contemporary notions of theatricality, subjectivity, self-consciousness, and death.

[3]

BECKETT'S PURSUIT OF EMPTINESS:
THE CONCENTRATED (EMPTY) IMAGE
BEHIND THE FRAGMENTED STORY
IN THE LATE PLAYS

Samuel Beckett's dramatic corpus has made a major creative contribution to the phenomenology of human language; and not only verbal language. On Beckett's stage, the visual is not secondary to the written and eventually spoken text. On the contrary, the language of Beckett's texts, the dialogue as well as the stage directions, constructs original stage images[1] which are much more than material support for Beckett's verbal witticism or his inspired if unorthodox form of "storytelling." One could certainly argue that the reason why Beckett moved from prose fiction toward an increasingly theatrical form of artistic expression is that he realized he could make a deeper impact on the world through a medium culminating in live visual image than through a medium circumscribed by the printed word, i.e., by "naturalized preconstructions."[2] A pictorial retrospective of the productions of Beckett's dramatic works reveals the dramatist's effort to articulate stage images powerful and compact enough to perform on the spectator's mind a spiritual holocaust, one which arouses, below the symbolic realm of ideology and verbal language, some extra-intellectual inner cosmos of self-awareness.[3] Clearly, Beckett's ingenious, and often ironic, manipulation of language is not an artistic end in itself, but an artistic means to an end which would transcend any conventional understanding of either language or art. For him, the theatrical stage was the best vehicle to achieve a more authentic artform, the "literature of the unword," as he called it; and the necessarily self-conscious language spoken on that stage was doomed to self-destruction.[4] As we shall see, Beckett's ultimate goal was not to eliminate either visual image or language, but to discover images as well as utterances which, instead of telling a story, would convey to the spectator a profound and complex sense of emptiness and silence.

Many scholars have described the evolution of Beckett's theatrical corpus in terms of increasing abstraction, on the one hand, and more concentrated economies, on the other. Yet most still persist in emphasizing the "fragmented" aspect of these works. In Beckett's work we see an increasing metadramatic focus on the empty space of the mind, one which shifts the overall quality of the stage illusion from one of fragmentation to one of concentration. In this chapter, I pursue the case of Beckett by examining in some detail two of his final works, *Rockaby* and *Not I,* and I conclude the chapter with a brief discussion of others of his late plays. First, we consider rather broadly his developing interest in emptiness. Then, we consider the ever-evolving techniques he used to focus the spectator's attention specifically on the empty psyche of one central protagonist. This discussion also considers the problems with arguments of fragmentation as opposed to concentration in Beckett. In other words, Beckett is an author of quality rather than quantity—quality of images and words. The quality of his drama rests on what the Austrian playwright Thomas Bernhard refers to in the title of his last play: "Simply complicated."

BECKETT'S ARTAUDIAN INTEREST IN DRAMATURGICAL EMPTINESS

To truly appreciate the concentrated, visceral poetic images of Beckett's theatrical works, one must adopt the particular perspective on the function of emptiness in twentieth-century Western theatre which I described in the introduction and first chapter of this book. Since the revolution of realism and naturalism at the end of the nineteenth century, and despite the continuing popularity of these movements throughout our own period, emptiness in theatrical space, whether evidenced by the dramatic text or manufactured and processed for the stage, has literally come into its own. Beckett's theatre is on the whole one of an isolated character surrounded and virtually consumed by empty space. Of course, since the beginnings of recorded theatre history and Oedipus and company, we have abundant examples of characters isolated on a relatively empty stage. Tragic monologues are commonplace in the classical canon; and the signifying potential of the existential outpourings of Hamlet, Phèdre, and Lorenzaccio are largely conditioned by the "echo" and cosmic mystery of emptiness. Where it was once exploited as a "conditioner" of psychological or early expressionist discourse, however, in Beckett's theatre it establishes the primary condition of drama. It took an avant-garde twentieth-century novelist to create a character like Malone who would both say and mean "Nothing is more real than nothing" (*Malone Dies* 16). It took the same novelist-turned-dramatist to spatialize images which could effectively and affectively convey this idea. Since the 1950s and the lonely tree of *Waiting for Godot*, the relative emptiness in the plays of Samuel Beckett has been at the forefront of a self-conscious and direct progression toward a mise-en-scène of emptiness.

To understand emptiness as a high-culture reaction to realism's often uninspired quest to replicate the clutter of reality—which on the stage includes language as well as objects, sets, architecture, costumes, etc.—is only a beginning; it is only a part of the truth about what Livio Dobrez, in his attempt at a definition of the "Irreducible" in Beckett's prose works, has described as Beckett's desire "to do the impossible, to *touch* the *void*, to be able to *point* to the intersection of silence and speech, nothingness and existence."[5] On the stage, Beckett discovered and exploited the point of another intersection, one in which the French theorist Antonin Artaud also had expressed a burning interest: the one connecting the void of space with the void of mind. As much as any twentieth-century artistic genius, Beckett fathomed Artaud's dicta concerning the link between "poetry in space" and "poetry in thought." He was, of course, well aware that "true" expression lies deeper than verbal language. But, perhaps more than any of his peers, he was especially responsive to Artaud's insistence on the connection between the power of the void within the space of the theatrical stage and the void that dwells within the space of our mind, at the core of our being:

> All true feeling is in reality untranslatable. To express it is to betray it. But to translate it is *to dissimulate it* [Artaud's emphasis]. True expression hides what it makes manifest. It sets the mind in opposition to the real void of nature by creating in relation to the manifestation-illusion of nature it creates a void in thought. All powerful feeling produces in us the idea of the void. And the lucid language which obstructs the appearance of this void also obstructs the appearance of poetry in thought. That is why an image, an allegory, a figure that masks what it would reveal have more significance for the spirit than the lucidities of speech and its analytics.
>
> That is why true beauty never strikes us directly. The setting sun is beautiful because of all it makes us lose. (*Theater* 71)[6]

Over the "lucid language" of the psychological, the social, and the ideological, Artaud opted for an extralinguistic, metaphysical account of "true" psychic experience, which he believed could translate to the stage. Criticizing the "storytelling psychology" of the "purely descriptive and narrative theatre" to which the West had been accustomed since the Renaissance (he includes Shakespeare under this rubric) (*Theater* 76), he turned from the language of the physical world toward a search for "one image that will shake the organism to its foundations and leave an ineffaceable scar" (*Theater* 77). This image would provoke in the spectator an awareness of the void; it would connect the extended extralinguistic regions of the mind of the spectator with an extended theatrical space focused on the empty mind of an isolated central character.

To be sure, Artaud's metaphysical vision of theatre endowed the human body with new power, to the extent that Robert Abirached interprets the Artaudian ideal to be a *"corps-théâtre."*[7] But he was not particularly interested in the *physical* nature of body. In Mark Johnson's turn of the phrase, Artaud "put the body back into the mind," in a simultaneously hyperphysical and metaphysical way. In fact, there is no clear mind-body dichotomy in Artaud's writing, not in any conventional sense. In his study of *différances* Jacques Derrida confirms this con-fusion when he defines Artaud's theatrical vision as a "metaphysics of flesh which determines Being as life, and the mind as the body itself, as unseparated thought" ("La parole soufflée" 179). Susan Sontag puts it another way, saying that "each statement [Artaud] makes about his consciousness is also a statement about his body" (xxiv). The body on Artaud's stage represents not so much an exterior as an interior, not so much an expressive anatomy as a psychic space. The neuro-metabolic unity is consummated through corporeal and theatrical extension of the space we think of as our mind. The point I would like to emphasize here, however, is that, from Artaud's metaphysical point of view, the basic substance of mind-body unity is emptiness; from his theatro-metaphysical point of view, psychological human "texts" on stage were to yield to the construction of an image of body as an empty human icon. As we saw in our examination of *Endgame* in chapter 2, Beckett too had an eye for emptiness, a rather sharp eye which eventually focused on the potential, reflective emptiness of the dramatic character. Grounded as it was in visual image, Beckett's artistic venture involved a highly articulate process of "loss" through reduction and erasure.[8] Beckett abandoned conventional reality by a process of elimination, an emptying out of theatrical space as well as a silencing of language, not only for purposes of deconstruction, but primarily to achieve a level of acuity in an Artaudian "figure that masks" (see above quote) in order to promote the artistic relevance of inner emptiness: the image of mind to which we all resort in the most stimulating of our "absentminded" and "thoughtless" moments.

A META-PHYSICAL APPROACH TO BECKETT'S DRAMA

Again I ask: How does the visible, concrete emptiness on the theatrical stage make the connection to the psychic void? How does it create meaning or feeling and elicit an affective or intellectual response by doing so? Though these are massive questions, in this chapter I continue to formulate a response by positing that there are at least two ways of looking at theatrical empty space: from either a "physical" point of view, or from a "meta-physical" or "hyperphysical" one. From a physical point of view, one considers this space as potentially fillable, believing that it is meaningful with respect to its potential to be filled. For the scholar or practitioner who approaches emptiness from this angle, the emptiness is essentially an *absence,* usually the absence of the "weight" of naturalistic illusion—the lamp, the wall, the painting on the wall, the trompe l'oeil background painting, or the fluid discourse of narrative. Even productions of Beckett's "empty" theatrical spaces can be more or less realistic with respect to this physical "weight." Consider certain productions of Beckett's first dramatic work to make it to the stage, *Godot,* a work which came early in his agenda to "touch the void." As his theatrical career developed, Beckett himself became progressively more conscious, more in "touch" with the aesthetic depth and complexity of his own textual design of the space for this work. Toward the end of his life, having accomplished the extreme emptiness of plays like *Not I* and *Rockaby,* Beckett was more concerned with reducing rather than increasing the illusion in *Godot.* Quoting Beckett's comments to Walter Asmus, Gerhard Hauck has noted that "By 1988, [Beckett] even insisted that the country road in *Godot* be eliminated: 'There is no road . . . Only tree and stone! As simple as possible!'" (97). Yet, based on a "physical" approach, some theatre directors have produced and continue to produce an illusionistic *Godot* in a way that detracts from—Shall I say it?—the latent authorial intention to explore the aesthetic richness of loss and emptiness.

Consider Jonathan Kalb's comparison between the two Alan Schneider *Godot*s, one produced for television in 1961 and the other produced at the Sheridan Square Playhouse in 1971. (Though the later production was not explicitly "for television," it was recorded as a commercial video.) As Kalb explains it, the essential divergence between these two productions begins with spatial setting. He describes the first as "a cartoon-like setting, that resembles a fairy-tale illustration: a few beautifully rendered, wispy clouds interrupt the emptiness of the sky; ridiculous pillowy hills, all about chair height, flank the road as it winds gently for at least thirty feet upstage, and a flagrantly artificial tree" (27). Ten years later, Schneider turned from what Kalb calls the "illusionistic self-sufficiency" (28) and the "atextual stylizations" (29) of the television version, and created a set of "a level stage of wooden planks, completely bare except for a real tree upstage, behind which are black curtains—no mound or rock" (29–30).[9] Thus Schneider has removed naturalistic illusion in a (no doubt) Beckett-sanctioned move toward more absolute emptiness.[10] Too many productions of *Godot* sacrifice emptiness for illusion, even for an illusion of emptiness. Most importantly, the "fullness" of the illusionistic trompe l'oeil setting of the 1961 *Godot* subverts the empty space–empty character connection so essential to the metaphysical reading of Beckett's work. Kalb's criticism of the illusionist production includes the following observation: "Beckett once commented that it is essential for the characters in *Godot* to appear trapped, yet this environment, like all fantasy, implies a potential for escape" (27). Yet we know Estragon and Vladimir are trapped ("Imbecile! There is no way out there," Didi tells Gogo), not within a fantastic illusion, but within emptiness. There is no way out of the endlessness of emptiness;[11] and the inward turn that Beckett's characters eventually take leads to entrapment within an inner empty space. Yet the directors of illusionistic productions cannot avoid filling the absence, albeit with a "physical" depiction of emptiness.[12] Their primary referent remains fullness, the fullest possible weight of realism, the most detailed portrait of conventional, material reality. There is, I think, a parallel between the directors who struggle to uncover and spatialize illusion in Beckett's texts and the critics who struggle to read into them an illusionistic "story." These directors and these critics are entitled to be judged on the merits of the illusion they create and the "story" they assemble. At the same time, however, our fascination with their stories should not impede the pursuit of the image behind the illusion.

The visual portrait of reality has structure, of course, just as language has structure. Trompe l'oeil background enhances the perception of structure within the stage tableau. Realism ignores Artaud's warning concerning the untranslatable aspect of "all true feeling" (see above quote). Expression that catalyzes into both content and structure, including narrative structure, "dissimulates" what Artaud so idealistically and metaphysically expressed as the nonmaterial "real void of nature," and it fails to create the connection between this and the "void in thought": "All powerful feeling produces in us the idea of the void." Beckett and Artaud based their stand against realist illusion on a belief in the presence of an extralinguistic mind-space in opposition to a language space. A vital principle of realism is the referentiality of language, the connection between the language space (rather than the empty space) of the mind and the material (rather than the immaterial) world.

As Artaud and Beckett knew all too well, a simple verbal utterance, or even a series of them, can leave room for the emptiness of silence. However, whether through the artless efforts of author or director, or through the ingenuousness of the spectator, when utterances become connected sequences comprising a comprehensive whole, a story, then the perception of the *whole* story tends to alienate the spectator's thoughts from the "real void of nature." The more the theatrical dialogue structures—or is believed to structure—a narrative story, the more it completes and "exposes" story through exposition, then the more physically and realistically full the work.

Most scholars who discuss Beckett's work as either "theatre of the body" or "theatre of language" fall into this realist category, the "the-stage-is-half-empty" or "the-story-is-half-told" variety of critic, since their primary interest is most often the fragmentation of a complete body and conventional language in this

65

theatre, or, on another level, the incompleteness (or indeterminacy) of subject. Their perception of the fragmented occurs with respect to the perception of the whole, the whole body and the whole narrative story, the whole subject. This is why a distinguished scholar like Enoch Brater chooses to argue against narrative wholeness in Beckett's late works with respect to some narrative whole, a story. After an enlightening discussion of the priority of "visual impact" over "theme and variation" in *Not I* (23), and the analysis of the protagonist (Mouth) as "the minimal image of a panting orifice" (31), he remarks that "Exposition is delayed indefinitely as Beckett spares us the art and craft of denouement" (34). Yet, as I will show below, Brater seems to placate his scholarly readership by addressing—albeit in a cursory fashion—questions of exposition, narrative, and plot in this minimalist work. For obvious reasons, the "physical" school of criticism remains so influential that, for too many Beckett scholars, the extra-physical, meta-physical, extralinguistic dimension of the visual image—the crucial component of Artaud's "poetry in space" (*Theater* 38)—cannot stand alone; it cannot free itself from the aesthetics of story or merit some degree of primacy with respect to it. Consequently, for the "physical" critic, Brater's approach will imply that Beckett's unorthodox theatrical fiction still coalesces around the idea of story even as it elaborates a story "untold."

But, other than this "physical" approach, one could also consider empty space from the meta-physical, sur-real perspective of the "the-stage-is-half-full" kind of researcher—not as potentially fillable, but as potentially and therefore essentially empty, and supra-representational. This is my interest, to examine ways in which emptiness is meaningful as emptiness, and ways in which the stage is essentially emptiable (depletable) instead of essentially fillable. My primary referent is not so much the detail of structure as it is the meta-physical, sur-real essence of emptiness, and its effect on the consciousness of the spectator. While most research on Beckett—much of it quite inspired—privileges language and the narrative story, or the narrative *whole* that the language haltingly sketches or implies, my approach leads to a focus on the visual, material image of the empty *hole* in Beckett's stage space and in his language (narrative), and on those words and objects and other verbal and nonverbal signifiers that, instead of "filling" the stage, reinforce our perception of the hole insofar as they co-operate with the emptiness that contains them.

To be sure, Beckett tows a tenuous line between theatrical presence and ontological absence: How does one use the presence of theatre and living image to induce spectators into an awareness of the void? All his analysts (directors, critics, scholars, spectators, and readers) have an obligation to at least recognize this line. From this critical position, I believe that if the practitioner who stages *Godot* translates Beckett's request for "a country road with a tree" as a call for a background painting, that practitioner transgresses Beckett's inviolable desire to signify emptiness in a way which will make the connection with the empty human psyche.[13] Despite the *illusion* of barrenness in the background added to this kind of *Godot* production, the material artificiality of the illusion restricts the open-endedness of the stage. It diffuses an impression of realistic structure onto the erasure of reality that Beckett textually imposes on the stage in his search for an image just this side of the metaphysical void. The illusionistic background is evidently intended to provide structure to some kind of story, a formal relic marked by Beckett for obsolescence.[14] In Beckett's works, especially his late works, spectators should sense simultaneously the sheer materiality of the image of void, and conversely, the voided materiality of the image. The illusion of a barren, de-structured physical reality and a de-structured linguistic space should yield to a hyper-present material manifestation of metaphysical inner experience. Only then will totally new meanings emerge which exceed story.

I believe that a truly Artaudian metaphysical approach to Beckett's theatre—one which reveals rather than obstructs our awareness of the void, of the hypercorporeal, of the extralinguistic—would *fundamentally* prioritize visual image over narrative story and concentration over fragmentation, as well as emptiness over fullness. In this chapter, I deal primarily with the aesthetic and self-referential nature of Beckett's concentrated (empty) image. Many scholars have discussed the importance of the emptiness of the stage in Beckett's theatre, and many others have argued the importance of the body within the stage.[15] However, since they have approached these topics from a "physical" point of view, they have largely ignored the reflective emptiness of the dramatic character, a concept that helps to explain both the process of concentration and the self-referential, metatheatrical nature of the work. The dramatist uses the visible (outer) stage space to evoke an image of inner space for the spectator. As Jane Alison Hale puts it, Beckett has "drawn audiences further away from the concrete, stable space of the stage, and deeper into the abstract, fluctuating space of the characters' minds" (150). The most remarkable feature of this process is the mind-space connection and its resistance to the dialectics of psychologization in keeping with the tenets of Artaud. Beckett marks the space of his theatre by the pervasive visibility of its emptiness, and the most powerful image within it is that of the hypersubject, the *mise en abyme* of empty space.

BECKETT'S INCREASING INTEREST IN THE EMPTY SPACE–EMPTY MIND CONNECTION

After *Godot*, Beckett created plays that by retrospective comparison seem to shed more and more of their naturalistic veneer. From the exterior setting of *Godot*, Beckett moves through the interior of *Endgame*, to an increased ambiguity between exterior and interior in his late plays. His settings become 1) increasingly emptied of objects and architecture; 2) more concentrated in terms of an increase in the monologic allocation of text, the reduced number of characters, the limited dimensions of stage space, and the restricted range of action; 3) and perhaps, more fragmented. Yet, as we have seen in the above discussion of the *Godot* productions, it is probable that Beckett too waited all his life for Godot, that is, he waited all his life to truly comprehend and properly produce the play's emptiness.[16] *Godot* (1952) established a barren countryside for a space, was relatively dialogic, and had an identifiable if bare bones "story." Martin Esslin noticed early that the "absurdist" movement had moved away from story in that the dramatists were not so much telling what's going to happen next, but "what's happening" (*Theatre of the Absurd* 366). Yet, relative to Beckett's other works, especially his later ones, *Godot* does have a story, however minimal it may appear: two men await the arrival of Godot. If we accept that "The one merit of *story* is its ability to make us want to know what happened next" (Holman and Harmon 456), then, by setting up at least a perception of structural sequence with a remnant of suspense, the objective of expectancy in *Godot* sustains (and feigns) an aura of story up to the last moment of the dialogue. In an initial introduction to *Godot,* what spectator does not really expect some kind of arrival throughout the "story"? After *Godot,* however, the expectancy has disappeared and structural sequence has become totally obscured. In *Endgame* (1957), Hamm and Clov await no one and nothing because, as the first word of the play suggests, it is always already "finished." They even verbalize their fear of becoming "story": "We're not beginning to ... to ... mean something?" (32). The intercalated, unfinished "stories" with which Hamm interrupts the "action" of the play from time to time represent an additional ironic challenge to the notions of a complete narration and meaningful reference: in this work they are not "stories within a story." Though the play takes place in a room instead of outdoors, and though the stage architecture is more elaborate relative to *Godot,* as we saw in chapter 2, the play focuses on the imaginary inner space of the paraplegic blind protagonist, Hamm, whose verbal superiority over Clov results in a reduction in the dialogic quality of the text. Despite the presence of Nagg and Nell and the movements of Clov, Hamm is more isolated and more static on stage. Later, in Beckett's last "full-length" work, Winnie of *Happy Days* (1961) is even more isolated, monologic, and introspective. Engulfed by a barren mound of dirt, she "in-habits" an extremely focused spatial field. By the 1970s and 1980s, short works like *Not I* (1972) and *Rockaby* (1980) have attained an extreme in terms of emptiness, isolation, the focus on one dramatic character (a focus articulated largely through stage architecture and lighting effect), the cryptic quality of verbal language, and the so-called fragmentation of corporal image. I think it too reductive, however, to say that Beckett has participated—in a semi-predictable way—in the destruction, deconstruction, or fragmentation of the subject. The evolution from the beginning to end of Beckett's dramatic corpus is not a question of an increasing mysteriousness and indeterminacy resulting from the reduction toward emptiness, for it is there in *Godot;* but rather, it is a question of an increasing clarity of the empty space-empty mind connection, a process which involves the effacing of the trace of story and the radical, chiaroscuro focus on one human icon (or its remnant). Through his contextual staging of the protagonist's body, Beckett has formalistically produced an ironic image of "hypersubject."

ROCKABY

In Beckett's theatre, the characters are not naturalistically integrated into a functional setting, but are reduced to an image of a *theatrical figure* at the center of a visual field. Stanton B. Garner's recent work on the spatial phenomenology of the theatrical image explains how in Beckett's late plays the visual field is characterized by "the formal predominance of shape" and how objects—those "vestiges of naturalism," says Garner— "gradually surrender their utilitarian value for the more strictly aesthetic value of shape." He further explains that "In keeping with this formal conception of mise-en-scène, the characters of Beckett's late plays are themselves objectified as aesthetic components of the visual field, reduced from person to figure, or less . . ." (63), so that "the geometry of figure forms part of a larger geometry of field" (64).[17] Consequently, as shapes, the characters begin to relate to language in a new and paradoxical way: the shapes on the stage and their proxemic context orient and organize the verbal language of the text, providing a kind of secondary syntax for it. "Fragmentation," whether corporeal, linguistic, cognitive, sociocultural, or ontological, is a highly suggestive label that is often hastily and uncritically applied to the bodies and the language that constitute the subject. Unlike most critics of Beckett's theatre, however, I believe that the reduction of the character to form implies a serious argument against claims of corporeal fragmentation. There is a considerable difference between the literal value of a body part illustrated in a medical dictionary and the metaphorical value of one featured on a theatrical stage. This means that architectonically, pictorially, and theatrically, Beckett's figures, even those figures such as the mouth of *Not I* and the head of *That Time* that scholars are hasty to label mere bodily fragments, become a concentrated, embedded *mise en abyme* of both theatrical subject and theatrical space. In the case of Beckett, fragmentation represents a conceptual "stage" (or mode) of the protagonist's existence rather than an interpretive absolute.[18]

Curiously, while Garner does not reach the conclusion that the head of the protagonist serves as a metaphorical empty space, his incisive analysis of the postmodern stage as a "bodied space" does support this argument, especially since it infers that the body of the protagonist is promoted above a purely intellectual rank to a poetic realm of spatial form. The strategically positioned body on stage is not simply a source of language, but an aesthetic form in its own right, one which derives from a living, breathing, blood-pumping body. In *Rockaby*, for example, the extreme economy of structure reveals the particularly striking focal point of an aging woman entrenched in a rocking chair on an otherwise empty stage (see fig. 7).[19] With this kind of concentration, stage lighting takes on a whole new meaning. Garner points out that in Beckett's drama light is an "active, aggressive determinant of the theatrical image. . . . light offers the primary articulation of the mise-en-scène" (65). In one sense, the lighting creates a chiaroscuro effect that enhances our perception of the "undifferentiation of the void."[20] In another sense, lighting detaches the body from the surrounding stage space. This detachment helps to divert the meaning of the character from the intellectual and the psychological to the formal; it also promotes the meaning of the unlighted space from peripherally ancillary to peripherally primary; and it helps to connect hermeneutically the emptiness of the unlighted space with that of the lighted space as well as that of the character. Beckett's work makes it clear to us that it is in fact light that creates darkness. As Garner puts it, "light throws into relief the darkness around it," and he speaks of "the comparative vastness of the 'nonseen' (stage not seen, bodies not seen)" (66). From a physical point of view, we consider darkness to be less "physical" than lightness, and consequently, we perceive it as less substantial, more mysterious, and ultimately, less consequential. We simply overlook the fact that, in a primarily undifferentiated, empty universe, lightness is as metaphysical as darkness.

A metaphysical point of view, however, would prompt a different regard for darkness as it would for emptiness, so the obscure or out of focus periphery becomes more alluring and functional than otherwise considered.[21] Beckett uses both darkness and light to divert the spectator's attention from world as well as from *theatrum mundi* and to draw attention into the self-conscious theatrical illusion of headspace, *theatrum mentis*. Fortunately, Garner's phenomenological approach to theatrical space has its metaphysical side, so he does not categorically dismiss darkness as nonessential just because it is nonseen. On the contrary, he argues that it "acquires pressing visual weight" and he speaks of "the paradoxical and innovative fullness of Beckettian stage darkness," a fullness which to some extent depends on "the *conditions* in which theatrical objects acquire or fail to acquire visibility" (66; Garner's emphasis). To be sure, human bodies and their organic parts are special kinds of objects, and the forms they constitute create special kinds of meaning. So Beckett's notes on the stage lighting for *Rockaby* focalize very obviously W's head as the first and last element on stage to be illuminated, ending with "Long pause with spot on face alone. Head slowly sinks, comes to rest. Fade out spot" (*Rockaby* 21). The head is much more than a body part or fragment and its form is not simply central to the visual field, but its very "meta-center," its very source. In Garner's words, "light seems to sever the head of the Woman in *Rockaby* (like that of Listener in *That Time* or the Protagonist in *Catastrophe*)" (65); but he bases his analysis largely on stage directions, on the rough equivalent of what Michael Issacharoff calls the mimetic space, that which is seen on stage, derived mainly from didascalia as opposed to the diegetic space, that which is communicated verbally through the discourse of the characters ("Space and Reference" 215–20; see chapter 2). With the understanding that diegesis invokes the act of "telling" as opposed to a mimetic "showing," in Beckett's works, the intensification of visual image through lighting is accompanied by an intensification of verbal sound images that diegetically overdetermine the emptiness of the visual image. The text's words do more to "tell" the image than to articulate or narrate some story.[22]

Enoch Brater, too, offers an excellent analysis of the play of light in this piece, and he extends his analysis to the diegetic space, the space evoked by the recorded and live language uttered by the lonely woman in the chair: "A striking visual metaphor materializes before our very eyes as we watch a poem come to (stage) life. . . . A visual image created by words . . . Sound therefore structures sight in *Rockaby*, just as sight structures sound" (169). I basically agree that to a large extent sound structures sight and vice versa in this play, but I do not believe that sound equals story. Though Brater's analysis of this work by and large emphasizes the visual over the linguistic, he nevertheless answers the rhetorical question "What does the poem reveal?" with the following observation: "A story develops from scene to scene. And as it does so, the figure 'moves' gradually inward" (170). This remark seems to apologize for the meta-physical argument that the "emptiness" of visual image hermeneutically precedes and undermines the fullness of language (narrative). Despite the overall merits of Brater's analysis, I would like to coax his critical groundwork in a different direction by doing with language and oral sound what Garner does with visual image. Let us critically and doggedly pursue the empty aspect of language that, in resisting narrative structure, fuses with the suprareferential flux of visual image. As with Garner's inquiry into the "emptiness" of darkness, let us avoid understating the "emptiness" in the form of silence that punctuates and effectively counteracts and neutralizes the linear flow of the referential sequencing on which story depends. A meta-physical point of view, one which foregrounds emptiness in all its manifestations, reveals that the sound that structures sight and image is the "fundamental sounds"[23] of verbal language at a more primitive semantic level, a level at which sound and detached, unconnectable signifiers overpower the signifying function of concrete, connectable signifieds.

71

The sound of *Rockaby* is monologue, but it is not mono-logic. Refining a technique employed in earlier works such as *Krapp's Last Tape,* the monologue surging from the protagonist's head is a recorded play-back that concludes each of the four segments of the play with the echo effect of live voice and recorded voice together uttering "Time she stopped." After a long pause, the recorded words are reactivated by the live voice's "More." This gives an impression of displacement from head to stage with the echo effect emphasizing the communication between and the conjunction of the emptiness of the three spaces evoked (head, stage, off-stage periphery). Interestingly, Beckett's stage directions are unclear as to when W should open her eyes, but he insists on fluctuation: "Now closed, now open in unblinking gaze. About equal proportions section 1, increasingly closed 2 and 3, closed for good halfway through 4" (21–22). In his world premier of the play,[24] Alan Schneider organized a rough pattern for the opening and closing of the eyes. At lights up, W's eyes remain open for the uttering of the first "More." For each succeeding sequence, her eyes come to a close in anticipation of the "More," they reopen immediately before the utterance and come to a close after it, and continue to fluctuate between open and closed. Finally, in accordance with Beckett's instructions, the eyes stay "closed for good" before the conclusion. This fluctuation helps to incapacitate any remnant boundary between outer and inner space by constantly shifting the spectator's attention from the physical body on stage (eyes open) to the inner space of the protagonist's psyche (eyes closed).

We should never take too literally the words of Beckett's drama. Indeed, in many instances they have only slight literal value and tend to signify primarily at a metaphysical level that transforms their physical aurality as well as their "story" into a visual image of internal mental process. "Downward" is a trope for "inward" in this play.[25] The words resounding out from and back within W's head do not so much tell a story as offer a graphic description of an end-less downward journey or progression through a memory space as vast as the outer cosmos where endless space coincides with infinite time: Space does not stop!:

> Right down / into the old rocker / mother rocker / where mother sat / all the years / all in black / best black / sat and rocked / rocked / rocked / till her end came / in the end came / off her head they said / gone off her head / ... / dead one night / in the rocker / in her best black / head fallen / and in the rocker rocking / rocking away / so in the end / close of a long day / went down / in the end went down / down the steep stair / let down the blind and down / right down ... (17–18)[26]

The "story" seems to "narrate" the idea of the perennial daughter reflecting on the turn toward infinity of the perennial mother.[27]

This quote shows us that, unlike the story of waiting for Godot, in *Rockaby* we are dealing more absolutely and transparently with a *process* of reflection, a process that resists conventional structure and replaces a conception of narrative whole with one of a denarrativized, psychic hole. This is the "de-territorialized" kind of art lauded by the philosophers Deleuze and Guattari: "something that achieves a breakthrough—art as a process without goal, but that attains completeness as such" (*Anti-Oedipus* 370).[28] Structural deter-minacy collapses into an aural and spatial void. The staccato presentation of the highly concentrated poetic assertions which are dispersed, truncated, repeated, shifted, and otherwise manipulated ("in the end came," "so in the end came," "in the end went down," "right down," etc.), tends to spatialize the discourse by creating the impression of words which, unsupported by syntax, are, shall we say, "lost in space." Structural details of reality, language, and life are suspended in a "thick" atmosphere of emptiness, one which coincides with the volume of silence in *Rockaby*. Silence is as meaningful as emptiness in a referential as well as supra-referential way. It is not simply present but operative and foregrounded. The destructured extension of silence cooperates with the extension of emptiness. Emmanuel Jacquart comments on the role of silence in Beckett's theatre: "Since silence is char-acterized as a zero-degree signifier (absence of sound), one could expect it also would have a zero-degree signified (absence of meaning). In fact, like the zero in the series of numbers, silence is not nothing" (238). More than this, silence establishes the difference between language and thought, it signifies thought by contextualizing it; and silence is a partner of empty space, extension; it, too, constitutes the raw material of our conscious and subconscious lives. We become aware of silence contextually in the theatre. It resides in the interspace from curtain to curtain and the interspace be-tween two utterances or two syllables. As with emptiness, silence is focused into the headspace of the character. Like the forms that emerge from a background of emptiness, the sounds emerge from a background of silence.

In contrast to normal, fluid narrative that ordinarily conceals the gaps of the thoughtlessness we all experience, gaps that betray the infinite vastness of our mind that backgrounds mental imagery and linguistic pattern and system, W's uttered thoughts create the impression that there exists a visual space all around them, a space that becomes more tangible and meaningful as words lose their articulating structure and become *thought-sounds*. The text calls for W's "More" to become a little softer each time. In Schneider's production, however, Whitelaw magnifies the decrease in volume, and her "More" becomes increasingly inaudible, the final one seeming no more than a gasp or a grunt. Thus a well-defined linguistic sign disintegrates into a signal-like psychic event.

On the aural rather than the visual side of theatrical art, through his use of pauses,[29] echoes, aural displacement, and poetic articulation, Beckett has reversed the narrational function of the monologue, transforming it, quite "visually," into "a path of sounds suspended in giddy heights, linking unfathomable abysses of silence."[30] The aural becomes visually concrete. In this, Beckett's only work in verse, the pauses at the end of each apocopated utterance,[31] enforce an overwhelming silence that overpowers literality, referentiality, and signification, one which blocks the story and gnaws away at the linguistic realm of the mind. As the action and imagery appear *within* the empty space, the utterances occur *within* the silence. The discourse is plasticized into an image of mind, a technique that induces the spectator into concentrating on the picturability of thought processes instead of on the anatomical, biological, or intellectual attributes of body, or on the actions of the protagonist, or on whatever surrounds the body. Beckett challenges his audience to confront theatre at its most experimentally and experientially figural and formalistic, a formalism that denarrativizes and deterritorializes structure. Garner explains that "Beckett's late plays manipulate depth, that dimension of visual field extending perpendicular to the audience's line of sight" (73–74). He does not expressly include *Rockaby* among the examples he gives, but certainly could have. The impression of depth—de(a)(p)th?—here is visually, poetically, and cerebrally spectacular.

The emphasis on the (empty) head tends to refute the postmodernist argument on the side of a systematic destruction or deconstruction of the subjective focus through a technique of fragmentation in the work of Beckett and other avant-garde dramatists. The notion of corporeal fragmentation loses its impact if we examine the upper body (the head) of the protagonist in a hierarchical relation to the lower body, a hierarchy implied by Mikhail Bakhtin's ideas on subjectivizing trends in modernist art.[32] Formalistically, the head of Beckett's marionette-like dramatic character no longer functions as a part of the body, but as an iconic index[33] of the body, an empty and framelike, yet *concentrated, mise en abyme* of empty body, of empty stage, and of the empty off-stage periphery. In this sense the head serves as a focalized vanishing point of two separate but analogous theatrical tableaux: an exterior empty space (stage and off-stage) which is duplicated as psychic inner space. If in Beckett's late plays the reduced and immobilized body (or body-head) remains a speaking body, the speaking body becomes the mysterious keeper of words—not Word—words that, as we have seen in *Rockaby,* plasticize the idea of mind as they deconstruct not so much the wholeness of subjectivity as the wholeness of story. This process is evident in *Not I,* as well.

NOT I

As Enoch Brater describes it, the visual image produced by Beckett's *Not I* is one of "a mouth staring out at us from otherwise 'empty' theatrical space . . . [D]isembodied, suspended in space" (18) (see fig. 8). Brater immediately checks this oversimplification by acknowledging the presence on stage of the Auditor who, "at the other side of the stage is a silent, elongated, hooded figure" (18) which in one production of the play struck Brater as "a wordless giant who stood in mute contrast to the minimal image of a panting orifice" (31).[34] Once again, despite his expressed interest in the silence and emptiness in the work, one gets the impression that, like most of Beckett's "analysts," Brater feels compelled to address the idea of story in the text, and to eventually subordinate the image of silence and emptiness to it. Consequently, in demonstrating the futility of the "story" told through Mouth's tortuous, segmented, and relentless monologue, he judiciously winds up with more questions than determinations: "What really happened to the woman in the field, resulting in her uncontrollable talking? . . . What happened in the courtroom and what happened to her in the supermart? . . . Why does she have 'no idea what she's saying . . . imagine! . . . no idea what she's saying!'?" (34). No matter how much and how well critics like Brater and Garner prioritize and explore the visual image in Beckett's theatre, in an attempt to get the "whole" story, they forge on in search of either hidden verbal reference or deep grammatical patterns in the text.[35] Their work is truly illuminating, and their linguistic connections are sound; but, I believe that any approach that circumvents the supra-referential, extralinguistic vortex of the (w)hole of Beckett's work (that "sucks us all in"), forestalls some level of meta-physical and extralinguistic discovery.

What if we were to prioritize the interpretive dimension of *Not I* with respect to the empty stage-empty mind connection? Brater says of the subject-Mouth: "All she seems able to acknowledge as her own is a painful 'roar in the skull'" (23). I would like to take this more literally than Brater seems to do and argue that *Not I* is fundamentally rather than circumstantially a theatrical presentation of a "roar in the skull," an empty skull, that, as in so many of Beckett's other plays,[36] provides an anthropomorphic metaphor for the emptiness of stage space. From this point of view, the dominant aesthetic effect of the play is that the spectator will somehow grasp that Mouth is helplessly hyperconscious of the bio(onto)logical and bio(geo)graphical source of her incoherent, unassimilable monologue: the headspace, microcosm of the empty theatrical space. Thus, words and phrases sacrifice much of their referential value as linguistic signs and derive a uniquely plastic and visual quality as *psychic signals*,[37] suspended like so many astral bodies within the personal, inner cosmos of the protagonist-spectator. Even without eyes, especially without eyes, Mouth performs as an even more postmodern avatar of Hamm of *Endgame*, observing her own emptiness which she para-diegetically reproduces for her spectating counterpart in the audience. In the monologue of *Not I*, we are once again dealing with poetic image. More fundamental and more significant than the sequential referentiality of story is the mimetic and diegetic construction of an image of empty inner space. We should *imagine* Mouth not as a fragmented part of a body, but instead, as a whole psyche (or psychic hole), as a monument to the formalistic self-consciousness of postmodern humanity.

Despite the repeated claims of fragmentation, the visual image is more substantial and complete than the narrative story line. Like the stage it occupies, the image represents a (w)hole, or, more precisely, a (w)hole within a (w)hole. The play's "action" is reduced and focused on thought processes liberated from conventional narrative structure. While the language of the play is still referential to the extent that for the most part utterances signify things and concepts, the things and concepts do not produce a comprehensive narrative. There is no determinate structure to the story, no referential whole (story), but rather a supra-referential "hole" (image). Image as signifier is liberated from story as signified. Much of the language fulfills a poetic function by organizing and emphasizing the locus of its creation, the same locus as the play's action: explicit references to mind, brain, and skull recur in a steady flow, heavily punctuating what Brater sees as a story about a "woman in the field" (34). The "action" of the play itself, the psychic impulses within the mind, takes the form of either visual signals ("thoughts," "sudden flash," "moonbeam") or auditory signals ("buzzing in the skull," "roaring," "scream"), signals that signify only to the extent that they "point toward" supra-referential meaning. These are the signals Mouth senses and expresses, the signals the audience is induced into "seeing," "hearing," or "feeling": not the linguistic but the imagistic; not the signifying word, but the punctuating brush strokes that paint a picture of inner space, or the vowel sounds that become not so much signifieds as plasticized psychic debris. One recurring utterance refers to words: "words were coming . . . imagine!" (80). Yet these words are "odd" (84), ultimately incomprehensible to Mouth, oddities reduced to subjectively produced "vowel sounds" even visual objects: "words were coming . . . a voice she did not recognize . . . at first . . . so long since it had sounded . . . then finally had to admit . . . could be none other . . . than her own . . . certain vowel sounds . . . she had never heard . . . elsewhere" (80). To draw attention to the independence of "vowel sounds" is to play havoc with the sequential connectedness of narration in a turn toward an image of disordered thought immersed within and overwhelmed by an irrational, anti-structural field of emptiness. If Mouth's autistic and barely visible stage partner is named Auditor, she herself is not the Speaker, but, more appropriately, the Contemplator, a mirror image for the "contemplator" in the audience. Having disengaged herself from the referential whole, she becomes an image (the new "ground")[38] of nonsequential, chaotic, psychic process.

In Beckett's plays words "matter" to the extent that they are matter, matter in a spatial vacuum. The echo effect contributes to the impression of internal, eternal emptiness. In *Rockaby* the echo is expressly indicated in the stage directions and further suggested by the constant repetition of utterances. In *Not I* the repetition alone enhances the effect of residual resonance in an empty chamber. This (re)sounding of silence exposes the referentiality of the echoed words as ultimately illusory, and the very idea of story collapses with the incessant intervention of words and phrases that function as "metaphysical" signals, i.e., as sensory stimuli lacking the comprehensive binary and dialectical referentiality of signs. Another recurring utterance, "stare into space," applies to both Mouth and to her audience, to the "spectator" on and off stage. Mouth, is as much a spectator of her own psychic impulses as the off-stage spectator staring into the dark space of the Mouth, gateway to the psychic heart of darkness. Martin Esslin calls the mouth the "point of intersection between a non-material world and the world of flesh, of matter" (89).[39] The monologue diegetically completes the embodiment of the sus-pended, isolated mouth, metaphor for psyche. No matter how you look at it, either the cerebral body of Hamm, the head of "W" in *Rockaby,* or Mouth, they are all frames for an inner psychic space that undermines the spectator's familiar impression of a corporeal, material, socially oriented world.

Like the passionate, consummate lover who teases their mate, or the true patriot whose protest challenges the democratic political structure of the nation, or the theatre critic whose severity entrains doubt of his love of theatre, Beckett taunts our professed social consciousness as he derisively reinvents the language and imagery through which it is constituted. Western society spent decades deciding that Beckett was not a nihilist. Despite his challenge to language and to the social foundation of the individual, there is no reason to doubt his compassionate commiseration with (and understanding of) humanity at its most primitive social origins. The distinguished Italian director, Georgio Strehler, avows that his most vivid memory of the director Bertolt Brecht was his high regard for Beckett's work. According to Strehler, Brecht, the quintessential socialist theorist-practitioner of theatre, confided that, "behind the void that engulfs Vladimir and Estragon, he would have liked simply to invent something in the process of construc-tion."[40] It is certainly not the sterility or stasis of the empty mind that Beckett sought to expose, but its potential for de-constructive process, though arti-ficial it may be; or its potential for the artifice of creative contemplation.

So just how fragmentary is Beckett's world after all? From how many critical angles can we view its fragmentation? To be sure, the text can be described as fragmentary; but the image that, ironically, the fragmented text helps to create and complete is quite the contrary. I can agree with Paul Lawley that "Whatever Mouth is, it is a godforsaken hole" (410). But I dis-agree with his contention that "Throughout the play, the fragmentary dis-course throws up a fragmented body, the image of the fragmentary self" (411). I can only reservedly agree that Mouth is, as he puts it, "*an emblem of absence*" (412), since "absence" is a "glass-is-half-full" kind of concept that implies a referential presence. Rather, Mouth is also—and even more powerfully—an emblem of emptiness; and we cannot ignore this attribute when we consider absence in Beckett's work to be the result of fragmentation, a fragmented presence. As an image the French would call "placed in *abyme*," Mouth is the result not so much of fragmentation but of multidimensional, metatheatrical concentration. Consequently, absence is rendered more graphic and organic. At the beginning of the romantic period in the nineteenth century Victor Hugo claimed the dramatic work should function not as any ordinary mirror providing simple reflection, but as a "concentrating mirror, which, instead of weakening, concentrates and focuses the rays of color, which makes of a feeble glimmer a bright light, of a light a flame" (74). A little more than a century later, Beckett's flame has burnt a hole right through the center of the stage, one that connects to the phenomenal subjectivity of the spectator.

As I have argued, in Beckett's works the perception of subjectivity is not a psychological phenomenon;[41] it is reduced to the association of the image of the human mind with that of the stage image. The substance of mind and stage is extended emptiness. I have examined his works from this angle in order to flush out his metadramatic strategies for expressing the material emptiness and extension of the mind. Like no other twentieth-century dramatist, Beckett broke with the naturalistic economy of theatrical space and especially with the way the spectator perceives the dramatic character's relation to the space it inhabits. His corpus demands a reconceptualized emphasis on the ways in which he uses black background and silence to draw the spectator's attention through an isolated character toward the interior space indicated by the dark background.

(META)MEANINGFULLNESS IN BECKETT

Just as light points toward darkness and sound to silence, local meanings can point to the fascination of universal, immanent meaninglessness. The meaninglessness orchestrated by Beckett's theatre signifies a meaning beyond convention. All art suggests this in some way, but most art (like most progressive theory) emphasizes deconstructing the system rather than truly pointing beyond it. A sophisticated glimpse at emptiness beyond space results in a *prise de conscience* of the empty psychic slate on which meaning inscribes itself. In a groundbreaking essay on the "achromatic" aspect of Beckett's texts and Georgia O'Keeffe's paintings, Jennifer M. Jeffers examines the use of achromatic colors in painting and in prose through an approach that resembles my examination of empty space for theatrical art. She makes a similar distinction between the utilitarian, representational use of achromatic colors in classical artforms and its more essential, nonrepresentational role in some of contemporary art: "Thus, da Vinci's discovery of chiaroscuro meant that achromatic colors were essential on the painter's palette but mainly because of their contribution to the goals of verisimilitude" ("The Image of Thought" 61). She develops the following thesis:

I am interested in exploring how achromatic art and literature attempt to think what has not yet been thought or the way that they try to depict what Deleuze calls "the image of pure thought." . . . Deleuze thus opens up an epistemological space that must be negotiated from a perspective other than one that is dependent upon chromatics and representation—it must be negotiated from the plane of immanence. (65)

That which has not yet been thought amounts to that which cannot be thought in conventional terms of structure, system, and logic.[42] She emphasizes the preeminence of the principle of "unboundedness" in the Deleuze/Guattari theory of "pure immanence," arguing that "Deleuze and Guattari's idea of immanence picks up where Kant's idea of the sublime leaves off. . . . Kant's realm of the sublime is also always already 'bounded' by the attempt to find a symbol for or the attempt to make reasonable the boundlessness of the experience" (65). This line of reasoning obviously connects to Greimas's theory of unbounded extension versus structured, bounded space that I discussed in chapter 1. Colored space is representational, whereas the achromatic space of a painter like O'Keeffe or a writer like Beckett constitutes an "unencumbered image of thought—image devoid of category—that requires that we view and read the coordinates on the plane of immanence prior to the formulation of transcendental, representational or universal meaning" (66–67). The lack of color in Beckett's work corroborates the lack of representational fullness in the form of the narrative and its material articulation of the image; the achromatic emptiness causes a critical anti-structural tension for the reader as well as for the spectator: "We want color, and more than anything else we want color to represent or to mean something we already know" (67). (This would help to explain the dominance of the physical point of view toward Beckett's theatre.) We enter the supra-representational mind of Beckett's protagonists, where it is dark and empty and where flashes of prelinguistic signals signal a primordial awareness as they contend for immanent "meaning." This meaning appears meaningless in the context of logic—any logic.[43]

How compatible is this concept of "pure immanence" with Patrice Pavis's evaluation of postmodern drama as a text that revels in its "narcissistic self-contemplation" (66; Linda Hutcheon's term) and one "emptied of meaning, or at least of any immediate mimetic meaning" ("Classical Heritage" 59)? Because of the text's refusal to connect to an extrinsic system of values, Pavis argues that we should approach it not as an interpretable text, but as

an object of questioning, the workings of codes, rather than a series of situations and allusions to a subtext which the spectator ought to feel. The text is received as a series of meanings which contradict and answer one another and which decline to annihilate themselves in a final global meaning. ("Classical Heritage" 60)

Pavis, of course, feels that the only legitimate approach to a dramatic text is through its performance,[44] and he emphasizes that the postmodern performance of a classical text must intend to "undo the rhythm of the text in its first (habitual or self-evident) reading" (61). More important, as a postmodern work, the value of Beckett's text resides in its ability to ward off interpretation: "The text has become signifying matter awaiting meaning, an object of desire, the hypothesis of a meaning (of one among others)" (61).[45] Consequently, the spectator is fascinated with the work's "process of fabrication," one which behaves, not to create meaning, but, on the contrary, to deliver us into a psychic region where meaning is irrelevant. Pavis's ideas on the postmodernist effort to produce no more than an hypothesis of meaning (based largely on Lyotard's metaphysics of desire) is not entirely compatible with Jeffers's and Deleuze's theories of pure immanence. However, when Jeffers explains that, like O'Keeffe's paintings, Beckett's texts "always seem to stop short of the absolute achromatic monochrome," and that his prose "always leaves open a margin of ambiguity" (74–75), in this respect, she suggests that these artists are aware that pure immanence is more a method than a goal, that the contemporary mind is not prepared to create perfectly or to accept fully any absolute as art—for more than a moment. In this respect, Beckett's theatre is a celebration of "immanence awareness," generated by the absence of color, of structure, and story—achromatics and extension.

Jeffers's examination focuses on Beckett's short prose fiction, but as Jonathon Kalb has pointed out, "[Beckett's] prose fiction is no longer perceivable entirely apart from his drama" (Kalb 117).[46] She completes her "achromatic" analysis with *Ill Seen Ill Said* (1981), where "The text actively flows, even in its calm pictorial achromatic movement, toward a state of non-narrative—not the *end* and not the obliteration but toward a new space where language stops and the pure image of thought begins" (77). Thus the reader must adopt a new receptive approach to Beckett's referral to a different, unfamiliar region of the mind. It is significant indeed that in this work the narrator challenges the reader to an act of contemplation rather than interpretation, a contemplation of emptiness rather than the fullness of structured reality: "Nothing but black and white. Everywhere no matter where. But black. Void. Nothing else. *Contemplate that.* Not another word. Home at last. Gently gently" (*Ill Seen Ill Said* 31; my emphasis).

Beckett emphasized thinking as contemplation and his art teaches us that we need to become more aware of the empty spaces of our universe and our mind. Jon Erikson has explained the importance of the act of contemplation in the reception of truly creative art:

> Contemplation is a distancing that allows one to see the relation of figure to ground. . . . Autonomous art, through its defamiliarizing process, places us in a contemplative attitude that calls into question the conventional

ordering of reality in which we are immersed. It turns the figure of the object, conventionally defined by our social ground, into a new ground upon which we must construct new figures of meaning. (30)

Beckett's hypersubjective humanoid figures differ from Oedipus, Hamlet, and Phèdre. They differ in the way that they function as a new ground, one which disallows the interpretable meanings one draws from heroic symbols of humanity, supercharged symbols of the existential absurdity of life. On the contrary, they are empty hypotheses that require the prolonged contemplation that permits an awareness beyond understanding. When we contemplate Beckett's human icons as the *mise en abyme* of empty space, the very idea of figure to ground relationship is "sent into *abyme*." Immanence awareness is a critical game we play with Beckett to get beyond representationalism. Ultimately, what we contemplate is not just an image but a hyper-image/ meta-image, a hyper-meta-image, one that guides us away not only from the referentiality and connectedness of language, but also from the representationalism of the human form—from the representationalism of the earth toward the pure immanence of the extended universe.

A HYPERSUBJECTIVE (EMPTY) GLANCE AT OTHER LATE PLAYS

In others of Beckett's late plays we see a similar self-conscious experimentation with the breakdown of story as well as similar dramaturgical strategies intended to merge the image of the human figure with the material emptiness of stage and scenery and to infuse referential language with the sounds of silence. These strategies include a stage design based on an economy of emptiness; the architectonic embedding of and focus on the character, framed by darkness; a telescoping lighting effect that begins and ends with a perceptive focus on the head of the isolated character;[47] a language consisting of signifieds that semantically suggest the focus on the headspace and invoke the image of an empty psyche—signifieds that are meaningful in the "meta" mode of directing our attention to the headspace; and a form of linguistic expression that is syntactically, morphologically, phonetically, and rhythmically fragmented and recast into modulated ("soundbite") signifiers that create the impression of spatial suspension and extension.

A Piece of Monologue (1979)

The stage directions of *A Piece of Monologue*[48] tell us that Speaker, the only character of the play, "stands well off centre downstage audience left." Speaker appears in a "Faint diffuse light" with "White hair, white nightgown, white socks." While we might get the impression that the off-center position of the protagonist undermines focus, there are at least two good reasons to believe that this position is not intended to divert focus from a human icon representing empty psychic space. First, on this empty, achromatic, dimly lit stage, the perception of a geometrical center is less relevant. The second reason is the presence of the "skull-sized white globe, faintly lit" that takes a more "centered" position on stage ("Two meters to his left"). The lamplight, which is faintly lit at curtain up, "begins to fail" thirty seconds before the end of Speaker's speech, and then it goes out ten seconds before the final curtain. Thus, *A Piece of Monologue* is yet another experiment in the material, theatrical representation of the contemplating subject. This time Beckett has moved from a strategy of using light to focus on the head of the human icon to one of allowing the light source to collaborate with the human figure in *co-articulating* the psychic space he wants to evoke. In effect, what remains of the "humanity" of Speaker transfers to the lamp, the icon for Speaker's psychic activity; the light fades as the activity decelerates at the end of the piece. This play was written one year prior to *Rockaby*, a play in which the human icon is fully visible and the voice is primarily produced by a recording. Thus *Rockaby* is likely a return to an emphasis on human presence, one complexified by the mediated voice.

There is the remnant of a story told by Speaker, the story of a man, who, alone in a room, reminisces while gazing into the empty space of the room: "Could once name them all. There was father. That grey void. There mother. That other. There together. Smiling. Wedding day. There all three. That grey blot. There alone. He alone. So on. Not now. Forgotten. All gone so long. Gone" (266). But we soon realize that the primary purpose of Speaker's narration is to create a theatrical image, not a story. From the beginning, the precise details of a virtual stage activity, though in the form of monologue, appropriate the nature of stage directions. In the course of the illusory narration, the "stage direction effect" becomes more obvious. "Stands stock still staring out. Into black vast. Nothing there. Nothing stirring. No such thing as no light. . . . Hand with spill disappears. Second hand disappears. . . . Pale globe alone in gloom. Glimmer of brass bedrail. Fade" (267). Almost imperceptibly the monologue transforms into its own stage directions, which in this work are—atypical of Beckett—not set off from the monologue of the character, because they are the monologue of the character. The directions describe the activity of a solitary male figure within an empty stage scene. Speaker's expression of this activity weaves into an act of perception, a highly intricate and nuanced perception of "nothing," "light," "dark," "empty dark," and "white" (266–67), and one which is shared jointly by the male figure and the reader/spectator. In the empty space of the theatre, limits dissolve. Not only the borders between fictional and metaphysical language and between the theatrical and the metatheatrical disappear. It becomes quite difficult to distinguish between the borders of stage and mind (mind of protagonist, mind of spectator), and just as difficult (and irrelevant) to distinguish among the borders of dark and light, white and black, nothing and something. The work is a masterpiece of the poetic detailing of nothingness; the theatre of the empty mind.

Toward the conclusion of the piece, once the empty stage has been set, the monologue's topic turns to the speech act and words. Language, the expression of something, and reality, the expressed existence of things, are simultaneously exposed as artifices that are unequal to the awareness and the perception of nothing. Beckett accomplishes a theatrical demonstration of how the transfiguration of thoughts/perceptions into words—from internal awareness, through internal process, to external expression—is a degenerative process indeed, one which represents the loss of essential, primordial awareness. We remember Beckett's confession to the effect that his verbal construction of theatrical event (image and words) is at once a necessary and necessarily futile attempt to touch the void. Thus Speaker says that the words "fall" from his protagonist's mouth, that they merely "make do" with his mouth, a pathway to the world: "Stands staring beyond half hearing what he's saying. He? The words falling from his mouth. Making do with his mouth" (268). The act of speech creation is a birth in the sense that it separates us from the void: "Stares beyond into dark. Waits for first word always the same. It gathers in his mouth. Parts lips and thrusts tongue forward. Birth. Parts the dark" (268). This recalls Artaud's warning cited at the beginning of this chapter: "All true feeling is in reality untranslatable. To express it is to betray it. . . . All powerful feeling produces in us the idea of the void. And the lucid language which obstructs the appearance of this void also obstructs the appearance of poetry in thought."

Consequently, words are banished, and Speaker speaks of dying as a process that is connected to words: "The dead and gone. The dying and the going. From the word go. The word begone" (269). Finally, the playlet concludes when the "stage directions" of Speaker coincide with Beckett's instructions at the beginning of the text. Beckett's directions explicitly call for a fading of the lamplight, then a lamp out and silence with "Speaker, globe, foot of pallet, barely visible in diffuse light" (265). The monologue concludes with the quintessential image of the hypersubject. First it focuses on the protagonist of the monologue: "Into dark whole again. No. No such thing as whole. Head almost touching wall. White hair catching light. White gown. White socks" (269). (The equivocation between "whole" and its homophone "hole" is significant here.) Then the monologue draws attention to the lamp whose light dies out: "The unaccountable. From nowhere. On all sides nowhere. Unutterably faint. The globe alone. Alone gone" (269). The image of the globe exceeds verbal expression. Its afterimage survives as the icon of empty psyche, paradoxically dissolving into the dark silence of the stage.

Ohio Impromptu (1981)

In this piece, there are two players, to be sure, Reader and Listener. But they are "As alike in appearance as possible." There is a "Light on table midstage. Rest of stage in darkness." The players have "long white hair" and they wear "long black coat." At the center of the stage there is a "black wide-brimmed hat" (285), an index of a headspace that points to the dark periphery of both the headspace and the stage (see fig. 9). There is even action: Listener periodically knocks on table; Listener's left hand checks Reader's left hand when he tries to turn back the pages of the book he is reading; Reader turns a page (286). We can glean a remnant "story" about a man who "Day after day he could be seen slowly pacing the islet" (286). However, metadrama overwhelms Reader's narration, which closely describes the character, action, and image we see before us: "Then drawing a worn volume from the pocket of his long black coat he sat and read till dawn" (287). Thus the story, "the sad tale a last time told" (287), becomes frustratingly but poetically pointless before the power of the image and the words used expressly to empower the image:

> So the sad tale a last time told they sat on as though turned to stone. Through the single window dawn shed no light. From the street no sound of reawakening. Or was it that buried in who knows what thoughts they paid no heed? To light of day. To sound of reawakening. What thoughts who knows. Thoughts, no, not thoughts. *Profounds of mind.* Buried in who knows what profounds of mind. Of *mindlessness.* Whither no light can reach. No sound. So sat on as though turned to stone. The sad tale a last time told. [*Pause.*] Nothing is left to tell." (287–88; my emphasis)

The empowered image suggests at once the mind and "mindlessness": "Thoughts, no, not thoughts. Profounds of mind." Reader's magnified gesture of closing the book ("makes to close book . . . Book half-closed . . . closes book") betrays the mental locus of the inward turn. The above quote describes a mental effort to move one's consciousness from outer world progressively toward the nothingness of psychic depth. The final utterance, "Nothing is left to tell," in the context of this and all Beckettian drama, implies the "telling" has just begun, since "nothing" is what Beckett tells so well. This theatrical impromptu has taken us through the material confines of the external stage to the borders of the internal stage, from a necessarily bounded empty space to the border of unbounded extension. The "nothing" that is left to tell is at once the end of the narration and the beginning of hypersensitive awareness. The piece comes to a close when "Reader closes book," thereby shutting out the world of language. Then "Simultaneously [Reader and Listener] lower their right hands to table, raise their heads and look at each other. Unblinking. Expressionless. Ten seconds. Fade out" (288). Reader and Listener fuse into one image of psyche that fuses into stage.

Catastrophe (1982)

This is, as Beckett's stage directions tell us, a rehearsal: "Final touches to the last scene. Bare stage" (297). There are four characters, not two, not one; but there is only one protagonist, in this play rehearsal within a play.

Protagonist is "midstage standing on a black block 18 inches high. Black wide-brimmed hat. Black dressing gown to ankles. Barefoot. Head bowed. Hands in pockets" (297). This time the black hat is not on the table but on the head of Protagonist; since Protagonist has his head bowed, it dominates the showcased human figure at the beginning of the play (see fig. 10). Director asks Assistant, "Why the hat?" and Assistant replies, "To help hide the face." Subsequently, to the question, "Why the gown?" Assistant replies, "To have him all in black" (297).[49] Then Director asks "How's the skull?" and Assistant replies "You've seen it." To which Director retorts: "I forget . . . Say it" (298). The artifice "say it" exposes the illusion of the adequacy of language (as well as the reality of its inadequacy), especially in view of language's subservient role in this kind of theatre, a kind of theatre that Ubersfeld refers to as one where "Image overwhelms the text, exhausting it at all points" (*L'Ecole* 298).

In the service of the image, the dialogue actively renders the spectator conscious of the opposition between face and skull. Director makes Assistant remove Protagonist's gown and hat. When Assistant asks, "Like that cranium?," Director replies "Needs whitening." Likewise, Protagonist's speech will be "whitened," i.e., effaced, since Director is disturbed by "This craze for explication! Every i dotted to death!" (299).

Finally, as the play concludes, once the black hat is removed and the "black" headspace is uncovered, the lighting progressively comes to a focus on the head, a maneuver that reminds us of *Rockaby*, despite the fact that, unlike *Rockaby*'s text, Beckett gives no lighting directions for the beginning of this play. In an interesting twist on the dramaturgy of the headspace—the outer, visible frame for the mind-space—this text consciously probes the opposition between head and face, suggesting Beckett's increased interest in the head as an icon. Towards the conclusion we have a carefully plotted sequence of lighting changes that begin when Director states: "Blackout stage" (300). This direction provokes a fade out that first leaves Protagonist's entire body illuminated, until Director specifies, "Just the head" (300). But Protagonist's head is bowed. Assistant "timidly" queries: "What if he were to . . . raise his head . . . show his face . . . just an instant." Director's immediate response is one of annoyance: "Raise his head? For God's sake!" After a reflective pause, however, he reconsiders: "Good. There's our catastrophe. In the bag. Once more and I'm off" (300).[50] Consequently, the light fades up first on Protagonist's body, then to a general light. Finally, when Director calls "Now . . . let 'em have it," the general light recycles through a focus on Protagonist's body to a focus on the head alone. Once the light is refocused on the head, there is a "long pause" followed by a "Distant storm of applause," until Protagonist raises his head and fixes the audience (see fig. 11). The applause falters, then dies, and the light fades out on face (301). Thus, the "story" of the image of the human figure, told primarily by lighting effect, demonstrates that Beckett has evolved in his revelation of the head-space. This play acknowledges and demythifies very concretely and explicitly what Maeterlinck and Craig knew very well. The human face, with its irrepressible personality, tells a story while the skull-like form of the head has the potential to present a virtual space. With the alternation of general lighting, focus on the body, and focus on the head, the category of time serves a telescopic spatial strategy to "move" the spectator's attention into the headspace—but this time with resistance (the return to general lighting), a strategy to increase the "force" of movement.

Beckett continues to experiment with the theatrical disclosure of the headspace. His distinction between the face and the head indicates progression toward an increasingly focused model of character-space connection through emptiness. In *Rockaby*, the face represented the head, whereas here, the expressive aspect of the face foils its ability to evoke an empty space. When the face is shown, the effect of empty space falters, and the applause of the audience "falters, dies": Catastrophe!

Quad (1982) and *What Where* (1983)

To complete this chapter, I have just taken another look at the video version of *Quad 1, Quad 2* (an alternative version of *Quad*), and *What Where*.[51] My wife enters the room. She's a nurse with a refined appreciation for all forms of art, especially dance and theatre, and she would like to see late Beckett. Ah! Here's a renewed opportunity to rehearse my "empty" approach to Beckett before an objective, critical audience. (She is acquainted with my approach, but she remains reserved.) First we view *Quad 1*. Together we observe the four players mechanically pace the illuminated grid. They wear hooded gowns: three that are each of a different primary color, one of the pure, neutral color, white. In varying combinations they cross the stage according to a pattern consisting of varying geometrical angles that approach a center point in the grid, "Point E." The players move from one of the outside corners of the stage toward an inner square surrounding Point E. Their course of movement along a diagonal deviates to follow at least one of the sides of the inner square before an exit that completes a diagonal toward another of the outside angles. The illustration in Beckett's text shows the apparently inviolable area of the inner square (293). See fig. 12, where, heads bowed, the players corporealize this space by hovering around Point E.

Immediately my wife's attention is drawn to the colors of the hooded players and to the choreography of their movement. I explain that this display of color is quite unusual for Beckett and that the primary function of the choreographed action is to undo or derealize our perception of space in order to reawaken our awareness of extension.[52] In my view, the colors as well as the choreographed pattern and the frenetic, percussive music are significant primarily for their ability to set off the fourth dimension of the emptiness of the space, a space that represents the essentially unstructured extension of the mind. She remains skeptical—until we see Beckett's alternative version to *Quad 1: Quad 2.*

By way of introduction to the performance of *Quad 2,* the actor Chris O'Neill explains that Beckett's idea for the new version of *Quad* occurred when, by chance, he saw a technician play *Quad 1* in black and white and without sound. Thus, in *Quad 2* color is removed (the costumes become four identical white gowns) and the only sound that remains is that of footsteps; and the tempo is slower. Beckett's move to achromatic display and his removal of the percussion are symptoms of his experimentation with the progressive unveiling (and valorization) of the empty space. Can he draw the spectator into the empty space without the use of color and music to set the perspective? To be sure, my wife and I realize that the shadows of the figures are more prominent in this version. Undisturbed by the expressive distraction of color, form takes precedence. Most important, however, in his comments on *Quad 2,* Beckett makes the following revelation: "E supposed a danger zone. Hence deviation" (293). By signaling clearly and unambiguously this deviation, Beckett produces a *mise en abyme*–like "grid within a grid" pattern of choreography. I reiterate to my wife that, in light of my hypersubjective theory, the stage represents an empty mental space and, as in all Beckett's works, the hooded figures have the dual role of representing both thinkers/contemplators (who are in the act of thinking/contemplating) and the "profounds of thought" themselves within the empty psyche of these thinkers. The "danger zone" presents the final extended abyss of inner theatrical space, or, in Artaud's words, "the dead center of space through which the mind must pass." . . . "Always the void, always the point around which matter thickens" ("Le Théâtre et les dieux" 206, 204; see chapter 2). There is no "Quad 3" because Beckett's genius was limited to delivering us to the threshold of the abyss, to Point E ("E" for "empty"?). It was enough that he made us so hypersubjectively aware of its possibility, of its latency, and of its relevance to conscious life, thereby producing the ontological and sociocultural contradiction or tension that genuine art is supposed to produce.[53]

At this point my wife began to accept the critical soundness of my theory; yet she still resisted the apparently "fatalistic nihilism" of it. Finally, when we saw the video of Beckett's last voluntarily published work, *What Where* (1984), it was relatively easy for me to explain the mask-like faces emerging from darkness. (In figure 13, we see the cerebral dramatist flanked by his "empty-headed," cranial cast.) But my wife challenged me to explain Beckett's apparent return to what seemed like an indicative, meaningful language, out of which a good detective might piece together a complex narrative.

How long would it take for a good detective to realize that the bulk of the language of *What Where* is at once an ironical wink at the storyline of a cops and robbers film and to the "story" of *Godot*? This is, in fact, Beckett's farewell wink at the use of language in the theatre, or more accurately put, the ironic use of language in the empty space of theatre. The playlet begins with references to time ("It is spring. / Time passes.") and with a naming of the speech act, of the consciousness of words ("First with words") (310). Like so many illuminated "profounds of thought"—or, as Breton described the surrealist excursion into oneself, "the systematic illumination of hidden places and the progressive darkening of other places"—the talking heads appear and disappear in a field of darkness. Once the skeletalized "narrative" gets underway, the character Bam has brief exchanges with each of the other three "heads," Bim, Bom, and Bem. The exchanges could suggest a bout with the Gestapo; but, more likely, they ironically evoke the superficial storyline of one of Edward G. Robinson's (black and white) films of the 1940s. For example:

> *Bam:* He didn't say it? . . .
> You gave him the works? . . .
> Begged for mercy? . . .
> Take him away and give him the works until he confesses.
> *Bim:* What must he confess?
> *Bam:* That he said where to him.
> *Bem:* Is that all? (312–13)

Bam presides over an interrogation that is framed by metadramatic commentary at the beginning and conclusion of the work. The final lines seem like Beckett's farewell to the world . . . of narration:

> *Voice of Bam:* Good.
> I am alone.
> In the present as were I still.
> It is winter.
> Without journey.
> Time passes.
> That is all.
> Make sense who may.
> I switch off.

There is a lights off on the playing area, followed by a pause, then a lights off on the Voice of Bam ("in the shape of a small megaphone at head level"; 309). Since Beckett has "switched off," so many of us continue to make sense of his nonsense. As a dramatist he made sense out of nonsense, but not the kind of sense that first comes to mind, one based on language and story. With the creation of his intricately organized playlets at the end of his career, Beckett has drawn scholars ever closer to the detail of the stage image and to the undifferentiated mystery of the emptiness that the image too often masks. The "after-image" of his entire theatrical corpus is one of empty psyche.[54]

FIGURE 1. *L'Harlequino
Bergamasco.* Late-17th-
century engraving.
Munich, Deutsches
Theatermuseum.

FIGURE 2. *Pierrot* (*Gilles*).
Jean-Antoine Watteau.
Paris, Louvre.

FIGURE 3. *Italian Comedians.* Jean-Antoine Watteau.
Samuel H. Kress Collection. Photograph © 2000 Board
of Trustees, National Gallery of Art, Washington, D.C.

FIGURE 4. *Harlequin.* Paul Cézanne. Collection of Mr. and Mrs. Paul Mellon. Photograph © 2000 Board of Trustees, National Gallery of Art, Washington, D.C.

FIGURE 5. An Übermarionette. Plate 8 from Gordon Craig's *Scene,* 1923. Edward Gordon Craig Estate and Bibliothèque nationale de France, Paris.

FIGURE 6. Roger Blin as Hamm in *Fin de partie* (*Endgame*). Dir. Roger Blin, Studio des Champs-Elysées, Paris, 1957. Collection Roger Pic. Paris, Bibliothèque nationale de France, Dept. des Arts du Spectacle.

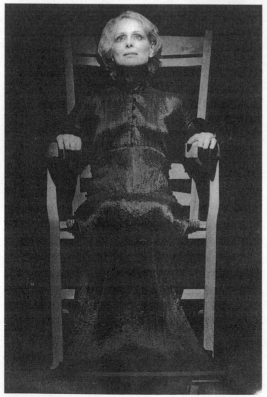

FIGURE 7. Catherine Sellers in *Berceuse* (*Rockaby*). Dir. Pierre Chabert, Théâtre du Petit Rond Point, Paris, 1983. Photograph © Brigitte Enguérand.

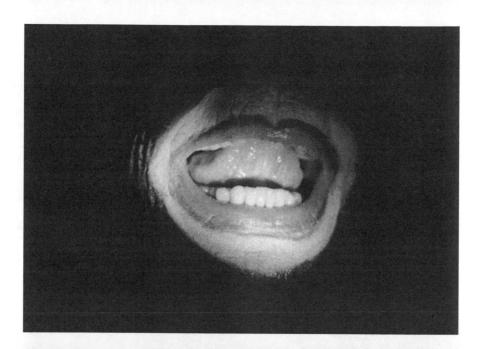

FIGURE 8. (above) Madeleine Renaud in *Pas Moi* (*Not I*). Dir. Samuel Beckett, Théâtre Petit Orsay, Paris, 1975. Photograph © Marc Enguérand.

FIGURE 9. David Warrilow as Reader and Rand Mitchell as Listener in *Ohio Impromptu.* Dir. Alan Schneider, Harold Clurman Theatre, New York City, 1983. Photograph Martha Swope © Time Inc.

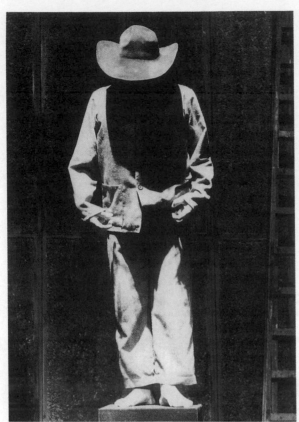

FIGURE 10. Jean-Louis Barrault in *Catastrophe*. Dir. Pierre Chabert, Théâtre du Petit Rond-Point, 1983. Photograph © Brigitte Enguérand.

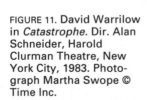

FIGURE 11. David Warrilow in *Catastrophe*. Dir. Alan Schneider, Harold Clurman Theatre, New York City, 1983. Photograph Martha Swope © Time Inc.

FIGURE 12. (above) Helfrid Foron, Jürg Hummel, Claudia Knupfer, and Susanne Rehe in *Quadrat* (*Quad*). Dir. Samuel Beckett, SDR, Stuttgart, 1981. Photograph Hugo Jehle © Südwestrundfunk.

FIGURE 13. Samuel Beckett with F. Becker, E. Dorner, W. Laugwitz, A. Querback, the cast of *Was Wo* (*What Where*). Dir. Samuel Beckett, SDR, Stuttgart, 1981. Photograph Hugo Jehle © Südwestrundfunk.

FIGURE 14. Klaus Herm in *Damals* (*That Time*). Dir.
Samuel Beckett, Schiller Theatre Werkstatt, West
Berlin, 1976. Photograph: Archives Ilse Buhs/J.
Remmler © Deutsches Theatermuseum, Munich.

FIGURE 15. John Bottoms in *That Time.* Dir. Paul Draper, Guthrie Lab Theatre, 1994. Photograph Michael Daniel.

FIGURE 16. M. Chikly, C. Combe, Y. Gourvil, P. Larzille, and A. Rais in *Force de l'habitude* (*Force of Habit*). Dir. Jacques Kraemer, Théâtre de la Tempête, Paris, 1986. Photograph Agnes Courrault/Enguérand.

FIGURE 17. Marc Chikly as Caribaldi in *Force de l'habitude* (*Force of Habit*). Dir. Jacques Kraemer, Théâtre de la Tempête, Paris, 1986. Photograph Agnes Courrault/Enguérand.

FIGURE 18. Al Carmines as Caribaldi in *Force of Habit.* Dir. Paul Draper, Mann Auditorium, Columbia University, New York City, 1987.

[4]

AVATARS OF THE HYPERSUBJECTIVE
DRAMATIC CHARACTER

In this chapter I move from Beckett's drama to the broader perspective of the dramatic movement in which he was often placed. The wellspring of the movement was located in the postwar culture of Western Europe, particularly in France. Furthermore, I will argue that the hypersubjective mode of this movement was more prevalent among dramatists who were native or adoptive children of French culture.[1] In the 1960s and 1970s many studies appeared which placed Beckett's drama within the critical-creative framework of a movement called variously "theatre of the absurd" (Esslin), "theatre of derision" (Jacquart), or "nouveau théâtre" (Serreau). Since the 1970s many scholars have criticized these labels, cautioning against the interpretive pitfalls of comprehensive labeling, the use of umbrella terms, and pointing out the many differences among works by Beckett, Ionesco, Adamov, Arrabal, Genet, Obaldia, Dubillard, among other nouveau dramatists working in France. To make a case for disparity, one has only to consider the differences mentioned in the preceding chapter between Beckett's early works, like *Godot* or *Endgame,* and the extreme minimalism of his later works.

One interesting argument to have arisen from the critical determination of the "absurdist" drama of the postwar period is the one centered around realism. The idea of realism inevitably arises in discussions of unrealistic theatrical art. Scholars of the 1960s and 1970s were quick to hail the new "irrational" theatrical forms as unrealistic or non-mimetic. As time goes on, however, scholars become increasingly more comprehensive in applying the label of realism to art forms. In other words, the more scholars discover worldly relevance for the absurdist vehicle, and the more we accept the absurd as a real part of life, the more generous and inclusive scholars become in qualifying realism. Eventually, many are willing to accept much of absurdist drama as no more than an aberrant form of realism. The concept of realism does more to help us formulate our approach to art when we evaluate art not for its surface verisimility but for its deeper relevance to society.[2] (Perhaps the twenty-second century will hail the twentieth century as a boiling pot of artistic realism!) In the rewriting of the history of drama, Beckett's work gets special treatment in part because of the considerable evolution of its form from the beginning to the end of his career.

At the same time that we continue to reassess the "absurdity" of nouveau théâtre, we also discover new approaches to distinguish between the "absurdist" styles of the authors of this theatre. Yet, our graduate students and even many of our colleagues who specialize in the twentieth century still are largely unwilling to seriously distinguish the work of Beckett from that of Ionesco. Moreover, too often we hear the epithet of "anti-theatre" uncritically applied wholesale to the so-called "absurdist" authors. Non-specialist colleagues, those whose research focuses on another historical period, another genre, theme, or movement, draw even broader brushstrokes on their analytical canvas. One has only to check the Ph.D. reading lists in twentieth-century French theatre to realize this.

The nouveau théâtre works of Beckett and company are not simply a new self-absorbing approach to the fantastic or the nonsensical. Very early on, Martin Esslin argued that the realism of the absurd theatre is based on the exploration of a deeper, personal reality, and that, in the theatre of the absurd

> we have always seen man stripped of the accidental circumstances of social position or historical context, confronted with the basic choices, the basic situations of his existence. (*Theatre of the Absurd* 401)
>
> While former attempts at confronting man with the ultimate realities of his condition projected a coherent and generally recognized version of the truth, the Theatre of the Absurd merely communicates one poet's most intimate and personal intuition of the human situation, his own *sense of being*, his individual vision of the world. This is the *subject-matter* of the Theatre of the Absurd, and it determines its *form*, which must, of necessity, represent a convention of the stage basically different from the 'realistic' theatre of our time. . . . It is a theatre of situation as against a theatre of events in sequence, and therefore it uses a language based on patterns of concrete images rather than argument and discursive speech. . . . The action in the play of the Theatre of the Absurd is not intended to tell a story but to communicate a pattern of poetic images. (402–403)
>
> The endeavor to communicate a total sense of being is an attempt to present a truer picture of reality itself, reality as apprehended by an individual. (404; author's emphasis throughout)

Up to the time of the nouveau théâtre, theatregoers were accustomed to watching a story revolve *around* a single individual, a story about civilization based on the essentially outer (sociocultural, mytho-social, or psycho-social) experience of the individual. For millennia, the civilized human race has been telling these stories, and so narratives always have been at the forefront of our culture. Not only books tell stories, but so do dance, and painting, and even sculpture. "Story" is practically synonymous with civilization. So the practice of storytelling—first oral, then written—forms the basis of culture. But, as Esslin points out, one thing many of the nouveau dramatists had in common was their magnified interest in the individual experience. Consequently, the magnified image of the individual took precedence over story and they began to experiment with space, time, character, metadrama, and even story and language to get to the powerful theatrical image behind and beyond the narrative. As I have tried to make clear in this book, the most powerful images were largely extralinguistic as well as non-narrative. The category of space, including the spatialization of the dramatic character and the emptying out of the stage space, was the primary extralinguistic strategy of these dramatists.[3]

How do the authors and the plays of nouveau théâtre relate to one another with respect to empty space and to the metadramatic construction of a hypersubjective protagonist? One could, I think, successfully argue that, in the postwar period in the West, the hypersubject was "in the air" of all artistic circles. In the next chapter I deal with important non-naturalistic dramatists whose work with empty space, character focus, and language has not produced a clear hypersubjective design. In the final chapter, I will to some extent discuss the hypersubject's ramifications for the world of plastic art; and, in my discussion of the marionette-like qualities of the hypersubjective character—or, in other terms, the marionette-like characters of Beckett and company as a *mise en abyme* of empty space—I will resume the examination of the historical background of this figure as image, revisiting symbolist dramatic theories like those of Maeterlinck and Craig. For now, I would like to make it clear that the hypersubject is not a motif that is exclusive to any one author or to all the works of one author. After the theoretical vision of Maeterlinck and the theory-practice of Craig, as early as Cocteau's *La Voix humaine* we see a clear prefiguration of Beckett's empty character.[4]

In this chapter, I examine other models of characters and space with traits that are clearly hypersubjective. Nowhere will we find such an absolute hypersubjective form as in the work of Beckett. Yet in a number of plays of other authors of nouveau théâtre, we find solid evidence of a strong tendency to construct such a character. In the words of Ionesco himself, "In reality, the concerns, the obsessions, the universal problems are in us all and, one after another, we all encounter them. . . . Several of us react in the same way."[5]

101

IONESCO: THE PROBLEM OF REFERENTIAL ABSENCE AND
THE HIDDEN HYPERSUBJECT IN *EXIT THE KING*

On the subject of empty space, perhaps the first Ionesco play to come to mind is *The Chairs*. Shortly after its publication, Geneviève Serreau remarked that the elderly couple is present on stage primarily to "signify the void, to give it its indispensable contour, the immediate density of its absence" (45). As was perhaps too often the case, however, objective evaluations such as this were often complicated by the fact that Ionesco took the liberty to unravel the mystery of his own fiction. He defined the subject of the play as follows:

> The subject of the play . . . is not the message, nor the failures of life, nor the moral disaster of the two old people, but the chairs themselves; that is to say, the absence of people . . . the absence of matter, the unreality of the world, metaphysical emptiness. The theme of the play is *nothingness*.[6]

Despite these remarks, when analyzed through a hypersubjective formula, i.e., the character as a theatrical representation of the empty psychic space, this work falls far short of conveying a sense of emptiness such as we have witnessed in the works of Beckett. There is no sense of spatial closure as with Beckett, and no remarkable isolation of the individual human form at any phase of the action. This is because Beckett more successfully distinguished between absence and emptiness, partially through his reticence on the subject and meaning of his art. In Ionesco's work, the on-stage presence of the empty chairs does not so much signify emptiness as absence, especially in view of their proliferation, a constant dramaturgical strategy in Ionesco's theatre. Curiously and perhaps unfortunately, the emphasis on absence, on the absent human referent, detracts from the metaphysical depth of Ionesco's drama. To be sure, absence is an important theme in all of so-called nouveau théâtre, Beckett's included. But in Beckett's drama, the notion of absence is entirely subsumed and subverted by a supra-referential emptiness, and one which is oriented through the union of space of the stage and mind of the character.

The Chairs is a story, albeit a story without a conventional ending. The title stands as a metonymy of absent people rather than a metaphor of an empty psyche. Indeed, the proliferation of people, things, and language predominates here: the absent bodies of the invisible visitors with whom the Old Man and the Old Woman dialogue, and the invisible objects that they see and evoke. In the typical Ionesco style, the space is encumbered and the text is verbose. Consequently, when the spectator imagines a mind-space of the character it is one that is filled with language; it is therefore a language space. The couple carries on a rather functional, referential dialogue, one which addresses themes of sexuality and money (*The Chairs* 132). In a stage direction, Ionesco details the lewd behavior of the Old Woman who "shows her underskirt full of holes, exposes her old breast . . . makes little erotic cries, projects her pelvis, her legs spread apart; she laughs like an old prostitute." Grotesque as this behavior might seem through the worn body of the aged woman, it enacts a reference to sexuality that we would not see in Beckett's drama, early or late. In the same stage direction, Ionesco explains that this abrupt change—this aberrant interlude—in the Old Woman's behavior "must reveal the hidden personality of the Old Woman" (132). The *idea* of personality, harking back to psychology, is constructed obliquely, perhaps absurdly, from the abundant language of the text. In the end, the point Ionesco wants to make is a referential one. While in his abundant theoretical writing and the criticism of his own work he tells us that he does not believe in personality, and that the stage is not a proper place for personality, in artistic practice he cannot restrain his referential habits in his texts.[7] The stage directions tell us that the movement on stage "culminates in an intensity" (doors open and shut, the protagonists "come and go" and they "appear to be gliding on roller skates") (141). This intensity of action reflects the intensity of language.[8]

At the conclusion of the play, the stage directions first tell us that the protagonists "throw themselves out the windows, shouting 'Long Live the Emperor'" (159). Then, in an interpretive act typical of Ionesco, and unimaginable in the work of Beckett, the directions refer to the "the scene of the double suicide" (159). This explicit announcement of suicide at the conclusion of the play renders the protagonists' action entirely unequivocal, at least in the eyes of Ionesco, the absurdist artist who, ironically, touted the uninterpretability of his dramatic art. To be sure, anxious "physical" critics of Beckett's work are hasty to discuss the death and suicide of his protagonists—take *Rockaby*, for example.[9] But Beckett's abundant stage directions do not deal with interpretation, theme, and referentiality, as do those of Ionesco. Nowhere does Beckett expressly suggest the death of his characters. The death we perceive is never a physical one but a metaphysical one. My point is that, in stark contrast to Beckett, Ionesco is often too willing to defuse the mystery of his art. He trivializes it by referentializing it. To put it another way, in *The Chairs* Ionesco betrays a need to abandon emptiness for absence. The body of his protagonist is a caricatural body, and it is assuredly a theatrical, "performing" body; but only rarely is it an empty body that could connect to the idea of an empty mind.

Another Ionesco work that has hypersubjective potential is *Amédée*. Unlike Beckett's work in which the action of the play takes place either entirely outside (as in *Godot* and the radio play, *All That Fall*) or, in the later works, entirely inside,[10] *Amédée* begins inside and moves outside. Though, as Esslin has observed, the inside is "claustrophobic" (*Theatre of the Absurd* 163) it doesn't suggest enclosure in the same way that Beckett's late plays do. Unlike Beckett, Ionesco's design often is not to empty the space but to overfill it. The huge cadaver that haunts the entire course of the play represents to some extent the envelope of a human icon with a potential for emptiness. Thus, Elizabeth Klaver speaks of the "textuality of the corpse" that "encodes a language which springs from and points to a language of absence.... The corpse is, paradoxically, both substantial and vacuous, a hollow text—as Ionesco says about the word itself, a 'sounding shell of meaning'" (185–86). However, for Ionesco, the idea of humanity never entirely eschews its mimetic, realistic orientation as it does in Beckett's work. Near the conclusion of the first act of the play, Madelaine, at wits' end because of the rapidly advancing body of the corpse, sums up the crisis with respect to humanness: "You don't realize that it is no longer human? No, no longer human, really no longer human!" (286). She continues to repeat obsessively her charge for several lines. This provides a key to much of Ionesco's theatre in that while it is true that his characters are no longer conventional, they still cling to human referentiality, and to the signified of the story over the signifier of the image. Despite his claims to a profound awareness of the absurdity of life and art, to the contrary, Ionesco often betrays his fear of meaninglessness. Significantly, Esslin *interprets* the corpse in a rather conventional way: "The flashback scene makes it fairly clear that the corpse in the next room is the corpse of the couple's dead love, the victim of their sexual incompatibility" (162). There is so much of this text that can be readily inserted in any conventional realist drama.

Despite the overwhelmingly physical side of Ionesco's drama, as many other eminent dramatists of his time, his artistic sensibility was nonetheless predisposed to the metaphysics of hypersubjectivity. There is certainly a good deal of emptiness in the ensemble of his corpus. Furthermore, as Marie-Claude Hubert has pointed out, there is a clear connection between the space of the stage and that of the character. Quite appropriately, Hubert refers to the character in Ionesco's theatre as "this envelope that hides only emptiness, is alone perceptible" (*Langage et corps fantasmé* 67). Hubert's thesis suggests that the space of nouveau théâtre is not a place of action, but an "extension of the character" (68), or, more precisely, the extension of a hollow (hypersubjective) character. I believe that *Exit the King* is the most hypersubjective of Ionesco's works. *Exit* is most assuredly a discourse on and depiction of the death of the human individual. Later in this chapter I will address the relation between metadramatic hypersubjectivity and death (supra-referentiality and antisocial death). For now, I would like to demonstrate simply how hypersubjective Ionesco's drama can be.

An initial comparison between *Exit* and Beckett's *Rockaby*, or between *Exit* and any other of the hypersubjective works I deal with in this chapter, would reveal more differences than similarities. *Exit* has multiple characters, its language is fairly verbose and referential. It is caricatural and has multidimensional humor. As I pointed out briefly in the introduction to this book, at the outset of the action the theatrical space is abundantly furnished and populated and one cannot readily detect a precisely focused protagonist equal to Beckett's W. Yet the space becomes emptier as the action progresses and the work concludes with the image of an isolated and radically introspective character embedded in empty space.

Quite simply, and on the surface, in this play without scenes or acts, the action takes place in the throne room of King Bérenger. At first, in the absence of the King, the characters, including two queens, the guard, the maid, and the doctor, observe the decay and the disintegration of the kingdom, which includes the universe as they know it. Then the King appears. His first wife Marguerite tells him of the imminence of his death; but the King, bolstered by his second wife, Marie, refuses to believe it and wrestles with the idea. Nevertheless, he increasingly becomes aware of his progressive loss of physical strength and political power. Though he continues to resist, he begins to comprehend. He must accept death and break with his affection for and attachments to the world. The characters progressively disappear from the stage, leaving the King with Marguerite, who helps him penetrate into death. Then she disappears, along with the scenery.

Critics have frequently discussed the play's metatheatrical aspect in terms of the explicit parallels between life and performance, of death as a successful performance; and of the compression of time and space on the stage. King Bérenger advances simultaneously toward the end of his life and toward the conclusion of a "death-spectacle." The process of death exposes itself explicitly as a theatrical exercise, as theatrical plot development. The King's first wife, Marguerite, reminds him: "You're going to die in an hour and a half, you're going to die at the end of the show" (*Exit* 24). The direct correspondence between "real" time and theatrical time is also suggested when the dying king compares himself to "an actor on the first night who doesn't know his lines" (39). The French critic Jean Claude explores still another angle to the relationship between the King's death and his theatrical performance. He believes that the treatment of death in this work is quite unconventional and original since, instead of implying death as an event (*événementielle*), it is a poetic meditation on death in the form of a *spatialized* projection of an interior world: "Death is a fusion to an undifferentiated reality that is space. . . . Man retreats within himself" (248). The life on stage becomes a function of death, and death, which we generally perceive as a purely temporal limitation of life, here translates into spatial terms.

Thus, one can speak of a "theatricality of contraction" articulated through the contraction of a visibly shrinking, progressively denser space. This shrinkage culminates at the end of the play where the isolated and focused image of the King disappears into a "kind of mist" (95). The King is helplessly drawn into the abyss of a death in the form of a "mirror in my entrails where everything's reflected" (85), a mirror which acts as a powerful magnet for the protagonist's hyperactive consciousness. Death is portrayed as a magnetic force that, as we shall see, is motivated by a particularly powerful form of subjectivity. The image of an exterior world fades in cadence with the protagonist's surrender to the interiority of his consciousness, that is, with the increasing intensification of his inward-turning. The vertical axis of the subjective abyss runs counter to the horizontality of the external world, as Marguerite explains:

> *Marguerite:* He will have to stop looking about him, stop clinging to pictures of the outside world. He must shut himself up and lock himself in. (*To the King:*) Not another word, be quiet, stay inside! Stop looking around and it'll do you good! (57)
>
> [T]hink hard, concentrate on your heart, keep right on, you must. (72)

In this work, the "spatialization" of the protagonist's internal awareness (psyche) is clearly articulated and asserted, yet this is not a question of simple spatial reference. The work's spatial self-consciousness is such that it allows the space–character relationship, the "center" of the metaphorical *mise en abyme,* to be examined from many different perspectives. The most evident of these is, of course, the portrayal of the King in a rhetorical relationship to his space. The King is both metonymy and metaphor of this kingdom. As the King is seen in physical degeneration, so too is his kingdom. As the "crack in the wall" (9) begins to widen and the kingdom begins to "plunge into the bowels of the earth" (14), so too the King's failing physical condition forces him to withdraw into his own consciousness. Examples of this spatial effect emanate from actual as well as virtual space and, at one point, towards the end of the play when the King draws near to his apotheosis of self-conscious death, the stage directions tell us that "The beatings of the King's heart shake the house" (81).

A king's identity resides in his power, and so another dimension of the protagonist–space relationship is seen in the King's power over three different types of space: natural space (nature), social space (his subjects), and interior space (his own self-awareness). Early in the play, we see that the first two of these powers are failing. In an attempt to prove himself to himself, the King gives orders to natural phenomena that, up to this point, he always has been able to control: "I order trees to sprout from the floor. (*Pause.*) I order the roof to disappear. (*Pause.*) What? Nothing? I order the rain to fall. (*Pause—still nothing happens.*)" (33). To prove his sociopolitical power, his power over social space, he orders Marie to come to him and kiss him; but "*Marie does not move*" (32). Likewise, his orders to the others, to the Guard, to Juliette, and to Marguerite, all prove ineffective.

Finally, we see that his power over his "personal space" is dualistic, power over body and power over mind. The first of these has also failed him, as expressed by the Doctor who refers to the King's failing health: "It's happened all at once and you're no longer your own Master" (30). The only power remaining to him is a fairly autonomous kind of power. It is not so much his "power" as it is a deeper order of awareness, of awareness of consciousness, that has preceded him and will survive him. Consequently, his relationship to this phenomenological potency is not one of control but release. The power resides in the extension of his mind, in his ability to uncontrol his own mind, his own mental space, which will eventually reassert itself simultaneously as *him* and his universe. If not completely dissipated, this power has transformed from "power over" into the "force of" his own consciousness. The idea of having control over one's consciousness yields to an impression of an overwhelmingly autonomous power of consciousness, one which resists mediation. Just as the subject becomes (pure) consciousness, consciousness (or psychic space, or the consciousness of psychic space) *becomes the subject*, becomes the unique subjective force. The adage "to control oneself," suggesting the disjunction of subject and consciousness, loses its meaning. To conclude the play, and his life, the King ultimately must uncontrol himself. No longer involved in the illusion of exerting its will over an exterior reality, the mind is fated to draw inward upon itself. From a metadramatic point of view, since it is no longer tenable or appropriate to exert its mimetic power over the exterior world, the stage turns inward on the metaphysical source of its raison d'être.

If the King's political, social, and existential powers have diminished or reoriented themselves, his *dramatic force,* directly linked to his mortality, has increased. In addition, the King's moribund condition is all the more significant to the play in that he is, in effect, the only character to whom we can attribute the quality of mortality. This is, indeed, a very curious and significant aspect of the text. While all the other characters are directly or indirectly perceived to be contemporaries of the King—who, by the way, is supposed to be a fantastic several hundred years old—their mortality is never brought into question. Yet their mortality is directly linked to the King's. The one point at which the destiny of another character becomes a topic, it is briefly presented as a sort of collective phenomenon near the end of the text where characters openly consider the consequences of the growing abyss. This abyss, we remember, is the breach of the universe that corresponds to the King's inward turn toward death.

Marguerite: We're poised over a gaping chasm. Nothing but a growing void all around us.

Guard: We're still clinging to the earth's crust.

Marguerite: Not for long!

Marie: Better to perish with him.

Marguerite: There's nothing but the crust left. We'll soon be adrift in space.

Doctor: And it's all his fault! He never cared what came after him. He never thought about his successors. After him the deluge. Worse than the deluge, after him there's nothing! Selfish bungler! (78)

The King is indeed an egoist, but an egoist in transition. We define the trait of egoism in relation to a social context. As an egoist, the King resists death because he is still tied to a social context that he exploits by wielding power. Throughout the course of the play, he labors through a transition from an egocentric subject—who selfishly and consciously considers himself to be more important *in relation to others*—to the type of hypersubject we have seen in Beckett's plays. The existential identity of the hypersubject is based on a refusal even to acknowledge the social context, and it is only here that the advanced stages of the psychic abyss can be imag(e)ined, i.e., brought into the imagination of the individual on both sides of the curtain.

The final category of space–character relation relevant to our study plays out through the King's relationship with each of the female characters of the play. In spatial terms these can be characterized generally as a relation to immediate space (Juliette), to exterior, cosmic space (Marie), and finally, to interior space (Marguerite). When Juliette, the maid, speaks to the King about the tragic reality of her life as a servant (60–64), the King is unable to understand her, proving himself unresponsive or insensitive to immediate "realist" space. On the other hand, Marie, in an attempt to prevent the King's inward-turning death, speaks to him of the heavens, of constellations, and of the universe (68–69). But she fails in her attempt to orient the King's mind to this particular (symbolic) exterior. He is already too far "in": "Do you love me?," she asks. He replies: "I always loved myself, at least I can still love myself, feel myself, see myself, contemplate myself" (71–72). Juliette's reference to realistic space and Marie's reference to symbolic space have become mean-ingless to the King, because, as foreseen, he has come under the spell of Marguerite's surrealist vision, one that seeks a new, interior and supra-refer-ential, psychic symbolism independent of any social or natural exterior. The vision is one that turns inward: "He'll see better if he looks inside himself" (85). But it is also one that paradoxically rejects the exterior by seeing through and beyond its immediate reality: "Cast your eyes beyond what you can see. Behind the road, through the mountain, away beyond the forest, the one you never cleared for cultivation. . . . Look deep inside of [things]" (85). In a sense, Marguerite acts as a twentieth-century surrealist Beatrice, guiding the King not to heaven or hell, but to his own inner self. She carries out her duties admirably and delivers the King to his own inner space.[11] At the conclusion of the play, all the characters disappear, along with all of the decor and objects.

All that remains is the King on his throne, an image that ultimately gives the impression of fusing with emptiness, of "sinking into a kind of mist" (95).[12] A spatial abyss could not be more clearly articulated.

The King is quite unlike any authentic Beckett character. Yet one has the impression that, having accomplished the "abyss," he has a certain potential to be reincarnated into Beckett's theatre. Throughout the play, his personal closure has maintained a well-balanced descent along the vertical axis of his *mise en abyme*.

BORIS VIAN'S *THE EMPIRE BUILDERS* (1957): THE ASCENT BEFORE THE DESCENT

Boris Vian's *The Empire Builders*[13] is about a bourgeois family subjected to a progressive restriction of living space. From one act to the next, we see the members of the family execute a vertically ascendant retreat within their apartment building. Apparently, this retreat is a curious reaction to a mysterious, threatening noise. One could straightaway articulate this as a movement away from (exterior) society in response to an (interior) psychic fear. However, as the play progresses we realize the noise itself is more of an interior phenomenon than an exterior one. The family, consisting of a father-mother couple, a teenage daughter (Zenobia), and a maid (Mug), is obliged to occupy living quarters which are consistently more squalid and reduced in size. The image of framing, a spatially embedded form of framing (*emboîtement*), intensifies as each of the play's three acts brings the family to a smaller space in a higher floor of the building. Moreover, after the start of the second act, the individual members of the family themselves begin to disappear into a lower part of the building: first the maid, then the daughter, then the mother, and finally the father. They essentially disappear with the space. At the end of Act 2, the horizontal shrinkage, accompanying the vertical ascent, accelerates when the door to the hall slams shut, leaving the daughter, Zenobia, outside. At the end of Act 3, the Father is the only one to make it to the tiny room of the top floor. On the one hand, the disposition *en abyme* that we have seen in other hypersubjective plays curiously reverses as it manifests a vertically ascendant, rather than descendant, movement. The play does, however, conclude with the vertical descent of the Father which very effectively counters and controverts the play's ascendant structure.

At the end of the play, when the Father is alone in a one-room attic we realize that the totality of this world is concentrated within the solitary consciousness of this one character who begins a seemingly unending soliloquy:

> So I had a family. (*He reflects*) . . . Sometimes I feel as if I'm remembering things that happened to somebody else. (*He laughs.*) Somebody else! Whereas in fact I'm all alone. (66)
> I always had the impression that I was alone, in any case. (70)

Recognizing the isolation of his interior vision, he decides that: "There seems no reason why the world should extend very far beyond the walls which surround me; what is quite certain is that I am its center" (71). In effect, he assures himself that, having little by little "closed-in" on his interior consciousness during the action of the play, it is only at the end that he begins to recognize this. The structure of this play has become increasingly focused on the Father, until it is finally reduced to taking on the identity of the psychic economy of the protagonist. Enclosed by the restricted physical space, personal consciousness becomes the final space of retreat. With the last sounding of the mysterious noise, the Father jumps through a small window, an act that many critics interpret as a suicide.

Martin Esslin has characterized this play as "a poetic image of mortality and the fear of death" (276). Although one might agree that death is quite significant in this play, I believe that the emphasis should be placed, not on its *thematic* importance, but rather on the circumstance of *death as structurally determinant because of its link to hypersubjectivity*. We should view death as a contradictory[14] artistic and sociocultural spatial function, that is, as a consequence of the (dramaturgically designed) rejection of social space in favor of psychic abyss, as is the case with Beckett's characters.

At this point it would be helpful to expand on the fundamentally "abysmal" nature of the play's spatial configuration, and to demonstrate the degree of the codification present in the different categories and dimensions of the theatrical space. In chapter 2 we used Michael Issacharoff's dichotomy of mimetic space versus diegetic space to analyze the space of *Endgame*. Very simply stated, mimetic space is visible on stage whereas diegetic space is communicated verbally and not visually. For Michel Corvin, the former is "actual space," the latter is "virtual space."[15] The virtual space of *Empire Builders* complements the orientation *en abyme* of the basic structure of of the actual space.

First a look at the actual space. Defined within the stage directions for the setting of the play, the actual space presents a three-tiered (the three acts that develop and convey a sense of *emboîtement*) "material" or formal—as opposed to "actantial"—macrostructure. In Act 1, for instance, we see that the "framed" set is designed to convey and overdetermine the notions of closure and vertical ascendancy. The author emphasizes that the windows of the setting are closed ("windows with closed shutters"), and he gives particular indications as to the disposition of the stairways: "the top of a staircase apparently leading up from a room which one presumes to be underneath, linking up with a staircase apparently leading to a room which would be on the floor above" (7). But perhaps the most important contribution to the effect of vertical ascent is realized by the author's method of introducing the characters into this space. The stage is to be empty of all human presence for a short time *before and after* the rise of the curtain. The first sign of the characters will be their voices as they ascend the stairs: "From the staircase, approaching voices can now be heard from below" (7).[16] This should create the impression of a dynamic verticality, of a *verticality in motion* which the spectator will reference back to the more static verticality of the play's multi-leveled and convergent macrostructure.

The creative conceptualization of the virtual space makes an interesting contribution to the articulation of actual space. This play presents a full and creative use of auditory imagery. Not only does the mysterious noise—which threatens the characters with some unestablished danger—instigate the vertical retreat, but it also provides the most significant indicator of exterior space by defining the outermost spatial frame of the work: the street. The stage directions tell us that "The Noise can be heard once more in the street, that is to say outside the windows" (8). Given the restrictive quality of the space of this play, this would indicate a definitive limit of exteriority. The noise contributes to the dynamic aspect of space as well, to the effect of spatial "telescoping," a device that reminds us of Beckett's work with lighting. We see, for example, at the end of Act 2 that the modulation of the noise is also capable of conveying a sense of spatial closure. When Zenobia, the daughter, is caught outside in the hall, and the door of the apartment is mysteriously closed and locked, the noise begins to execute its "movement": "The Noise can be heard: a faint and distant echo. . . . The Noise grows louder and louder . . ." and finally, "The Noise grows fainter again" (58). It is at the end of the play, when the Father is completely isolated and enclosed, that the noise begins its most elaborate articulation. Starting softly, it increases its volume and then suddenly stops only to reassert itself at the conclusion of the play as "The Noise suddenly recommences very close at hand" (76). After the Father's disappearance through the window, a black-out accompanies the noise, bringing the play to a close as "The Noise invades the room, and darkness descends" (76). So we perceive the noise, which is responsible for the family's progressive ascent as well as the Father's descendant plunge through the window, as both spatialized and spatializing. The noise complements the effect of spatial compression and closure. It begins as a marker of the most exterior spatial field of the work and it winds up converging on the *huis clos* of the Father's psyche. It collapses all the spatial frames—from the frame of the apartment building to the frames of the floors of diminishing size—into the psychic frame of one isolated protagonist.

Before a discussion of the protagonist as space, let me offer one final example of virtual space that is derived by virtue of the discourse of the characters: the evocation of "lower space" in order to reinforce the category of verticality. One particular character, Zenobia, the daughter, seems more closely allied to this lower space when she attempts to question her parents about it. Her parents exhibit a curious reluctance to refer to their previous ("lower") quarters; but Zenobia insists on comparing present "higher" space with past "lower" space: "We had six rooms . . . we were alone there . . . trees in front of the windows" (13). She is, moreover, the only character who dares to hypothesize a return to the lower space as well as to question the mystery of the space that these people have abandoned: "And what's going on downstairs at this moment? We can't hear a thing. . . . We never hear a thing. . . . Why don't we listen to what's going on down there? Why don't we go down again?" (36). Her reference to this space contributes to the sense of verticality.[17]

Finally, let us consider the possibility of a spatialized character. If, as I maintain, the image of the *mise en abyme* comes to a focus within the consciousness of one single, dominant protagonist, and since we have established the *mise en abyme* as a spatial signifier, then we should be able to speak of the protagonist in spatial terms. What then are the aspects of the work that serve to induce the spectator to perceive the protagonist as space? We remember that at the very beginning of the play the characters are introduced to the spectator aurally, through the use of voices that are ascending: "From the staircase, approaching voices can now be heard from below" (7). The Father's voice, his discourse, and the references made to the Father by the other characters dominate, in fact, this introduction:

> *Father's voice* (*urgently*): Come on, Anna, hurry up . . . only five more steps.
>
> *A sound of stumbling can be heard, then a cry.*
>
> I've told you already not to put your hand just where I put my feet, Zenobia . . . you've no sense of discipline, that's *your* trouble.
>
> *Zenobia's voice* (*trembling*): And why do you always have to be the first one up, eh? (7)

It is evident that the Father is obsessed with space and that he is the determining agent of the vertical movement of the family. He always has to be "the first one up." Immediately after their arrival within the new space, the Father, "carrying a toolbox and some planks" (8), isolates each succeeding space, each of the family's new quarters, by boarding up the access to the descending stairway. The Father is a deviant form of "empire builder," so to speak.[18] His mysterious, fearful attitude toward exterior space, having led to a rejection of real social space, is directly responsible for his fatal entrapment within interior space.

The Father's interior space is determined and described by the text. The fact that he suffers from a serious loss of memory (10–11) initiates the impression of interior space. Memory is, after all, metaphorically regarded as either an "interior space" itself or as occupying interior space. A general law of physics, relating to the constitution of a vacuum, suggests that empty space (void) tends to generate a (pulling) force of attraction. If we somehow empty mental space of (social) memory, it will develop a force to replenish itself. Consequently, the Father increasingly directs his attention toward his "inner" space. He becomes progressively ignorant and negligent with regard to the exterior spatial "frames." After rejecting the outermost frame ("the street") evoked by the noise that he refuses to acknowledge, he subsequently denies the existence of the ("lower") interior space within the building. Finally, his family is the last exterior "social frame" to be sacrificed to his "self interest," and this brings him to the solitary conclusion of the play. It is he who proposes that Zenobia leave the apartment to go to the neighbor's when she gets fatally trapped outside. It is he who rather deliberately leaves his wife behind as he climbs to the attic at the beginning of the final act.[19] His will to solitude has become increasingly manifest as his rejections are increasingly categorical. Having trapped himself in the attic to which he refers as a "cell" (64), he asks: "Who am I?" (63). He becomes fascinated by his solitary condition and begins to consider it very seriously: "Question: what does a man alone in his cell do?" But he quickly reconsiders his choice of the word "cell" because he remarks that in his "cell" there is a window big enough for a man to pass through (64). This prefigures, of course, his final plunge which indeed will represent a very particular kind of escape from solitude, if for no other reason than because the space from which the Father is escaping is a special kind of space.

After describing his radical sense of solitude ("I always had the impression that I was alone, in any case") and defining himself in spatial terms ("There seems no reason why the world should extend very far beyond the walls which surround me; what is quite certain is that I am its center"), the Father's monologue evokes the important difference between simple "social" solitude and a hypersubjective condition:

> Is it possible for the feeling of loneliness to develop in an adult individual except as a result of contact with his fellow creatures? No. If such is the case, this feeling of loneliness which I have always experienced was doubtless derived from one or more of the hypothetical personages by whom I was—perhaps—surrounded. I venture this opinion in order to assist the process of ratiocination that I am in the throes of formulating . . . at this moment. If I felt alone, it was exactly because I was not alone. It follows, therefore, that if I continue to feel alone. . . . (74)[20]

As we have seen, perhaps a bit more clearly, in *Exit the King*, solitude represents a symptom of social egocentrism. One is egocentric or selfish by virtue of one's social relationship, and one's feeling of solitude is a function of a desire for the Other. The Father's transcendence of "social solitude" becomes clear when his line of reasoning brings him to rather dispassionately conclude: "I am not alone, here" (75). We can interpret this statement to mean that he is no longer "lonely," not because he has identified his social context, not because he feels the presence of another, but, paradoxically, because he believes, or wants to believe, that he is *truly and absolutely* alone. If he continued to *feel* alone, it would indicate that he was not alone because this feeling would only operate in a social context: "this feeling of loneliness which I have always experienced was doubtless derived from one or more of the hypothetical personages by whom I was—perhaps—surrounded." The radically asocial closure of the Father into himself renders him sensitive to the social nature of solitude. After his long soliloquy, one has the impression that when he finally slips through the window he is not at all moving into exterior space, but instead, that he is describing a vertical descent into the artistically "fatal" depths of psychic hypersubjectivity. This dramatic final plunge does not simply contrapose or contradict the exclusively ascendant verticality of the play's action, it annuls and supersedes it.

From a semiotic point of view, the hypersubjective pertinence of the Father's conclusive fall might, of course, depend upon the absolute nature of his actantial role vis-à-vis the other characters of the play, his functional relationship with respect to the other character-functions of the play. One might, at this point, question why I have not considered the mysterious and fantastic—even surreal—presence of the puppet-like Schmürz in my analysis, especially since so many critical interpretations focus on this figure. The reason for this omission is my hypersubjective point of view, which obliges me to concentrate on the determinant role of one *hyperprotagonist*. From this point of view, the role of the Schmürz is no more than a contributory motif. Nevertheless, it would elucidate my argument to comment on Marie-Claude Hubert's more traditional interpretation of the role of the Schmürz:

> [The Schmürz] is at once the punching-bag and the bringer of misfortune. He figures the irremediable. He obstinately blocks the passageway that would allow a downward flight toward more clement places, which are henceforth off-limits, and he prevents the rescue of the three women, now permanently lost. Insensitive, he attends the Father's death. (*Langage et corps fantasmé* 291)

While Hubert's study illuminates much of the text, given her psychoanalytical approach to this theatre it is not surprising that this account of the Schmürz errs on at least two principle points. First, it is the Father, and not the Schmürz, who blocks the downward return by boarding up the "down" stairways. According to the stage directions, the Schmürz is, more often than not, situated in a corner of the room and not near the stairway. Secondly, we cannot say that the Schmürz witnesses the Father's death, because the stage directions quite clearly declare him to be "dead" well before the moment that the Father slips through the window: "The Noise stops suddenly. The Schmürz collapses, visibly dead, alongside the wall where it had been standing" (75–76). Furthermore, Hubert's conclusion—which is shared by many other critics of the play—that the Father's fall through the window is indicative of his death, is the conjecture of her global interpretation. There is, in fact, no specific mention of the Father's "death": "He slips and falls, screaming" (76).[21] After the Father's fall, the play concludes with the suggestion of two possible endings: "The Noise invades the room, and darkness descends. And perhaps the door opens, and perhaps schmürzes enter, vague outlines in the dark" (76). Given the first scenario, where the play ends in a blackout, there is little question of the consummative nature of the Father's fall. Admittedly, though, for the second scenario, where the blackout is accompanied by the suggestion of the reappearance of more Schmürzes, the Father's plunge might seem less determinant for the action. But not from my point of view. The Schmürzes would constitute no more than so many signal-like signifiers ("vague outlines in the dark") within the empty psychic space of the Father.

The Father's plunge is *into*—and not "out of"—an interior space. The realization of this plunge essentially and retrospectively divides the dramatic space into three different fields: a social exterior / exterior world (the Noise), a social "interior" / personal exterior (the family within the building), and a personal interior (the psyche of the hypersubject). As discussed at the beginning of my analysis, the all-important, mysterious "Noise" begins the play by indicating at the same time the outermost spatial frame and the definitive limit of exteriority for the work. This outermost frame is constantly in movement (modulation) throughout the progression of the play; it creates a sense of closure and figures a spatial *mise en abyme*. The Noise's invasion of the stage at the end of the play has a double function. It represents the ultimate stage of physical closure of the work's spatial embedding since it essentially "moves" the exterior limit or outer frame inward. In addition, accompanied by a general blackout, it creates the effect of a "black hole," which parallels the Father's plunge through the window. Metaphorically speaking, the exterior space of the work has been "sent into *abyme*," compressing the space of the street and that of the family into the psyche of the Father. At the conclusion of the play the darkened stage signifies no less than the mise-en-scène or the dramatization of the dark inner space of the Father's psyche. It is from this perspective that we must interpret the suggestion of the presence of any schmürz within this space. The Father has sacrificed himself to his own inner space, an act which, through an apparently different motivation, becomes the very *raison d'être* of *Exit the King*.[22] Like the King, the Father has plunged into the hypersubjective world of Beckett's characters, where language, story, and outer reality are effaced. Of course, Beckett had rid his drama of the psychological veneer (especially the *idea* of fear) that is still present in the works of Ionesco and Vian. He had more thoroughly sacrificed the "surface" social reality for the sake of a deeper one. Whereas in Beckett's works the characters evoke and experience the world of an empty psyche, in *Empire Builders* and in *Exit*, these hypersubjective avatars, King and Father, worked their way into it. The King's demise (dé-*mise?*) and the Father's plunge remove them from a stage that is cluttered relative to Beckett's stage. This is a beginning of extended empti-ness. Both protagonists exchange the illusionistic fullness of reality for an empty space.

ROLLAND DUBILLARD'S *THE HOUSE OF BONES* (1966)

Rolland Dubillard's creative genius was likewise predisposed to the hyper-subjective bug. As with Ionesco and Vian, Dubillard's drama presents a distinctive dramaturgical design of this simultaneously metaphysical and dramaturgical condition. In his *The House of Bones*,[23] the space is a house, or, to be more precise, "the inside of a house" and the protagonist is the "Mas-ter" of the house.[24] No question that, here, as in all the other hypersubjective plays we have discussed, the textual web is strewn with many fundamental and significant literary and philosophical themes such as faith versus reason (religious dogma), the master-slave relationship, life versus death. However, most, if not all of the principal discourses of this work are conditioned by a hypersubjective core, by a structure of *mise en abyme* focused within the interior depths of one unique psyche.[25]

The selection of the spatial structure of *House*, the interior of a house, is, of course, far from neutral, far from arbitrary. The "inside of a house," fits into the same paradigmatic grouping as that of the other plays (the throne room, the apartment); and just as an apartment or apartment building for an apart-ment dweller, and a kingdom for a king, it constitutes, in more ways than one, a physical, social, and existential frame for the modern subject. The text emphasizes the spatial, interior, and vertical[26] nature of this house, categories which contribute to the text's surrealist-phenomenologist bent.

The text privileges space over time, a space that is primarily vertical (as opposed to horizontal) and interior (as opposed to exterior). In conformity with the spatial designs of hypersubjectivity and with Michel Corvin's theory concerning the spatial properties of *mise en abyme* (*emboîtement*), temporal sensitivity is effectively paralyzed and "encapsulated" within the interior of the house as we are told that: "Day and night don't exist for [the Master] any more. It's always the same, never-ending day, you don't even notice the sun any longer" (71). If the *theme of time* is important to this work, it is to a great extent, subordinate to the *structure of space*. At the very beginning of Scene 1, the stage directions tells us that a servant "gets up and goes and starts polish-ing a grandfather clock on wheels, which he pushes out of sight. He passes a slight, swift-footed MAJOR-DOMO," who says "Dust! Dust!" (7). This act of "making time disappear," or perhaps of "turning it into dust," orients the general theme of time versus space. As the play progresses, we realize that the paralysis of time operates to advance the dynamism of the category of space.

116

The protagonist also complements those of the other plays (King and Father) to the extent that, as the master of the house, he becomes the center of the theatrical space. Furthermore, like the others, he is overly preoccupied with the phenomenon of interior space. Secluded in an upstairs room, which at one point a valet refers to as the "strong room" (30),[27] he constitutes the cerebral center of the house and its forty-odd domestics. Dubillard opposes the Master's singularity to the multitude of domestics (forty odd) whose roles are played by "as few actors as possible" (6). Thus, we see the Master against a uniform field of characters. The Master's attitude toward his singularly centered position closely resembles that of the Father of *Empire Builders*. Despite the prior existence of the family he has abandoned, the Father concludes that "I've always felt I was alone." In a similar tone, but relatively early in the play, the Master remarks that "The more I think of it, the more I'm the only one. Who exists" (26).

The visual image of the Master isolated in a house finds support in what I loosely term the "narration" of this work, i.e., the interweaving of the monologues of the Master with the dialogues between the domestics, which suggests the central theme of interiority. The very concept of "house" initiates the interior-exterior opposition; it divides the space into exterior and interior. As the narration develops, one is struck by the interplay of references to the concepts of "house" and "man" as phenomena defined by their interiority. Houses, after all, are constructed by people *for* their interiority; and to this end we endow the idea of home with a certain amount of autonomy. The Master's own autonomous existence closely relates to that of the interior of the "house of bones," which is no less than the metaphorical equivalent of the Master's interior being, his inner psychic space.[28] The text deals with the difficulty of access to the autonomous interior—the difficulty of its very conceptualization—and the characters seek a resolution to this problem through the intervention of representation. "I want them to give me my house," says the Master, "I haven't got it. I'm inside it. The outside—we still have a coherent idea about that. But the inside—it's incoherence personified. I can't see it. . . . what I want is to get a picture of the inside of my house as it is" (25).[29] The idea of material representation, the essential premise of theatre, is particularly important since the Master explicitly desires some kind of material spatialization: "[G]ive me a model of the inside of my house. D'you understand? So that I can manipulate the inside of my house. Get a proper grasp of it, something clear and definite" (25). Later, one of the valets states the obvious: "A House is like the inside of a man. . . . A House makes the distinction. In space. In a House, space is divided into an outside, and an inside that Man can inhabit" (58).[30] The image of the house as "man's inside" provokes a (virtual) series of successive frames revolving around the man-house relation (self and other?): "Man—the house of the soul. (And I—the house of another me)" (58). The Master has interiorized the house as it has interiorized him, and the chain of interiority continues with respect to the Master's framelike body/skull that divides the outer space of the interior of the house from the metaphorical inner space of the mind.

Despite the unusual length of this work, from a narrative point of view the basic story is both extremely simple and firmly grounded within the interior of the house. Precious little reference is made to the exterior, and consequently, the spatial field dichotomy of "unseen versus seen"[31] dramatically alters its mechanical framework. Whereas in a typical realist work, the unseen space would refer to a *natural exterior frame*—to the action that occurs in a place outside the space represented by the stage—in this work its point of reference is more clearly and directly a psychic interior frame unmediated by metaphor. The Master of the house—who might actually be more "dead" than alive—is secluded in his room for the duration of the play. The existence of the numerous domestics of the house (divided into the two categories of "simple" or "superior") is contingent upon that of the Master; it is no more than a veritable reflection of or reaction to the notion or image of the Master. Consequently, the essential "action" of the play is made up of references to either the house or the Master, on the one hand, and, on the other, of physical movement toward and away from the Master who is secluded in his room on the top floor of the house. One could say that the domestics lead a "satellite-like" existence. Most of the eighty-three, very brief scenes of the play are based on verbal exchanges between either two or three domestics or between domestic and Master. Some consist simply of a monologue by the Master whose lines are often more monologic than dialogic. Even in a dialogic situation the Master's lines are frequently disconnected from the presumed topic, and so they acquire a monologic tone. The text makes it obvious that the monologic Master is self-consumed, to the extent that in many scenes the text is deliberately ambiguous as to whether his "conversation" takes place in the presence of others. In Scene 25, for example, the stage directions specify the Master is "alone or not." The physical presence of "other" discursive agents changes its interpretive value because the entire text concerns an interior hypersubjective monologue.

One important dialogue of the work also reveals the connection between the concepts of head, house, and empty space. At one point, two valets engage in a rather existential conversation on the subject of the house as a modern dwelling that replaced primitive ones, which they refer to as "holes" (*trous*).[32] According to them, houses rise, holes descend (81–82). Valet-2 personifies the house, which he defends as the proper habitat for the modern individual: "A house—a house is a head. That's it. With windows, doors, gutters, a head held high" (82). Finally, in an argument contradicting the hole's viability as a domicile for the modern individual, he disparagingly refers to the "infinite nostalgia for holes" (83) [*re-nostalgie du trou; Maison* 91], a notion which both reiterates and complements the leit-motif of memory in the work. Earlier in the play we discovered that, like the other hypersubjective avatars, the

Master suffers from a serious loss of memory, and memory becomes an important topic of discussion throughout the play as the Master's pretension to oblivion—or, shall we say, inner emptiness—contrasts with the "strong memory" which the domestics believe is built into the walls of the house (35, 59). The dialectic of presence and absence here becomes entangled in the web of representability initiated by the discussions of interior versus exterior. The Master seeks to resolve the absence in his mind, not by filling his psyche, but rather through the quest for a clear representation of its emptiness. Where the hole once descended, the house now rises; where the human individual once descended into the hole, he now rises within the house. Yet the empty interior of the Master's mind clearly reflects the emptiness of the hole, a primitive space that will haunt the representation of the interior he so obsessively desires. The Master will represent the inside of his house/head as a primitive fathomless hole (or abyss) into which he will have to descend—like other hypersubjective protagonists.[33]

The descendant hole becomes an important conceptual force within the vertical configuration of the house. The conception (as well as the construction) of the house "moves" on a vertical plane and it is not simply a question of "it rises" as V-2 would have it. At the beginning of the play we learn from the Priest that there is a hole in the roof: "Yes. Downstairs. Well: Upstairs. That sort of cubby-hole, where there's a hole in the roof. For a telescope, I suppose. The stars" (11).[34] In the next scene, a valet, speaking to the Architect, reinforces this image. According to the stage directions he "points his index finger up towards the sky and shouts": "There! there! there! You see! It's cracking, it's cracking! (12). Soon after this, Scene 7 consists of a conversation between the Mason and the Architect who reveal some essential information concerning the house as a structure. According to the Mason, the roof of the house is at the same time quite solid and in a state of collapse: "Oh! but that's sound. It's falling to bits, but it's sound" (15). Evidently, this is because the roof is made of lead. It was, moreover, the first part of the house to be constructed: "Lead. Flat. On the ground. That's where they started, and then bit by bit. . . . A stone a day, you slide it under yesterday's stone, it's under the front left one tomorrow. . . . Like that, bit by bit, the house grew" (16).

It is significant enough that the construction of the house is alluded to at all, but it is all the more interesting and relevant to our study that this construction has been carried out in such a way that the vertical axis is emphasized: the horizontal lead roof, the first integral part of the structure to be completed, has progressively elevated vertically. Finally, this roof, which has acted as the embryonic origin or cerebral center of the structure, is pierced and has begun to reverse its ascendant movement to one of descent. The roof carries the mark of the primordial *re-nostalgie du trou*.

The interior frames of the inside of the house—which figures the interior of man—join in the descent. In Scene 31, the Major-domo voices his concern to the Architect: "And that extra storey built on at the end of the last century, as if that weren't enough! We're caving in. The ground's caving in. The floor" (53). This idea of the "extra storey built on at the end of the century" reflects and reinforces a somewhat "outdated" will to ascendant verticality. At present, the characters' will to prevent descent is merely a question of "patching things up" (53), which can only function to retard—rather than prevent—the inevitable collapse.

The house has grown as a human would grow, the growth of a child being, of course, predominantly vertical: *homo verticalis*. Onto-archeologically speaking, the human being was born at the advent of consciousness—the primitive "hole." Since this birth, civilization continues to deposit layers of cognition on the clean slate of consciousness. Nevertheless, our *"re-nostalgie du trou"* yearns to return to the primitive state of clarity, a form of "total consciousness." So the theatre-like house evidences the same surrealist effect as the protagonist, i.e., an interior descent into its own depths, into its original, primitive "hole." The roof and floors give way as the psyche yields to the weight of its own will to self-consciousness. This identification of human icon and house is not simply a metaphysical blending of subject and object, but an important example of an icon that translates into a hypersubjective *mise en abyme.* In contrast to Beckett's drama and the way in which Beckett prepares and articulates for the audience an illusion of transference into an empty psyche, like the other avatars, Dubillard pursues the image discursively, even narratively. The avatars feel its relevance, but only at the conclusion of their works are they able to present the visual image with which Beckett's later works begin. Beckett's extreme economy for the visual image was indeed unique.

Nevertheless, Monsieur, the Master, is a hypersubjective protagonist. His depiction as a hypersubjective construction, his descent into a vertical, multi-tiered interior, relates both metaphorically and metonymically to that of the house. Metonymically, the house represents an existence, as well as an existential frame, contiguous to the Master's. Metaphorically and paradoxically, the house—which in this case has no "exterior" value—does not so much "represent" as "present" an inner space duplicating the hypersubjective *mise en abyme* of the protagonist.

As the house has its floors, the Master has his masks. I have already alluded to the idea of supplementary floors added to the house with time. The Master, too, as he grows older, appropriates supplementary layers, but in the form of "masks." In a discussion with a valet (Valet Thing) the Master says that old age is a part of him "as if I'd always been old" (114). But not content with this overly simplistic thought, he desperately asks the valet to come up with something better: "What is it? Think for me, Thing" (114). In his philosophical attempt at "thinking for"—and, perhaps, appeasement of—the Master, the valet expresses the following:

Old age, for you, is a sort of race—there are old people, like there are negroes. When you say you're old, you don't believe it. You belong to the race of the young. You would say in the same way that you were a negro if a negro mask had come and stuck itself on your face. It's an old man's mask that someone's stuck on your face. (114)

Subsequently, assuming that the mask is a purely exterior phenomenon, the Master asks about his interior, engaging the following dialogue:

VALET THING. The inside, the outside! . . . —it's also stuck, as you might say, on the inside.

THE MASTER. But underneath?

VALET THING. It's stuck underneath, too.

THE MASTER. No: I mean underneath this whole mask I have on the inside and everywhere. What is there there?

VALET THING. There's—there isn't anything, there's no room for anything other than the mask.

THE MASTER. Yes there is.

VALET THING. Memory?

THE MASTER. Youth.

VALET THING. Monsieur, in his memory, has always been, and will never stop being—young. (115).

The dialogue explains the idea of mask(s) as an infinite ideological or existential chain. The Master's preoccupation with his "interior" has engendered the articulation of a possible form of this chain resulting in the suggestion that there might be some innermost core constituted by memory, which can also be defined as "youth." This memory/youth, however, will remain an image of the house. Beyond all intermediate layers of floors, the "memory" of the house is, after all, concentrated in the memory, or psychic space, of the Master: "I was brought up in this house. No. I grew up in it" (29). Since the Master, has been isolated all his life in this house, the house has become his "interior mask." He has interiorized the house as it has interiorized him. Whereas the realist subject is preoccupied with exterior masking, with the exterior layers of ideological or psychological framing, the surrealist hypersubject *idealizes* the interior layers of phenomenological, existential illumination. "The vertiginous descent into ourselves, the systematic illumination of hidden places" (A. Breton, *Manifestoes* 36).

Unlike the Father of *Empire Builders*, who did not fully realize nor seriously try to "experience" his social isolation until the conclusion of the play, the Master is immediately seen as a subject apart. If the Father is only morally separated from the other characters at the beginning of *Empire Builders*, the Master is situated, throughout the duration of the work, in the "strong room" at the very top of the house. Immediately contiguous to the falling roof, the strong room represents the "cerebral center," of the house. Yet the Master's presence remains, until Scene 9, a part of "unseen" space, the unseen focal point of discourse. When he finally appears he is "on all fours" chasing a mysterious mouse that has invaded his strong room:

> THE MASTER. No but really! where's it got to, that mouse?
>
> THE VALET. Monsieur shouldn't be on all fours.
>
> THE MASTER. I shouldn't! And what about the mouse. It's the same every evening. I can see it. (19)

The image of the Master on all fours is significant. The Master's quality as *homo verticalis* is called into question as he takes on the horizontal identity of the mouse (animal) that he seeks. But this horizontality also acts as a theatrical foil for the verticality of the play's protagonist as well as the house. The Master is an entity that is "up there" [*là-haut*], but which is nonetheless in vertical collapse.

One of the earliest and clearest articulations of the vertical-horizontal dichotomy finds its expression through no less than the subject of death. Stage directions tell us that, in Scene 5, when a valet conveys the very ambiguous "latest news, which is of some gravity," the two other valets "can't believe their ears." The news is, "He's dead." The valets are evidently stunned because they believe the news refers to the Master (12–13). It is only after a particularly arduous clarification of the information that the other valets realize it is not the death of "MONSIEUR" ("Monsieur-MONSIEUR") which is meant, but the death of another "Monsieur Whatsisbloodyname." What is important here is that the distinction made between the two "Monsieurs" is one of horizontality versus verticality, and this is reinforced with a suggestion of "descendant verticality," or the eventual fall of the Master.

> THE FIRST. Monsieur! . . . Not "Monsieur-MONSIEUR"—of course not! Mr. Whatsisbloodyname, the one from the house near the Reservoirs.
>
> THE SECOND, THIRD. Ah! the stupid bugger!
>
> (*They turn their backs on him and exeunt*)

THE FIRST. (*alone*) Yes, in his bed. Over there. (*he points to the far-off place*) As for what's going on (*pointing to the ceiling*) up there . . .

(*Enter a FOURTH VALET*)

THE FOURTH. What are you looking at?

THE FIRST. Nothing. I was just thinking about this and that.

THE FOURTH. (*looking up*) About this and that?

THE FIRST. About things. Things that fall. About apples. . . . (14)

What makes M. Whatsisbloodyname and his death different is that they are placed "over there" [*là-bas*] on the horizontal axis in opposition to the "up there" [*là-haut*] of the Master. The death of the former is necessarily a horizontal death and therefore a less significant, and certainly less (hypersubjectively) "perpetual" one. Vertical death is not an event but a timeless condition of the psychic abyss.

Whereas the Father of *Empire Builders* only begins to accomplish (to grasp and express) the full impact of his isolation at the end of the play, the Master is clearly conscious of his "exceptional" status from the very beginning. In *Empire Builders,* the Father's egocentricity is alluded to at the beginning of the work and its eventual transformation or translation into a hypersubjective condition is progressive and consistent as it reaches its apex at the conclusion of the play. In *Exit,* King Berenger's transformation is likewise progressive, if more clearly programmed and imminent. In *House,* the Master's awareness of his social isolation is, from the beginning, more concretely established, and, as a result, his hypersubjective psychic condition is less climactic. The Master certainly does not await the dénouement of the work to express his extreme isolation and to interrogate his relation to the Other(s), to his social situation.

At the end of Scene 9, the Master's first physical appearance, where we see him on all fours, a valet helps him up and then, for Scene 10, "MONSIEUR finds himself in the presence of a PRIEST" (20). Despite the priest's presence, Scene 10 is not a dialogue, but a long soliloquy in which the Master expresses the primacy of his role in the economic relationship of Master to domestic:

> This is what's going on all around me, people being paid, bought, sold, and they buy each other, isn't that what they call: being together [*être ensemble*]?

> And here I am, in the middle, and I'm not together. (21)

From the Master's point of view, the economy has replaced society as a catalyst for the "being together," which, for him, directly opposes his solitary existence. Consequently, the arbitrary notion of "being together" becomes a very sterile conceptual device. Opposed to this idea of the "ensemble," is the Master's position "in the middle," a position which, for all its capacity to avoid the negativity of the "ensemble" (of the all too unsubstantial economic collective), if not artificial, is extremely exclusionary:

> If I don't pay one of them, he'll pay me back! You see! Tell him to come in. (*calm*) They simply don't exist. The more I think of it, the more I'm the only one. Who exists. (*he manipulates*) And that. The relation of an object. (23).

Egocentrism can be easily and directly expressed by language; it can readily translate into a (superficial) sociocultural concept of master-slave or reification. The more radical hypersubjective message, more structural than thematic, is achieved instead by a "linguo-spatial" code specific to the visual art of theatre. So we are not dealing here with a simple variation on the theme of master-slave, or on the phallocentrism of the Father figure. Beyond these themes lies the deeper hypersubjective structure imposing a formal expression on the work that pushes beyond the limits of conventional language to find a spatial articulation sufficient to evoke the aesthetic conflict.

We recall that the Father of *Empire Builders* finds himself in a remarkably similar conflictual asocial context which is without the evident economic pretext.[35] The thoughts of the Father, those of the Master, and those of King Berenger are all *structurally* forced inward in an aesthetic process which, if a good deal less schematic and deliberate, is not unlike that experienced by Beckett's characters. Beckett's characters are more consistently and more closely "enclosed" by obvious theatrical devices that establish a highlighted central frame for their psychic *mise en abyme:* a wheelchair, a rocking chair, a mound of dirt, and finally, a dark stage. The monologue of the Beckettian character echoes through empty space, articulating a spatial image of *centripetal mise en abyme*. While the King is framed by his throne at the climactic conclusion of *Exit,* the Father and the Master find themselves relegated to a "cell." The Father's cell is the result of a progressive diminution of space, of spatial closure. The effect of spatial enclosure on the Master is, however, not as progressive or cumulative, but rather it presents a focal point of discourse from the very beginning of the play. In this play, the effect of enclosure, cooperating with vertical movement, is therefore not so much physically or materially intensified as it is discursively reinforced.

At the conclusion of the play, if the Master is not entirely alone he is certainly the only character who "exists." Paradoxically, his existence is a condition of his perpetual, asocial, hypersubjective death: (A Valet says) "It's always been like this. Even years before I came here. Monsieur is dying, dying, dying. And then he comes back to life" (157).[36] The Master is, in the tradition of the Beckettian character, "astride a grave" (*à cheval sur une tombe*). Condemned to a *mise en abyme* of space, he will remain a prisoner of a space that he refuses to recognize as social space. His hypersubjective abyss

124

is asocial to this extent. When he tells the valet who is with him in his "cell" that "I'm not here" (159), he implies that, drawn inward, he does not feel he belongs to social space. He is instead a "black hole" of theatrical imagery which, as Pirandello has made quite clear, is immortal in its own right. The Master's final words are: "I'm waiting" (159).

RENÉ DE OBALDIA'S *CLASSE TERMINALE* (1973)

The brief but instructive synopsis with which René de Obaldia prefaces *Classe terminale* evokes the "surrealist" nature of the work. It also deceptively persuades us that the play constitutes a real story. The story concerns a group of high school seniors (*classe terminale* students) who, rebelling against sclerotic academic tradition, have just killed their teacher because, they assure themselves, he was already "dead" in the sense that he lived an existential lie. The libertarian ideas he espoused in class had no effect on his personal life. The students celebrate their newfound liberty: "They finally will be able to give free rein to their nature: singing, dancing, inventing poems that no one will be able to explain" (*Classe terminale* 171).[37] To fulfill their joy, one of the students goes to free "Le Cancre," the class dunce, who for the past seven years has been locked away by the teacher in one of the school's underground jails. When Le Cancre actually appears on stage, the play's action takes a crucial turn: "Le Cancre has really changed! He appears as an immense clown, represented by a marionette" (171)." His schoolmates question him, but "His presence is terribly silent" (172). Is he perhaps "an incarnation of God? God, willing to accept humanity in its current derisive state: Clown-God, Marionette-God?" His troubling, muted presence alters the behavior of the group because "he acts as an enlightener." Each of the students ultimately expresses his or her most profound desire which is that, in view of the present state of the world, they would prefer to die young "in the exaltation of beauty and the gratuitousness of life" (172). The immense marionette will grant their wish.

No interpretation of this work should underestimate its post-soixante-huit, anti-scholastic message. Consistent with my subject, however, the objective of my analysis will be to demonstrate the hypersubjective framework within which this theme finds a context. From this vantage point, the anti-scholastic theme relates closely to the solitude of the modern subject, an especially intense solitude based on psychic intimacy. At the point where the solitude of the play radicalizes, it also spatializes, becoming more structural than thematic, more hypersubjective, more like Beckett.

At first sight, *Classe* resists any comparison with any of Beckett's works. On the one hand, it has a fantastic dimension which is altogether lacking in Beckett's work. Beckett's setting, his characters and their language break from realism not in a fantastic or uncanny way, but a more nonsensical way.

125

The ludicrousness of the characters in his early plays is largely of a meta-theatrical design, such as Hamm's famous first words in *Endgame*, "Me—to play." The imaginary is wholly an internal affair, an "inside job," so to speak. If Beckett's characters represent marionette-like humans, and if "marionette-like" suggests the unnatural, their mysteriousness originates in the positioning of their bodies on stage, in a wheelchair, a garbage can, a mound of dirt, a rocking chair that rocks itself. The visual distortion affects not only our perception of the situation and the action, but also our reception of their language.

The basic design of Obaldia's work and the spectator's initial processing of it takes place on a more naturalistic level. The realistic, representational nature of the space, described as a classroom; the referentiality and lyricism of the language; the story; the actions and interactions of the characters, as well as their numbers, give the impression of a "natural" world that is all but rejected in any of Beckett's works, early or late. However, if the play begins as a reflection of a tangible outer world, this world rapidly transforms. It develops a dramatic turn inward on the part of one very imposing, isolated character and a concomitant reordering of the stage space, processes which bring the work into the Beckettian order of the theatrical world. Toward the end of the play, the space is emptied, and the seven original characters are magically erased by and illusionistically transformed into one bigger-than-life marionette, Le Cancre. At this point the hypersubjective connection between Le Cancre and W of *Rockaby*, though not crystal clear, begins to come into focus. The final stage direction of *Classe* advises that "An intense light illuminates for a moment the great Clown-God-Marionette, standing, towering above the dead at his feet, in all his tragic solitude" (216). Both plays conclude on a very similar note with the image of a highly singularized, focused, human icon. Though the role of W is played by a human actor who must repress natural human gesture, while the role of Le Cancre is for a marionette whose purely iconic humanity derives from context and reference, the theatrical function of both these figures converges into image.

On a primary level, the classroom of *Classe* constitutes a solitary space, that is, a space that is as isolated from the world at large as are the spaces of the other avatar works of our study. The classroom figures within the same paradigmatic grouping as the King's throne room, the Master's "strong" room, and the Father's apartment, spaces which function as theatro-worldly frames. There is a marked absence of concrete references to the contemporary world outside of the classroom. One actually gets the impression that the children have neither home nor home life outside of this space. On a secondary, deeper level, constituting an interior spatial frame, we are made aware of the protagonist-Cancre's personal solitude as a *mise en abyme* of the physical space he inhabits. In all the previous works examined, we are dealing with a form of solitude that leads to a form of hypersubjectivity. Each play presents a particular concrete space capable of conveying the isolation of one principle figure: the king within his kingdom, the father within his family (home), the master within his household. *Classe* presents an interesting variation since it treats the space of the classroom, a space capable of suggesting the intense solitude of either the teacher or the class idiot. Indeed, by emphasizing the important parallels as well as the points of binary opposition between the images of the two principal characters of a classroom, this play identifies and illuminates the paradox of the "Cancre." Le Cancre represents a purely empty mind. The translation of *cancre* by the word "dunce" is far from adequate. In contemporary French, the term *cancre* signifies the kind of student we would call a "zero," one that is incapable of, or absolutely resistant to, any formal or traditional acquisition of knowledge. What is more, the etymology of the word suggests an original meaning marked by a radical sense of social alienation. Before it came to refer to a "class idiot," its original meaning of "a species of crab" was applied figuratively and familiarly to a "rapacious, detestable miser"[38] or a "being that vegetates, down-and-out."[39] Yet the extreme state of this being produces the potential for power.

The dynamic opposition of teacher to class idiot is based on the potential of the one and the other to assume the leadership of the class, or, at least, to become the principal figure in the class. While the teacher is supposed to be the students' intellectual leader, the class idiot has the potential to become a sort of moral mentor. Both are individually opposed to the class as a whole as well as to each other. In *Classe* the antithetical and paradoxical relationship of the two figures is taken further. It is made clear, for example, that the teacher has claimed to teach whereas the Cancre's role is to "unteach." The students' dialogue contrasts the sterile, pedant verbosity of the teacher, particularly odious for the students, with the dynamic, catalyzing silence of the Cancre. The postmortem presence of the teacher on stage is as inanimate as that of the Cancre, represented by a marionette. One of the students uncovers the teacher's cadaver inside the bathtub and we see his legs which "hang in empty space" [*pendent dans le vide*]: "Impenitent professor, who died of not being alive" (179). Finally, toward the end of the play, just before the Cancre begins to work his deadly skills, the students execute a ritual that recognizes the Cancre's ascension to the role of the teacher: "Yves takes the teacher's baton and places it between his arms. Francis places his bowler hat on his head" (210).[40] One cannot help to think that the teacher's fundamental defect was his failure to embody surreality, to comprehend the surreal sense of life: "he was incapable of going mad" (182). Too much the scholastic realist, he lacked the imagination and creative frenzy to evolve existentially with the surrealist youths of this play: "Ours is a life of provocation" (185).

This play is an excellent example of the transformation of the irrationalist form of surrealism into its hypersubjective form.[41] At the beginning of the work the students completely reject the logical, the rational, the traditional forms of reality. Fond of the linguistic play so dear to the surrealists, the youths want to be "free to invent poems that no one will be able to explain" and to "Nail to every door the owl of universal stupidity" (184). The liberty the students seek is surrealist in nature: the liberty to refuse the (exterior) historical past: "Latin, Greek, Massachusetts, Gilles de Rais, Tintoretto, the Adriatic, the neolithic economy" (176); a past with which the teacher was so "puffed up": "All that which swelled his head, swelled his head" (176).[42] The students are not "puffed up" like the teacher because their surrealist nature has induced them to reject conventional culture and history in favor of a more present, internal, deeper form of intelligence.

The arrival of the Cancre galvanizes the students' fascination for the absurd, rendering it more serious, more profound, more interior and hyper-subjective. As the catalyst for this change in the surrealist mode of the play's theatricality, the Cancre focuses the play's spatial structure. What sets him apart from the other students is the radicality of his anti-scholastic, anti-rational surrealism: "he had the courage to affirm his dunceness, his funda-mental dunceness" (189). His absolute refusal of instruction carries him beyond the absurd into the realm of the hypersubjective. Consequently, the Cancre is represented by a larger-than-life marionette, the ideal figure for the hypersubject. The extent of his psychic "void" surpasses the mere impli-cations of the severe loss of memory suffered by the hypersubjects of the other works of our analyses. This "Dieu-marionnette" is an unequivocal image of the "emptiness of mind," the psychic vacuity associated with the paradox of intelligence rekindled by the surrealists: "by virtue of his not knowing anything, he must possess a colossal intelligence!" (189). The psy-chic vacuity of the marionette is indeed the most dynamic, determinant aesthetic force of the text.

In conformity with my hypersubjective structural model for "psychic abyss," the Cancre is marked by the qualities of interiority and verticality. Imprisoned within his own mind, he was already considered to be (subjec-tively) "introverted" when he was sent to his underground cell.[43] After his long confinement "in total darkness" (187), his introversion becomes all the more "total": "Oh how introverted he has become!" [Comme il s'est intro-verti!] (192).[44] The verticality of his imprisonment is also evident. Annick, for example, tells us that when she went to free him, "I found him at the bottom. At the very bottom of the depths of the tunnel" (190–91). Finally, when the Cancre is re-presented to his classmates, his enormous vertical stature plays a key role in the creation of his new image: "a marionette more than two meters tall" (190).

The Cancre's imposing stage presence adds new meaning to the vacuous stare of the marionette, a stare that becomes, in effect, an inward-turning postmodernist mask framing and enclosing inner space. The Cancre has become pure hypersubjective image. Surrealist hypersubjectivity does, after all, find its substance in the visual image of the inner dark spaces. Having lost "the power of the Word" [*L'usage du Verbe*] (192), his force intensifies through his existentially profound, vacuous expression: "And his stare . . . that stare without expression" (192) . . . It's quite impressive, someone who says nothing!" (196). It would be, I think, impossible to overstate the import of the visual force of the image of the Cancre in this work. Strongly evocative of an interior space, it conveys a concentrated, hyperspatial hypertheatricality.[45]

The theatrical space of *Classe* is clearly structured by a form of *emboîtement*-telescoping that eventually telescopes into the visual image of the marionette as concentrated space. The play begins with an expansion of the theatrical space. According to the stage directions, "The students run out from the audience at the back of the theatre; they invade the stage" (173). Then, once on stage, the stage borders are no longer breached; but, during the festive, surrealist phase of the work, the stage directions allow for liberal movement throughout what is projected as the stage space. With the entrance of the Cancre onto the stage, the theatrical space changes character as it begins to redefine its organic unity through the figure of the marionette as space. Just prior to the Cancre's entrance, the students, fearful that the intense light might blind him, signal the stagehand to cut the lights: an obvious subversion of the limits of theatrical space. Once the lights are cut, each of the students then lights up a small flashlight and they all begin to dance "in the light of the flashlights" (170). This reduces the theatrical space to the surrealists' dark, empty image of the extended psyche. Breton's "vertiginous descent within ourselves, the systematic illumination of hidden places and the progressive darkening of other places," Caillois's surreal "personal abyme," and Artaud's notion of nodal void (see chapter 2), all find their way to the stage in yet another expressive form evoking the infinite extension of emptiness.

This image does not last, however, and the theatrical space again realigns and reasserts itself when the students all focus their lights on the Cancre: "More precisely, on the face of the Cancre. The great face of the sad clown, singularly disturbing. Then the lights come up and we discover the Cancre, in his entirety: marionette more than two meters tall" (190). This meta-theatrical act of ostension signifies the *spatial* significance of the figure of the Cancre. The sequences of spatial framing, initiated by the formulation of an expanded space that included the audience space, have systematically reduced to the figure of the Cancre. Once the stage is relighted, the magnitude of the original stage space is deemphasized in favor of the image of the Cancre: "Attention is drawn to the Cancre" (194). His troubling, overwhelming, muted presence modifies the behavior of the group because, we remember, "he acts as an enlightener" (171–72). Anne Delbee, stage director and actrice, explains what happens when a marionette figure is transposed to a conventional stage and integrated with human actors:

> [I] believe that the marionette is exclusive. I mean that when it enters on stage, it fascinates the audience and polarizes its attention. If a marionette crosses a stage where live actors are performing, a strange phenomenon occurs, one which truly belongs to fascination, which relegates the human actors to secondary importance. . . . [T]he actors are placed at risk [*mis en danger*] by the marionette, and they are very uneasy with it, in general. (52)

The entrance of Obaldia's *cancre-marionette,* more than two meters tall, has the polarizing power to turn the play's structural economy from one of story to one of image, from the naturalism of world to the emptiness of psyche.

The final stage of compression or *emboîtement* will be realized at the conclusion of the play when the Cancre remains alone on the stage after having granted the fatal wish of each of the students. The progression toward that end is marked by the intensification of the students' fixation on the image of the marionette. Withdrawn into his own consciousness, the Cancre is more a spatial image than a social subject. He apparently has renounced all obedience to the social imperative. The surrealist youths themselves, who never quite attained the *cancralité de base* of their former classmate, want to believe that they desire no more—and no less—than freedom from the realist oppression of society: "Free us from all who want to do well by us" (212). But their anti-social fervor is such that it ultimately demands a form of hypersubjective communion with and through the image of the Cancre: "King of Dunces, King of the Night, teach us about darkness . . . you who totally masks yourself" [*toi qui te masques éperdument*] (210–11). Consequently, the hypersubjective metamorphosis will take place in two clearly defined phases. First, the students realize the charm of their own personal "self-absorption" or *mise en abyme.* Subsequently, the consummate stage of hypersubjective *mise en abyme* will occur when the play's unique, absolute hypersubject, the Cancre, annexes the students' subjectivity. In effect, at this point the students have become *intermediary spectators* of the hypersubjective image. Like the audience, they are drawn into the illusion of an empty psychic space.

In the first stage the students lose their sense of solidarity, their group identity: "Lost within themselves, they all begin to appear like sleepwalkers" (213). These students, who initiated the play's action by killing their teacher for not being "alive," will become the victims of a hypersubject who proves to be exceedingly alive in his deathliness. The marionette initiates his ritual-like process of execution in response to the students' ardent desire for total surrealist self-consciousness. As the students dance and chant, *one at a time* they are put to death at the point of a finger by the marionette. Each student dies as he or she is in the process of making some sort of wish: "Me, I want

130

to travel. . . . Me, I know what I don't want; what I want. . . . Me, I want to die free . . . erotic, erotic, erotic, erotic. . . . The song of the young man who prefers to die young rather than to. . . . Me, I want . . . " (214–15). The students represent so many scattered signals in the extended, empty universe of the Cancre's psyche, where they are extinguished one after another.

The synopsis that prefaces this work might suggest to some readers that the students' death represents no more than a will to avoid aging and conformity: "they prefer to die young, they say, in the exaltation of beauty and the gratuitousness of life. That's when the Dieu-Clown (?), in answer to their wish, will extend his pointer finger and put them to death" (172). If this is what the students express, it is not their ulterior motive. It is only acceptable from a more superficial, anti-intellectual, surrealist viewpoint. The play closes with the following didascalia:

> All the students are dead. An intense light illuminates for a moment the great Marionette-Clown-God, standing, towering above the dead at his feet, in all his tragic solitude. Then it's a BLACKOUT. (216)

Thus, the play closes in much the same way as *Rockaby* and *Exit the King*. The lighting signals the passage from the global stage space *through* its core, the inner empty space of the Cancre. It also emblematizes the passage of realistic stage space from story to image, and the passage of the dramatic character from a local, surface form of humanity to the universalizing depth of hyper-social art, from the external and finite framework of society, reason, and convention to the internal and eternal emptiness of psyche. In the absence of society and conventional intelligence, the force of emptiness engulfs the stage space. Artaud's strange fascination with the void and his hope to discover a Western equivalent of the Balinese central dancer have found yet another concrete rendering on the stage.

Existentially and phenomenologically, this image of the marionette, devoid of any "deflective" personality traits, is endowed not with subjectivity, but with hypersubjectivity, which, in a sense, is so radical as to approach a phenomenon of "anti-subjectivity." The hypersubjectivity of the marionette, characterized by vacuous inner space, is capable of "absorbing" or appropriating the subjectivity of any spectator, on or off the stage, character or audience. Aesthetically, this marionette is a curious compression of hypertheatrical presence, of non-life, of hyperspace: the "black hole" of theatropsychic space.

ON DEATH IN HYPERSUBJECTIVE THEATRE

It is usually in the context of artistic nihilism that scholars have spoken of the theatre of Beckett and these avatars as a theatre of death. Both death and nihilism carry a negative connotation, at least when they are considered as the "end" (pun intended) of a particular work of art. When we consider death and nihilism as the "means" of the work, however, our judgment is altered. In all forms of art, artists generally evoke a sense of mortality in order to ponder more profoundly the condition of life, in the same way that dramatists have created hypersubjects in order to ponder and to pioneer new understandings of the sociability of civilized human beings and of the concept of being human. As I pointed out in chapter 2, because of the fundamentally contradictory nature of art, we must continue to strive to understand all conventional themes, such as love, death, family, war, and society, in a different light. Adorno was right in saying that art "is social primarily because it stands opposed to society" (*Aesthetic Theory* 321).

The theme of death is essential to all the plays examined in this book. Many scholars believe it to be the predominant theme. Martin Esslin, for example, defines *Empire Builders* as "a poetic image of mortality and the fear of death" (*Theatre of the Absurd* 276). Clearly, in the play not one of the characters survives through the conclusion. If they don't die before the spectators eyes, their disappearance suffices to induce a reflection on the idea of death for sure, on our own death, perhaps. However, the deathly atmosphere here is different—it is not "terminal." The absurdist nature of the work calls into question a real demise, death as an event. Since no one visibly perishes and none of the characters' discourse addresses the topic of death in a direct or conventional way, death is not an event.

Theatre scholar Thérèse Malachy rightly speaks of a more pervasive "situational death" in contemporary French theatre: death as a *condition* as opposed to the more traditional theme of death as a tragic event. "Death becomes a 'lived' situation," writes Malachy, "It is no longer an end or a rupture, but a state; it is no longer exorcized by mourning, embellished by remembrance, sterilized by the grave" (30–31). This "situational" death is directly linked to the concept of theatro-psychic empty space. In hypersubjective drama, death is antisocial to the extent that it relates to suprareferential empty space of psyche and stage, conveying an antisocial message that antagonizes the social essence of theatrical art. No longer literal, death becomes the metaphorical challenge to the health and to the life of the social subject. Radical self-consciousness becomes an instrument of execution. Death is a hypermental process, not a hyperphysical state. In hypersubjective plays like *Empire Builders,* we are dealing with a poetic, surrealist image of non-life, with an asocial condition of life that resembles what we think of death. Consequently, we could effectively analyze death from a point of view that is at the same time surrealist, spatial, and theatrical, in order to demonstrate that the discourse on mortality, the message of death, connects to a surrealist notion of a hypersubjective theatrical space. The mortal thought is a consequence of the overdetermined spatial isolation of the Father, the King, the Master, and the Cancre, of the abstraction of their social context. In spatial terms, it is a function of their radical pursuit of the internal space of their psyche and of their aberrant refusal to acknowledge the external space around themselves. So, by figuring an aberrant, antagonistic social situation, the theatrical space evokes a surreal(ist) demise.

The concept of empty space challenges what we might call the "social imperative" recognizing that all space is perceived, constituted, and understood in terms of its a priori social nature. According to the early twentieth-century Marxist-formalist theory of Mikhail Bakhtin and Vladimir Voloshinov, the human individual is essentially a social being. The way in which this individual perceives reality is absolutely mediated by convention established within a social context. All that this being senses—conscious or unconscious—of its individuality or subjective existence requires a social referent to be meaningful. Consequently, any antisocial denial of this absolute is problematic for our very conception of life.[46] In artistic (extra-ideological) defiance of this social imperative, new metatheatrical constructs attempt to create an anti-mimetic (super-mimetic, hyper-mimetic) empty space in which inwardness appears on a new aesthetic register. A theatre that suggests the idea of a supra-referential realm of human awareness, along with the structural focus on the self-reflexive psychic space of a very singular dramatic character, is a conceptual threat to human social existence. Consequently, self-conscious theatre becomes a "theatre of death" not because it signals any weakening or disappearance of the aesthetic subject as many theorists believe, but rather because it threatens the viability of the social context that defines both the subject and the theatrical space the subject inhabits.

We recall Jean Claude's argument that the death of the King in *Exit the King*, is a veritable spatial construct: "Death is fusion to an undifferentiated reality that is space. . . . Man retreats within himself" (248). The primary example Claude gives of this semiotic conjunction of death and space is that the "deterioration of the kingdom . . . suggests the shrinking of the individual's field of consciousness to the point where this consciousness is lost, or the progressive capitulation of thought" (247). The point where consciousness is lost is the point where it loses sight of the referentiality of its social context—the point where some personal, imaginary, aesthetic vacuity is supposed to signify, or, more precisely, not signify but "unsignify," to make itself known but not understood, to signal the possibility of meaninglessness in the absence of a referential (social) world. Life is referential, death is not. Likewise, life is *physically* determined, whereas death takes the physical presence of life into the realm of the *metaphysical*. The death of the hypersubjective protagonist is a result of a dramaturgic *mise en espace vide*. Immobilized and introspective, the protagonists we have seen have a particular obsession with their inner psychic space into which they are drawn along with the theatrical space of the work.

133

The paradoxical concept of theatrical empty space comes into metaphysical and aesthetic confrontation not only with the essentially social nature of humankind, but also with the essentially social nature of theatre. Historically, we have considered theatre to be a uniquely concentrated form of social space, or, in Victor Hugo's terms, a "concentrated mirror" of social space. Jean Duvignaud's social theory of theatre suggests that theatre does not so much reflect society as constitute a radically oriented but bona fide part of it (*Sociologie du théâtre* 560–62). Elizabeth Burns supports this argument when she writes that "the peopled dramatic world is autonomous and represents a temporary reality equivalent in its significance—its consequentiality—to that of the social world outside the theatre" (14). And Jean Alter's "sociosemiotic" theory of theatre is all the more "socio-semiotically" relevant because it "reflects the highly social nature of theatrical activity" (15). I think we can assume that theatre, the one artform that is at the same time an iconic enactment of a sociocultural event and a sociocultural event in its own right, is a particular kind of social space because it is a particularly social kind of space. Any attempt to question objective social reference in favor of subjective emptiness would be especially antagonistic for the theatre.

If, historically speaking, dramatic art was originally born of a natural need to represent social space, much of contemporary metadrama responds to an artistic desire to articulate the creative empty space of a solitary psyche. Challenging the idea of social space, theatrical empty space contradicts the very concept of space itself. In his study of the "topoanalysis of dramaturgic space," Darko Suvin expresses a point of view that, recalling Voloshinov's socialist epistemology, is relevant here. Affirming that space cannot be neutral, Suvin offers the axiom that "in a wider sense all spaces are social spaces . . . their qualities and properties can also be understood as variant possibilities of people's relation to each other and to the universe" (316). Evidently, his conception of space does not embrace or recognize an awareness of "extension" in Greimas's sense of the term (see chapter 1). Moreover, his endorsement of theatrical space as socially bound is unequivocal: "Within dramaturgic space, sociohistorically contingent signifiers and signs always and without exception signify and refer to some type of human relationship imaginable by the audience in an empirically possible space" (324). Strictly speaking, for scholars like Suvin, theatrical space, a concentrated form of social space, can never be truly empty and the "space" of the psyche can never be more than an obscure metaphor. Yet, as an "interior" theatre, the psyche itself is really no more than an extended concentration of social space. The stage—for which the nouveau théâtre's texts are written—is an empirically possible space that corresponds closely to a post-Freudian, spatialized conception of the psyche. Thus, as we imaginatively represent it to ourselves or through the mediation of the theatre, the psyche relates to some image of empirically possible space. It is the second dimension of concentrated social space within the already concentrated social space of theatre; and in hypersubjective théâtre it becomes the empty space within the empty space of theatre—the postmodern equivalent of theatre within theatre.

To escape space, theatrical or worldly, would be to disavow one's essentially social nature, to escape altogether from society. If this escape is cognitively as well as ontologically impossible, its artistically induced hypothesis engenders a "resistance" (in Adorno's sense of the term) that is essential to positive socioaesthetic evolution. No space of our world can be "empty" space, and by extension, no space is truly "interior." But what about Greimas's distinction between extension and space, wherein extension is non-space, since the category of space only comes into thought through referentiality and structure (see chapter 1)? The fundamental yet acquired interdiction against emptiness in theatre as in human consciousness can only encourage the most original of contemporary dramatists to push back the envelope of representations of the extra-representational or extra-referential by producing images that create an awareness of primordial extension.

THOMAS BERNHARD'S *FORCE OF HABIT* (1974)

How about death in Thomas Bernhard's work? When scholars describe the Austrian writer's dramatic corpus, they seldom fail to emphasize death and disease as major themes. Bernhard himself has remarked that "Everything we say is always about death" (*Ténèbres* 35). In a chapter in his book on "intimate theatres" from Strindberg to Marguerite Duras, Jean-Pierre Sarrazac refers to the theme of death in Bernhard's "intimate" drama in terms similar to those I have used to explain the new kind of "situational death" for hypersubjective French nouveau théâtre:

> But, in intimate theatre, death cannot be simply stated; it must be present and "in labor." . . . It becomes the spokesperson for the dramatic character and its shadow. . . . [I]t controls and supports the character and sets him up as a vertical figure, as a *standing monument of death.* (133; author's emphasis)

Death is a function of hypersubjectivity.

More than any one of Beckett's French nouveau théâtre contemporaries, Bernhard's drama attains a hypersubjective intensity comparable to what we saw in Beckett. In fact, since Bernhard's work has a recognizable anti-fascist political bent that Beckett's work lacks, in general it is socially antagonistic in a more explicit way. Comparing Bernhard to Beckett, Sarrazac refers to one of Bernhard's plays, *The Eve of Retirement* (1979), as follows: "The Bernhardian 'endgame' is just as *condensed* but even more *socialized* than the Beckettian one: theatre of the world and theatre of history are both specularly embedded [*mis en abyme*] in this intimate theatre" (141; author's emphasis). For his part, Martin Esslin went so far as to call Bernhard the

Austrian Beckett. Bernhard began writing seriously in the early 1960s, accomplishing his most prolific output in the 1970s and 1980s. He died the same year as Beckett (1989); but, unlike Beckett, he is perhaps more famous for his novels than for his plays. However, speaking of the theatricality of his novels, Bernhard has said: "In my writing . . . everything is artificial, that is, all figures, events, incidents, occur on a stage, a theatrical space that is plunged into darkness" because "in obscurity, all becomes clear" (*Ténèbres* 62). Scholars have yet to appreciate fully and appropriately his major innovations in dramatic form. One glance at a page of his *Force of Habit*[47] proves that he has pioneered a new method of showcasing language, of exposing its gaps and barriers and of experimenting with its rhythms, in short, of framing language theatrically in a theatrical space that is "completely dark." These strategies in many ways link him to Beckett and in some ways exceed Beckett's theatrical ventures on many levels.

We can compare Bernhard not only to Beckett but also to other playwrights of the nouveau théâtre tradition through the hypersubjective connection, through the ways in which Bernhard's work focuses on the empty mind-space of a central character. Bernhard's experiments with language are an important part of this strategy. Though his theatre still has not received the attention it deserves in this country, in Europe, directors regularly perform his plays on major stages. I would argue that, in France, the extraordinary success of his work is due as much to its hypersubjective, metaphysical structures and strategies as to its anti-fascist themes. It is, of course, the hypersubjectivity that places it very neatly in the context of this study on empty space and empty characters.

We are reminded of Charles Lyons's remark concerning the critical significance of the aesthetic union between the dramatic character and space. Strangely enough, spectators tend to be more attuned to the potency of the stage's emptiness on the one hand and to the spatial aspect of the character on the other, in plays whose characters have been called marionette-like. Scholars have long discussed the marionette-like traits of Bernhard's characters, a judgment that helps to place his work in the context of nouveau théâtre. These traits also place his work in the realm of hypersubjective theatre. Martin Esslin, though evidently deeply intrigued by Bernhard's drama and the characters that inhabit it, has spoken of their marionette-like qualities in rather derogatory terms. His remarks emphasize the aesthetic value of their mechanical behavior and downplay the possibility that the marionette-like aura can in some way represent the consciousness or psychic dynamism of the characters.

> Any interaction that takes place is thus purely mechanical, as that between puppets. Bernhard's earliest dramatic efforts were written for marionettes. He regards and deliberately designs his characters as basically no different from puppets—simply because he is convinced that people in real life are,

with very few exceptions, barely conscious, let alone able to act otherwise than as merely propelled by mechanical instincts and reflexes; that, in fact, living human beings, in the mass, are no better than marionettes. ("A Drama of Disease and Derision" 377)

If the mechanistic absurdity of Bernhard's characters intrigues Esslin, he seems to warn us that from a psychological angle they are "no better than marionettes" because they are "barely conscious." William Gruber too calls Caribaldi and the other characters of *Force* "puppets" (141), pointing out that Caribaldi's "mechanistic behavior is a metaphor for broad social or aesthetic matters" (146). In the next chapter I challenge this somewhat apologetic form of judgment about the marionette traits. But for now I deal with the idea of the metadramatic consciousness of Bernhard's characters, agreeing instead with Stephen D. Dowden that Bernhard's break with psychological portraiture or depth has created not a "barely conscious" character—as Esslin qualifies it— but a "hyperconscious world" (*Understanding Thomas Bernhard* 7): an extra-linguistic hyperconsciousness of the hypersubject. In his book defending the concept of character in postmodern drama, William Gruber sets out to "discuss Bernhard's characters in ways that describe as fully as possible their mental landscapes" (110). This is precisely what I would like to do; but, unlike Gruber, I am more interested in the metadramatic design of extended emptiness than in some contoured map of the mental space. In the text of *Force* there is abundant evidence that when Berhard wrote this play his principle point of reference was *an image of his own creative (or, creatively empty) mind.* Like Beckett, Bernhard's artistic genius reached beyond the language space of his mind to seek out the extralinguistic dimension.

In what follows, I focus primarily on Bernhard's design of three aspects or structures of the *Force of Habit:* the social (socio-spatial) structure that immediately connects the play to the outside world; the structure of the character-in-space that provides a visual template guiding the spectator's attention toward the mind-space of the character; and finally, the structures of the language spoken by the character-in-space in a form and rhythm which exposes its psychic locus and draws attention to the mind-space.

In terms of social structure, the play is about the megalomaniac ringmaster, Caribaldi, who maintains a tyrannical control over his circus troupe, consisting of the Juggler, his granddaughter the tight-rope walker, his nephew the Lion-Tamer, and the Clown. For twenty-two years, Caribaldi has attempted unsuccessfully to get his troupe to rehearse and eventually perform Schubert's *Trout Quintet,* a rather absurd idea that creates an absurd situation, one that makes some profound revelations about human relationships and habit, about art, and about thought processes. The themes of art (high art versus low art), habit (bad habits and rehearsals), family, master-slave relationships, the human beast, isolation, decay, and death are preeminent in this tour de force of the human comedy. However, a hypersubjective approach to the play will help demonstrate that all these themes are in large part articulated less through dialogic or diegetic argument and story than through the structural configuration (syntactical arrangement) of visual and acoustic imagery. All these themes are backgrounded and contextualized by the social structure of the troupe. As in all the previous plays treated in this study, one central figure stands out among all others, one who wields an extraordinary control over the very existence of the other characters, one who controls and translates their thought processes and determines their death, whether this death be situational (in terms of a deathly condition) or physical. We are dealing in effect with another hyperconscious, maniacal master whose thought processes form the critical mass of the play's action, creating on the stage a virtual locus of inner world. The stage directions indicate that this play takes place in Caribaldi's caravan; but it is usually staged as an interior set with the actual caravan in the background.

The social-familial structure underlies the organization of secondary characters around a central "master," the one character whose "after-image" never leaves the stage. The corporeal, or more precisely, the cerebral presence of Caribaldi sets up a force of attraction for all the stage activity as well as the dialogue. It is the element of the text that regulates for the spectator the unfolding choreography of character(s) in space. Caribaldi makes no entrance at the beginning of the play and no exit at its conclusion, but, what is more, his presence on stage works as a gravitational force of attraction for all the other characters. The play consists of three scenes. The first scene of the play begins with Caribaldi flat on the floor, searching for the rosin that has fallen under a chest. The Juggler is the first character to enter. A long expository dialogue ensues, dominated first by the Juggler and finally by Caribaldi. The Juggler carries out the bulk of the movement and physical action. He either responds nervously and spontaneously to the tyrannical temper of the master, such as when he bends down to help Caribaldi look for the rosin, or when he arranges and dusts Caribaldi's cello, or when he "jumps up and rushes over to a picture hanging crooked on the wall" (6),[48] or when he responds to Caribaldi's orders to get him another cello. Caribaldi, on the other hand, is relatively immobile. Furthermore, at the very beginning of the play the dramaturgical strategy of having the Juggler narrate while Caribaldi interjects "Augsburg tomorrow" (18) helps focus the spectator's attention on Caribaldi's retreat into his mind-space. Consequently, due largely to the master's immobility and his blank stare that produce a sense of intense introspection, we begin to associate the Juggler's nervous verbosity (which is instigated by Caribaldi's presence) with Caribaldi's mind. Toward the end of the long scene, the Granddaughter enters, (mechanically) approaching Caribaldi with a basin of water for his foot-bath. At her grandfather's command, she stations herself in front of him and executes "the exercise" "exactly like a puppet, with ever-increasing rapidity" (29). On another command, she exits, then shortly thereafter, with Caribaldi and the Juggler on stage, the text calls for a "curtain."

Scene 2 begins with only the Lion-Tamer and the Clown present. Yet the spectator still senses the strange presence of the oppressive master, not only in the subject matter of the expository dialogue between the Lion-Tamer and the Clown, but also as an after-image resulting from the master's immobile dynamism in the first scene. The Lion-Tamer eats "bread, sausage and radish," occasionally throwing the Clown a morsel, and he rails against the tyranny of the master, while the Clown, a sort of chorus of one, punctually iterates some of his remarks. Caribaldi enters and interrupts their "feeding"—not only the feeding of their bodies, but also the feeding of their minds through their conversation about their oppressive existence—and immediately orders them out. The Granddaughter enters. She too carries out her grandfather's commands to bring one or another of his cellos and to do her exercise. Then the Juggler enters (54), and he obeys Caribaldi's commands to straighten a picture and rearrange the shoe-cloth in his pocket (60). At the end of the scene, the Lion-Tamer and the Clown reenter. The scene concludes with all characters present at the "curtain" (62).

The third and final scene of the play begins with "Everyone apart from the Lion-Tamer on the chairs tuning their instruments, rubbing the bows with rosin" (63). Caribaldi's first word is "Crescendo" (63). The rhythm of this scene is punctuated by the playing of various notes by each of the "musicians" and it is stimulated by the Clown's gag with the falling hat, until the Lion-Tamer appears near the end in a drunken stupor. Finally, Caribaldi orders them all "Away" (94). After emptying the stage of characters, he acts "as if he wanted to clear everything away—all of a sudden, faster and faster, with incredible haste" (94). He drops into the armchair, hangs his head and repeats one last time the primary verbal motif of the play: "Augsburg tomorrow." Five bars of the *Trout Quintet* ring out of the radio. Curiously, with Caribaldi alone on the stage, there is no curtain indicated for the end of the play. This is a hypersubjective image, a powerful spatial commentary on the force of one individual mind, a reminder of the concluding images in the other plays of this study. The spectator is left, not with the erasure of the stage image that comes with the fall of the curtain, but with the image of an empty stage marked—and duplicated—only by the presence of a solitary super-thinker imbibing musical notes into his mind-space. One does not have to be an irrepressible dreamer, or an insomniac like Caribaldi, to realize that *there is no curtain for our mind-space*. Accordingly, the image of Caribaldi's mind does not disappear. In the absence of the other stage characters, the illusion of psychic empty space intensifies, drawing into it the spectator's consciousness.

In the Théâtre de la Tempête French-language production of *Force de l'habitude*[49] in the spring of 1986, the director, Jacques Kraemer, added some material touches that contributed to the spectators' reading of the image of an empty psychic space. Within the dimly lighted, gray-hued (achromatic) stage setting, a most remarkable sign was centered on the back wall behind the place where Caribaldi was seated with his cello: a painting representing a death's-head (see figs. 16 and 17).[50] Kraemer's production provides an immediate signifying context for the death's-head. To begin the action of the play, the Juggler enters and rushes directly to Caribaldi, stops abruptly and elicits the first lines of the text: "What are you doing there / The quintet is on the floor / Mr Caribaldi." He then picks up the composition and replaces it on the floor, but this time under Caribaldi's chair, where it will remain throughout the action of the work. This creates the vertical alignment extending upward from the written Quintet on the floor, through Caribaldi's seated body (upper body and head most prominent), to the painting of the death's-head on the wall: an interesting rapprochement of signs of art, of mind, and of death. A material display of *mise en abyme* of the hypersubjective character.

Now for the language of the text. The "choreography of human relationships" (Gruber) is the spatial template onto which the language of the characters inscribes an image of the chaotic emptiness of Caribaldi's psyche. The characters' language accomplishes this inscription first perceptually and materially, through the display of its mechanical rhythm and the self-conscious manner of its articulation, then conceptually, through its obsessive reference to the process of thought. Furthermore, we cannot underestimate the signifying power of the isolated, disjointed musical notes that integrate into the acoustics of the spoken language. Paradoxically, we are more apt to ideate these notes as a referential form of language in the context of the truncated, fragmented utterances.

Syntactically, the language of *Force* is the language of thought rather than speech. Bernhard's text undermines the grammatical convention of the sentence, exposing the fact that human beings do not think in sentences, hence, in this respect, grammar is artificial. Indeed, as in the case of Beckett's late plays, such as *Rockaby*, there is something more profoundly realistic, even hyperrealistic, about this language since it is not so much language as thought. Whereas Beckett's late plays rely more heavily on at least one principle visual image to illustrate and invoke extralinguistic thought process (articulatory functions of the mouth in *Not I;* "close-up" of facial expression in *Rockaby* and *What Where*), in *Force,* Bernhard attempts to distill from what Gruber calls the "naturalistic subtext" (125),[51] those elements of language that are isolatable signals of the individual resonance of language in context, i.e., the context of its construction—like the hydrogen atoms that came together to create the universe. Like Beckett, Bernhard works with the distinction between language and thought. He portrays language as the artificial, external, social phenomenon that it is, thought having the extralinguistic potential to be a more natural, primitive, internal, less conventional phenomenon. In short, Bernhard's characters are not so much talking as thinking; they are not so much concerned with communicating their ideas to others as to themselves as other. Bernhard's formatted foregrounding of language—one syntactical element such as a noun and its article, a verb, a clause, then the break on the written page—induces a pause, a rupture, a rhythm, a gap, revealing emptiness to be the primary substance of our mind. Since the language is less full, and the repeated patterns tend to fuse into an image of psychic background, it is ultimately the emptiness of the mind-space that is foregrounded. As Gruber puts it "Such repetitions give rise to the peculiar impression that certain thoughts are 'in the air,' part of a Zeitgeist, possibly, or at the least an identifying structural feature, like a rhyme in poetry or a song's refrain" (125).

We can also explain the repetition of the language another way. In normal, "artificial" conversation, we avoid repetition because we are subjugated by the temporal, linear dimension of logic. In thought, which is an internal, spatial phenomenon whose visual image remains undiminished by the linear processes of language, repetition is irrelevant. To put it another (yet still paradoxical) way, thought is theatrical whereas language is narrative; theatre is the more appropriate venue for thought, whereas the page is the more appropriate venue for language. Repetition in language is a throwback to the constancy of the visual mental image presented in thought.

Take, for example, Caribaldi's words to the Juggler after Caribaldi has taken control of the monologic dialogue near the end of Scene 1. (I should note here that, because of the highly solipsistic quality of the text, it matters little to whom Caribaldi speaks.)

> How we switch our intelligence
> to any channel we choose
> Magical astronomy
> Grammar
> Philosophy
> Religion
> Chemistry and so on
> Notion of contagion
> Sympathy of the sign
> with the signified
> The rosin has probably
> rolled right up against the wall
> right up against the wall
> right up against the wall
>
> *Plucks the cello. Juggler looking back at Caribaldi as he searches for the rosin with his hands under the chest.*

Every arbitrary
random
trivial thing
seems to create a whole system of relationships.

Puts his ear to the cello and at the same time plays a low note. (26–27)

If these syntactical groupings of words, these utterances, were not physically divided on the paper, they would not seem quite so unnatural. Yet conventional transitions between ideas are missing, especially in the shift from the thought about "the signified" to the observation about the rosin. Consequently, the observation of the external world is colored (grayed) by its situation within the overwhelming amount of text devoted to thought—it is effectively absorbed into the internal context and refashioned as thought.

Bernhard exposes the arbitrariness of language's "system of relationships," to be sure. The locus of language shifts from an external world—a place, a situation, a conversation—to the head. It is curious that the final sentence is not divided after the complete grammatical unit "seems to create." This is not the only place in the text where grammatical units are joined, but it is more exceptional than the tendency to divide units. Consequently, in this instance, Caribaldi's final verse leaves the impression that it is an ironic, rational-intellectual summation of the author's apparent attack on the rationale of language.

With the plucking of the cello, and the playing of the note—an activity executed frequently by all the "artists" and one that prevails throughout the text—musical notes acquire more linguistic-referential power as language acquires a musical aura. The border blurs between the primarily perceptual domain of music and the ultimately conceptual domain of language. The recurrent phrase "Augsburg tomorrow" becomes a powerful perceptual image that resembles the plucking of the cello. Conversely, the low note becomes more conceptual, evoking a comment on the fathomless absurdity of the situation as well as the inability of language to re-present the thought. In effect, the situation reduces to the presentation of a disordered, primitive *performance of contemplation.* Just as the quality of much music depends not on harmony or disharmony, but on the silent space from which the solitary notes are produced, so too the quality of "language" in the play—and consequently the entire theatro-aesthetic system—depends not on the fullness of narrative, but on the resonance of the highly charged emptiness echoed within the gaps.

Reading Bernhard's text, one gets the impression that the writing process for it consisted first of the notation and distribution of a number of highly charged linguistic signifiers (such as "Augsburg," "sabotage," "high art," "Casals," "onetwo," "out," "practise," "crescendo," "thoughtlessness," "fresh meat," "radish," "the sacred word," "perfection," "society," "sodomy," "insanity," "diseases," "death," "cacophony," "art-wrecker," "away") followed by a process of partially filling in the empty gaps with only enough words to fall short of the illusion of the plenitude of narration, thereby exposing the inadequacy of narration in the new drama.

Yet there are referential meanings attached to the signifiers. The words produce a subtle design of the headspace. To begin, there are a number of references to the mind-body dichotomy. As in Beckett's plays, the human body in this play is neither healthy nor whole. Caribaldi is infirm. The Juggler and the Lion-Tamer, characters through whom Caribaldi speaks, who closely approximate his monologic style and who partake in the exposition, are also maimed or infirm. Caribaldi refers to the Clown's complaining of "pains in his kidneys" (52), and the Juggler has an "indefinable illness." The Granddaughter and the Clown have bodies that are not visibly infirm, but they are mechanized and caricaturized. The relative health of their bodies corresponds to a reduction in the contribution of their language toward the conceptual. The illness and fragility of the body induces immobility, reduced rhythm, and lethargy, thus presenting an impressive, forceful, and "moving" visual and acoustic image.[52] The deconstruction of verbal language through fragmentation, disjunction, and de-rhythmization contrasts with the increased intensity of brain activity resulting from the "illness" of mind (madness).

Bernhard's stage directions refer to the characters as thinkers, thinkers who refer to themselves as such. In Scene 1, for instance, Caribaldi's interjection of "Augsburg tomorrow," is supposed to be uttered "thoughtfully" according to the direction (22). Caribaldi then refers to himself as *homo pensas* in the following terms:

> But if one thinks all the time as I think
> it is madness (22)

In scene 2, Caribaldi tells his granddaughter,

> I don't sleep
> I don't dream
> show me your legs (46)

He does not sleep because of his obsession to think.[53] He does not dream because of the psychoanalytical process it might initiate or the psychoanalytical system it might imply. (As I have already argued, though psychoanalysis was largely responsible for the twentieth century's image of the mind as space, its mechanistic, systematic principles have tended to obfuscate the essential emptiness of the mind.) Toward the end of Scene 2 Caribaldi says to the Juggler:

> Head and body
> bodies and heads
> under constant control
> Thoughtlessness
> is the most disgusting thing (57)

143

Despite this affirmation of "constant control," chaos prevails in the world of Caribaldi's mind. But Caribaldi's world *is* his mind. Despite his avowed determination to fill his empty psyche, his language betrays the irremediable, immutable emptiness of his mind. Besides these references to the act of thinking, the text is replete with references to the head as well as with the physical showcasing of the head. Early in the play, the Juggler, who virtually narrates for the static image of the master, associates language and headspace:

> The German language
> Stultifies as time goes on
> the German language
> clamps down on your head (11)

He then "Grasps his head in his hands, Caribaldi plucks the cello" (11). (One is reminded here of the reference to the dripping in the head by Hamm in Beckett's *Endgame*.) The auditory signal of the plucking of the cello transfers to the image of the Juggler's head, which, the stage directions tell us, is "watching Caribaldi" (11). Thus the signal also transfers to the primary image of Caribaldi's mind-space. The Juggler watches him "even more closely" when Caribaldi says:

> The posture
> of the upper part of the body
> was attained by Casals
> at his peak (11)

Since Bernhard's stage directions are generally much less detailed than other dramatists we have considered in this study, their design of a visual stage image focusing on the upper body and head of the characters is all the more significant. Furthermore, the implicit stage directions embedded in the dialogue—the reference in the above quote to the upper body, for example—become more determinant for the image.

Caribaldi's headspace haunts the other characters. His thoughts have found a path into their heads and they are obviously conscious of the locus of the tyranny. As the Lion-Tamer puts it in Scene 2:

> The madness
> of a single man
> into which this man ruthlessly
> drags everyone else
> Who has nothing but destruction
> in his head (39)

Subsequently, in Scene 2, Caribaldi appears and interrupts the Lion-Tamer and the Clown. He "hangs up his top-hat on the peg," repeats several times the phrase "Hang up my hat" and then "Beats himself on the head" (44). In

Scene 3 he warns the Juggler that "Your head will find no peace/ against society," followed by one word to the Clown, "Melancholic," to which the Clown responds by playing "three short notes back and forth on the bass" (67). This suggests, once again, the artistic conflict that hypersubjective theatre—its portrait of the empty mind—produces in response to the social imperative. This play is a cultural masterpiece that aesthetically and ostentatiously sets itself up *against* culture.

Likewise, the text links the persistent falling of the Clown's hat not to a behavioral or psychological problem, but directly to Caribaldi's headspace. The Juggler tells Caribaldi, "It is your brain-wave"; the Granddaughter "plays a long note on the viola," then Caribaldi concedes "It is my brain-wave" (86). The collusion among the acoustical, the visual, and the linguistic references points to a picture of what is going on in Caribaldi's mind.[54]

By the "empty" conclusion of *Force*, the spectator is prepared for the *mise en abyme*-like image of the solitary figure on the empty stage, one which subverts closure and draws the spectator's attention toward the recycling of the dramatic action and its reproduction within the extended empty stage of the protagonist's psyche. After clearing the stage of "everything," including the characters, chairs, and music-stands, Caribaldi "drops into the armchair, hangs his head and says": "Augsburg tomorrow." (In the Kraemer production he is positioned under the painting of the death's head.) He then turns up the radio to hear five bars of the *Trout Quintet* on the radio (94). The end? . . . But no curtain this time! Without the curtain, the notice of "END" presented on the page is as ironic as the rest of the text.

In a *Le Monde* review of a recent French production of *Force*, Brigitte Salino was struck by the stage design: "the space is immense. . . . [The designer] enlarges it, and—as if by magic—creates the impression that the stage disappears. . . . he elicits a place as vast as an enclosed world." The oxymoronic association of "vast" with "enclosed world" is perfectly relevant when expressed as an internal, hypersubjective concept, as the infinite extension of the empty psyche. The stage space represents Caribaldi's psyche, the *mise en abyme* of the theatrical empty space.

Yes, this work is about art, about habit, about disease and death, and about the incapacity of language to articulate the truth about these themes. Behind the highly creative articulation of these themes—and perhaps more important than the development of these themes—lies the highly creative visual and acoustical image of the locus of our consciousness of life and death. *Force* is a work not only about how we think, but *where* we think as well. Despite all the linguistic references to the outerworld and to the body of the subject (weather, food, behavior, pain), the text focuses, quite simply, on the mind-space of Caribaldi.

[5]

THE HYPERSUBJECT AVATAR MANQUÉ

In chapters 3 and 4 we examined plays in which the hypersubjective empty-space aesthetic was at its most articulate and its most determinant for the reception of the play. If the whole of Beckett's corpus represents an increasingly focused hypersubjective economy, the other selected nouveau théâtre works show strong evidence that their authors were interested in emptiness as a stage image connected to the mind of a singularly central protagonist.

At this point, I suspect that readers are inclined to deduce other avatars of this type of theatre among the avant-garde dramatists who are most familiar to them, especially the American and British dramatists who were not directly immersed in French culture as Beckett was. Pinter, Stoppard, Handke, and Shepard stand among today's most influential high-culture, non-naturalistic dramatists. Their plays are linked in various ways to French nouveau théâtre, and they all are at least mentioned in Martin Esslin's seminal *Theatre of the Absurd*. For the most part, they have explored dramaturgical techniques based on various forms and dispositions of empty space and non-discursive language. They increased clarity of focus on solitary characters, on a monologic style of discourse, and on the themes of solitude and death, which are ever-present in their works. Emptiness, silence, and immobility punctuate the meanings of their work as well as the most memorable images that weigh on our minds as we reflect on their work.

The theatrical works I examine in this chapter evidence hypersubjective elements which approximate those we have already seen. Nevertheless, they do not share the same focus. In fact, from a strictly hypersubjective perspective, the space, characters, and language of these texts have little in common with Beckett's consummate model. Consequently, the objective of this chapter is more contrastive than comparative, and to this extent, this chapter is more parenthetical than central to the thesis of this study. Yet, I believe it is a necessary undertaking. By holding up to these plays the template of focused emptiness we have developed, we can clarify and expand our reception of absurdist types of postwar theatre, especially with respect to the distinctions we can draw within this category of theatre.

The hypersubjective model serves as a double-edged critical tool. By showing more clearly to what extent many absurdist, avant-garde forms of theatre deviate from the more extreme models, we can increase our critical understanding of the comparative labeling (anti-theatre, pure theatre, metatheatre, metalanguage, nihilistic or existential emptiness, etc.) that scholars have sometimes too hastily applied to rather disparate forms of the so-called "theatre of the absurd." All forms of visual imagery marked by emptiness and metalanguage are not created equal.

I realize that some readers might feel that I am applying large, somewhat reductive brush strokes to this selection of authors. True, what follows is not meant to be a comprehensive analysis of these plays. But it will be a close one. My three primary objectives are 1) to expand my definition of what is hypersubjective; 2) to flesh out new understandings of these avatars manqués by applying to them the hypersubjective template; and 3) to present further evidence of how metaphysical and supra-referential dimensions co-operate with physical, referential, social, and aesthetic discourses. The metaphysical "black hole" does not merely co-exist with social themes and physical presence; more than this, it encompasses these referential dimensions of text and stage as it places them into perspective for the author of the work, for the character the author has created, and for the spectator of the work. Not all spectators of these works will have the same investments in socially grounded discourse like issues of race, gender, and class; but they do share the same metaphysico-phenomenological relation to the pre-referential regions of their consciousness. In short, by investigating further levels and designs of hypersubjectivity and of failed hypersubjectivity we can simultaneously reassert the integrity of the hypersubjective model and flesh out alternative deep structures in many of the works.

In examining these plays of the hypersubject manqué, it would help to keep in mind the concluding visual images of all the plays where we have seen the image of the human figure merge with the material emptiness of stage and scenery, and the theatrical tableaux in which, through a variety of strategies, the sounds of silence have infused referential language.

Harold Pinter

Harold Pinter's first play, *The Room* (1957), seems more focused on the theme of the couple than on the visual image of any singular character. Yet the play stages the emptiness of the "room in a large house" (*The Room* 91) where the action takes place (the mimetic space), and the characters discuss the dark emptiness of the diegetic spaces (those merely referred to) that surround the room: the house in which the room is located and the basement. There are six characters who appear in the room throughout the course of the action: Rose and Bert Hudd, the depthless, middle-aged couple who live there; Mr. and Mrs. Sands, who visit the house looking for a room; Mr. Kidd, who might or might not be the landlord of the house; and Mr. Riley, the "Blind Negro," who, before appearing in the room, loiters mysteriously in the dark emptiness of the basement. The lives of all the characters are characterized by an extraordinary paucity of detail and context. Consequently, their existence on stage reflects the mysterious barrenness of the house. The dialogue of all the characters promotes the sense of mystery surrounding the space of the house in which the room is located. When the visitors come from the outside into the house, looking for a room, they also bring to the dialogue an external point of reference that reemphasizes the unusual darkness that plagues the inside of the house:

Rose: What's it like out?

Mrs. Sands: It's very dark out.

Mr. Sands: No darker than in.

Mrs. Sands: He's right there.

Mr. Sands: It's darker in than out, for my money. (103)

Pinter himself has remarked that his two people in the room are "scared of what is outside the room,"[1] a remark reminiscent of the characters of Vian's *Empire Builders*. With regard to this fear, Martin Esslin makes an interesting connection of sorts between the emptiness of the space and the primordial emptiness that haunts the spectator's consciousness:

the room becomes an image of the small area of light and warmth that our consciousness, the fact that we exist, opens up in the vast ocean of nothingness from which we gradually emerge after birth and into which we sink again when we die. The room, this small speck of warmth and light in the darkness, is a precious foothold. (*Theatre of the Absurd* 235–36)

Hinting more at the work's nihilistic tendency than at the metadramatic, Esslin's comment illustrates the missed potential to interpret the more positive

148

function of emptiness, a metadramatic one which aligns the phenomenological awareness of the subject with the emptiness of the stage.

The reader-spectator of the play gets a sense of the void that is the universe
and he/she is likely to sense the emptiness within his/her own mind-space.
The stark characters, prisoners of a colorless language which has even less
meaning outside of this "room" on a theatrical stage, exude emptiness in
themselves, but it is an emptiness related to the "full" illusion of referentiality.
They are interesting theatrically because they "don't have a life" so to speak,
at least not what the spectator would see as a full, referential life. Perhaps the
emptiness the spectator senses, then, is an emptiness connected with the
language-space (rather than the extralinguistic space) of their minds. Do we
get into the minds of these characters? Yes we do . . . well, sort of, but late in
the play.

The conclusion of the work has the potential to consummate the fusion
between empty stage and empty character, and to produce its own original
suggestion of this connection. Like Beckett's Hamm, Mr. Riley's blindness,
immersed within the opaqueness of the dark stage, reverberates psychic
emptiness. When he enters the room with a message for Rose, like the
Cancre (*Classe terminale*) he presents a focused, statuesque human icon,
attracting attention to his mind-space. He conveys a perplexing message to
Rose: "Your father wants you to come. . . . Come home, Sal. . . . I want you to
come home" (114). By undoing the name of this not-so-round central character—one who gives the impression she was born middle-aged—this coup
de théâtre is obscure enough to deliver the spectator's consciousness not
only from the reality of an identifiable world, but also from the murky
referentiality of the second-degree reality constituted by the stage, and toward the awareness of a hypertheatrical realm.[2] Despite the stark realism of
Rose's initial reaction to Riley in the form of racial slurs, the hypersubjective
potential of the conclusion subsequently increases when she "touches his
eyes, the back of his head and his temples with her hands" (115). One page
later, the last line of the text informs us that, consequent to this act (of
touching and drawing attention to the head-space of the blind character),
Rose herself is blind. Riley, in effect, transfers the "vast ocean of nothingness" to her mind-space. Will this ocean have the power—and will Pinter
show the determination of focus—to supplant the meaningless referentiality
of Rose's life?[3] Not quite. The metaphysical spell is broken by the entrance
of Bert, Rose's husband. First, with Bert's hackneyed report on his little
sortie in his truck, then with the violent physical abuse he inflicts on Riley,
the reality effect returns into focus and dissolves the hyper-metatheatrical
effect created by the newly blinded Rose, a less empty figure on a less empty
stage. Themes of social realism, such as racial bigotry in particular and the
breakdown of communication among human individuals in general, were too
powerful for Pinter when he designed the dramaturgy of this play. Melodrama

overtakes metadrama. Esslin criticizes the play, writing that "The weakness of *The Room* is clearly its lapse from horror, built up from elements of the commonplace, into crude symbolism, cheap mystery, and violence" (*Theatre of the Absurd* 237). Perhaps more serious than its "lapse from horror" is its ultimate retreat from hypersubjective focus. Pinter cannot push his quest to create an original (absurdist) form of social realism over the brink of a second-degree world of reference.

Subsequently, Pinter produced short pieces, sketches, and radio plays with titles that suggest emptiness as well as the mind as a vastly extensive memory space: *Landscape* (1968), *Silence* (1969), *Night* (1969), and *Monologue* (1973). Yet it is difficult to turn up an image of a truly intense focus on one protagonist within an empty theatrical space. Furthermore, the language of the plays does not point clearly toward the extralinguistic regions of the mind. Memory remains a theme associated with discursive intelligence, and we are not drawn into the locus of the *theatrum mentis*. Our attention seems to dwell on the outer space. Esslin points out that many of his plays show that one of Pinter's main preoccupations is "a room of one's own as a symbol for one's place in the world" (*Theatre of the Absurd* 249). This is to say that, unlike the hypersubjective plays we have seen, where the dramatist intends for the spectator to lose (or, to penetrate) the focus on the throne room, the classroom, the master's apartment, in order to refocus on the *theatrum mentis* within the room, the rooms of Pinter's plays are still connected to the world. Consequently, we are never really invited to pass through the hyper-referential plane of a spot-lighted memory-space into the supra-referential space of the character's mind, as well as our own mind. The "higher degree of realism" (Esslin, *Theatre of the Absurd* 242) that Pinter seeks is in fact his claim to be a serious partner in the non-realistic genre of theatre.

In *Silence* and *Landscape*, as many scholars have noted, the theme of memory is critical. Indeed, the memory mode of the language text is less structured, less discursive, than that of the earlier plays, such as *The Room* and *Birthday Party*.[4] Pinter is staging the memory space of his characters' minds. In *Landscape*, there is a middle-aged couple, a man and a woman seated in the "kitchen of a country house."[5] The stage directions tell us that neither character appears to hear the other's speech (*Landscape* 175). Though each of the characters often speaks at some length without pause before the "dialogue" changes voice, their utterances are spaced by numerous pauses and silences. But the text is not nearly as full of gaps as the text of Beckett's late plays. In *Silence*, we have three characters, two men (Ramsey and Bates) and one woman (Ellen), younger than the men. Pinter employs a setting that shuns at least immediate reference to a specific place: "Three areas. A chair in each area" (*Silence* 200). Thus the space simultaneously ostends its emptiness and its theatrical origin: metadramatically, the emptiness enhances the "meta-" dimension of the theatrical effect.

The dialogue is still fairly monologic, taking the form of seemingly telepathic narrations of the consciousness of each of the participants. In a detailed manner, the monologic dialogue deals with the relationship of either one mimetic character (present on stage) with another, or with the relationship of one of the mimetic characters with a diegetic one, a now absent participant in their lives ("absent" only in the metatheatrical sense of not being physically present within the "reality" of the stage space). But the dialogue is clearly less signal-like than that of Beckett's works, and it is less self-consciously metadramatic and phenomenological, i.e., it is less evocative of a "deep" (hypersubjective) awareness. Unlike the language of the hypersubjective protagonists of French nouveau théâtre, discussed in chapter 4, it is less focused on the supra-referential depths of the thinking process itself as an internal act of contemplation. Memory was also critical to these hypersubjects, but wholly as a visual image. Here, it remains referential, evocative of other "natural" places (beach, pond, bus), personal emotions (love), and physical sensation (erotica, physical touch, kiss), and events (wedding). These memory patches are not signal-like, and they are not successfully embedded in extralinguistic space.

Pinter's characters desire love more than psychic awareness. That is to say, they question the physiological sensations and social connections of love more than they seek an awareness of the supra-referential thought processes beneath these sensations. In *Silence,* Ellen begins to get in touch with her mind: "Around me sits the night. Such a silence. I can hear myself. . . . Such a silence. Is it me? Am I silent or speaking? How can I know?" But she winds up appealing to the space outside her mind: "I must find a person to tell me these things" (*Silence* 211). So Bates seems to speak for Pinter's dilemma as an avant-garde author seeking to provoke an awareness of a deep consciousness when he says: "I walk in my mind. But can't get out of the walls, into a wind. Meadows are walled, and lakes. The sky's a wall" (208). These characters are frustrated in their search for an unadulterated phenomenological connection to the stage and a higher ground of metaphysical emptiness.[6]

At the end of *Landscape,* Beth describes her physical position and expresses her mental attitude toward the man on top of her:

He lay above me and looked down at me. He supported my shoulder.

Pause.

So tender his touch on my neck. So softly his kiss on my cheek.

Pause.

My hand on his rib.

Pause.

So sweetly the sand over me. Tiny the sand on my skin.

Pause.

So silent the sky in my eyes. Gently the sound of the tide.

Pause.

Oh my true love I said. (198)

The beauty of this inner monologue resides in the fusion of the tense of memory with the diegetic visual imagery evoked by Beth. Beginning in the past tense ("He lay above me . . . "), Beth and the spectator visualize the masculine face. Immediately, however, time is frozen into an image of changing perspective, one which is evoked more intensely without verbs. Beth's awareness and physical sensation progressively turn from the physicality of the masculine face and body, first toward her immediate environment (the sand, the sand on her skin), then to the empty silence of the sky and the silent, vacuous, repetitious sound of the tide. Finally, at the border of a referential world, Beth relapses into a trite "Oh my true love," framed by the referential past tense of memory, "I said."

Of course, these final lines of the play function ironically as the coup de grâce to language of love, laying bare the inadequacies and ambiguities not only in the language of human individuals, but also in the depth of their feelings and sensibilities. This is one of the ironies of the absurd. Unlike Beckett, who succeeds in transcending this level of absurdity by means of a hypersubjective break from language space, Pinter leaves us at the border of a referentially absurd world and the language that represents it, without a clear signal to move outside language space and deeper inside our psyche.[7] Beckett's works, on the other hand, searching for a much deeper plane of awareness beyond the conceptual, do not induce us to rethink love, the flesh, or death, at least not on a conceptual level. The hypersubjective character does not suffer from loneliness, melancholy, despair, or the superficiality of a need for hope.

Let us make one final comparison between Pinter and Beckett. In 1973, Pinter's *Monologue* was televised. This could have been Pinter's best opportunity to produce a hypersubjective play. The two short lines serving as stage directions place a solitary figure on an empty stage, opposite an "empty" chair: *"Man alone in chair. He refers to another chair, which is empty"* (271). Despite the persistent signal to "pause" during the monologue, however, the lone thinker addresses quite obviously the absent (not empty) interlocutor. In an original take on tenderness and self-sacrifice, "Man" beautifully encapsulates a relationship of love, and the pitfalls of human emotion and human attachments.

If we compare *Monologue* with Beckett's *A Piece of Monologue* (1979), we are immediately struck by the strategies Beckett has employed to break with the effect of story and to turn the spectator's attention from an empathetic response to human relations. As we saw in chapter 3, Beckett uses staging techniques, lighting effects, and a monologic language that never permits a clear glimpse of a picture-like story of a human situation. Furthermore, the monologue is replete with supra-referential references to darkness, silence, emptiness, and immobility. The monologue self-consciously transforms into stage directions that design a mind-space.

In sum, Pinter sought to paint a deeper picture of human, social relationship. He wanted to do it in a way that was original, profound, and more universal. So he was attracted to the empty medium of the mind wherein we human individuals "entertain" notions of social identity. Out of this empty medium he produced a penetrating story of human relationship. Whereas Pinter has the talent to rouse a story out of nothing, Beckett evoked the emptiness underlying the human story.

Tom Stoppard

Tom Stoppard's first and most famous play, *Rosencrantz and Guildenstern Are Dead* (1967), immediately invited comparison to Beckett's *Godot*.[8] In fact, the play seems to pick up on the "route" where *Godot* left off, but not on the route to emptiness, the one that Beckett took. Instead, the play beats a rapid "retreat" into the language space of farce pushed to its outer intellectual limits. This is super-intellectualized, existential burlesque at its most complex. On the whole, Stoppard devised a brilliantly comic assimilation of a Pirandellian type of metadramatic discourse, challenging the borders between life and art, with existential questions of a reality produced through human language and displayed on the theatrical stage. Thus, the play's emphasis on language is at least partly owed to Stoppard's search for comic effect through a linguistic playing out of existential reality and metatheatrical method. Stoppard's Polonius reiterates the words of Shakespeare's character: "Though this be madness, yet there is method in it" (*Rosencrantz and Guildenstern* 52). And Guildenstern confiscates the words of Shakespeare's Hamlet: "Words, words. They're all we have to go on" (41). As in *Godot*, there is a discourse on the reality of absurdity in the form and content of this play, in the words and the actions of the characters, and there is likewise a discourse on the absurdity of dramatic realism, which follows from the former. In this play, however, the "realism" is produced and challenged almost entirely by discursive means and it is never imagistically undone. No image of emptiness intervenes to erase the picture of an outer world. No image of silence to counteract the spectator's perceived desire for more language.

Structurally, the text frequently calls for a "pause" in the dialogue; but this device is used more often for comic effect, or to metadramatically call attention to the *art*-ifice of theatrical language, and not to evoke a sensation of extralinguistic emptiness. Thematically, unlike the authors of hypersubjective works, Stoppard handles the awareness of death purely and strictly discursively. Unlike the "immortal" hypersubjective protagonists whose corporeal substance transcends the mere thought of death, the "mortals" of this work deal with death as a form of conceptual brainstorming:

> Ross: We might as well be dead. Do you think death could possibly be a boat?
>
> Guild: No, no, no . . . Death is . . . not. Death isn't. You take my meaning. Death is the ultimate negative. Not-being. You can't not be on a boat.
>
> Ross: I've frequently not been on boats. (108)

Yes, there is, in the end, a stinging satire of the referential, of the referential character of language that, for Stoppard, constitutes the whole of our referential world. Thus we can call the work meta-referential, or hyper-referential, or even super-irreverential, but not supra-referential.

Stoppard's next major play, *Jumpers* (1972), generates a different type of character set in a different type of space. Instead of the historical and literary associations of *Rosencrantz and Guildenstern,* we now have a contemporary social ground for the characters: professor, actress, dandy, secretary, police inspector. Even the misplaced Jumpers, dressed in yellow uniforms, have a socially referential dimension, one that is wholly lacking in Beckett's corpus, and one that, while it might make a nominal, formal appearance in the avatar works (king, teacher, father, master) is rendered all the more absurd in that the identity lacks concrete development within the works. The detailed introductory stage directions announce "three playing areas, the study, the bedroom, and the hall" and "There is also a screen, ideally forming a backdrop to the whole stage" (*Jumpers* 7). Interestingly, however, this bizarre yet referential world is not presented on an equally referential playing field. It is not framed as either an illusion based on reality effect or as a mediated illusion based on theatrical effect, because none of the theatrical space "is visible for the first few minutes of the play, for which is required an empty space" (8). The play begins with a potpourri of absolute emptiness and darkness, spotlighted characters and objects, voices of unseen characters, and a character who "Like a pendulum between darkness and darkness . . . swings into the spotlight, and out" (9–10). All this is accompanied by a variety of assaults on silence: drum roll, cheers, applause, singing. Thus, either wittingly or unwittingly, Stoppard makes the spectator aware that the referential space they are about to see, together with the dialogue—which, in the style of Stoppard will quite thoroughly fill the space—emerge from the extralinguistic empty space of the *stage-mind.* Especially interesting is Stoppard's use of the ellipsis after "empty space" in his directions.

Peter Handke

Peter Handke is Austrian, like Thomas Bernhard. Like Bernhard, he is haunted by language. Unlike Bernhard, he seems almost totally obsessed by language, and by a primarily discursive form of it. He, too, questioned words, even as words remained the dramaturgical emphasis of his plays. His interest in empty space would function as a sort of microscopic slide through which the spectator could get a better look at the essence of language, irreconcilable though it may be.[9] Given his interest in the staging of language, one might argue that instead of trying to build on the new poetics of extralinguistic empty space which began in the 1950s, he was trying to discover a fit between a poetics of language and a "language of space." In a "Note on the Sprechstücke" in his *Plays: 1,* Handke himself says that these plays are

> spectacles without pictures, inasmuch as they give no picture of the world. They point to the world not by way of pictures but by way of words; the words of the speak-ins don't point at the world as something lying outside the words but to the world in the words themselves. . . . They employ only such expressions as are natural in real speech. . . . Therefore they need a vis-à-vis, at least *one* person who listens; otherwise, they would not be natural but extorted by the author. It is to that extent that my speak-ins are pieces for the theatre. (*Plays. 1,* 308, author's emphasis)

Despite this insistence on the linguistic dimension of theatre, there is evidence in Handke's *Kaspar* (1968) that, beyond his interest in emptiness as a background for the staging of language, he sensed the connection between the empty figure and the empty stage.

Kaspar is most apparently the "story" of how a child acquires simultaneously a personal identity and a relationship to world through the acquisition of language, an acquisition which is not necessarily positive.[10] Beyond his obsessions with language and the language space of Kaspar's mind, Handke betrays his own struggle to understand the void, to apprehend the contemplation of it. In this play, the stage reveals itself to be a fundamentally empty mind-space. Introducing the play, Handke advises that "The stage represents a stage" and that the many and varied objects on the stage "look theatrical" at first glance "not because they imitate other objects, but because the way they are situated with respect to one another does not correspond to their usual arrangement in reality" (*Kaspar* 54). They are not part of a "story" but of a "theatrical event." He also tells us that "Centre stage is empty" (54). In his abundant and detailed stage directions, Handke goes to great lengths to reprogram notions of dramatic reference and to deconstruct the notion of communication. Yes, his theatrical work is super self-conscious, and yes, it is even more than this.

Handke is very concerned that the spectator notice his strategy of ostending the objects: Thus, from the time of the spectator's arrival at the theatre, "Nothing moves on stage. Every theatregoer should have sufficient time to observe each object and grow sick of it or come to want more of it" (55). In effect, these "play" objects, shunning reference to world and relation to one another, lose their force as signs, their sense of belonging to a signifying system, and they take on a signal-like allure. Handke's strategy was to break the signifying chain between objects as well as to disconnect them from world, and consequently, to break down the illusion of logic and natural flow that comes with discursive reference and referential discourse. The use of objects in *Kaspar* resembles the use of language in Beckett's late plays, where the semantic "distances" or gaps between words and expressions coordinate with the syntactic gaps created by directed "pauses" and points of suspension. At times these gaps are enormous.

As the lone figure on the stage, Kaspar's first words produce a full sentence, which he utters "over and over," though "he has no concept of what it means": "I want to be somebody like somebody else once was" (58). It is clear by the stage directions that Kaspar's initiation into language is realized in conjunction with his intricate interaction with the objects on stage (60). The arrangement of objects within and around empty space will orient *all* the language of the play, its birth in the protagonist's mind, and its evolution. Handke uses a constantly fluctuating lighting scheme to further ground the imagery of loosely interactive words, bodies, objects, and empty space. The stage constantly goes from dark to bright, and the successive images of Kaspar and his clones (which appear late in the first half of the play) are illuminated and darkened. Even during intermission, Handke relentlessly maintains his assault on language by piping an "intermission text" through loudspeakers in the form of "mangled sentences" (111).

Finally, towards the end of the play, Kaspar I tells us: "I learned / to fill / the void / with words / I learned / who / was / who / and to still / everything shrill / with sentences / no empty bed / confused my head /.... / I shudder / before an empty wardrobe / before empty / boxes" (125). The disjunction of syntax on the written page resembles the texts of Beckett's *Rockaby* and of Bernhard's *Force of Habit*. Yet, unlike these hypersubjective texts, this text tends to draw us into the language-space of the mind. How ambiguous, how ironic, is the message these words convey and the feeling and awareness they provoke, especially given the "medium" through which they are conveyed, and the context in which they are spoken?[11] If, as Tom Kuhn has suggested, Handke sensed the threat of language to self-perception as well as our perception of reality, one wonders if he also sensed the supra-referential void? The language "trap" only works in a linguistic world. It only works if artists, scholars, and protagonists *fear* the void and consequently "a-void" the *risk* of tunneling toward its alternatively rich inner sanctum. If Kaspar were Beckett's character, and he certainly could have been, he still would have perceived and presented the void in his head, and he still would have treated this perception as a primitive form of awareness; but he would have done so with more essentialist contemplation than naïve rationalization.[12]

Sam Shepard

The "reality-challenged" plays of the American Sam Shepard have a style that distinguish them from the European authors we have discussed above. On the whole, it is arguably the violence of America's reality which takes them in a different direction from Stoppard's intellectualized burlesque and Handke's linguistic deconstruction of individual personality. Instead, Shepard deconstructs the myth of Johnny Rebel and the American Heartland through brutal action as much as through a violent language, whose complex vulgarity undermines the myth of good old American "Just-do-it-ism." Shepard, too, employs language against itself. He challenges the language of human relationships. He, too, tries to take protagonist and spectator into the protagonist's mind.

In his recent book on Shepard's theatre, Stephen J. Bottoms smartly weaves his way through Shepard's corpus, making astute observations on his place among contemporary playwrights. He also improves on concrete guidelines for our distinction between what we call modern, and what we would like to call postmodern. Very interestingly, he argues that the play *Action* (1974)

> clearly demonstrates the effects of Shepard's prolonged stay in Europe, in that it is almost entirely lacking in both overt American pop culture references and the American-style high modernist spontaneity of Pollock or Kerouac. Instead of being yet another fast-and-loose exercise in improvisatory creativity, *Action* is far more *controlled and precise* than any of his previous work, suggesting the much starker influences of late modernist writers like Samuel Beckett. Indeed, *Action* is closer in spirit to the European theatre of the absurd than anything else Shepard has written, presenting a remarkably spare examination of a state of existential crisis, which makes no appeals to redemptiveness of any kind. (115–16; my emphasis)

I agree wholeheartedly with Bottoms's overall assessment of this play. Particularly remarkable is that, beyond the "absurdist" and the Beckett connection, this is the Shepard play with the strongest hypersubjective connection, primarily because of its "controlled and precise" use of emptiness, suggesting a connection between stage and mind, but also because of its language, which discursively and poetically suggests the division of inner space into language and extralinguistic space. Thus Bottoms refers to Shepard's praise of the "dark rigor of Beckett's work" and his hope to produce a "similar impact." He cites Shepard's remark that *Action* "represented a new move toward 'the heart of what [I'm] after . . . the real meat and potatoes'" (116). However, though he delves deeply into Beckett's influence on Shepard, Bottoms often resorts to conventional labeling, referring to nihilistic notions of a "postapocalyptic wasteland" and to the "empty existence" of the characters in *Godot*. He also makes an interesting case for the contrast between *Godot* and *Action* by saying that Shepard's play is more postmodern because it models Jean-François Lyotard's theory of the postmodernist "incredulity toward meta-narratives" (117).[13]

Bottoms's analytical point of departure, which seeks a postmodernist account of nihilism, leads him into discussions of the following: the "atomized environment in which the most basic precepts of human existence—community, conversation—are problematic or meaningless" (121); "a kind of schizophrenic condition in which the characters try out a succession of fragmentary roles" (122); and of the "schizophrenic instability of character" (124). He concludes his analysis as follows:

> Shepard had nowhere to go with this existentially based, (post)absurdist approach unless he were to follow the Beckettian lead in distilling the same basic ideas down to a point of almost complete self-erasure. . . . But Shepard proved unwilling to pursue such minimalism further. Shaking off the European influence, he headed back to America to find fresh inspiration. (124)

In my analysis of this play, I would like to discuss at some length the hypersubjective dimension of Shepard's work, one which escaped Bottom's critical scrutiny, primarily because of his physico-psychological approach, albeit a postmodernist one. Bottoms has not read this play with an eye toward the *au-delà* of language space, beyond the tableaux and the actions of the characters to the empty background. Likewise, he has not metaphysically or phenomenologically visualized the mental locus of the language of the characters. This is in part because Shepard himself could not focus on it. Despite this breach of focus, the empty field has had a great effect on Shepard's text and on Bottom's reading of it.

First, let me say that the two male characters of this play, Shooter and Jeep, like the author himself, make a serious attempt to engage the extended empty space of stage and of mind. For instance, Bottoms rightly notes Shepard's "detailed attention to movement and gesture . . . leg scratching, arm gnawing, fish slicing," which he judiciously dubs "momentary diversions from their sense of emptiness" (118). However, I believe these "diversions" indicate something deeper still. Shepard and his characters "sense" the positive artistic, ontological, and ultimately social power of emptiness; yet, since Shepard is artistically unprepared to focus on it, he creates characters who are functionally unprepared to consummate the radical focus it demands, the one we see in the immobile W of Beckett's *Rockaby*. I suspect that it is not the negative, nihilistic "sense of emptiness" that is at stake here. Rather, it is the character's sense of impotence with respect to the awareness of the essential void.

The characters of this play resist hypersubjective focus. Their actions and their references to their consciousness often divert from this focus. For example, they quite literally have abundant "food for thought," that is, they eat and drink a wide variety of food and beverages. And their dialogue implies that they think about it often. To be sure, Shepard's insistence on the presence of real foodstuffs (turkey and fish) and on the character's attention to these foodstuffs, goes far beyond the naturalistic dramatist's desire to place a beef quarter on stage in order to produce a reality effect. In the context of this play, given the exaggeration of this naturalistic presence, it produces the opposite effect, i.e., a theatrical effect. But this effect remains a local device which does not directly serve the metadrama of hypersubjectivity.

Beyond these questions of content, the form of their language also diverts from the hypersubjective focus. Bottoms calls attention to the "inchoate 'um' and 'uh' sounds that show the failure of language and the blockage of communication" (118). In effect, these sounds are quite special. Dictionaries are hard-pressed to categorize them as parts of speech (interjections?), but describe their function as "expressing hesitation." Surprisingly, there is a marked absence of these sounds in Beckett's works, despite the seeming inarticulateness of the language, despite the persistent gaps and pauses disrupting the normal flow of discourse, despite Beckett's interest in the material quality of speech sounds. Why then do these particular "interjections" not suit the speech patterns of Beckett's characters? Beckett does not use these sounds, and Shepard does, because they evoke the misfire of "real" linguistic discourse, the presence of an absence (the differed presence of conventional language), rather than the existence of emptiness. Unlike Jeep and Shooter, Beckett's characters are not hesitating before language, they are not so much at a loss for words as they are signaling an awe for the extended vacuum beyond words.[14]

Despite these hypersubjective "blockages," there is significant evidence that Shepard had clear glimpses of the empty "plate" beneath the "real meat and potatoes" he so desired to achieve through meta-physical processes of European dramaturgy. Despite Shepard's failure to set the consummate focus by making an unequivocal connection to empty mind, *Action* contains moments of attention to an empty economy in the architectonics of the stage (the human character as stage-within-a-stage), in the lighting, and in the speech of the two male characters. First, let us look broadly at the forms and the contents of the stage. Introductory stage directions tell us that the stage is effectively divided in half by a lighting technique that keeps upstage in "complete darkness except for the blinking lights of the Christmas tree," and "downstage is lit in pale yellow and white light which pulses brighter and dimmer every ten minutes or so." Furthermore, at the beginning of the play, "The stage is in darkness for a while with just the tree blinking"; and even after the lights come up downstage, "Nothing happens for a while except the slight movements of the actors drinking coffee." The stage space not only radiates emptiness because it is so sparsely furnished, as indicated in the stage directions, but its emptiness is supported, backgrounded, and extended by the ever-present darkness of upstage. The blinking Christmas tree lights only enhance the darkness by the contrast of the light flashes and by their distributed, signal-like quality, creating the effect of a sort of interior "starry night," gateway to the universe. Most important, the two male and two female characters of the play, their corporeal forms, continuously emerge from and re-immerse themselves into empty space: "All exits and entrances occur upstage into or out of the darkness" (125). Numerous stage directions remind us that characters disappear into darkness and come back into light on their entrances and exits. Thus, the theatrical space comprises the universe. It is not, as we might first conclude from the stage directions, merely a divided space. It is especially not divided into two parts, upstage and downstage. On the contrary, given the configuration, the lighted downstage is a playing space which is randomly and arbitrarily situated within (and not in front of) the dark outer reaches of a theatrically ostended empty world. This is a self-conscious illustration of the process of ostension.

Let us now examine the characters and the language as they are set contrastively into emptiness. The characters are more ostended than they would be in a more naturalistic setting, in which they would tend to blend in with their surroundings. They are signals emanating from a dark universe. But not all characters are ostended equally. I will argue that Shooter and Jeep, the two "male" "consciousnesses" of this universe, are the principal focus of this world, and that they are so largely because they have the most hypersubjective potential. The two female characters, Lupe and Liza, talk about worldly topics (food, dance) from a pragmatic perspective. They are more active on stage and make more exits and entrances than the males. In sum, they are more dialogic, whereas the males, more given to other worldly, introspective reflection, are more monologic. Lupe and Liza function as signal-like facilitators for the revelation of the deep psychic realms of the male characters. Consequently, as the play progresses it focuses increasingly on male speech. The vocal participation of the females first flags and then it completely disappears in the conclusion. In many ways this resembles the hypersubjective focus we have seen in the avatar works. Despite the fact that the text alternates and stalls between the voicing of the two male characters, it leads us into a unitarian kind of "shared" male psyche.

Consequently, these males are more iconic, more outlined, more figural than the females. According to the stage directions, "they are dressed in long dark overcoats" and "they both have their heads shaved," an appearance which contrasts with the females: Lupe wears a "flowered print dress" and Liza, "a long full, Mexican type skirt" (125). The women are more ornately and more "dialogically" presented than their (darkly) formalized male counterparts. If the bodies of the males are dark spaces within the global dark space of this stage, their heads project another type of frame-within-a-frame. Their naked skulls would seem to be mounted on the top of the dark drapery of their overcoats, drawing attention to the male head-space.

Not surprisingly, the first words of the play recall the monologues of the Father in Vian's *Bâtisseurs* and the Master in Dubillard's *House of Bone.* Jeep says: "I'm looking forward to my life. I'm looking forward to uh—me. The way I picture me." And Shooter retorts: "Who're you talking to?" (125). Jeep is talking to himself, of course. He focuses on a self-centered mental image of himself, on his own personal psychic theatre. One will note, however, in contrast to Beckett's characters, Jeep's internal images refer concretely to outer references, such as a "picture" of himself: "I pictured myself being different than how I was" (130). Moreover, his initial thoughts lead to violent thoughts remembered ("Then I exploded") and to violent acts committed, i. e., to the smashing of chairs (130–31). Yet his introspection is not connected to a naturalistic outer world, nor is it clearly a psychological function. He does not evoke a sense of loneliness, melancholy, frustration, or desperation, as say a Willy Loman does. Within the frame of the play, his violent rage derives from the metaphysical inside rather than from the physical inside or outside. Outside the frame of the play, I would go so far as to say that at least part of the rage derives from the author's frustrated attempt at hypersubjectivity.

The audience might identify with much of what the women feel and with how they express their feelings, such as when Lupe expresses the self-conscious embarrassment-turned-dejection she felt on being criticized by Jeep for her "soft shoe" dancing: "I mean while I was doing it. . . . it made me feel funny. You know what I mean. It was like somebody was watching me. Judging me. . . . It started off like it was just for fun you know. And then it turned into murder" (129–30). But spectators, male or female, cannot identify, not in any conventionally referential way, with the "personality" of the male figures. Yet, in part despite this fact and in part owing to it, they are drawn into their mind-space. The stage directions present these characters as introspective thinkers. Thus, at one point, Shooter is "staring out into the audience" and Jeep seems "hypnotized by his own [repeated] action" (136).

Shepard relies heavily on a discursive path to the mind-space. In a supercharged allegory of a hypersubjective world, Shooter seems to speak for Shepard in describing the paradoxes of the extralinguistic regions of the mind. Digging into his own mind, Shooter speaks "quietly to himself":

Just because we're surrounded by four walls and a roof doesn't mean anything. It's still dangerous. . . . You go outside. The world's quiet. White. Everything resounding. . . . You see into the house. You see the candles. You watch the people. You can get a cold feeling being outside. Separated. You have an idea that being inside it's cosier. Friendliness. Warmth. People. Conversation. Everyone using a language. Then you go inside. It's a shock. . . . You lose what you had outside. You forget that there even is an outside. The inside is all you know. You hunt for a way of being with everyone. A way of finding how to behave. You find out what's expected of you. You act yourself out. (133)

The "outside" here is in an inverted relationship to what we normally think of as inner psychic space. It represents the empty, extended extralinguistic region of the mind. The house, on the other hand, stands for language space. Outside, all is "quiet" and "white," and there is no light. Yet we thinkers get sucked into the "light" (candles) of the referential world, the space of the mind where we join "Everyone using a language," because we feel "separated." But the real crisis occurs when, through the act of acquiring language, we become "separated" from the original, primordial extralinguistic space: "You lose what you had outside." Language is insufficient. It destroys our original authentic belonging to the universe, forcing us to create artificial, conventional, social identities in order to survive: "You act yourself out." The house, "four walls and a roof," a super-ficial social system, is but a minute portion of the greater ontological universe. Shooter's discourse frames society for critical analysis. Existential malaise stems from our grasp of the true, innermost sociocultural roots of our consciousness. It is not that we must deny that society (sociocultural relationship) is everything, that we are sociocultural beings to the core. Rather, the malaise ensues because we fail to comprehend that our sociocultural identity has a relation to the universe. Depending on how you look at it, our consciousness of the universe, internal as well as external, forms a part of our social reality.

Shooter's allusion to the mind-space changes character positions at the conclusion of the play, with the effect of fusing the individual mind-space of the two male characters. Jeep closes the action with the longest monologue of the play, in which his consciousness turns toward "something bigger" (144) than the surface referentiality of a good-boy-gone-bad in society. He remembers a dream from a time when he was in jail. But neither he, nor Shooter, nor the audience can determine what kind of "jail" this is, its reality, its significance. Jeep's "jail" resembles Shooter's "house." Both are metaphors for the "prison-house" of the language space of the mind. Paradoxically, to escape this space Jeep had to perform an "inner" leap, which would result in a "crash against the wall" (145). Thus, like Shooter, he senses that to "break in" to the extralinguistic realm of his psyche, he must "break out" of a referential consciousness, one which includes family, school, and the 4-H Club, because this

162

was, "Something bigger. Bigger than the family. Bigger than the 4-H Club" (144). Yet, like Sam Shepard who writes his lines, he demurs before this hypersubjective leap of faith. Does he understand that this "new world" is even bigger than "A vast network. A chain of events" (144)? Does he fear the chaos that surely underlies consciousness? Does he fear a loss of consciousness altogether? If so, is this fear linked to Shepard's fear of a loss of artistic relevance? The thought that draws Jeep closest to the supra-referential world was/is "FOREVER," which "wasn't just a thought" (145).

Through his stage directions, Shepard tries to reconcile himself and his character with the inner space where no "man" has gone. He tells us that "The words animate [Jeep] as though . . . he's attempting his own escape from the place he's playing in" (145). Here, Shepard makes a metaphysical connection between the language space of mind and theatrical space, a connection which might have led him further into fresh metatheatrical territory, to the boundaries of *Rockaby* and *Ohio Impromptu*.

In the context of this action, still within the memory of his dream, Jeep says, "I'd start to make sounds. It just came out of me. A low moan. An animal noise. I was moving now. I was stalking myself. I couldn't stop. Everything disappeared. I had no idea what the world was." This leads to the final words of the play: "I had no references for this" (145). He freezes, the other characters continue their actions, the lights fade to black, and the "Christmas tree keeps blinking." With a goal of stalking his hypersubjective self, Jeep's animal noises are an improvement over the "inchoate 'um' and 'uh' sounds," which are so suggestive of language space. Unfortunately for the hypersubjective project, however, in naming both the animal noises and the lack of reference, the text draws the spectator's interest into a referential disturbance that will not settle for awareness over understanding, for apprehension over comprehension.

While Beckett was content to design stage images on a model of the emptiness he sensed in his deep consciousness, in this play Shepard tried to comprehend emptiness and to half-explain it on the stage. Like the other dramatists of this chapter, Shepard was unable to match Beckett's dramaturgical "breakthrough," because he was unable to "break through" the barrier of language as Beckett did. I cannot help but see Jeep and Shooter as Beckett wannabes, who have not settled into the reality of emptiness. This tends to lend credence to Bottoms's observation that Shepard balked at the thought of designing "almost complete self-erasure" and he "proved unwilling to pursue such minimalism" (124).[15]

[6]

THE HYPERSUBJECTIVE MARIONETTE-LIKE LEGACY OF PIERROT: FROM THE SOCIAL SPACE OF THE *COMMEDIA* TO THE EMPTY SPACE OF NOUVEAU THÉÂTRE

In this final chapter, my primary interest is to revisit the notion of "marionette-like dramatic character" as so many scholars have applied it to works belonging to nouveau théâtre and especially to Beckett's and Bernhard's characters. To date, scholars overwhelmingly have concentrated on the mechanical, automatic, robotic traits of these so-called "marionettes." We read that they are marionette-like because, content-wise, they lack personality, and formally, their reduced, unnaturalistic behavior is "robotic." At a textual level—and most scholars deal with the textual rendering of these characters—scholars examine primarily the lack of psychological motivation and conventional conversation/dialogue. To be sure, Ionesco has explicitly indicated the marionette-like behavior of some of his protagonists in his stage directions; and the protagonist of Obaldia's *Classe* is a huge marionette. But the King of *Exit the King*, and the Cancre of *Classe* are not automatons. They have other traits that link them to the marionette figure and to the protagonists of Beckett and Bernhard; the only clear "robotic" behavior of Beckett's and Bernhard's protagonists that has strong textual support is the reduced mobility, including immobility.

Though Beckett, Bernhard, and other authors of hypersubjective characters do not explicitly or consciously design them to behave like machines, or like the puppets or marionettes of children's theatre, these characters are nonetheless marionette-like. This is in part, if not largely, because of their hypersubjective empty-space connection. There is an historical explanation for why we perceive marionettes and marionette-like characters as empty forms and why, when they speak, we focus our attention not so much on the space of some psychologically motivated and socially contextualized body as on some virtual representation of their mind-space and thought processes. Hypersubjective characters are visually distorted in the sense that they are prominently displayed, even forced upon the attention of the audience. The visual distortion affects not only our perception of the situation and the action, but also our reception of their language.

The historical explanation for this distortion begins with its remote connection to the theatrical and metatheatrical conventions of the Commedia dell'arte. To show the rise of the hypersubject, I will deal with the marionette-like connection between nouveau théâtre and the *commedia,* primarily in contrastive terms, instead of the comparative terms employed by theorists like Martin Esslin.[1] As with Esslin's study of the absurd, my study benefits from the nouveau théâtre's connection to the theatrical and metatheatrical conventions of the *commedia.* By developing a contrast between two of the most enduring marionette-like archetypes of the tradition, Harlequin and Pierrot, I will show how this connection is more complex than most of us have thought it to be.[2] Pedrolino, the early version of Pierrot, was the same type as Harlequin, one which was true to the popular culture of the *commedia.* Pierrot, however, is strange, and not just from a psychological perspective, not simply because of his "melancholy." Pierrot has lost his all-important socially caricatural connection to the *commedia.* Like the modern Pierrot, the hypersubjective character only distantly relates to the *commedia* in its original form. Consequently, Beckett's characters are, for the most part, not avatars of the popular and caricatural Harlequin but of the metaphysical Pierrot.

It was inevitable that the denaturalized bodies of the new characters of the 1950s, 1960s, and 1970s, having relinquished their conventional status as purely discursive agents (in which they participate in conversations that form part of a story), would increase their value as image. In his search for a common denominator to apply to the nouveau théâtre calculus for the dramatic character, Robert Abirached examines the process of depersonalization, whose source he locates in the theory of Antonin Artaud and which he describes as the act of reducing either the character's personality "to the zero degree" (393) or the category of character itself "to the essential" (395). Indeed, despite a shared trait of depersonalization, there is an extremely wide variety of characters who are "reduced to the essential" in an even wider variety of situations in which they may or may not interact with other characters. The anonymous, robotic Smiths of Ionesco's *Bald Soprano* seem, at best, distant cousins of any of Beckett's tramps; and moreover, many of the characters created by a single author, such as Ionesco's Berringer from *Rhinoceros,* or his King of *Exit the King,* do not fit within the same family of depersonalized characters because they represent different types of "individuals." The hypersubject belongs to a specific subtype of the depersonalized characters of nouveau théâtre, one which, on the level of the text, has become more visually profound, more of an image than all the rest.

The corporeal, material form of the hypersubjective character is the consequence of an historical shift in the artistic sensibility of Western playwrights and theatergoers, of the creators as well as the beholders. The present century's penchant for the theatrical and the metatheatrical has resuscitated the two great archetypes of the Commedia dell'arte, Harlequin and Pierrot. We tend to downplay the differences between the two, simply describing Harlequin as more mischievous and Pierrot as more melancholic. We are inclined to think of both these characters in comparative terms of caricature, the first principle of the *commedia*. Much of their original caricature was visual, figural, and probably physical. However, when we study these two characters from a figural point of view, the contrast becomes quite vivid. If we examine how, visually, Pierrot differs from Harlequin, we will understand more concretely the social as well as the aesthetic significance of the hypersubjective character.

The major distinction between Harlequin and Pierrot originates in their material form. As a preliminary step to explaining this formal distinction, I will call on art history and refer the reader to the illustrations of the *commedia* characters shown in figures 1, 2, and 3. To be sure, there is something theatrical, something metatheatrical, denaturalized, and marionette-like about the images of both Harlequin and Pierrot in these portraits. They both are on display, so to speak. But, more particularly, even a casual glimpse at these portraits reveals a stark contrast between the two figures in question. Figure 1 shows a typical seventeenth-century rendering of Harlequin: crouched and prepared to spring into interaction; figures 2 and 3 show the typically static and statuesque image of Watteau's eighteenth-century tragic clown, Pierrot, who essentially isolates himself from action as well as interaction with his peers. In a sense, Harlequin is "at play" while Pierrot is on display. Following the theatrical tradition of the *commedia,* both these figures defy gravity, as would a marionette, but in different ways. The romantically pathetic, modernist mutant of the popular version of the *commedia* character has come to serve a divergent aesthetic end that we can better understand in terms of form and space, questions I will deal with in greater detail later in the chapter.

Despite the usual tendency to associate rather than to dissociate these characters, there is something more dialogic, physical, and demonically sociable about Harlequin, while Pierrot is more monologic, metaphysical, and introspective—and, for reasons that should become clear, I will refrain from insisting on the term "melancholic." Harlequin and his image can be traced to the origins of *commedia* in the sixteenth century and to a truly popular and carnivalesque aesthetic sensibility. His theatricality stems from his caricatural stage existence, his exaggerated and active physicality, his stylized gestures and expression and overall playfulness. Pierrot, on the other hand, an eighteenth-century mutant of the *commedia* stock character, acquired first a melancholic, *mal du siècle*, romantic dimension, and later an extra-psychological, phenomenological presentation. If we examine the visual history of Pierrot's image, we will find that the Pierrot paradigm is not simply different from the Harlequin one, but it stands at the other end of the spectrum of dramatic character types.

Our century has embraced the Harlequin and Pierrot paradigms of corporal spectacle. Between these two paradigms there is an array of types, mostly psychological. The contrast between the poles is one of near absolute opposition: social to the metaphysical; empty to the full, social caricature to metaphysical form. Much like Pierrot, the nouveau théâtre characters constitute more of an iconic image than socially interactive agents.

The figural contrast between Harlequin and Pierrot coincides with another contrast developed in the aesthetic theory of Mikhail Bakhtin. The spatial aspect of the Harlequin-Pierrot dichotomy becomes clearer thanks to Bakhtin's theories concerning the historical shift in aesthetic sensibility toward the idea of the *grotesque* from a popular historical period to a post-romantic period.

BAKHTIN'S FORMALIST THEORY OF THE MASK: FROM SOCIAL FULLNESS TO THE ASOCIAL EMPTINESS BEHIND THE ROMANTIC MASK—THE DEPERSONALIZATION OF THE DRAMATIC CHARACTER IN TERMS OF FORM AND SPACE

The *commedia* model of the stock character subverts naturalist conventions primarily due to its innate theatricality. The primary virtue of the *commedia* characters lies not in the lives they lead or the stories they tell, but rather, in the activities they perform. They are more important as stage image than as narrative agents. One could argue that the *commedia* character has become increasingly important in our century probably because, unlike the naturalistic character, including those of Ibsen, Strindberg, Claudel, and Sartre, the image of the character never gets lost or disguised in a world of discursive textual order, or bourgeois ideology. If the *commedia*'s stock characters did exploit, either wittingly or unwittingly, the metatheatrical aspects of character that conveyed a sense of the metaphysical through techniques of caricaturization (including exaggeration, stylization, and depersonalization), Mikhail Bakhtin's study of a very unnaturalistic, popular realism brings the "meta" dimension back to earth by inferring that the form of this figure was generated by and aligned with the collective social consciousness of the period. Medieval and Renaissance popular culture was more *socially* committed to the kind of dramatic characters that *commedia* scholars such as Giacomo Oreglia have typically described as follows: "Like comic strip characters, they seemed unreal and ageless, masks without souls or nerves" (xi). Yet, despite their lack of "souls or nerves," which probably means their failure to indulge or convey complex processes of psychological motivation, their grotesque presence was more socially "full" than existentially or metaphysically "empty."

In his work on folk carnival culture, Bakhtin developed a theory of the grotesque that traces the change in the relationship between art and society from the time of the *commedia* to the present century. He suggests that the *commedia* characters, born of a more "realist"[3] sociohistorical moment, represented a communitarian, popular, and therefore realist notion of the grotesque. Through a process of distortion, carnival masks along with distorted sculptures and linguistic deformations reflected a parodical mode of social consciousness that mocked, deformed, and deconstructed conventional forms of identity, subverting the hierarchy formally inherent in the sociopolitical system of the time. The ambivalence, incongruity, and distortion generated by grotesque art forms—whether in the plastic arts, on the pages of a book by Rabelais, or in the theatrical space of the marketplace—helped to break down formality and social barriers. To this extent, the grotesque characterized the fundamentally carnivalesque perception of the world held by the least common denominator in this society: the uncultured and "common" peasant.

Bakhtin's formalist approach to aesthetic history, illuminating for a study focusing on material as well as linguistic form, is replete with structural concepts such as his idiosyncratic notion of "corporality," a notion that links the sociocultural consciousness to the production and reception of visual imagery. Popular grotesque imagery is primarily constructed around a dualistic sense of "corporality." Louisa E. Jones explains succinctly this duality as follows:

> the grotesque "body" is social as well as individual. Carnival gives individuals a higher awareness of body, of their own bodies, but also a sense of participation, of belonging to a larger social body—the kind of giant body represented by Gargantua. (20)

On the one hand, we have the metaphor of an organic "social body"; on the other, in a direct and concrete relation to the social, the material awareness of personal anatomy: the personal, biological body grounds the social orientation of this common culture. The organic flesh connected the individual to the earth and to fellow human beings. In touch with its flesh, its anatomy, the popular culture exhibited, shared, and communicated it in "grotesque" ways that would soon become "vulgar" (i.e., obscene) to more civilized versions of Western society. According to Bakhtin, the "grotesque body is not separate from the rest of the world. It is not a closed, completed unit; it is unfinished, outgrows itself, transgresses its own limits" (26).[4] More specifically, Bakhtin recognized the significance of the lower body as a vital metaphor for the motif of social exchange, social interpenetration, and social regeneration. The early grotesque vision of the world was constructed around the semiotic capacity of the individual's private parts, excretions, and bodily orifices (including the female womb) to represent fertility and regeneration as well as so many openings to the social exterior. We see this vision clearly reflected in the *commedia* where "the Sexual/Scatological Lazzi, the so-called 'stage crudities' of the *commedia*, were among the most popular routines" (Mel Gordon 31).[5] The *commedia* was as much an anatomical theatrical genre,[6] a corporal spectacle, as it was a physical one. The theatricality of the genre proceeded not only from its physicality, its penchant for gestural hyperbole and acrobatic tour de force, but, first and foremost, from a culturally dynamic, primitive, graphic image of the body.

The idea of social "body" suggests a rather spatial and theatrical perspective on society; and the spatial implications become even more graphic when Bakhtin illustrates his theory of the grotesque through what he calls the "theme" of the mask. He believes that our attitude toward the mask as an aesthetic, cultural—and, I would add, theatrical—motif emblematizes the essential shift in our conception of the grotesque. In the carnivalesque tradition, the mask is "related to transition, metamorphoses, the violation of natural boundaries" and it is based on a "peculiar interrelation of reality and image, characteristic of the most ancient rituals and spectacles" (39–40). Social subject, mask, and society enjoy a sort of symbiotic aesthetic relationship. We can detect no formal break between mask, its wearer, and the sociocultural context that it signifies, so the motif is an entirely social phenomenon that does not constitute a barrier or "frame" at this point. On the contrary, Bakhtin's theory implies that the mask symbolically iconizes a dynamic, dialogic interaction among all seemingly heterogeneous elements of society: human individuals and their dramatic stereotypes (lecher, maiden, buffoon, etc.), ritual materials, and daily activities.[7] From a formal point of view, there are no clearly defined barriers or frames, and consequently, no empty spaces (behind the mask), frames and empty space being key metaphors in Bakhtin's theory of the modernist, subjectivist corruption of the carnivalesque. Essentially social caricature, the mask is marked by the fantastic nature of a popular grotesque. It makes a statement about a popular absurdity of life, about the interplay and exchange among life's multiple faces, so to speak. In this respect, not just his mask, but the entire body of Harlequin, typically clothed in a multicolored costume, has a signifying function that visually replicates that of the carnival mask.

Historical changes in political structure and social reality, however, take their toll on the popular collective consciousness. According to Bakhtin, only after the advent of the romantic, modernist artistic temperament does the notion of the grotesque lose its original social richness and break away from folk culture's "organic whole." Consequently, as an emblem of the grotesque, the mask loses its open, derisive quality and begins to conceal: "now the mask hides something, keeps a secret, deceives" (*Rabelais* 40). Likewise, it begins to induce the perception of an empty space. Bakhtin implies that at this point the mask acquires a framelike quality and becomes a barrier enclosing an inner space that he describes as "a terrible vacuum, a nothingness" (40).[8] Although Bakhtin does not expressly link the form of the mask to the form of the marionette, his allusion to the romantic version of the marionette as a "tragic doll" (40) suggests that he recognizes the marionette as no more than an autonomous, integral mask.[9]

These spatial parameters complete Bakhtin's theory of the coming to age of the modernist-formalist sensibility toward the spectacular. Far from the historical period which produced the popular, yet highly theatrical Commedia dell'arte, an art form that thrives in contemporary theatre, the space and the forms of an art based largely on the caricatural presentation of the human body have come to a confrontation with a more metaphysical style of presentation. There is some kind of irony to the fact that, through his formalistic approach to the spatial dynamics of an authentic state of social realism (carnivalesque) and to the disruption of this state by post-romantic subjectivism, Bakhtin prophecies one of the most controversial forms of imagism in nouveau théâtre. He does not veil his warning concerning what he saw as the inherently antisocial and therefore misguided trends toward modernist subjectivism. He accused authors like Alfred Jarry of participating in a "new and powerful revival of the grotesque," one "connected in various degrees with the Romantic tradition," and one which "evolved under the influence of existentialism" (46).

I will argue that the construction (author) and perception (spectator) of the dramatic character evolve along a path which is similar to that taken by the mask. The shift is theatrically "personified" in the contrast between Harlequin, the caricatural clown, and Pierrot, the metaphysical tragic doll. The romantic mask represents a different aesthetic process, one in which the individual (rather than social) body of the character becomes more of a signifying presence: the body's flesh turns to frame, corrupting its superphysical quality and becoming the bearer of a deep metaphysical message that sets the tone for the entire work. This formal image eventually comes to insinuate itself into certain modernist and postmodernist theatrical movements, including the hypersubjective plays we have analyzed. The romantic mask's tendency to evoke—to construct and enclose—an empty space eventually imposes itself on the comprehensive corporeal form of Pierrot before extending to a Pierrot type, or Pierrot-like dramatic character in certain kinds of modern and postmodern theatre. While Bakhtin criticizes the symbolist-subjectivist theatrics of Jarry, one would assume that Bakhtin's contemporary, Antonin Artaud, would have endured the same fate. A comparison of Bakhtin's socialist, dialogic aesthetic theory with Artaud's metaphysical theatrical theory reveals a curious enigma, one which attests to the multidimensional dynamism of the isolated hypersubjective character.

ARTAUD'S MODERNIST-SUBJECTIVIST OBJECTIONS TO BAKHTIN'S SOCIALIST PROJECTIONS

If, on the artistic side, Harlequin and Pierrot stand as symbolic banners against naturalistic forms of theatre, on the theoretical side, Bakhtin and Artaud were both militant adversaries of the bourgeois conformism that bolstered much of the most sclerotic forms of naturalism. Because of their fundamental philosophical differences, however, they fought the battle against conformist naturalism from very different fronts, even opposing fronts. Concerned with the idea of art as a reflection of some recondite ideology, Bakhtin fought from the outside in, articulating the sociohistorical imperative and elucidating the capacity of ideology to mold the human individual's self-perception as well as its world vision. Concerned with the metaphysical source of aesthetics and its organic link to theatre—or, to put it another way, with theatrical art as an organic manifestation of life—Artaud fought from the inside out. He struggled to construct poetically a more or less a priori metaphysical imperative imposed on the individual within society through a universal deep consciousness, a category which Bakhtin and his school refused. Clearly, Bakhtin's social theory is more aligned with the carnivalesque nature of the physical image of Harlequin, while Artaud's theory pursued a Pierrot type. The Balinese central dancer alone on the stage touching his head is more Pierrot-like than Harlequinesque. Though contemporaries, to my knowledge there is no evidence that either theorist was aware of the other's work. Bakhtin was a Russian socialist philosopher turned literary scholar, while Artaud was more thoroughly a rather apolitical metaphysician of theatre. Despite his more literary orientation, however, as we have seen in his work on the carnivalesque, Bakhtin had a unique understanding of the spectacular, theatrical, material, imagistic, formal value of the human body in space, one that begs a comparison—or confrontation—with Artaud.

The major differences between the two thinkers stem from their vision of a prototype for the quintessential character, based on a concept of individual subjectivity or intersubjectivity as conveyed through the formal image of body in spatial context. They both would agree that the artistic representation of the body became more formal and more empty in the twentieth century; but the one has a negative opinion of this development while the other has a positive one. We have seen Bakhtin's argument in favor of a carnivalesque conception of the body and his consequent case against the "subjectivist" tendency to isolate and outline the body as a figural frame enclosing a metaphysical empty space: the tragic doll. Now, in the light of

Bakhtin's theory, let us reconsider the other side of the coin: Artaud's metaphysical, essentialist, and organic vision of the empty body on the stage. Let us reconsider its impact on the "new" dramatic characters of our study, the "newness" of the characters being linked to the figural.

I do not mean to suggest the absence of a metaphysical dimension in the carnival, in the popular perception of the carnival mask, and in Harlinquinesque "grotesqueness" in general. On the contrary, as I argue below in the discussion of Harlequin and Pierrot, the theatricality of the Harlequin figure provokes a deeper metaphysical awareness of social life. Artaud was aware of this. In Jarry's indomitable Roi Ubu, Bakhtin saw a selfish, greedy theatrical subject, while Artaud saw the metaphysical side of Ubu's hypercaricatural stage presence, the very same "boiling anarchy, an essential disintegration of the real by poetry" that he praised in the comic routines of the Marx Brothers (*Theater* 142–44).[10] Though Bakhtin criticized Jarry's subjectivist tendencies, Roi Ubu was a highly complex stage presence, quite as complex as the contrast between Bakhtin and Artaud.

Antonin Artaud's condemnation of what he referred to as the "psychological" theatre that dominated the stage of his time and up to his time implies that spectators had become more readers of text than true theatrical "spectators." The human body on the stage was a mere pretext or agent of not so much social as ideological discourse motivated by "bourgeois conformism" (*The Theater* 76). Placed in a naturalized setting, readily identifiable characters engaged in discourse structured by and permeated with bourgeois psychological motivation, the psychological trials and tribulations of modern society. He railed against "purely narrative and descriptive theatre—storytelling psychology. . . . Psychology, which works relentlessly to reduce the unknown to the known, to the quotidian and the ordinary" (76–77). Even Shakespeare did not pass Artaud's muster! Artaud blames "Shakespeare himself" for this "aberration and decline, this disinterested idea of the theatre which wishes a theatrical performance to leave the public intact, without setting off one image that will shake the organism to its foundations and leave an ineffaceable scar" (76–77). In his more derisive moments, Artaud viewed these psychological portraits to be so much ideological gibberish, a gibberish that obfuscated equally the "idea of the void" and the metaphysical dimension of the stage image. The one powerful image that Artaud thought necessary for the stage had to be constructed around a dramatic body rather than a dramatic character, a paradoxical human icon emptied of psychology, a powerful empty envelope. We remember his remarks about the theatrical void:

> All powerful feeling produces in us the idea of the void. And the lucid language which obstructs the appearance of this void also obstructs the appearance of poetry in thought. That is why an image, an allegory, a figure that masks what it would reveal have more significance for the spirit than the lucidities of speech and its analytics. (*Theatre* 71)

In the idea of the "figure that masks what it would reveal" we see an un-equivocal example of Bakhtin's subjectivist "terrible vacuum." Bakhtin, too, rejected psychological discourse, but not in favor of some metaphysical void. Bakhtin, too, pursued his theory through physicality, through what he called the "material bodily principle" and the dialogic physicality of speech; but the corporal image he had in mind did not and could not stand alone. So the two theorists believed they were correcting the same error, but, unlike Bakhtin, Artaud believed the individual human body could stand alone. More important, however, is that, in the above quote, Artaud places Bakhtin's "terrible vacuum" in a positive light, a void which Artaud hoped would awaken a primal psychic organ in the spectator, thereby eliciting not Word, but what Derrida has called "psychic utterances."

Let me repeat that Artaud worked from inside the human body (body-mind) to the outside, and this explains his break with the communist sympathies of the surrealists of his time, a break that emblematizes his world view:

> The communist revolution ignores the interior world of thought. But it does take account of thought, it takes account of it through experience, i.e., through the outside of phenomena. . . .
>
> Like life, like nature, thought goes from the inside to the outside before it goes from the outside to the inside. I begin to think within a void and from that void I proceed toward fullness; and once I've attained fullness I can fall back into emptiness. I go from the abstract to the concrete and not from the concrete toward the abstract. ("L'Homme contre le destin" 191–92)

For Artaud, as for Bakhtin, the corporal image is at the center of the essence of both life and art. For Bakhtin, this essence is social, for Artaud, it is metaphysical: when presented as theatrical icon instead of as discursive agent, the physical presence of the body on stage, its presentation as pure image, conveys a deeper metaphysical awareness of life. Robert Abirached sees the Artaudian ideal as a *corps-théâtre* around which the scenic apparatus is simplified. Furthermore, Abirached implies that the body of the dramatic character becomes the "keystone" of the stage architecture and, in the extreme, an empty theatre within the theatre, a body-within-a-body which reflects and extends the profound emptiness of the stage. According to Abirached, on the "cruel" stage envisioned by Artaud, the body signifies "skeletally" through its form and its volume: "the skeleton is [the stage's] only practicable scenery [*son unique praticable*] and the volume delimited by its walls is its exclusive labyrinth, erected within the void or propagating its noise on the immaterial waves" (Abirached 377). Thus, the body as signifier transcends not only the fringes of the purely discursive—for Baktin, the dialogic—but also the fringes of heretofore closed semiotic systems.

This is precisely how the avatar of the *commedia* character, the image of Pierrot, deviates from the popular Harlequinesque type. We can construe both types as metathcatrical, calling attention more to theatre's self-reference than to its external references to social reality (theatre as signifier as well as signified, rather than as a signifier pointing to some off-stage signified). But Harlequin is socially oriented, his metatheatricality functions through the assumption that theatre is a fundamentally social phenomenon. Pierrot's metatheatricality is metaphysically oriented. This is where the greater social body of the carnival separates from the focused body of the stage, and two theorists of corporal spectacle part ways. Bakhtin's world view, with its theatrical point of departure, relied on a semiotics system whose signifying processes were consummated at a simultaneously plebian-social and artistic level. The artistic and the social are complementary and equal. All meaning and communication, even the innermost, apparently individualistic, thoughts, begin with a dialogically conceived and referentially oriented sign. Artaud, however, resists referentiality.[11]

As we saw in chapter 2, for Artaud, the central, quintessential sign ultimately reduces to the "one powerful image" of the central character, the cycloptic Balinese dancer, the "central eye" or "intellectual egg." His hieroglyphics of the corporeal architecture of the stage, apparently semiotic in nature, depends ultimately on a theatro-metaphysical phenomenological base, one which antagonizes the socially referential identity of the human individual as well as the socially referential nature of theatre. Artaud had graduated from the referentiality of semiotics to the supra-referentiality of a phenomenological vision of theatre, what Bert States calls "a naïve perception of the thing." Despite the desire to discover surreality they share with Artaud, his Marxist cronies of the time, like Breton and Aragon, simply could not understand Artaud's extremist approach to transcending the visible world, the material body, the psychoanalyzable mind, and especially the border between body and mind. Abirached writes that "If [Artaud] kills the dramatic character" it is because it represents a "search for the origin of being," a search in which the character is shielded from "all social, historical, and cultural trappings" (381). For Artaud, artistic meaning is life itself; organically produced by the body-mind's symbiotic relationship with the primal world, it is not so much meaning as a vital awareness.[12] Emptiness is the essential substance of the individual psychic space in which this awareness is created. Consequently, not only is meaning extra-discursive, but also truly extra-linguistic and extra-semiotic.

Today, after phenomenological, poststructural theory, and after Beckett's theatre, it is perhaps easier for us to judge Artaud's vision as either pre-social or trans-social, rather than as anti-social or a-social. Perhaps *in the end* all relevant meaning is dialogic and socially generated. However, if we are still a long way from absolute knowledge of outer reality as well as inner reality, then, in order to push the envelope of our consciousness, we cannot afford to avoid truly radical challenges to intellectual convention or to the socio-cultural status quo. Perhaps there is a non-Freudian primal access to the human individual's social core. That is why nouveau théâtre dramatists pushed the envelope of the dramatic character; they re-staged its body, and foregrounded its mind, a mind which they rendered more complex by emptying it of language and by articulating in their texts subtle hints of an extralinguistic realm of the psyche. Ionesco's *Exit the King* is an example of a theatrically staged debate that the author negotiated with himself. The King had to let go of the outside, i.e., language and reference, in order to reach the inside. Ionesco had to let go of signification to truly signal a new—empty—theatre, to point to emptiness as Beckett has done.

Artaud's theory and Beckett's plays represent an extremely modernist-sub-jectivist attitude that disgruntled the Marxists, who were more interested in grotesque subversion than metaphysical indeterminacy or supra-referenti-ality. Since Bakhtin and his circle believed that human consciousness, and ultimately the human psyche, is entirely and absolutely socially constituted, they disallowed the validity of truly individual thought processes which were not preconstituted by some form of dialogue. So the human form itself also must be dialogic.[13] Even ultimate, primal metaphysical awareness was both social and dialogic, and consequently the individual human icon was never an absolutely personal one. Yet the Marxists were inspired enough to ex-plore a concept of depersonalization with respect to a concept of greater social body, i.e., as it applied to theatrical representations such as the popu-lar *commedia* character, which survived its original Renaissance form. Thus, placed in the context of a concept of greater social body, depersonalization is a self-contradictory artistic phenomenon. As we have seen with Bakhtin's warning of the "terrible vacuum" of the post-romantic period, he did not believe that the spectacular human form could exist either in or as a vacuum. The Artaudian notion of depersonalization, however, the notion of creat-ing and evoking the "zero degree" of the character, is taken to its vacuous extreme: de-personalization led to (metaphysical) de-socialization, an ar-tistically antagonistic form of metatheatricalization that was entirely unac-ceptable to a socialist world view.[14]

Like Artaud, but unlike Bakhtin, many twentieth-century playwrights and theorists believed that the nineteenth century's interest in social themes and forms was connected to a bourgeois ideology that had corrupted the extralinguistic aesthetic essence of dramatic and theatrical art. Because of its iconic nature, theatrical art had a special mission apart from the purely literary, from the narration of social reality. From the time of the symbolist drama of Maeterlinck and Jarry's symbolist-surrealist-absurdist *Ubu Roi*, a play that took place in the *Nulle Part* of the theatrical stage, dramatists as well as theorists took a greater interest in theatrical metadiscourse. They sought

175

new dramaturgical methods of exploring, exposing, and emphasizing the alienating *Nulle Part* of the stage—its potential to ostend not only the extra-linguistic, but more simply, the artistic frame provided by the borders of the stage.

   Much of twentieth-century metadrama was extra-social to the degree that it was metatheatrical—theatre-*as*-theatre, or, in Artaud's terms, life as the "double" of theatre. The focus shifted from the body-mind of the subject in social context to the individual mind as a theatrical body. W. B. Worthen seems to suggest that, from the time of Gordon Craig's *Übermarionette*, dramatic authors began to unabashedly dissociate the social from the aesthetic: "[Craig] shares with modern playwrights the sense that the individual privacy of the subject is what distinguishes aesthetic experience from the degraded routine of everyday social life" ("Of Actors and Automata" 9). But, more than a renewed interest in monologue, we should interpret the "individual privacy of the subject" in iconic terms. Craig's solution was to shift the focus from the linguistic text and naturalistic detail to architectural design, one in which the corporeal, spatial form of the individual was the human trait that was most assimilable to the stage. As the stage can represent the human psyche, so too can the body: the body as a theatrical mind-space (see fig. 5). Gordon Craig's theory of the *Übermarionette* for the stage actor is a plea for a break with a theatrical tradition wholly preoccupied with inducing "spectators" into reading the dramatic character in the reductive terms of naturalistically and psychologically stimulated literary discourse. In the progressive drama of the new century, psychological human beings on stage were to yield to the construction of metaphysical human icons. Spectators would increase their interest in the dramatic character as an isolated form, rather than as an "actor." This certainly prepared the way for much of nouveau théâtre, especially Beckett's, where the body sacrifices social activity for aesthetic form.

   But Artaud's theory goes farther with this idea of the human icon. The post-Artaud "crisis" in the theatre began when, instead of signifying in naturalistic terms as some place, the stage began to signify more radically on the level of art, as a strange, non-discursive void. The crisis intensified when the dramatic character's body, after having ceased to signify in conventional, naturalistic terms as a psycho-sociologically structured human, began to signify in theatrical terms (against the basic premises of signification) as a special kind of icon—as a metaphysically empty human icon. It was at this moment that the theatrical world *wholly* replaced the real world outside the theatre; the theatro-human subject/icon *wholly* replaced the human subject/*being*, a moment that occurs at the beginning of Beckett's plays, if only at the conclusion of Ionesco's *Exit* and Vian's *Empire Builders*. Furthermore, as we have seen in our study of the hypersubjective works of nouveau théâtre, this telescoping of essentially empty forms (empty theatrical space, empty body) continued through the iconized body to the focus on a psyche that was essentially emptied of language. If Beckett has "fragmented" anything in his theatre it is the social agency of the body; his (ab)use of the body epitomizes the culminating modernist shift away from the patently social aspect of art.

HARLEQUIN VERSUS PIERROT

Once again, it would help to examine the portraits of Harlequin and Pierrot. If we compare the former (fig. 1) with the latter (figs. 2 and 3), we could characterize Harlequin as a socially oriented figure and Pierrot as mysterious and metaphysical. Why? And what about the later painting of Harlequin painted by Cézanne (fig. 4)? How does it compare with the others? Confusing, is it not? The dress is harlequinesque enough, but the bodily attitude, posture, and contextual form tend to indicate more a Pierrot than a Harlequin. Bakhtin assuredly would have considered this painting a modernist corruption of the popular figure. The carnivalesque tradition would not portray or perceive Harlequin as that mysterious, framelike, or empty.

Harlequin, we know, was present at the very beginnings of the *commedia* in the late sixteenth century. When we think of the popular grotesque of the Renaissance, we likely think of him: scatological, puerile, the icon of all human weaknesses, a symbol—or victim—of human instinct, yet a champion of physical and mental agility. In this respect, we could say that a large part of his artistic presentation might even seem "superhumanized." He possesses a superhuman capacity to symbolize popular culture:

> Arlecchino is always hungry and represents, among other things, the wishes and desires of the common people. He embodies their rebelliousness against authority and power and their will to survive in the face of adversity. Numerous other servants appeared under different names, but most were variations on Arlecchino. (Fisher 4)

His early portrait conveys his insatiable appetite for food and the social interaction it suggests. Since he personifies Bakhtin's idea of transformation and metamorphosis, he is not a simple character. Allardyce Nicoll remarks on the complexity and ambiguity found in his moral and intellectual qualities:

> Harlequin exists in a mental world wherein concepts of morality have no being, and yet, despite such absence of morality, he displays no viciousness (70). . . . Although he may seem a fool, he displays a very special quickness of mind. (72)

Nicoll refers to a description of him as a "chameleon assuming all colors" and he apparently agrees with Jean François Marmontel's summarization of the impression Harlequin makes: "His character is a mixture of ignorance, simplicity, wit, awkwardness and grace."[15] Harlequin's behavior and appearance are mutually suggestive of the popular grotesque. To add to the complexity and volatility of his character, however, neither his behavior, nor his physical appearance will remain constant with time. According to Nicoll, "when we first meet [Harlequin] he appears in a costume heavily and irregularly patched; during the seventeenth century the patches become formalized, and, in the century following, his characteristic costume becomes even neater and more elegant. So, too, with his personality" (23–24). So the continued "formalization" of his costume was accompanied by a spiritual change: "At the beginning he was less refined than he later became, and it would seem that he was definitely duller and less animated" (70). An essential part of his image that remains constant, however, is the kaleidoscopic color of the costume. Based on his costume alone, Harlequin is not uniform but multiform; he is not static but dynamic and changeable as is the kaleidoscope or the "chameleon assuming all colors." In short, despite the evolution in his character, which one could probably attribute to the modernist shift described by Bakhtin, Harlequin's raison d'être is to integrate on a formal level into the social body of the stage's world. He is at once catalyst and barometer for the kaleidoscopic shifts in relationship and attitude taking place among the stock characters on the *commedia* stage. If his costume represents the most exotic and ex-centric on the stage, it is not so much to make him stand alone, but rather to make him stand out, and, in so doing, to allow him to more visibly and "socio-theatrically" assimilate, creating a grotesque, kaleidoscopic image of the interpenetration of colors as well as personalities. In this respect, he symbolizes the chaotic web of social relations. This is not true of either Pierrot's appearance or his behavior.

Pierrot stands out on stage in a very different way. There is, of course, no early description of Pierrot, since he remains a relatively modern mutant of the *commedia*. As I pointed out at the beginning of this chapter, with respect to his *commedia* predecessor Pedrolino, Pierrot stands at the opposite pole.[16] His strangeness and his modernness are evident even in the following simple description offered by Martin Green: "Pierrot, at least in modern times, wears a black skullcap, white floppy pants and jacket, a pale gaunt makeup" (10). This is the appearance with which he "came into his own under the auspices of French Romanticism" (Jones 10). Consequently, we see him as not only more meditative and more introspectively independent, but also more isolated from his social context. His "black and white" chiaroscuro presence accomplishes an artistic presentation that contrasts with the socially interactive grounding of Harlequin: It deemphasizes the biological social body while emphasizing the body as form, a figural presentation that draws particular attention to the head; and, isolating his form on stage, it renders him more profoundly mysterious than spectacularly grotesque.

Unlike the traditionally half-masked Harlequin, Pierrot's face is not covered by a mask, at least not the traditional kind of mask which Bakhtin has labeled a "popular" emblem of transition and social caricature. Paradoxically, this absence of the *commedia* mask works to shift the spectator's focus from Pierrot's body to his head. In the case of the masked character of the *commedia*, explains David Madden, "With either the face covered or the voice muted, the body had to supplement those limitations" and "the inanimate mask and the animate body enhance each other" (112, 120).[17] So, with the half-masked Harlequin, the ultimately social function of the intersubjective lower body would necessarily predominate. But this reverse effect of the mask, this symbiotic relationship between mask and body, only works in conjunction with a grotesquely active lower body, such as that of Harlequin. In the case of the inert and statuesque Pierrot, however, his black skullcap[18] and white makeup constitute a new, more framelike, and modernist mask that actually emphasizes the head: the image of corporal interpenetration (of the socially constructed lower body) yields to the suggestion of psychic inner penetration.[19]

Pierrot's whiteness of face is the final complement to the theatrical emphasis on the head as an isolated image representing, in effect, the central core of theatrical space. Pierrot has become a stage-like image within a stage. Insisting on the metaphysical force of Pierrot's white face, Louisa Jones refers to *Moby Dick* where Herman Melville evokes the white whale's "blank dumbness full of meaning":

> For it seems that much of [Pierrot's] power lay in the very emptiness of his oval face, his expressive silence, his agile immobility, a great whiteness which lent itself to many styles, many forms, many interpretations. (115–16)

Here, we should not confuse the color white with the sensorial effect of light, and black with that of dark. While we might consider white to represent the opposite of black, it does not necessarily signify the opposite of dark. Whiteness suggests blankness and blankness can suggest darkness, as it does in the infinite blankness of outer space. On the other side of the material whiteness of Pierrot's face lies a metaphysical darkness, a space that forms a tangible barrier between social reality and the socially antagonistic emptiness of our psyche. Our post-romantic culture cannot help but perceive Pierrot's expressionless white face in the same way that Bakhtin has said we perceive the mask, i.e., as the hermetic curtain behind which lies the "terrible vacuum."[20] This is strikingly similar to the space that hypersubjectivist dramatists like Beckett and Obaldia invite us to imagine behind the borders of a prominent protagonist's skull. It also resembles the human space that Artaud evokes in poetry and through the portraits he sketches: "The human face / is an empty force, a / field of death" ("Le Visage humain . . . " 94).[21]

Bodily attitude and facial expression work together with costume and makeup to differentiate Pierrot from Harlequin. Harlequin stands out first and foremost for his acrobatic skill. The "harlequinade" was based largely on physical dexterity and stage acrobatics which might have rivaled the suppleness and perceived "weightlessness" of the marionette relative to the naturalized, humanized dramatic characters.[22] The *commedia* characters dynamically and physically commune on stage.[23] In the case of Harlequin, bodily attitude serves as an emblem for "socio-physical" dexterity, and bodily attitude is the one feature of Harlequin that remains historically constant, at least in the unambiguous illustrations of the figure. Nicoll insists that despite the evolution of his costume and despite the eventual "refining" of Harlequin's character noted above, "Harlequin remained the same from the start of his career to the end . . . he is recognizable in all his guises" (70). Yet, as we see in the images portrayed in figure 1, Harlequin's suggestiveness was not simply a matter of costume or of movement but perhaps even more one of posture: "we can always be sure of his identity," says Nicoll, "not only from the costume but also, and more importantly, from his bodily attitudes" (3). He goes on, however, to observe the following:

> No modern artist could paint a "Hamlet" which would be immediately discernable as such, but Cézanne and Picasso and Degas and Dérain have all created sketches or canvases which need no title to tell us the name of their sitter. (4)

These remarks are problematic since the only feature of Cézanne's portrait we might call harlequinesque is the costume (fig. 4). If there is one aspect of these Harlequin portraits that diverges, it is precisely bodily attitude. With Cézanne, Harlequin is clearly straight, upright, and "monumental," a posture that diverges enormously from the early, seventeenth-century version. Harlequin was never a straight, upright, linear figure; he was always bent if not contorted. In his famous—if overrated—essay on the marionette, Heinrich von Kleist touches on the inability of human dancers to find the "natural arrangement of the centers of gravity," (240–41) a quality inherent to the marionette.[24] Like the marionette, Harlequin's center of gravity is in his groin area, so his characteristic pose is the crouch.[25] This is the very opposite of Watteau's *Pierrot*.

While it is not within the scope of my study to examine the evolution of period styles of painting from the Renaissance through the twentieth century, the similarities between Cézanne's early twentieth-century Harlequin and Watteau's eighteenth-century Pierrot are striking, and they are significant for the notion of formalism as it relates to the aesthetic function of the dramatic character as image. Notwithstanding the inevitable variations on the *commedia* type from Watteau through Cézanne, we get a glimpse of the aesthetic shift from the popular to the metaphysical, from the elasticity of body to the body as frame. Nicoll describes Pierrot as "lazy . . . largely a static figure" (90) and Deburau's nineteenth-century rendering of Pierrot was "tall and straight as the gallows."[26] In contrast to the grotesque, even animal-like posture of

Harlequin, the clearly defined form of Pierrot's body does not suggest physical agility. One more glance at figures 1 through 4 will finalize the stark contrast between the two *commedia* figures: one is horizontal and curved, the other, vertical and straight, representing a clearly defined structure within space; one is physically active, signifies kinetically through action and implies interaction, the other is statically receptive, signifies through sheer presence and ostension; one, with minuscule, sequestered eyes, draws our attention to the lower body (its center of gravity in the groin area), the other draws our attention to its gaze; the one is not only dialogic but clearly vocal, it must have a voice (or at least a sound to complete the body), the other is evidently speechless and perhaps even thought-less, it draws our attention first to the head and then to the interior headspace. Harlequin is exaggerated, Pierrot is understated; yet the "monumentality" of Pierrot renders him more of a "clearly defined structure," more spatial and, consequently, less human.[27]

The advent of a Harlequin type character and the late intrusion of Pierrot, as well as the pictorial images portraying them, help us to distinguish the two very different ways in which audiences could perceive the marionette: the full-bodied carnivalesque form and the empty-bodied, "empty-headed" psychic form. Just as one might speak of a socially derived artistic sensibility as opposed to a more metaphysical one, or of a socially committed theatre of, say, a Bertolt Brecht or an Armand Gatti as opposed to the cerebral theatre of Beckett,[28] we might equally speak of a socially oriented caricatural image as opposed to a more cerebral, metaphysical one. During the essentially popular culture of the medieval and renaissance periods, when spectators were confronted with the more-or-less-than-human theatrical character of the *commedia*, they likely were not induced to a metaphysical perception of it, one which would "see" beyond the body to an isolated metaphysical emptiness (a focused visual field). So they probably interpreted the character, as Bakhtin suggests, primarily on a bio-social level. On the other hand, the Pierrot figure signifies through a delineating geometry of figure that shifts the perceptive focus from social body to individual psyche, radically transforming into the socially antagonistic expression of what Bakhtin refers to as the new "subjective, individualist world outlook. . . . It became, as it were, an individual carnival, marked by a vivid sense of isolation" (36–37); "this *interior infinite* of the individual was unknown to the medieval and the renaissance grotesque" (44; Bakhtin's emphasis).

Beckett's characters have not sprung from a bona fide carnivalesque tradition. With the shift from the original, dynamically clownesque duo of *Godot* to the highlighted Hamm of *Endgame*, Beckett takes a giant step away from the harlequinesque in the direction of Pierrot-like emptiness. Stanton B. Garner Jr. argues that in the early plays Beckett dresses his figures to "streamline the visual irregularities of the human shape," and in the later plays "anatomical reduction further diminishes figural irregularity" (63).

We can read the diminishing "irregularity" to imply the effacement of the social—and the socially grotesque—body. Beckett's figures are more like Giacometti's ironic human icons and George Segal's plastic plastercasts than the freakish humans of Jerome Bosch or Bruegel the Elder. Watteau's *Pierrot* (figs. 2 and 3), whose central character already represents an autonomous visual field within a greater field of darkness, exemplifies an intermediary stage of the mutation leading to Beckett's figures. No longer representative of the irregular, incongruous, distorted, and disfigured corporality of the popular grotesque exemplified by Harlequin and theorized by Bakhtin, Beckett's "marionettes" have become figures of reduced kinesis embedded in and reflective of the shape, substance, and context of the greater visual field, the stage: "the geometry of figure forms part of a larger geometry of field" (Garner 64).

I am not suggesting that Pierrot-like dramatic characters replaced, wholesale, Harlequin-like dramatic characters. I am suggesting that, when we spectators confront a play in which one single dramatic character occupies such a large part of the textual and visual focus of an essentially empty visual field, we are likely to perceive him/her as a spatial field in its own right, just as the romantic mask was for Bakhtin.

Prior to the nineteenth century, the most acceptable manner of denaturalizing the stage character was through the *commedia* style, a style that has survived the increasingly symbolist artistic tendencies of the twentieth century. In his volume on "symbolism, surrealism and the absurd," J. L. Styan underlines the twentieth-century revival of the Commedia dell'arte in the symbolist-inspired, stylized French theatre of Jacques Copeau and Charles Dullin from the twenties through the forties. He points out that this revival occurred in the personage of Harlequin: "It is curious with what frequency in these years that rascal Harlequin reasserts his fundamental right to return to the stage" (2:94). Like Martin Esslin, Styan feels that this clownesque *commedia* influence can be traced into at least the earliest of Beckett's drama (2:126). But we should not lose sight of the alternative anti-naturalistic turn in the early twentieth century that in many ways imposed itself on many of the same theatre practitioners and playwrights who had a soft spot for the *commedia:* Craig's *Übermarionette,* a figure we can trace to the whole/"hole" of Beckett's corpus.[29] Beckett's characters are not simply marionette-like, but rather *hyper*-marionette-like.

THE MARIONETTE-*COMMEDIA* CONNECTION

We have always associated one form or another of marionettes with the *commedia.* Marionette theatre precedes and in many ways survives the *commedia.* Many scholars who seek the most ancient of predecessors to explain the theatricality of modern and postmodern characters look beyond the *commedia.* We have seen, for example, Esslin's argument that what the theatre of the absurd borrowed from the *commedia* the *commedia* had already borrowed from the mimus of Antiquity. Other scholars have suggested that the source for the mimus was the marionette. Charles Nodier, for example, believed that the most primitive of theatres was the marionette theatre, and the most primitive of actors and dramatic characters were marionettes. He expresses plainly the *commedia*'s link to the figure of the marionette:

> But *marionettes* had their destiny. They went on the boards. The multitude followed them. They embodied the grand comédie of the world. . . .
>
> Drama, as we know it today, is not progress. It is plagiarism. Live comedy was only a reckless transformation of the wooden comedy. The theatre got a bit larger, going from the size of a two-square-foot box to one of a tipcart. But the buffoons of old Athens covered themselves with wine sediment like *Punchinello,* with lampblack like *Harlequin,* or with flour like *Pierrot.* The marionettes took flesh.
>
> Everything disappeared, monuments, people, religions. Everything changed, men, times, and places. Primitive art did not change, and primitive art is the *marionette* comedy. ("Les Marionnettes" 73–74; author's emphasis throughout)

Nevertheless, despite their formalist roots, marionette and *commedia* characters have changed with "men, times, and places." Robert F. Storey traced the evolution of Pierrot from his Harlequinesque roots as Pedrolino to his introspective metamorphosis, which scholars largely attribute to Jules Laforgue in the post-romantic nineteenth century. He suggests that this evolution created a polarized critical perception that became the great dilemma of an entire aesthetic movement at the end of the last century.

> In the end, Laforgue's *zanni* (we might even say the "Laforguean voice") confronts the basic question facing Pierrot and his interpreters at the close of the nineteenth century: how to escape the Hamletic prison of the skull, to recover an equilibrium between the self and the world. (155)

The comparison of Pierrot to Hamlet, which has progressed beyond the simple melancholic aspect of the figure, is the point at which the critical debate on the Pierrot-like image has stalled. To my knowledge, to date scholars have not connected in any clear way the Pierrot figure with Maeterlinck's and Craig's ideas on the *Übermarionette.* This is primarily because they have not taken a critical enough look at the form of the figure, on the one hand, and the formal relation between the dramatic character and the stage on the other.

In the modern period, especially since romanticism, we begin to have second and third thoughts about the possibility of reality; theatrical fiction focuses less on art as reality, and more on reality as *art*ificial. Instead of reality, symbolist-expressionist forms of art take the illusion of imagination as their subject, one which can foreground and undermine the conventions of reality. Maeterlinck and Craig rightly maintained that the human element on the stage tends to obstruct the *art*ificiality of the theatrical project as do the mimetically social and psychological aspects of a textually produced character who behaves as if he or she must eat, drink, and socialize (copulate, swindle, laugh) in order to survive. Harlequin and his cohorts were denaturalized to the extent they were veritable social animals. They represented larger-than-life clowns that presented a stronger stage presence and a more prominent image than naturalized characters. One could make an excellent case for theatrical self-consciousness in the *commedia,* but the self-consciousness was more of a social (and professional) construction than a formal one, and the theatricality primarily focused on stylization and exaggeration. With their improvisation and masks, comedic actors playing characters such as Harlequin and Pantalone transcended the illusion of reality and called attention to their artistic function, but they did so by "socially" playing off and playing with each other as well as with the audience.[30] The artform was based on the socio-logical (rather than psychological) character and the exaggerated if stereotypical story of this character in social intercourse.[31]

As we have seen, while we might speak of an imaginary, fantastic element in the *commedia,* the self-consciousness of the *commedia*'s fiction was a good deal less formalistic, because it consciously materialized as a stylized product of social rather than aesthetic process. In the modern period though, the prominence of artistic image and the concomitant skewing of the life of/in the body have entirely transformed the phenomenology of the dramatic character and its double, the marionette. A very particular marionette-like connection between Pierrot and the hypersubjective "marionettes" of nouveau théâtre arises in the form of a denaturalized, de-socialized, and even dehumanized image. The Pierrot-like avatar evolves, through the *Übermarionette,* into the hypersubject of nouveau théâtre, which has three essential traits: its relative immobility (instead of either dynamic acrobatics or "normal" social or biological motion and gesture); its central (not necessarily "centered," especially in the case of Beckett), detached, and highlighted presence on stage (instead of an interactive relationship with other characters); and consequently, its focus on the head as a metaphorical empty space (instead of the mimetic—ideological or psychological—focus on the whole body, or the popular, carnivalesque focus on the lower body).[32]

The mutation of the Harlequinesque *commedia* character into Pierrot was only a beginning. The degree of hypersubjectivity in the character increased with the model of the *Übermarionette* and it subsequently redoubled with characters of nouveau théâtre. Much of today's so-called intellectual theatre has harnassed and transformed the metaphysico-metatheatrical energy of the *Übermarionette,* precisely because of its capacity to echo emptiness by installing an empty envelope within the empty space of the stage—precisely because of its formalistic marionette likeness (see fig. 5). Set off from its social and natural surroundings, the Pierrot figure controverted social interaction and interpenetration. It also helped to produce a mystical aura that became mutatis mutandis one of the most powerful images on the avant-garde theatrical stage of the 1950s through the 1980s. The *Übermarionette* has extremely deep theatrical roots, and represents the most radical of forms of the marionette and the *commedia* character. First and foremost a relatively inactive stage image, it represents in many ways the antithesis of Harlequin, a very different marionette-like type. It is indeed the child of Pierrot as well as the grandfather of Obaldia's Cancre and Beckett's W. But, from the early part of the twentieth century to the 1950s, the evolution produced an extravagant mutation. More than the introspective self of the nineteenth-century Pierrot, more than the personalized, metatheatrical architectonics of the *Übermarionette*, the hypersubjective character of nouveau théâtre portrays inner emptiness.

THE (POST)MODERNIST, (HYPER)SUBJECTIVIST, METAPHYSICO-THEATRICAL PERCEPTION OF THE MARIONETTE: ÜBER-, META-, HYPER-MARIONETTES OF NOUVEAU THÉÂTRE

At the turn of the century, philosophers, theorists, and dramatists were clearly affected by the post-romantic perception of the mask and the marionette. In an essay examining Gordon Craig's fascination with the mask, Denis Bablet points out that an exhibition of Craig's theatrical projects included an elaborate collection of his masks. On the cover of the catalogue for the exposition, Craig placed the following epigraph, excerpted from Nietzsche's *Beyond Good and Evil*: "All that is profound loves the mask" and "All profound minds need a mask" ("D'Edward Gordon Craig au Bauhaus" 137).[33] Speaking of profound, Nietzsche also said something to the effect that "If we contemplate the abyss long enough, eventually we are drawn into it." The symbolist contemporary of Nietzsche, Maurice Maeterlinck, for his part, tells us that "Art always seems a detour and it never speaks face to face. You might call it the hypocrisy of infinity. It is the provisional mask under which we are intrigued by the faceless unknown" ("Menus Propos" 331). For him, the mystery of the mask applies as well to the mystery of the marionette: "it seems that any being that has the appearance of life without being alive calls on extraordinary powers" (336) Both Nietzsche and Maeterlinck had developed a fundamentally Western, subjectivist-modernist vision of art that exceeded not only the popular, carnivalesque sensibility, but the ritualistic as well.

One wonders if we inhabitants of Western culture are capable of contemplating the mask or the marionette from either a popular or even a ritualistic

185

point of view, since our post-romantic civilizations have been cut off from both. Does the funeral mask of a "primitive" African tribe or the ceremonial mask of a Chinese dancer enclose an empty space for the indigenous spectator? Do they represent the gateway to some metaphysical abyss? Do they instill metaphysical, ontological fear rather than spiritual awe, as I believe they do for the Western spectator?[34] In accord with Bakhtin's theory, our turn-of-the-century subjectivist symbolism spawned first the hyper-marionette (*Übermarionette*), then an increasingly hypersubjective response to mask and marionette. It also cleared the way toward the creation and the reception of a hypersubjective type of marionette-like character. So what does the marionette do for contemporary spectators, creators, and scholars of theatre? Today the marionette's metatheatricality definitely has acquired a new twist, one profoundly associated with the image of the empty abyss, the double of the stage.

The marionette is not simply an object and it is certainly not human; but, as an inanimate icon of life, it can function as a dramatic character, though a less-than-human one. When a dramatic character is marionettized or marionette-like, it signifies something less than *naturally* human; but to say that a dramatic character is marionette-like could mean a wide range of things, because the marionette figure can convey a wide range of meanings. When representing a dramatic character, the inert but highly versatile marionette can present an acrobatic tour de force or it can create a formidable vertical presence; it can "talk" (with the help of a human voice) or remain silent; it can smile, smirk, or frown; and some theorists and practitioners believe it can do any of these things more effectively than the human actor. To be sure, the art of the harlequinade, the acrobatic and kinesthetic style of the marionette, is still strong today and quite evident on stage and screen. Nevertheless, in the "high-culture" theatre of the twentieth century, the text-based theatre that one reads more frequently in university classes and sees more frequently in the government-sponsored national theatres of Europe, the marionette-like figure has taken on a formalistic, metaphysico-metatheatrical, aesthetic allure, one which was probably inconceivable in the sixteenth and seventeenth centuries when the *commedia* was in full bloom. Reflecting the Harlequin–Pierrot dichotomy, today the marionette figure has the capacity to work in one of two very different aesthetic modes. The famous silent actors, Charlie Chaplin and Buster Keaton, who to this day likely are more celebrated in Europe than on this side of the ocean, owe much of their fame to their hybrid ability to move from one marionette-like mode to another, from superhuman acrobat to tragic doll. At its most extreme, the tragic doll assumes an asocial and ahuman allure; it antagonizes the social nature of the civilized human individual. Critics, especially American critics, have not considered seriously the distinction between these two modes; so most who write on or around the *commedia* do not openly acknowledge the two styles.[35] What can we add to this discussion of what produces this allure, best described as the image of a tragic doll? What do critics see in this type of humanoid figure?

The critical, intellectual, and phenomenological interest of the French in the *commedia* is equal to their interest in the art of the marionette. In France, the Italian *commedia* thrived in the sixteenth and seventeenth centuries; and the *commedia* character eventually was appropriated into the French Pierrot in the eighteenth century. It is no coincidence that France is also the country where nouveau théâtre saw its greatest success. (As we have seen, the transmutational birth of Pierrot represents an essential shift in the image of the *commedia* character; and this is the marionette-like image that was most appealing to dramatists of nouveau théâtre.) French intellectuals, theatre scholars, and practitioners alike view the marionette as an alien aesthetic being capable of enormous metatheatrical power.[36] One of the most widely held views is the metatheatrical notion of the marionette as a theatrical icon that represents pure role, pure image. Unlike the human and personal flesh-and-blood character, the marionette figure makes a direct statement about theatre *as* theatre. In fact, many scholars view it as a kind of corporal "mini-stage."[37] This aspect of the theatricality of the marionette helps diagnose Gordon Craig's enchantment with the unity of expression that, in his opinion, could only be attained by the "Übermarionette." Craig certainly inherited Maeterlinck's disdain for the human actor, feeling that the human body, with a personality—or personal psyche—of its own, tended to distort the formal purity of the aesthetic image.[38] Since his time, French scholars have elaborated on this position in the wake of formalist and semiotic theory. Annie Gilles, for example, writes that:

> Marionettes are not like actors, who confer their own corporal reality on the fictional characters they play. They are truly pretense, simulacra that are not what they evoke, but signs. . . . they are indicators of fiction. . . . they are no more than signifiers of humans. (16–17)

Thus, for the contemporary scholar, marionettes become the corporeal equivalent of Alfred Jarry's idea of how the stage should function as a *Nulle Part* ("Discours" 21). The nature of the marionette joins with the duplicitous, self-conscious nature of the stage: whereas the stage is more a signifier of space than it is any real place, the marionette is not a human individual but a paradoxical signifier of the human.

The conceptual correspondence between the theatricality of the marionette form and that of the stage space is particularly tenable when we compare the artistic form and the artistic space from the angle of aesthetic self-consciousness. In the second half of the twentieth century, the stage, which up to this point conventionally had been considered a non-space that signified a "real" place, began to unveil its artistic value as a non-functional non-space whose primary mission was to explore its creative value as a non-space, as a *Nulle Part*. As for the form that inhabits the stage, up to this century, the dramatic character in the text was generally destined to be incarnated by a human actor: one human being signifies another (scripted) human being who is either entirely fictional (as in the naturalistic drama of, say, Strindberg) or a fictional-historical-mythical composite (as in the romantic theatre of, say, Hugo). The human actor does indeed *incarnate* the character, whereas the marionette disincarnates, iconizes, plasticizes, and denaturalizes it. Both the costumed human actor and the marionette are, to a certain degree, icons for the human character; they both resemble and stand for an obviously fictional (non-)being. But the human actor cannot help to signify simultaneously as a real human being as well as a sign.[39] Because of the metatheatrical component of its figurative nature, the marionette is the true icon, and in this sense, the more truly theatrical. Consequently, the naturalized character represented by a human actor is less than a "true" icon of life because it is life, and the marionette-like character is closer to the signifying work, closer to pure signification. So the dramatic character conveying a marionette-likeness is a co-extensive step in the metatheatrical direction of the self-referential stage space. Furthermore, since we must add to the phenomenon of the self-referential, metatheatrical bond between stage and human icon the metaphysical ingredient of emptiness, the marionette-like character is also a step in the direction of the supra-representational and the supra-referential. The modernist-subjectivist vision imposed an impression of emptiness within the coextensive, coterminous envelopes of stage and body.

So it is that scholars refer to the strangeness of the marionette in strange, rather metaphysical and extra-referential ways, the metatheatrical being part and parcel of the metaphysical. The mystery generally is more closely associated with the likes of Pierrot than with Harlequin. Brunela Eruli sees the marionette's presence as striking, to say the least. Evidently agreeing with Annie Gilles, she finds that the image of the marionette is "Second-degree imitation.... This body whose functions are entirely theatrical seems above all the place of an imitation of reality." "But," she is hasty to warn "the referent is unknown, elusive." The marionette stands out like a three-dimensional dinosaur. It is a "unique presence" [*une présence à part*] ("Ruptures" 7), and an "in-between space [*lieu de l'entre-deux*].... a hybrid body" (11).[40] More prosaically, Philippe Découflé has called it "a form that moves" (62). This "form that moves" for which "the referent is unknown," is both strange and exciting to the twentieth-century critical eye, which cannot help but see it as a pure, hollow, ultimately empty form. Thus, the American Martin Green has expressed his belief that the marionette is one form among others (circus, carnival, freak shows, etc.) that is linked to the *commedia* as distinct from legitimate theatre. He cites Duchartre's description of the marionette theatre as "the last vestige of the *commedia*" and, remarking that marionettes "represent the idea of stereotypes more clearly than any other form," Green obliquely refers to the denaturalization of this figure by hitting on what I believe to be the epitome of a contemporary view of the marionette: "[The marionette's] inhumanity constitutes a hollow space, inside which the human meanings reverberate and swell to thunder, and the audience that identifies with them feels those meanings become larger than life" (19–20). This is it in a (hollow) nutshell, the perception of the marionette figure as an empty space.

In the twentieth century, when the stage became emptier and emptier, the spectator's perception of the dramatic character was radically altered. The stage also came to more closely resemble not only the idea of the marionette, but the very idea of dramatic character as well. Without the detail, the "flesh," of the setting, the stage becomes as it were an "organless" envelope of space—"organless," because, despite its emptiness, despite its relative freedom from the competing sign systems of scenery and objects, it remains a designated three-dimensional playing area (*aire de jeu*, as the French would say). This had to affect the way in which the spectator would perceive the dramatic character within the space. One important shift in perception is the tendency to relate the emptiness of the stage to the character, who we could see as a kind of empty envelope, or a *mise en abyme* of the parameters of the surrounding empty space. In conjunction with his idea of the stage as a *Nulle Part*, the pataphysician Alfred Jarry extended the idea of emptiness to the dramatic character. He claims that, through the use of a mask enclosing his head, the actor should attempt to attain "the effigy of the CHARACTER" ("De l'inutilité" 142). For Jarry, this impassivity of the mask was comparable to the "minerality of the skeleton hidden beneath the animal flesh" in its tragicomic effect (143). So the effigy would be deemed organless, as empty as a skeleton, or as an *Übermarionette*.

The dramatists of French nouveau théâtre took up this challenge at the level of the dramatic text. Quite appropriately, then, Marie-Claude Hubert says of the character in Ionesco's theatre: "this envelope that hides only emptiness, is alone perceptible" (*Langage et corps fantasmé* 67). Hubert's argument suggests that the primary function of the space of nouveau théâtre is not to present action but to "extend the body of the character" (68). Conversely, the more or less hollow body extends the space of the stage. Emptiness becomes a very potent form of metatheatricality.

The empty body of the dramatic character is at once an extension of the stage space, a theatrical form within a form (envelope within an envelope), and a figure for the empty mind, i.e., a further extension of the empty stage. The marionette's figural, formal capacity to construct a space within a space is clear. Its configured, tangible presence is especially effective when situated within an essentially empty space.[41] If some scholars and practitioners view the marionette as an empty body, others extend the metaphor to the mind-space, making it clear that the empty envelope draws attention to the head.[42] Roger-Daniel Bensky, for example, argues that

> In his struggle to manifest his being, the marionette . . . must concentrate to a supreme degree the symbolic value of his expressions. For his part, the spectator must furnish a very intense effort to project onto the doll his subjective universe. The concerted action of these two psychic "courants" creates a veritable magnetic field that privileges hallucination. (64–65)

In accord with his idea of the hallucinatory effect of the marionette, Bensky cites Tancrède de Visan, who, referring to his experience with the guignol theatre, argued that, "From the animated puppet there emanates a sort of psychic irradiation, an enormous power of suggestion" (66). Bensky concludes: "Hypnosis, psychic irradiation, suggestion: these are the elements that are supposed to constitute the fascination exerted by the marionette" (66). The spectator is extraordinarily fixated on the image of the marionette, and he projects onto this figure the degree zero of referentiality, the *mise en abyme* of the *Nulle Part* of the stage.

Thus, the denaturalizing process of the marionette-like character begins with ostension, the conscious intention of the author/text to put the figure on display, or, more precisely, an aberrant display of and focus on the figure. To figure prominently is to disfigure—the reference to social context is "ostensibly" severed and the focus shifts to the metadramatic figure as a signifier of psychic irradiation/penetration deep within the borders of the stage. On the empty stage, the signifier produces an ultimately hollow echo that phenomenologically irradiates to the spectator the image of an empty psyche. The apparent dramaturgical objective is to cause the spectator to cross the border from a "world of reference" to the extensive, empty, suprareferential world of signal-like thought.

Though scholars have argued the significance of the emptiness of Beckett's stage and the significance of the body within the stage, they have largely ignored the reflective emptiness of the dramatic character, a process that, we have seen, helps to explain both the marionette-likeness of the character and the metatheatrical nature of the work.[43] Because scholars have emphasized the *exterior,* automaton quality of the marionette-like character, they primarily have discussed the impression of an absence of thought in this character in terms of a lack of personality and intentionality, pointing to the external evidence of the absence of intentionality and personality rather than to the suggestion of the interior image. It is, of course, my interest to open up the interpretation of the forms of this theatrical figure to include the suggestion of metadramatic emptiness. It is not so much the automaton movement of the character as its relative immobility that orients our "empty" perception of the image.

Immobility is one of the principle denaturalizing, marionette-like traits that I cited above for the hypersubjective character. It compliments the strategies of emptiness and silence in hypersubjective theatre. The human actor can never attain either the acrobatics of the marionette or its superb immobility. We remember that the hypersubjective marionettes of *nouveau théâtre* find their most powerful signifying presence in some form of immobility. Progressive inactivity characterizes all the plays of this study; and the bulk of the "movement" at the conclusion of Beckett's late plays is operated by a lighting effect that focuses on the headspace of a stationary character transfixed by the inner "activity" of his or her mind. In his study of the body in Beckett's theatre, Pierre Chabert addresses the important topic of immobility, making it clear that in Beckett's works it is a paradoxical, complex strategy: "In eliminating all the customary properties pertaining to the body, Beckett reaffirms the irreducibility of the body, and reminds us that it remains an agent of disclosure" ("The body in Beckett's theatre" 27). "In Beckett," he explains, "immobility becomes a scenic entity" (24), so the Beckettian actor's gestures and movements "must always be seen to arise out of immobility and return to it" (26). In another essay, Chabert explains that, in short, the "apparent immobility" in Beckett's theatre "provides an unusual perception, a totally new vision of the body" ("Samuel Beckett: lieu physique, théâtre du corps" 93). Chabert concludes his argument concerning the immobile body with the following sentence: "Mind becomes body" [*L'Esprit fait corps*] (97). This summons not only the images of Hamm, Winnie, Mouth, and W, but also those of the other hypersubjective protagonists of this study, including Obaldia's Cancre: one striking irreducible image that draws us deep within the empty, radically focused field of the stage.

In a sense, Beckett articulated for the stage what Alberto Giacometti designed in sculpture. In an article titled the "Poetics of immobility," Pedro Kadivar identifies for the concept and phenomenon of immobility what my study has attempted to demonstrate for emptiness: its dynamic, hypermeaningful potential. Through the example of Giacometti's sculpture, particularly *Man walking*, Kadivar explains that paradoxically, Giacometti has endowed this seemingly static work with "not a fraction of movement but all movement in its essence, its origin, its impulsion" (12). In tune with the "dense" form of emptiness that Beckett designs for the stage, this is a dense form of immobility, which, Kadivar assures us, has nothing to do with the sentiments of either revolt, submission, or resignation. In speaking of the immobility of the gaze [*regard*], he says that it is "the very opposite of resignation and impotence in that it is the maximum attention accorded to the world" (13). It is, in fact, the "excessive glance" [*l'excès du regard*] that commands the attention of the beholder (14). Likewise, the immobility of body and the fixed glance of the head of the dramatic character draw the attention of the spectator toward an inner empty space.[44] Referring to Plato's writings, Kadivar argues that "The immobile body is not inanimate, it receives its movement from the inside. . . . Immobility summons up emptiness. To sustain immobility is to refuse any voluntary manifestation of life. . . . It is to accept the void and to heed the barely audible yet powerful murmur of life" (16). Immobility joins silence to complete the *mise en abyme* of empty space. Thus, instead of communicating the referential, the immobility of a live marionette-like character on stage co-operates with silence to "point toward" the mystery of the supra-referential by sustaining our intense focus . . . on emptiness.

Having dealt more at length with the question of *how* nouveau dramatists have created hypersubjects, in this brief conclusion I reconsider the question of *why* they have created them. I will also attempt to summarize the place of the "empty" protagonist with respect to what came before it and what might come after it. I have no doubt that, after all the critical debris has settled, the future will judge the hypersubjective work of Beckett et al. to be a revolutionary, extreme, "hyper" form of realism, a necessarily contradictory and antithetical, "extra-socially social" form of realism.

In the beginning of Western drama, Aristotle's formula for the perfect tragedy involved man *acting* in a mythico-political environment. In Aristotle's world there was a *logical* sense of justice and meaning associated with the immediate political reality.[1] Two millennia later, through a world view that has exceeded conventional, logical meaning, Beckett's formula involves man/woman *contemplating* emptiness while situated in an empty space. Beckett's great dramaturgical challenge was how to present both the act of contemplation and the empty mental space and how to draw the spectator's imagination into the act and the space. Between Aristotle and Beckett, there was Shakespeare. The hypersubjective dramaturgical project, especially in its most developed form in Beckett and Bernhard, was equal in artistic innovation, theatricality, and existential and social relevance to Shakespeare's dramatic work. Shakespeare created a highly innovative dramatic form that questioned the social and artistic logic and conventions to which

Aristotle subscribed. Without Shakespeare, twentieth-century theatre could not have reconciled itself so creatively with emptiness and meaninglessness. Unlike Beckett, however, Shakespeare did not propose to transcend language, and his protagonists still occupied an existential position between heaven and earth. They onto-logically questioned the logic of language and reality, fostering turbulent political situations and exhausting their physical and intellectual energies in the process: "A horse! a horse! my kingdom for a horse!" Connected to history, their thoughts and behavior always evolved into a sense of an ending and a new beginning. Even as they questioned reality, Shakespeare's rulers were learning to govern and their subjects were learning to become ever more civilized and socialized in this absurd world. These characters carried on their stage business through an elaborate use of "words, words, words" (*Hamlet* II, ii), words which provided fodder—brilliant and complex schemes—for explorations into human psychology, collective as well as individual: Shakespeare was a genius at weaving and unraveling the most intricate web of human relations.

But the words of Shakespeare's text, issuing from his protagonists' minds, obscured the image of the body as a form as well as the mind as a space. In *Hamlet* we have the material image of an empty human skull ("Alas, poor Yorick!"); but Hamlet's task was not to evoke the virtual space of the empty psyche; the skull is not yet the metaphorical showcase for, at once, the empty human icon and the theatre of the mind. It has not yet become—as it became quite literally in Beckett's *Endgame*—wholly equal to the empty stage. It is instead a metaphor for the mysterious—yet linguistically reproducible—search for the meaning of life through the meaning of language. Like Antonin Artaud, Shakespeare had a vivid vision of the organic relationship between life and theatre; but he did not see the void at the center of the stage and life. In Shakespeare, the theatricality of the mind was limited to the linguistic mental space. All the world was a stage, but the mind was not so much a theatrical locus as a source of inspiration, anguish, and cruelty:

> . . . O Lear, Lear, Lear!
> Beat at this gate that let thy folly in [*Striking his head*]
> And thy dear judgment out. Go, go, my people. (*King Lear* I, iv)

Antonin Artaud rejected wholesale Shakespeare's theatre because Shakespeare filled the void. Artaud knew that the system of language presented a peril to art, because it placed the emphasis on the word as a signified rather than as a free falling, free-wheeling signifier. Like Artaud, Beckett understood that too many words, as well as the narrative template that links them, close the empty gaps between them, covering up the important reception of the empty space of the mind. In addition, the more Beckett rid the stage of objects and infrastructural detail, and the more he emptied the human body—or human icon—on the stage of narrative content, the more we perceived that body as space. When this body speaks a rarefied language, exudes a vacuous stare, or immobilizes itself at the center of a dark stage, the effect intensifies, and the body becomes a mind-space. At the end of the twentieth century we can still appreciate Shakespeare's genius; yet we also see that Shakespeare was, in essence, trapped by the binary network of language and by a human psychology based on this network. From Shakespeare to Beckett, the most hypertheatrical of Western drama progressed from the depiction of psychologically grounded human characters and stage space, to the post-romantic *Übermarionette*, and finally to extra-psychological empty space and unconnected thoughts of psyche. Both Shakespeare and Beckett had something profound to say about reality. Three centuries after Shakespeare, Beckett discovered an even deeper, extralinguistic reality.

Beckett manipulated referential language primarily to produce supra-referential visual imagery, imagery with a brand new, highly unusual connection to society. The continued existence of mystery in our daily lives presents evidence that we human individuals have not lost sight of our extra-referential psychic space, an integral part of our reality. In its now proverbial inward turn, theatrical art has the potential to become a picture of the mind's extended dark space, especially as it relates to the juncture between character and stage space: the character's dehumanization (its extra-referential nature) augments the image-in-ary nature of the stage's formal image. Contrary to what we might believe at first glance, however, there is something strangely realistic about this formalism, since, as Patrice Pavis puts it, "forms are never innocent" ("Parcours au bout du sens" 229). In this insightful essay on avant-garde experimentation in theatre production since the late 1970s, Pavis elaborates on the shift from story to image, or, more precisely, the shift from traditional forms of (mimetic and diegetic) narrativity, to the power of visual imagery. As part of his argument, he makes a case for the realistic nature of even the most metaphysical of aesthetic forms, such as the one I have outlined in this book. Through the example of a stage production by Richard Demarcy, Pavis argues that, since the 1970s, the primary aesthetic principles that structure stage imagery are multiplication, heterogeneity, and polysemy. Consequently, to respond to a veritable orgy of meaning production, the spectator is forcibly drawn into a new mode of reception of mise-en-scène. Of course, Pavis focuses on the work of the stage director rather than the playwright; and the imagery of the production in question is based more on material and technical complexity, as opposed to the apparent "textual" synchrony and congruity of the character–stage image I have discussed here. In addition, he curiously but not surprisingly claims that fragmentation plays a part in the composing of these images, believing that "fragmentation is often no longer experienced as alienating and strange, but as normative and almost comfortable" (227). Yet, Pavis's argument sheds light on the dominance of visual image in dramatic texts, and, in explaining the realistic nature of polysemic stage imagery, he concludes his essay on the side of concentration. For him, the "travail formel" (228) of contemporary polysemic theatre is not only metaphysical, i.e., it relates to some psychic, imaginary world, but it also relates integrally and directly to what we perceive as the real world:

> Perhaps it is time to approach theatrical representation as a subterranean discourse that, from the inside, changes our perception of the world, a world which is not only psychic and imaginary, but social, political, and economic as well. . . . Reading the forms of the imagery of our time: this is also one of theatre's objectives, a political objective, since ideology is found wherever we least expect to discover it . . . [I]mages too fashion our social unconscious and realism too is a question of form. (229)

If we accept Pavis's approach to formal image, we can apprehend the meta-theatrical, formal emptiness of stage and character in at least two socially oriented ways. On the one hand, as a product of our distinctly self-conscious century, the identity that Robert Langbaum claims "approaches zero" (137) in Beckett's theatre is not altogether the last vestige of a social identity; it is merely an outmoded, layered, and exterior form of social identity. On the other hand, since the formal emptiness of the character cannot exclude sociocultural or sociopolitical signification, since there is no such thing as a social vacuum either outside or inside the individual mind, nouveau théâtre dramatists like Beckett and Obaldia have discovered an intriguing and aesthetically fertile process to construct *antagonistic* models of a hypothetical vacuum. Philosophers from Lucretius to Bergson warn that reason abhors the void and will, paradoxically, attempt to "erase" it. As the nouveau théâtre playwrights moved away from the *rational*-realist realm of theatre, they demonstrated a desire to design theatrical images that can sustain the illusion of vacuum—and the paradoxical tension of the vacuum—that much longer. The artistic attempt to transcend or to erase ideology is, in some way, an ideological gesture—the most extreme one. In the words of Adorno, this artistic endeavor "is social primarily because it stands opposed to society." In other words, it only seems opposed to society when evaluated by prevailing scholarship. In the history of theatre, hypersubjective drama is the most extreme example of this endeavor.

Pavis concludes his essay by describing the final image of Demarcy's mise-en-scène, which, in Pavis's opinion, "summarizes the ensemble of scenic metaphor and recounts the end of the story in a single glance" (230). He calls this image a *"mise en abyme,"* an "apotheosis," "the moment where theatre turns into tableau, absolute space where all is *concentrated*. . . . the moment where reality signals to us one last time before disappearing forever" (230; my emphasis). I have argued, of course, that the consummate, concentrated image of the character–space relationship is present already within the hypersubjective texts I have examined, texts which have produced multiplicity and polysemy through the merely apparent simplicity of the empty marionette-like human icon, a form which functions as a *mise en abyme* of the stage-space: emptiness connecting emptiness, or, more to the point, the socially relevant emptiness of theatrical space connecting the socially relevant emptiness of dramatic character.

Emptiness in all its metaphorical manifestations, such as absolute death and nihilism, is the most naked and the most primitive of "truths," and its impossibility or its possibility is the most perplexing of thoughts. Since the beginnings of civilization, artists have created meaning, sensation, and impression through a wide range of artistic processes based on either the disguising or exposing of the empty subject. According to Nietzsche, we remember, the Greek tragedy was born as a "state of individuation" problem, it was an aesthetic response for the resistance of the individual to the "oneness" of all living things. The idea of "oneness" relates to emptiness. In essence, for two millennia Western drama primarily has pursued the construction of meaningful space out of emptiness, struggling to identify the individual against the background of oneness. With the empty space–empty character connection, Beckett, and dramatists like him, have discovered a new, more formal and truly theatrical, approach to emptiness, one which signifies metadramatically through the formal configuration and the spatial context of the essentially empty images instead of through their narrative content. Beckett's dramatic texts reflect the extralinguistic origin of human evolution, the reality that visual mental image precedes verbal language. The central image, that of a paradoxical human icon which both contemplates and represents emptiness, breaks through the artificial fullness of language and forces the spectator to confront the primordial void that underlies it. In nouveau théâtre, what the social body loses in identity the mind gains in theatricality, and therein lies the postmodern metatragedy.

Like the first painter to cover a canvas in black and give it a title, Beckett took a major risk in the production of theatre, especially since he knew that his theatregoing "clientèle" would have to pay to be held captive in a fixed seat and for a fixed period of time. His risk paid off. He developed the hypersubjective image to such a degree that we might skip a generation or two of dramatists and practitioners before someone comes along who can develop it even further. (Genius is truly precious and extreme forms are extremely rare.) Meanwhile let's keep an eye open for the avatars of the empty figure on the empty stage.

Introduction

1. "Nouveau théâtre" is an umbrella term for the avant-garde theatre movements of the 1950s, 1960s, and 1970s in France. It is meant to include the movements identified as "theatre of cruelty" (Artaud), "theatre of the absurd" (Esslin), "theatre of derision" (Jacquart), and the works of such dramatists as Beckett, Ionesco, Adamov, Genet, Arrabal, Vian, and Obaldia. See Geneviève Serreau's *Histoire du «nouveau théâtre»* (esp. 5–11) for an endorsement and explanation of this label. In order to focus on the theory behind the texts, in the chapters that follow, Samuel Beckett's dramatic works will serve as the quintessential paradigm of "hyper-subjective" nouveau théâtre, a term I will define in the discussion below.

2. This and all further translations from the original French are mine, unless otherwise noted.

3. The "supra" prefix aligns closely with the "hyper" and the "meta" prefixes (see below, note 5). Similar to the notion of the meta-physical and the hyper-theatrical, the supra-referential plane of human consciousness is creatively hypothesized by a conscious and ultimately artificial process that moves from the realm of the referential beyond the referential. While there is a remnant of the non-referential origin of human consciousness in all human thinkers and at all times, it is obscured, if not obliterated, by our referentially conditioned thought processes. Some art and some philosophy make an effort to reconnect us with the non-referential origin.

4. This also might help to explain the absence of female dramatists in this book. Female dramatists are disproportionately represented in postwar nouveau théâtre. In their authoritative works on nouveau théâtre neither Esslin, Corvin, nor Serreau

herself deals with any female authors. I would conjecture that until female authors achieve fully their own brand of "conventional," "realist" feminine drama (and sustain it), and until the more militant feminist authors have been able to neutralize the misdeeds of patriarchy, they will not excavate beyond and beneath the foundations of art and humanity in the universal way exemplified by hypersubjective works.

5. My use of "metaphysical" throughout this book emphasizes the "meta" prefix, one which, according to *Webster's Third New International Dictionary*, carries a range of meanings that are relevant to my study. "Meta" can suggest "situated behind" the physical (space, reality, language, etc.), or it can suggest "a specialized form of" or a "transformation of" the physical. It can also point to something that is "beyond" the physical, as with the term "metaphysical" that is "something that deals with what is beyond or the experimental." In this sense it relates closely, of course, to the "hyper-" (theatrical) and "supra-" (referential) terms I employ, and it suggests applications such as "metatheory," "metalanguage," and "metatheatre," which are concepts of a "higher logical type" that help us "deal critically with the nature, structure, or behavior of the original ones." The metaphysical nature of empty theatrical space is, at this point of the critical game, of a "higher logical type," because it "transcends" conventional and immediately comprehensible logic.

6. The representational-referential aspect of semiotics is probably best betrayed by the proposal of the highly reductive actantial model to account for the major representational forces of a given work. The purpose of introducing the actantial model in semiotics was to spatialize (graph) the principal forces of the work and to show their functions within the action. According to Patrice Pavis, the advantage of the actantial model is that "it no longer artificially separates the characters and the action, but reveals the dialectic and the progressive passage from one to the other" (*Dictionnaire du théâtre* 2). See also the chapter titled "Le modèle actantiel au théâtre" in Anne Ubersfeld's *Lire le théâtre 1* (53–97).

7. Bert States speaks of "the passage of the stage image into conventionality, or sign-hood. I suggest that conventions occur first as anticonventions, or antisigns (anti*studia* would do just as well)." He further suggests that the "antisign" becomes a sign by taking its place in the "informational circuitry. But how did it get there in the first place if not as an attempt to break into the circuit, to pester the circuit with nuance, to wound it with the resistance of its presence? In other words, it began as an image in which the known world was, in some sense, being recreated or revised out of its primal linguistic matter" (*Great Reckonings* 12). Unlike this concept of "antisign," the prelinguistic signal does not "attempt to break into the circuit."

8. One is reminded of Barthes's study of the art of photography, specifically his proposal of the *punctum* of the photographic image as opposed to the *studium*. The human icon on the stage is like the *punctum* in that it is not semiotizable or referential. But it differs from the *punctum* in that it certainly is not a detail of the image—though in hypersubjective theatrical images there may be details that tend to contribute to the phenomenological reading/awareness of the empty human psyche. The point is that the *punctum* is phenomenological rather than semiotic.

9. See my "Beyond the Structuralist Language-Space."

10. In the afterword of his book, Garner argues the phenomenological importance of the Derridean concept of deferral, which is really a part of the idea of suspension: "The concept of 'trace' has been appropriated not by phenomenologists, but by

poststructuralists, who have employed the term as a challenge to Husserlian and other ostensibly 'metaphysical' notions of presence. Derrida writes, 'The living present springs forth out of its nonidentity with itself and from the possibility of a retentional trace. It is always already a trace.' But . . . the recognition of traces and nonidentity is by no means at odds with the phenomenological project. Deferral signals not the closure of presence and subjectivity, but the *dis*closure of them in a new field of manifestation. Far from representing a movement beyond presence and subjectivity into some new arena, this disclosure establishes the terms with which the contemporary study of these phenomena may genuinely begin" (*Bodied Spaces* 229–30).

11. In his *The Tao of Physics*, Fritjof Capra explains how all our scientific theories and the "laws of nature" they produce are "limited and approximate": "Physicists have come to see that all their theories of natural phenomena, including the 'laws' they describe, are creations of the human mind; properties of our conceptual map of reality, rather than of reality itself. This conceptual scheme is necessarily limited and approximate" (287).

12. A metaphysical approach has allowed some theatre scholars to articulate hidden spiritual forces in the theatre, "spiritual" in the sense of theatre's connection to religion and religious ritual. This is the dimension that many scholars continue to explore in the writings of Artaud et al. Monique Borie's recent study, *Le Fantôme ou le théâtre qui doute,* is an example of this ultimately "spiritual" approach. But I want to take the metaphysical in a different direction, one which is not so historical and not connected to a discourse of ritual, religion, and death, i.e., of referential mythos. As complex as Artaud was, he was even metaphysically deeper than this. I hope to generate a sophisticated interest in emptiness *qua* emptiness, and not as a potential for some referential fullness.

1. Emptiness

1. For our Greek ancestors, chaos was a form of emptiness, as Rudolph Arnheim reminds us: "Chaos, from a Greek word referring to the 'yawning' abyss of the beginning, is described in the ancient myths as the original darkness, either empty or filled with shapeless matter. Ovid calls it a crude, unformed mass, nothing but an inert weight, the 'not well-joined' discord of the seeds of things" ("From Chaos to Wholeness" 117).

2. Foucault describes medieval space as "the space of emplacement" which was "a hierarchic ensemble of spaces" ("Of Other Spaces" 22).

3. Referring to our awareness and perception of space, Galileo and Foucault are simultaneously constructing a model for our awareness of psychic space. See my "Beyond the Structuralist Language-space," where I discuss Derrida's positing of psychic "space" as a "purely mechanical and chrono-logical *process* of space, space as *system*" (145). See also Erik MacDonald's discussion of Derrida's belief "that a 'text' is the primary structure of the psyche" (*Theater at the Margins* 1–2).

4. Cited in Hauck, *Reductionism and Drama in the Theatre*, 197, n. 34; author's emphasis throughout.

5. Emptiness also has social relevance in that it implies an alternative to the mundane materialism that gnaws away at our lives under late capitalism. It mocks

the wrongful, de facto denial that the best things in life are free and that the most creative, desirable, enrapturing thoughts in life are "empty."

6. According to Marie-Claude Hubert, "the stage became increasingly overloaded with useless signs from the end of the eighteenth century," and she cites Henri Michaux's highly critical comparison of the "illusionistic realism" of Western theatre with Asian theatre: "Only the Chinese know what a theatrical production is. For a long time, the Europeans have not been representing anything. They present everything. Everything is on the stage. Every thing, nothing is lacking, not even the view that one has from the window" (*Histoire de la scène occidentale* 114). Often, as Denis Bablet points out, with naturalism and with "academicism" the encumbered "fullness" of the stage was not connected to the meaning of the work, but only to the stage convention, a more or less gratuitous indulgence in scenography as an autonomous art (*The Revolution of Stage Design* 18–24).

7. Yet, for all the discussion of theatrical empty space since mid-century, I do not think we have come to appreciate fully empty space *qua* empty space. Keir Elam, for instance, states the following: "The stage is, in the first instance, an 'empty' space, to use Peter Brook's phrase (Brook 1968), distinguished from its surroundings by visible markers. . . . and potentially 'fillable' visually and acoustically" (*The Semiotics of Theatre and Drama* 194). Like Elam, most critics understand Peter Brook's definition of the stage as "empty space" solely in the sense that it is a "potentially fillable" space while ignoring the other—less naturalistic and infinitely more metatheatrical—sense in which the stage is seen as a potential vacuum in the midst of an irreverent world encumbered by the furnishings of rationalism.

8. Timothy Wiles illuminates another value of empty space, one which he believes is implied by Peter Brook's idea of empty space. From Brook's remark that "I can take any empty space and call it a bare stage," Wiles argues that Brook "points to a phenomenon of theatre architecture which has broader implications for our understanding of space in dramaturgy and in general aesthetics. Concern with empty space suggests the disavowal of an autonomous site of theatrical activity—a rejection of both the stage setting and of the auditorium, if the setting be understood as a scenic mimesis of some place other than what it is (a stage with decorations), and the auditorium be understood as an assembly hall set apart from the world and having no other function than that of paying homage to such mimesis. Instead of this separation, the empty space asks for a continuity between theatre event and life event—that is, it claims that the theatre event is a *kind* of life event, not a *copy* of one. And its more general aesthetic implication is to require us to pay as close attention to the empty space surrounding and shaped by the art object as we pay to the object itself" (*The Theater Event* 114; author's emphasis).

J. L. Styan, too, refers to the "belief that the *tréteau nu* would ensure that the play would seem to take place in the same room with its audience" (*Modern Drama in Theory and Practice* 2: 98). He also reminds us that symbolism, as we sense it, is very much a part of the "exhibitionist" nature of theatrical art, so it is "easy to see how drama moves easily from realism to symbolism, and it is significant that each of the great nineteenth-century naturalists, Ibsen, Strindberg, Hauptmann, and Chekhov, chose a more symbolic expression at the very time when he had apparently succeeded in being rigorously realistic. A symbolic stage can pass easily into surrealism and the absurd, and both the ancient and modern theaters have shown that when the creative impulse touches the deepest feelings we all share, drama can ignore realism entirely and move into ritual" (2: 1–2). Consequently, he argues that "Absurdist plays fall within the symbolist tradition, and they have no logical plot or characterization in any conventional sense" (2: 126).

9. McGuinness discusses Mallarmé's concept of the "theatre of the mind" as an entity that is perhaps more mechanical than metaphysical. For Mallarmé, the act of reading was a theatrical act in which the reader stages the imaginary space of the text. McGuinness says that, for Mallarmé: "Theatre and theatricality exist independently, they inhere in the mind as a faculty of thought, the inner theatre is the 'prototype du reste'. This 'théâtre inhérent à l'esprit' (*OC* 328) does not necessitate a real space or the various imaginative 'points d'appui' around which to form itself, be these fireplaces, empty frames, windowpanes or whatever. This is because they are not the models on which the inner theatre is based but the inferior material *replicas* of a way of thinking *already operative* in the poet's mind" ("From Page to Stage" 26; author's emphasis).

10. Bablet quotes the Russian director A. Tairov, speaking of his 1933 production of *The Optimistic Tragedy* by V. Vishnevsky at the Kamerny Theatre in Moscow: "When we say that 'simplicity is indispensable,' in all of our works and in this one in particular, we are thinking of a kind of simplicity that is the result of enormous effort, of a simplicity that is precise, crystal clear and directly reaches the spectator" (*The Revolution of Stage Design* 122; note to illustration number 218).

11. We can see the quest for symbolic simplification in the expressionist work of the Bauhaus Theatre under the direction of Otto Schlemmer in the 1920s. Symbolic simplicity was largely played out by an emphasis on architectural space, the human icon, and stylized gesture. Schlemmer comments on space and body in abecedarian, wholly conscious terms: "Begin with space, its laws and mysteries and let yourself be 'bewitched' by them. . . . Begin with the positions of the body, from its simple presence to the positions of standing, walking and finally leaping and dancing" (cited in Bablet's *Revolution of Stage Design*, 199). Schlemmer's ideas resonate in the titles of his creations, such as "Space Drama" and "Figure in Space" (1924). According to J. L. Styan, "Schlemmer conceived of the stage as a sculptor might, using actors as architectural and mechanical robots to 'transfigure the human form.' Costumes and masks were geometrical in appearance, and gesture and movement were angular and staccato, as if made by a clockwork mechanism. Acting was seen as a spatial form, to be designed and lit like the dance" (*Modern Drama in Theory and Practice* 3: 138). Thus the human figure increasingly became a human icon intimately fused with space and into the meaning of space.

12. R. E. Jones, the distinguished American stage designer of the early twentieth century, wrote that "The setting must be created for the mind's eye. There is the outer eye which observes and an inner eye which sees. . . . The designer must be careful not to be too explicit. A good setting, I repeat, is not a picture. It is something seen, but it is also something suggested: an emotion, an evocation. Plato said somewhere: It is beauty I seek, not beautiful things" (cited in Bablet's *Revolution of Stage Design* 240). This metaphor/metonymy of the "mind's eye" is of particular interest here. It suggests that we use our eyes as a door to the mind, and that we should not take the utilitarian, mediatory role of our eyes for granted. It also suggests direct perception, meaning that the mind is truly an *eye* in and of itself, one which creates a space. Finally, it implies the corporeal aspect of the mind, the phenomenological eye.

13. Cited in Monique Surel-Tupin's "L'Espace théâtral chez Copeau," 73.

14. The increased prominence—and therefore increased responsibility—of the actor on an empty stage is not new for this century, of course. Bert States, for example, raises the issue that the chief virtue of the Elizabethan stage was its "tabula rasa on which the actor could draw the ever-shifting pictures of text" (*Great Reckonings* 56).

15. In his essay on the themes of the symbol, Tzvetan Todorov explains that with the Romantic movement imitation (representation) was abandoned and production (presentation) was adopted as the chief end of art. It is with the *crise romantique* that imitation comes to an end as an art form, and that, in the Romantic view, imitation was no longer evident in the work of art, but only in the activity of the artist as creator, imitating the creative aspect of nature (God the creator). Contributing to the demise of mimesis in this sense was that, during the Romantic period, the irrational character of art predominated: "art expresses something that one cannot express in any other way" (*Théorie du symbole* 225). What is more, according to Todorov, it is here that the word "symbol" takes on a radically new meaning. The neo-Romantic aesthetic radiates from the symbol (235), which opposes the classical, rhetorical category of allegory—a category that is evidently more productive of the mimetic form. According to Todorov, unlike the allegory, the symbol signifies indirectly, it addresses perception and not intellection. It is non-utilitarian, non-functional and (curiously) unconventional in the sense that it is born of the "natural" (236–40). The Romantic movement diverts attention from imitation (works are determined by their referent, which is the world) to production (353). If the outer world no longer provides the referent, the poet turns to the productive inner world. The inward turn begins with the Romantic movement.

16. *La Poétique,* translated and annotated by Roselyne Dupont-Roc and Jean Lallot.

17. This "distance" is what Dupont-Roc and Lallot call *le recul de la fiction* (*La Poétique* 21).

18. Anne Ubersfeld argues that, in the most naturalistic, illusionist types of theatre, there is the "pleasure of the copy": "Theatrical space can be constructed in order to give the spectator the pleasure of the copy, of the representation, and if possible, of the unrepresentable" (*L'Ecole* 66). In the case of the most precisely elaborated reproduction or illusion (Ubersfeld offers the example of a staged volcanic eruption) a pleasure results from "the play between the ingenuity of the fabrication of programmed stimulation and the presence of concrete elements that are rare or difficult to obtain (live animals: horses or wild animals, strange or luxurious costumes). . . . this pleasure of the 'difficult figuration'" (66–67).

19. For an interesting examination of theatrical self-consciousness see Susan Wittig, "Toward a Semiotic Theory of Drama." She argues that "*all* artistic drama is metatheatre, drama cast in a self-conscious medium" (453).

20. Writing on the aesthetic reception of puppets and masks in the Bread and Puppet Theatre, Stephan Brecht argues as follows: "A mask . . . gives its life and its identity to the wearer of it. He or she becomes it, and all the wearer's vivacity is constrained within the bond of its inanimation. . . . when a person puts on a mask, the transformation is astounding, in fact, unbelievable. . . .

"The mask is a false face. The perceptor's conflict is between the illusion that it is a face and the knowledge that it isn't. This conflict makes encounter with a masked person delicious. . . . [T]he conflict in the case of the mask is metaphysical inasmuch as it raises the question of what a face is and whether it is what it is usually considered to be" (*The Bread and Puppet Theatre* 17–18).

21. David Grossvogel remarks on this unique relationship between theatre and life in his comments on the uniqueness of the human gesture in dramatic art: "the human gesture is its own ultimate extension and can be apprehended immediately by the human participant (spectator) without the imposition of thought and arte-fact. . . . Only one instrument is equal to the complexity and the sensitivity of man, that instrument is the theatre's own, the identical human being *within* the actor" (*Four Playwrights and a Postscript* 180).

22. The socio-aesthetician Jean Duvignaud discusses this as a dialectic between theatre and society: "Is not society theatrical and is not existence revealed through the duality it operates to represent itself?" (*Sociologie du théâtre* 5).

23. In Boal's theory, self-observation is one of three essential properties that constitute the "extraordinary gnoseological (knowledge-enhancing) power of the-atre": "1) plasticity, which allows and induces the unfettered exercise of memory and imagination, the free play of past and future; 2) the division or doubling of self which occurs in the subject who comes on stage, the fruit of the dichotomic and 'dichotomising' character of the 'platform', which allows—and enables—self obser-vation; 3) finally, theatre's telemicroscopic property which magnifies everything and makes everything present, allowing us to see things which, without it, in smaller or more distant form, would escape our gaze" (*Rainbow* 28). Boal probably refers to film when he speaks of a "smaller or distant form" that lacks this "telemicroscopic" property.

24. These theories of the connection between creative, re-creative, dynamic the-atrical production and life process are reflected as well in the theories of perfor-mance of the anthropologist Victor Turner. For Turner, performance is a kind of ritual text whose primary task is not so much to imitate culture as to produce it, to form a productive part of cultural process. See especially his comparison of "poiesis" with mimesis as the difference between "making" (poiesis) and "faking" (mimesis) (*From Ritual to Theatre* 93).

25. We are once again reminded of Mallarmé's thoughts on the theatricalization of the reading process. Philippe Sollers assures us that Mallarmé believed deeply in the "theatricality" of the reading process, amounting to the idea that, to be effective, the fictional form of a given text must somehow transform into a "theatrical form." Indeed, it is only in this way that the text can become a "part of life": "The book is nothing more than the passage from world to theatre, the theatrical apparition of the world as text, the 'raw exposure of thought,' the operation: not one work among others but the implementation of everything that is" (cited in Sollers, *L'écriture et l'expérience des limites* 82). According to Sollers, Mallarmé is affirming the existence of a "theatre inherent to mind": "In reading, we can perform any play 'within.' But if we want to become aware of the writing that is this reading, we must go through the stage (through life)" (84–85).

26. As an example of this obsession with illusion Abirached refers to the theory of the "fourth wall" proposed by Diderot. In order that the "comme si" ("as if"—illusion) be more effective, the actors on the stage must forget the spectator, pretending that the curtain had never risen (*La Crise du personnage dans le théâtre moderne* 108).

27. "Profitable" in the sense that individuals with a strong concern for their individuality actually make much better consumers and are much easier to exploit commercially than individuals with a greater respect for a collective identity and for a more collective consumption.

28. In correlation to the concept of "interior world" versus "exterior world" Elizabeth Burns has discussed theatricality in terms of the production of a reality that is "present" rather than "past": "Although all forms of fiction are imitation, dramatic representation of action is the most complete as it rests on the assumption that the peopled dramatic world is autonomous and represents a temporary reality equivalent in its significance—its consequentiality—to that of the social world outside the theatre. By being acted out here and now it claims to belong to the present rather than the past" (*Theatricality* 14). The theatre is as concerned with the actuality of its own fiction (present) as it is with the history of its mimetic model (past). It is evident that, for Burns, the autonomous "temporary reality" of the "peopled dramatic world" belongs to a "present" that opposes the "past" tense of other fictional art forms which rely on an "exterior" aspect to survive: the written page, the plastic image. The imaginative reality of theatre remains *present* because it is actualized within the interior self-consciousness of the theatre. The theatre that "knows that it is a play" also knows that its plastic image, its exteriority, can only be present in the present tense, so to speak. Thus the imaginative reality of theatre is indeed more directly related to the fiction. Cut off from the past, it is equally more self-concentrated.

29. In his work on the "metatragedy" of Euripedes's *Bacchae*, Charles Segal speaks of the "paradoxical nature of tragedy . . . paradoxical, because by creating illusion tragedy seeks to convey the truth; by causing us to lose ourselves it gives us a deeper sense of ourselves, and by representing events filled with the most intense pain it gives us pleasure." Part of this pleasure is the "metatragic dimension" of the *Bacchae* which Segal describes as the "self-conscious reflection of the dramatist on the theatricality and illusion-inducing power of his own work, on the range and the limits of the truth that the dramatic fiction can convey" (*Dionysiac Poetics and Euripedes' Bacchae* 216). With this in mind, we can say that the nouveau théâtre dramatists deal with a more complex paradox. The hypertheatricality of this theatre goes so far as to develop the important parallel between the theatrical work and the social subject.

30. The emphasis is mine throughout this citation.

31. Victor Turner writes on the liminal nature of performance that leads to cultural renewal. He explains cultural renewal, that is, the passage from an older and possibly obsolete cultural form to a new one as "a unidirectional move from the *'indicative'* mood of cultural process, through culture's *'subjunctive'* mood back to the *'indicative'* mood, though this recovered mood has now been tempered, even transformed by immersion in subjunctivity. . . . The subjunctive, according to Webster's Dictionary, is always concerned with 'wish, desire, possibility, or hypothesis'; it is a world of 'as if,' ranging from scientific hypothesis to festive fantasy. It is 'if it *were* so,' not 'it is so'" (*From Ritual to Theatre* 82–83; author's emphasis).

2. Surrealist Inner Space

1. Bearing in mind Ubersfeld's point that theatrical space never represents the world, but the "image of an image" of an essentially imaginary space, we can hypothesize

four possible points of reference for a given theatrical space: 1) as a metaphysical–imaginary reflection of the outer universe (classical Greek theatre); 2) as an empirical reflection of an outer world 3) as an inner space reflecting a self-reflective human individual reflecting an outer world—this might include the psychoanalytical model; and 4) as a metaphysical–imaginary inner space reflecting the extended universe.

2. Despite the many examples of memorable, fantastic, visual imagery created by some early-twentieth-century surrealist playwrights such as Apollinaire and Cocteau, most critics stress verbal and not visual inventiveness, because they believe that the process of automatic writing anchors all of surrealist theoretical as well as creative writing. Consequently, Martin Esslin declares surrealism to be no less than untheatrical: "In the theatre, the harvest of surrealism proved a meager one. The stage is far too deliberate an art form to allow complete automatism in the composition of plays" (*Theatre of the Absurd* 379). In his introduction to an anthology of dadaist and surrealist plays, Michael Benedikt stresses the connection between automatic writing and psychoanalysis: "Here [Breton] couched his definition of surrealism strictly in terms of psychiatric technique, drawing a literary parallel" (*The Avant-Garde, Dada, and Surrealism* xxiii). Remarking that Aragon's theatrical work demonstrates an "increasing stress on purely verbal inventiveness," Benedikt reminds us that "the most adventurous of the playwrights who followed Jarry were in fact poets: with Appolinaire, Cocteau, Radiguet, Tzara, Aragon, Soupault, and Breton" (xxv). He characterizes dadaism and surrealism as a "tendency toward what is perhaps an ultimately untheatrical, purely verbal brilliance" (xxvi). J. H. Matthews also supports this view: "At the very least, Dada and surrealist writing for the stage demonstrates indifference to the medium of the play" (*Theatre in Dada and Surrealism* 10).

3. Zinder criticizes Marinetti, Tzara, and Breton, remarking that "even when they did write plays, they seemed to have 'forgotten' the three-dimensional, visual, and dynamic nature of theatre, and concentrated mostly on only one aspect of the theatrical communication: language" (*The Surrealist Connection* 126).

4. We recall the phenomenological merger of outside and inside within Merleau-Ponty's theory: "We have said that space is existential, we might just as well have said that existence is spatial, that is, that through an inner necessity it opens to an outside, so that we can speak of a mental space" (*Phenomenology of Perception* 293).

5. For the purposes of this discussion, inner space, mental space, psychic space, and inner psyche are all synonymous.

6. The phenomenologist Gaston Bachelard might have labeled this representation of the psyche a "poetic image" of empty space. Furthermore, in defining his concept of "poetic image," Bachelard expresses the hostility of this concept to psychoanalytic methodology, which tends to "intellectualize the image" (*Poétique* 7–8).

7. We too often and too simplistically view surrealist art as a depiction of a dream state for which psychoanalysis can provide a code. Jon Erikson has cautioned against this tendency, remarking that "The use the surrealists made of the unconscious is not the use intended by Freud, for instance. What for Freud was a ground for the determination of behavior was for the surrealists a ground for the possibility of freedom" (*The Fate of the Object* 36).

8. "We assume that mental life is the function of an apparatus to which we ascribe the characteristics of being extended in space and of being made up of several

portions—which we imagine, that is, as being like a telescope or microscope or something of the sort" (Freud, *An Outline of Psychoanalysis* 14). Freud's reference to a "telescope or microscope" suggests succession of imagery as well as concentration and concentric focus.

9. I prefer to translate "descente vertigineuse" of the original French text (*Manifestes du surréalisme* 41) as "vertiginous descent" rather than the "dizzying" descent of the translation at hand.

10. At one point in his writing Breton describes surrealism as "this tiny footbridge above the abyss" (*Manifestoes* 146), suggesting perhaps that he does not consider the abyss itself as surrealist space. But at another point Breton betrays a certain awe for emptiness at the same time he suggests the analogy between mind and "hole," the emptiness of which facilitates the "look beyond" so essential to the surrealist method: "As has been proved to me after the fact, the definition of surrealism given in the first Manifesto merely 'retouches' a great traditional saying concerning the necessity of 'breaking through the drumhead of reasoning reason and looking at the hole,' a procedure which will lead to the clarification of symbols that were once mysterious" (300).

11. For a more detailed discussion of the surrealist conceptualization of mind-space as an extralinguistic space where non-representational "signals" (instead of signs) occur, see my essay "Beyond the Structuralistic Language-Space of the Mind," esp. 9–13.

12. The French term *mise en abyme* refers to a fragment or analogical enclave within a work of art (pictorial, literary, theatrical) which contains the essential elements of the work and therefore reflects the work as a whole.

13. The metatheatrical dimension of this self-concentration is the very topic of conversation in Robert Pinget's *Abel et Bela*. Having just seen a play (for which the title is not given), the two characters of the drama, Abel and Bela, discuss the meaning of theatre. Referring both to theatre as an art and to the particular work of which they are a part, they comment on how they can render their own performances more dramatically profound. Abel proposes that the key is in self-concentration and "descent": "Concentrate. Descend" (33) and "Get deeper. Go down lower" (37). Bela then protests, "That isn't theatre, it's psycho-psychi" (37), and she undertakes to show that Abel himself has trouble descending into his "inner depths" [*tréfonds*]. But Abel defends his method remarking that "They have forgotten the transposition. Art transposes." "Well what about my inner depths?" insists Bela. "Let's forget about inner depth, and let's transpose," replies Abel (39). So we see here the suggestion that, like the surrealist mind, theatre must concentrate on its own space and descend its own (inner) depth, not to produce some psychological order, nor simply to reproduce psychic imagery, but to articulate the transpositional relationship between the psychic and the theatrical—only then can the theatrical become "psychic" and vice versa. The language of descent reappears quite concretely in Beckett's *Rockaby*, as we see in the next chapter.

14. Bal, who was only considering the use of the concept in the more symbolic rather than iconic art of narrative literature, argues that, while not all icons are cases of *mise en abyme*, all cases of *mise en abyme* are icons ("Mise en abyme et iconicité" 128). Recognizing the iconic link between this semiotic concept and the art of theatre, Maria Voda Capusan argues for the increased acceptance of the concept in theatre

studies: "Unlike literature where any *mise en abyme* can exist only in terms of language, the theatre is capable of preserving the specific code. . . . iconicity in the graphic sense of the term" ("Theatre and Reflexivity" 107).

15. See, for example, Anne Ubersfeld's explanation of the "weakening of the subject" in contemporary theatre (*Lire le théâtre* 93–94). And elsewhere, in her work on contemporary theatrical "myths," Monique Borie concludes that Beckettian theatre "tends toward the obliteration of both space and time" (*Mythe et théâtre aujourd'hui* 67). Similarly, Elizabeth Burns suggests that the theatrical space of authors belonging to the tradition of nouveau théâtre (Artaud, Genet, Beckett) signifies a "rejection of specific space" and consequently evokes an idea of "placelessness" because it represents more a "condition of the spirit than a physical area." Consequently, Burns finds that "place is irrelevant to Beckett's apparently existential view of the human condition" (*Theatricality* 87).

16. Take for example, the contemporary French dramatist and theatre critic Gérard Lepinois, who, in a poetic essay, affirms his intent to create—and the general need to create—protagonists, with a dramaturgical view toward the fusion of the "empty" body of the actor with the material emptiness of the theatrical space: "In space, the actor appears as a hole. / Object or man. / When you bring emptiness to existence, you engender a gap. / The actor appears against the reign of space. / The protagonist begets the antagonist. / *Space closes on a body that opens it up*" (*L'Action de l'espace* 15; my emphasis). For Lepinois, the primary function of the theatrical space is, in effect, to expand the extension of the spectator's imagination by focusing her attention on the *empty* body of the character. The body of the character orients at once theatrical empty space and the subjective corporeal awareness of the spectator. Thus theatrical empty space is oriented toward the dis-closure of universal, essentialist emptiness, which remains acknowledged but undefined.

17. Sidney Homan refers to Hamm as "hyperimaginative" and "hyperconscious" (*"Endgame:* The Playwright Completes Himself" 131, 142). This "hyper" terminology is also analogically consistent with Robert Abirached's idea of "hypertheatricality" (*l'hyperthéâtralité*) in French nouveau théâtre (*La Crise du personnage dans le théâtre moderne* 417–19). There is, of course, another sense of "hyper" that comes to mind, the one applied to the "hypercard" in computer technology, the idea of the stacking of windows, one upon another. This sense too is useful in that the theatrical windows—world, stage, mind—are stacked and the spectator will tend to focus alternatively on one or the other while aware that all are simultaneously present.

18. On the discussion of the theatricality/specificity of the dramatic text see esp. Pavis's "Le texte (é)mis en scène" (*Analyse des spectacles* 182–204), Worthen 's "Disciplines of the Text/Sites of Performance," Pavis's "Du texte à la scène," States's "Performance as Metaphor," and the special number of *Theatre Research International* on theatricality: Vol. 20:2 (Summer 1995).

19. Ubersfeld has described the dramatic text as characteristically more full of holes than other literary texts (*Lire le théâtre 1* 23). She refers, of course, to the dramatic text's necessarily schematic structure. The dramatic text does not present the same (tyrannical) illusion of completeness or wholeness that narrative texts do. At least since the art of mise-en-scène came into its own in the late nineteenth century, we consciously write and read drama as a regenerative process whose reception implies the generation of another (performance) text, the mise-en-scène. Because of the "holes" in the dramatic

text, reader reception becomes both more complex and more active. All readers of drama are in some way metteurs-en-scène, producing and spatializing stage as well as text in their minds. For a more detailed discussion of the reader reception of the dramatic text, see my "Teaching Literary-Dramatic Texts," esp. 24–27.

20. The instance of Patrice Chéreau's productions of Bernard Koltès's texts comes to mind. Despite his untimely death in 1989, Koltès was considered the leading French dramatist of the 1980s. He fervently defended the autonomy of the dramatic text and criticized overly creative directors who did not respect the original text. One of the most important French directors of the 1980s, Patrice Chéreau, has creatively mounted many classical French works; but, in the case of Koltès's rather verbose works, he apparently was content that Koltès regarded him as the ideal producer of his texts. They thoroughly admired one another's work.

21. On the importance of "ostension" and "framing" for the theatre, see, for example, Umberto Eco's essay "Interpreting Drama." Eco explains ostension as follows: "You ask me, *How should I be dressed for the party this evening?* If I answer by showing my tie framed by my jacket and say, *Like this, more or less,* I am signifying by ostension. My tie does not mean my actual tie but your possible tie (which can be of a different stuff and color) and I am 'performing' by representing to you the you of this evening. I am prescribing to you how you should look this evening. With this simple gesture I am doing something that is theater at its best, since I not only tell you something, but I also am offering you a model, giving you an order or a suggestion, outlining a utopia or a feasible project" (103).

22. See, for example, Emmanuel Jacquart (*Le théâtre de la dérision,* esp. 37) and Robert Abirached (*La Crise du personnage dans le théâtre moderne,* esp. 423–24), who argue that the texts of authors of nouveau théâtre (Beckett, Ionesco, and Adamov, et al.) show a clearer vision of the stage action and exert a greater control over the eventual mise-en-scène. Abirached says that "All these stage directions demonstrate the clarity with which the authors see the concrete translation of the work which they are writing" (423).

23. There are, of course, many different categories of space for the theatre. Strictly speaking, I am primarily interested here in the *dramatic space* as opposed to the *theatrical space,* which is said to be realized only at the level of the concrete stage production. According to Patrice Pavis, the dramatic space "belongs to the dramatic text and can only be visualized by the spectator as a purely imaginary construction." As a "spatial image of the dramatic universe" motivated solely by a reading of the text, dramatic space is constructed from two sources: the stage directions of the author, constituting a sort of "pre–mise-en-scène," and the spatio-temporal indications within the dialogue (*Dictionnaire* 119). Despite the theoretical opposition between the concepts of dramatic space and theatrical space, however, I will follow the tradition of a great many theatre scholars by freely referring to dramatic space as theatrical space.

24. See Hugh Kenner, "Life in a Box" 41. Before Kenner, Ruby Cohn argued that "The interior of a skull, owner unknown, is a recurrent locale in Beckett's fiction" (*Samuel Beckett: The Comic Gamut* 237, 325 n. 9). Cohn's remark, however, moves beyond the text. She refers to the "vaguely oval" stage set in Roger Blin's French production of *Endgame,* which was supervised by Beckett. The text does not explicitly suggest this oval quality.

25. Blindness is a trait which, curiously, is not directly expressed in the didascalia.

26. "Ultimately, the stage in *Endgame* is a self-reflective metaphor of internal or inner space. Because Hamm is blind, his perception of space is already interior" (Shimon Levy, *Samuel Beckett's Self-Referential Drama* 24).

27. In an essay titled "Practices of Space," Michel de Certeau reminds us that "In his *Regulae*, Descartes made the blind man the guarantor of the knowledge of things and places against the illusions and deceptions of sight" (124, n. 5). For Beckett as for Hamm, "the illusions and deceptions of sight" include the in-sight, when it refers to the interior vision of referential language space, as opposed to the supra-referential, imaginary empty space of the psyche.

28. Shimon Levy gives a good account of another "empty" spatial field evoked by Beckett's text: the "extramural" stage space, the offstage. According to Levy, "Offstage is the black aura of stage, it is the specific emptiness that hovers around the stage, sometimes serving as the padding between outer reality and inner theatrical reality, or illusion. . . . Offstage—dramatically and theatrically—sucks us all in" (*Samuel Beckett's Self-Referential Drama* 48–49). While I would evidently prefer to argue that it is the innermost stage that "sucks us all in," one might judiciously remark that the *mise en abyme* generated by the headspace radiates outwardly as well as inwardly.

29. This perspective on framing coincides with Artaud's spatial approach to metaphysical meaning in theatre. Monique Borie, for instance, argues that Artaud's mythico-theatrical space, which is "totalizing," "oriented," and organized "around a center," takes on the structure of a "universe of layers operating on a principle of verticality": "it is also a layered space in which the different spatial planes are brought into play with one another, the center being, par excellence, the point where the planes begin to communicate" (*Antonin Artaud* 244).

We could, of course, distinguish between what Borie perceives in Artaud's theory to be the *site* of meaning and Corvin's idea that the *mise en abyme* is the actual *source* of meaning. Whether site or source, we should recognize that it is not just the idea of exact center that is meaningful in either Artaud or Beckett, but the "embedded" aspect of the central core.

30. "I was right in the center, wasn't I? . . . Am I right in the center? . . . Put me right in the center!" (*Endgame* 25–27).

31. Still, the diegetic space does not refer exclusively to inner space. One excellent example of how diegetic space helps to create the impression of the exterior frame is that when Hamm takes his "little turn" around the outer walls, he makes it clear that the enclosing frame itself reflects the emptiness of the space it delimits: "Do you hear? (*He strikes the wall with his knuckles.*) Hollow bricks! (*He strikes again.*) All that's hollow!" (26). There is, of course, no mention of the hollowness of the bricks—or of any bricks—in the external didascalia, so we might consider this either an internal or implicit stage direction.

32. Beckett's English translation of this work has led some commentators to interpret this dripping as blood rather than water. But the original, French version of this work, *Fin de partie*, is more instructive in this regard. The line "There's something dripping in my head" reads "Il y a une goutte d'eau dans ma tête" (*Fin de partie* 33). A literal translation of this would be: "There's a drop of water in my head." The idea of an independent drop of liquid is more clearly analogical to a gesture of

touching the head; and certainly, because of its transparence, water seems more "empty." Furthermore, the naming of the singular object (drop) instead of the act (dripping) is less contradictory for a concept of empty space because dripping implies the collision of drops against a surface or barrier. These drops have been present ever since the inception of Hamm's consciousness, "ever since the fontanelles."

33. Szondi's theories help refute the thesis that the so-called nihilism, first of early-twentieth-century surrealism and later of the nouveau théâtre of the 1950s, was an artistic reaction to the destruction of the two great wars.

34. In a guarded defense of subjectivity, Fredric Jameson points out another of its paradoxes: "the problem of expression is itself closely linked to some conception of the subject as a monadlike container, within which things felt are then expressed by projection outward.... Here too Munch's painting [*The Scream*] stands as a complex reflection on this complicated situation: it shows us that expression requires the category of the individual monad, but it also shows us the heavy price to be paid for that precondition, dramatizing the unhappy paradox that when you constitute your individual subjectivity as a self-sufficient field and a closed realm, you thereby shut yourself off from everything else and condemn yourself to the mindless solitude of the monad, buried alive and condemned to a prison cell without egress" ("The Cultural Logic of Late Capitalism" 15).

35. Lois Oppenheim argues that a certain female subjectivity derives from "the aesthetic presentation of consciousness in the *act of self-perception*" (author's emphasis) in plays like Beckett's *Not I* and *Rockaby*. To what extent is the "pre-cognitive self-awareness" of which Oppenheim speaks a perception of one's mental space? In this intriguing essay, Oppenheim also addresses "the problem of referential reference" ("Female Subjectivity in *Not I* and *Rockaby*" 219) and the referentiality of self-reference in Beckett's drama.

William E. Gruber too has articulated more complex notions of both the concept of dramatic character and subjectivity for non-realist theatre, including the work of Beckett and Bernhard. For Gruber, however, as for many contemporary scholars, neither character nor subjectivity are defined though interiority. Curiously, in accounting for subjectivity, Gruber's astute recognition of the increased figural presentation of the character and of the increased self-conscious presentationalism of space in "modern" theatre from Craig through Beckett takes him in an opposite direction from mine. While I identify subjectivity with a theatricalized image of psyche, claiming that our vision of character is propelled from empty stage (including the empty periphery), through the character's corporeal form into its empty mind, Gruber sees perspectival movement in the opposite direction. Contrary to Sarrazac, but reminiscent of Szondi, Gruber explains the break between the modern and the postmodern, the old and the new, in terms of a shift from a clear and elaborate interiority to an apparent lack of interiority, from a discrete personal psychology (interiority) to a "flat" one: "(I)n response to inherited dramaturgies that located personal identity *within* a discrete subject, modern and postmodern dramatists stage characters who sometimes lack 'interiority,' whose outlines and edges blur into the environment and whose chief characteristic often turns out to be a collection of qualities not private but public" (*Missing Persons* 9). For him, avant-garde dramaturgies shift from an emphasis on private psychology to public display, and from an individual identity to one that is amalgamated, integrated, or "synchronic" as he calls it. Thus, he argues for "intrapersonal (rather than individual) models for selfhood" (16), warning that "To equate the stage space even metaphorically with human consciousness sidesteps . . . the crucial relationship between body image and identity" (81). Though he skillfully builds on the figural, iconic, sculptural importance of the character, he writes of the "new definition of character as a function of the overall artistic environment. Here the blurred image of human presence resembles that diffusion of subject into background" (31). Clearly, he does not allow for a very different design of interiority in terms of self-reflexive empty space. Consequently, in his argument concerning the (intrapersonal) synchronic representation of the dramatic character versus its individual identity, Beckett's characters are supposed to evoke "a sense of pure existence" (79) or, in *Krapp's Last Tape*, for example, "a representation of the phenomenon of character itself" (85).

36. I hasten to defend the compatibility of my concept of a hypersubjective dramatic character with philosophical and sociological objections to the validity of the subject in terms of "personal identity," such as those of Pierre Bourdieu. Against movements hailing the "return of the subject," Bourdieu laments the difficulties this poses for work in the social sciences: "One of the reasons why the sociology of literature or of art is so backward is that these are realms in which investments in personal identity are formidable. And therefore when the sociologist arrives on the scene and carries out banal scientific operations, when she reminds us that the stuff of the social is made of relations, not individuals, she encounters enormous obstacles" (*Invitation to Reflexive Sociology* 179). Bourdieu principally criticizes theories bent on establishing "personal identity" (179). The hypersubject is not a personal identity, but a hyperpersonal, hypertheatrical, hypersocial awareness, an organic awareness that precedes and transcends, one that theatrically overreaches but in no way undermines the constitution of the social subject.

37. For Victor Turner, Beckett's hypersubject is not a fictitious "person" but an "individual" whose sociocultural value stems from its "liminoid" attribute. Our culture evolves and remains healthy primarily because of its passage through the "liminal period": "The liminal period is that time and space betwixt and between one context of meaning and action and another. It is when the initiand is neither what he has been nor is what he will be. . . . In our society we might see the 'Theater of the Absurd' of Ionesco, Arrabal, and Beckett as 'liminal,' though I would prefer the term 'lumin*oid*,' however gratingly neologistic, as being at once akin to and perhaps deriving from the liminal of tribal and feudal rituals, and different from the liminal as being more often the creation of individual than of collective inspiration and critical rather than furthering the purposes of the existing social order." Turner emphasizes the necessity of "antistructure" for cultural progress. When dramatists construct a multidimensional and focused impression of emptiness in their work, they are producing "antistructure." Turner cites Kennelm Burridge's "speculation about this *proto*- or -*ur* individual. He regards what he calls 'the self,' not as a static entity, but as a movement, an oscillating energy between the structured persona and the potentially antistructured individual" (*From Ritual to Theatre* 113). For Turner as for Burridge, "Man grows through antistructure, and conserves through structure" (114). It is the antistructural "individual" that has the potential to grasp, in Burridge's

words, "that symbols and symbolic activities contain a *mysterium*—a latency, a promissory note, an invitation to realize that which lies behind the obvious and overt" (114). A theory of hypersubjectivity can account for the "mysterium" in terms of essential emptiness.

38. See, for instance, Jacques Lacan, "L'Instance de la lettre dans l'inconscient," esp. 260–61. As Malcolm Bowie so aptly puts it, in Lacan's theory, "the 'vertical dependencies' of the signifying chain extend as far downwards into the hidden worlds of mental processes as it is possible for the speculative imagination to descend. Beyond the last outpost of signification there is nothing at all—or rather there is that boundless and inexpressible vacuity" (*Lacan* 72). We remember, of course, that this bent toward psychoanalytical theory was intuitively prefigured by the surrealists. Breton's notion of the perpetual, vertiginous descent (the successive "illumination of hidden places") suggests displacement along a signifying chain submerged in the inexpressible vacuity of psyche.

3. Beckett's Pursuit of Emptiness

1. As I pointed out in chapter 2, the debate on the extent to which the written text either suggests, provokes, evokes, orients, or determines the multidimensional mise-en-scène rages on, especially in France. Given Beckett's legendary control of the staging of his texts, his abundant stage directions and his scrutiny of the production of the minimalist images of his plays, I believe most scholars will agree that his texts do more to determine than to merely suggest their subsequent mise-en-scène.

2. The sociologist Bourdieu disparagingly refers to language as "an immense repository of naturalized preconstructions" (*An Invitation to Reflexive Sociology* 241).

Some might find it difficult to ignore Beckett's remark in 1965 to Colin Duckworth: "I'm not interested in the theatre." But Duckworth reflexively cautions that "This has to be viewed in the light of the fact that Beckett is very interested in seeing his *own* plays on stage" (*Angels of Darkness* 17; author's emphasis). So we might read Beckett's remark as a rejection of the type of theatre he was attempting to write against. After all, many scholars have credited Beckett with the creation of a new theatrical genre.

3. During the production of *Not I*, Beckett told the actress Jessica Tandy, who played the only voiced character (Mouth), that "I am not unduly concerned with intelligibility. . . . I hope the piece may work on the nerves of the audience, not its intellect" (quoted in Enoch Brater, *Beyond Minimalism* 23).

4. In a letter written early in his career, Beckett announced that "more and more my own language appears to me like a veil that must be torn apart in order to get at things (or Nothingness) behind it" (*Disjecta* 171). "Since we cannot eliminate language all at once," he says, the highest goal for a writer should be "To bore one hole after another in it, until what lurks behind it—be it something or nothing—begins to seep through" (172). He admits, however, that "On the way to this literature of the unword, which is so desirable to me, some form of Nominalist irony might be a necessary stage" (173).

5. Quoted in Hauck, *Reductionism in Drama and the Theatre*, 197. Author's emphasis.

6. See chapter 2 for my initial discussion of the importance of emptiness to Artaud's world vision.

7. See Robert Abirached's chapter on Artaud titled *"Le Corps-Théâtre"* (372–82).

8. For more on Beckett's "revisional reductions" (Hauck, *Reductionism in Drama and the Theatre* 144) which characterize the generative process of Beckett's entire dramatic corpus, and on his struggle to "create with erasure" (Gontarski, *The Intent of Undoing in Samuel Beckett's Dramatic Texts* 4), see Hauck and Gontarski.

9. Kalb engages an interesting analysis of the interplay among stage set, action, and acting style, explaining how the stage set conditions acting as well as action. He also discusses the merits and the drawbacks of both productions in this regard. In the first production, "Mostel/Meridth favored the beautifully theatrical over the metatheatrical and ended up creating a fantastic form of fourth-wall realism." In the later production, "Forsythe/Price emphasized cynical metatheatrical playing at the expense of theatrical illusion and ended up losing the play's emotional center and, hence, justification for their physical activity" (*Beckett in Performance* 32).

10. See Kalb's discussion of Beckett's own German production of *Warten auf Godot* at the Schiller Theater in 1975: "The audience sees the action occurring in a nearly empty space, which discourages perceptions of theatrical illusion" (*Beckett in Performance* 33).

11. Colin Duckworth has seen *Godot* as "an exploration of the fear of endlessness" (*Angels of Darkness* 65).

12. Two recent French versions of *Godot* provide another interesting comparison in this regard. Concise yet pertinent information (director's notes, commentary) and photographic illustrations related to these versions can be found in Jean-Claude Lallias and Jean-Jacques Arnault, eds., *Théâtre Aujourd'hui 3: l'univers scénique de Samuel Beckett*, 36–51. In 1993, Philippe Adrien's production at the Théâtre de la Tempête took place in a setting which Jean-Claude Lallias describes as "vast and profound, covered with ash-colored sand: a desert where characters come to inscribe their steps, their presence" (*Théâtre Aujourd'hui 3* 46). In 1992, at the Théâtre des Amandiers de Nanterre, Joël Jouanneau produced a controversial, contemporized *Godot*, set in a suburban industrial site in an advanced state of disintegration. The tree became a dilapidated, gutted electric transformer. The near absolute, vast emptiness of Adrien's production, enhanced by the sand-covered stage, is evident; whereas the spectator's first impression of Jouanneau's work seems a fully illusionistic contrast. Yet, Jouanneau attempts to obfuscate the material illusion on the stage through the use of subdued lighting effects and a constant, omnipresent pea-soup mist which permeates the set, effacing all illusionistic details. His use of this mist can be likened to the use of smoke in contemporary productions. Bernard Dort explains just how determinant this can be:

> Smoke as temptation: it plugs the holes of the performance. It unifies that which should remain separated. It casts powder into our eyes.
> Smoke as punctuation: it preludes the performance; it suspends it and puts holes in it. It prompts us to *see*. (*La Représentation émanicipée* 93)

It prompts us to "see"—and connect with—the emptiness of the stage.

13. An American production of *Godot*, at the University of Louisville's Belknap Theatre (March 6, 1992, Dir. J. R. Tompkins, Scenic Designer Brynna C. Bloomfield), used a trompe l'oeil background painting depicting a countryside landscape.

14. In *Beckett in Performance,* his examination of "concept productions" belonging to a "history of altered Beckett" (72), such as Alkalaitis's *Endgame* (American Repertory Theatre, 1984), Jonathan Kalb charges that the directors of these plays are frequently guilty, not of "narcissism and monomania" as is often thought, but of "bad old-fashioned conservatism—denial of newness to the truly new by blending it into the established" (94). Even after four decades of Beckett, we still find something new to discover about his subversion of traditional narrative structure and his search for an empty-space connection which would work on the audience's nerves.

15. See, for example, Pierre Chabert, who argues that Beckett's theatre is "a deliberate and intense effort to make the body come to light" ("The Body in Beckett's Theatre" 24). See also Marie-Claude Hubert's "The Evolution of the Body in Beckett's Theatre," where she argues that, after the 1960s, "instead of emphasizing its infirmity, Beckett's plays focus on the question of how to situate the body, or, in other terms, of how to find the place where the fragmented body can be integrated" (59).

16. "From *Waiting for Godot* to *Rockaby,*" writes Jane Alison Hale, "Beckett's theater has evolved consistently in the direction of reduction, compression, and the economy of artistic means. What he has to 'say' today is, in fact, not very different from what he had to 'say' in the beginning" (*The Broken Window* 145). She astutely adds that, "one of the most significant aspects of the evolution of Beckett's drama through the years is the fact that, as movement upon the stage has been minimized and/or strictly regulated, the imaginary mobility required of his spectators has progressively increased" (152). Thus, she contributes to the argument that the mimetic detail of realism—in this case, the mimetic detail of movement—tends to induce passivity and facility in the creation, practice, reception, and theory of art.

17. William B. Worthen agrees that Beckett's characters are "sculpted, hollowed out by the text of the mise en scène" (*Modern Drama* 136), and that Beckett's *Play,* for example, "deploys the actors' bodies for their imagistic value" (140).

18. Lois Oppenheim broaches the topic of fragmentation in Beckett in terms of corporal dismemberment as opposed to disembodiment. She too criticizes the exclusionary tendencies of the physical approach—what she calls the "objectifying and positivisitic tendencies"—to Beckett's texts: "Though much has been offered in the way of critical interpretation of Beckett's preoccupation with the dismembering of the body, little, if anything, has been written on disembodiment as such in Beckett's texts. This reflects the objectifying and positivistic tendencies of our critical traditions which seek to identify, from the perspective of stasis as opposed to process, symbolic and other signifying structures as the principle components of textuality" ("Female Subjectivity in *Not I* and *Rockaby*" 220).

19. Enoch Brater refers to this tableau as "an image almost holy, an image free of all non-essentials" (*Beyond Minimalism* 172).

20. "Black and white, the predominant colors of Beckett's latest works, evoke for him the undifferentiation of the void, towards which tend human life and all the perceptual efforts of which it consists from the very moment of birth" (Hale, *The Broken Window* 135).

21. Anne Ubersfeld explains that "a black or very dark background functions as the fundus of the eye, a *camera oscura,* and as such it renders a psychic space, an interiority. The black background interiorizes the performance, transports it into the psychic stage" (*L'Ecole* 104). One of Beckett's major achievements was to have

concretely, metatheatrically demonstrated the simple emptiness of this psychic space, and its darkness. On directing Beckett, Pierre Chabert emphasizes how important it is that the spectator gain a "physical and spatial experience of blackness and of listening to the voice in darkness" ("Genèse" 127).

22. Jane Hale seems to understand this when she writes that "the meaning of the words in *Rockaby* is less important than their form, their sound, and the visual image they envelop" (*The Broken Window* 133). Nevertheless, this does not prevent her from discussing at least the trace of story in *Rockaby:* "[W's] story, like that of all the other characters we have met, is an indication that human existence is nothing more nor less than a continual, albeit fruitless, struggle for perception" (135), a "story" that reiterates the thesis of Hale's book.

23. In writing about *Endgame*, Beckett remarked, "My work is a matter of fundamental sounds (no joke intended) made as fully as possible" (quoted in Kalb, *Beckett in Performance* 93).

24. See *Rockaby*. By Samuel Beckett. Dir. Alan Schneider. Film by D. A. Pennebaker and Chris Hegedus.

25. There is an interesting analogy we can make here between the textual pattern of theory and the body of an actress. Hauck notes that "the structural design of almost all Beckett's plays thus suggests a pattern similar to the way water moves in spiral-like fashion towards the increasingly narrow centre of an eddy" (*Reductionism in Drama and the Theatre* 140). On the acting side, Billie Whitelaw has lamented the physical pain she experiences in playing Beckett because of her attempt to personalize and "corporealize" this eddy-like configuration: "Now perhaps I'm being silly, perhaps I shouldn't do that, but I feel that the shape my body makes is just as important as the sound that comes out of my mouth. And that's the shape my body wants to take, of somebody who's spiraling downward" (quoted in Kalb, *Beckett in Performance* 147).

26. W's fixation on descent recalls the discussion of the interrelated tropes of descent, self-concentration, and inner depth in Robert Pinget's *Abel et Bela*. See note 13, chapter 2.

27. In his analysis of *Rockaby*, however, William E. Gruber concludes that Beckett's theatre remains nonetheless a "theater of representation" based on a merely more complex model of representation and that it is through this sustained link to representation that the category of character survives. Thus, in *Rockaby* he focuses on the meaning of the parent-child relationship: "The key to this pattern of increasing identification of child and parent goes beyond language to include a concept of body image and mimetic engulfment. It is a theatre of representation that is yet not mere representation because it is far too enveloping, far too troubling. . . . We confront a paradox of character: here it seems that Beckett's nonrepresentational theater best represents the real syntax of human identity as fusion of self and other" (*Missing Persons* 93). Gruber sees not the absence of mimesis but the evidence of a creative mimesis in Beckett's work, one complexified by its use of synchrony: "Thus character in *Rockaby* is not a self-sufficient subject but a being who is formed from beginning to end by mimetic interaction. . . . These intercorporeal synchronizations suggest that W has no continuous and coherent sense of separateness that differentiates her from her parent" (97).

Despite his revealing pursuit of the complexity of meaning in this work, a pursuit focused on the spatial, figural qualities of character, Gruber hesitates to reach beyond the margins of the representational. He almost parenthetically remarks, for example, that "Like *Oedipus Rex* and *Hamlet*, *Rockaby* is a play about parents and children . . . *Rockaby* shows that the relationship between parent and child is turbulent and deeply ambivalent" (92). This is not to say that Gruber is altogether wrong about this, but that his recourse to referentiality jeopardizes his argument for the figural impact of the image *beyond* its link to narration or story. The design of interiority or subjectivity in terms of self-reflexive empty space equates the stage space as well as the body image with a primitive state of human consciousness rather than the evolved state of story.

28. Deleuze and Guattari credit the nineteenth-century painter J. W. Turner with having achieved such a level of what they call "deterritorialized" art. They trace the genius of "deterritorialization" in the plastic arts back to the paintings of Tintoretto and Lotto, an art "whose force fractured the codes, undid the signifiers, passed under the structures, set the flows in motion, and effected breaks at the limits of desire: a breakthrough" (*Anti-Oedipus* 369). Curiously, the French word for "breakthrough" used by Deleuze and Guattari (*percée*) derives from the French verb *"percer,"* meaning literally "to make a hole in," or, by extension, "to open up a point of view," concepts that remind us of the opposition between narrative "whole" and visual "hole," on the one hand, and of Beckett's desire to "break through" the superficial barrier of language, on the other.

29. Jane Hale observes that the instruction to "pause" is "by far the most common stage direction in *Endgame*," Beckett's earlier full-length play. She believes that it "helps to structure the play like a chess game where each player reflects silently before proceeding with his next move" (*The Broken Window* 57). In the later, shorter plays, the "pause" is even more frequent, though often implicit and more discrete. In *Not I*, which chronologically precedes *Rockaby* in the corpus, Beckett seems to experiment with the profusive use of points of suspension, all of which indicate some kind of interruption or pause. In *Rockaby*, by structuring the text into the form of a dramatic poem, Beckett renders the "pause" implicit. This development of the treatment of "pause," which we should consider to be nothing less than the setting of language in a background of silence, is emblematic of Beckett's move toward both concision and emptiness.

30. Elaborating on his desire to transcend "literature," Beckett queries: "Is there any reason why that terrible materiality of the word surface should not be capable of being dissolved, like for example the sound surface, torn by enormous pauses, of Beethoven's seventh Symphony, so that through whole pages we can perceive nothing but a path of sounds suspended in giddy heights, linking unfathomable abysses of silence" (*Disjecta* 172).

31. What W. B. Worthen evidently referred to as the "poised periods of *Rockaby*" (*Modern Drama* 132).

32. See Bakhtin's *Rabelais and His World*, esp. 1–66. I will return to Bakhtin's argument in the final chapter, on the marionette-like dramatic character.

33. The head figures the body by virtue of its own empty, internal nature (icon) and also by virtue of being in a real relation to it (index). See Charles Peirce's distinction between icon and index, discussed in Ducrot and Todorov, *Encyclopedic Dictionary of the Science of Language* 87.

34. As a result of his study of the generative process of elimination in Beckett's work, Gontarski believes that the Auditor is non-essential to *Not I:* "But the Auditor remains only a physical representation of an internal force that is developed clearly in dialogue, and the fundamental discourse with the other works equally well without the additional icon" (*The Intent of Undoing in Samuel Beckett's Dramatic Texts* 148).

35. Garner discusses the "suppression of deixis in *Not I*" (*Bodied Spaces* 132). "[The] play on the grammatical category of verbal deixis" (134). "Mouth is equally the emblem of language's inescapable reference to utterance in its physical and subjective parameters" (136). The notion of subjectivity is essential to Garner's phenomenological point of view, so he examines it in all its manifestations.

36. Even in Beckett's early plays the idea of "roar in the skull" is fundamental. I have already pointed out that, as early as *Endgame*, critics like Ruby Cohn and Hugh Kenner saw the stage space as the inside of a skull.

37. Derrida might say *"paroles psychiques"* or psychic utterances. He gives the following explanation for Artaud's resistance to conventional language: "The word is the cadaver of psychic speech, and along with the language of life itself the 'speech before words' must be found again" ("The Theater of Cruelty" 240).

38. This recalls Jon Erikson's point about the figure-ground dichotomy for the art object, one which I cite below. Beckett's humanoid figures function as a new ground.

39. There is, of course, the monstrousness of the image of the mouth. Despite its location in and its metonymic, indexical relation to the head, Mouth could metaphorically and iconically refer to the lower body. Brater notes that in the film version of *Not I*, a black and white version where the Auditor was eliminated, the mouth strikingly resembled a vagina (*Beyond Minimalism* 35). Is this transfiguration of the head into a vagina to be regarded as an aberrant postmodernist reversal of the popular grotesque according to Bakhtin? (See chapter 6.) Has Beckett reappropriated and reversed the image of the lower body, placing the focus on the upper body? Perhaps this is another example of the contradictory nature of Beckett's art with respect to its social relevance. Conventionally, the orifice of the popular grotesque could not function out of corporeal context, in isolation from the body. The integral body, either represented or implied, is critical to the popular context in which the orifice figures as a passageway to the socially oriented body. I. Wardle, a critic for *The Times*, evidently remarked that "in isolation [the mouth] could be any bodily orifice" (cited in James Knowlson and John Pilling, *Frescoes of the Skull* 200). For the popular consciousness, the orifice, then, is nothing without the context of body, and the "socially challenged" body in Beckett's theatre is, in one way or another, absent. The absence of a personal body challenges our conventional understanding of collective body.

40. Interview by Olivier Schmitt ("Un entretien avec Giorgio Strehler").

41. I also have argued that Beckett's quest can be traced imagistically to postulations of psychic space by early-twentieth-century surrealist thinkers such as Caillois, Breton, and Artaud. These postulations differ from psychoanalytic theory. While Freud located fractured stories in the inside of our mind-space, the surrealists discovered something else, something that was not quite "story." They found instead poetic images that were separate from both the rational and irrational—an irrational that the psychoanalytical process systematically percolated into the rational—narrative networks of human thought and action. Artaud, we know, had considerable experience with psychoanalysis and psychiatry since he spent nine years toward the end of his life in an asylum. In his

essay "Van Gogh le suicide de la société," Artaud defines the state of madness as "a primitive force . . . a truth," and psychiatry as "a violence against this truth." He believed that "our degenerate society" had invented psychiatry in order to avoid having to deal directly with the primitive genius of madness, with the extralinguistic vortex. He believed society had the defensive objective of repressing madness by claiming to understand its illogic, in order to be able to systematically reassimilate it through the use of sophisticated terminology ("Van Gogh" 14–15). Given Artaud's interest in the connection between the void of nature and the empty space of the mind, he surely believed that madness was also a way to get in touch with the void.

42. See also my essay, "Beyond the Structuralistic Language-Space," where I argue that the property of "connectedness is as essential to structuralist and post-structuralist theories of meaning production as are concepts of binarity and *différance*" (esp. 2–15).

43. Jeffers also speaks of the "lack of emotive qualities" in O'Keeffe's and Beckett's achromatic texts ("The Image of Thought" 67). I cry when I watch a videotape of *Rockaby*. Thus, I react in the only—representational, rational—way my body knows how. Though the image and sound of *Rockaby* works primarily on the unemotional plane of "pure immanence," I have an emotional response which is triggered by the text's and the image's intellectual and artistic transaction of *referral* beyond the borders of reference. Beckett pushes back the envelope of rationalism to include the emotion that his images produce. How does one react "metaphysically" to a work of art?

Jeffers's "achromatic" analysis of Georgia O'Keeffe's painting *Black Abstraction* (1927) is revealing. The painting, in Jeffers's words, "seems at once to feature a concrete mindscape and an ephemeral, shadowy and unascertainable netherworld. . . .The thin band of grey separating the black and white . . . acts as a dividing band permitting the eye to capture the canvas's infinite series of layers and detailed brushstrokes . . . thought is given a new path" (69–71). Yet, like their literary counterparts, art critics respond to a physical, representational temptation. As Brater returns to a necessarily representational model of story for *Rockaby*, and as Gruber ultimately suggests for the work a highly complex *theme* of motherhood, according to Jeffers the art critic Edward Alden Jewell's analysis of this painting is one which invokes "the symbolic conventions of color theory" (71). Thus Jeffers accuses Jewell of "Eulogizing O'Keeffe as the maternal creator of a painting that serves to reflect the divine 'Mighty Mother,' a symbolic system of meaning historically associated with patriarchy in the West" (71). O'Keeffe's painting is like Beckett's late works: an incursion into the pure immanence of empty psychic space. Its artistic relevance lies not in its ability to participate in a symbolic system or even to cultivate new symbolic territory, but 1) to divert our attention from symbol-*ism* as well as rationalism; and 2) to creatively "paint" a psychic plane of immanence, an image of psychic emptiness wherein psychic signals burst in and out of our consciousness.

44. "[T]oday nobody believes in the specificity of the dramatic text" ("Classical Heritage" 59).

45. Translation modified. Pavis's original French text reads "l'hypothèse d'un sens (parmi d'autres)" ("L'Héritage classique" 222). The translation at hand reads "one hypothetical meaning among others." I believe Pavis's original intent was to emphasize "hypothesis" and not "meaning."

46. Jeffers notes that "Beckett is attempting to move from an alphabetical language to a language of image" ("The Image of Thought" 74), that in "Ping" (1967),

for instance, he "presents a colorscape which is dominated by white," and that "Lessness" (1970), a text marked by the suffix "-less," "maps its coordinates carefully onto a white topography of would-be stillness and silence—both 'less' sound and 'less' movement" (75). "Words function like the still, flat tints of an abstract painting: color escapes from a chromatic spectrum into a fresh and unique achromatic realm" (76).

47. In an article titled "Voyage à l'intérieur de l'être humain," Jean-Claude Fall reflects on his experience directing and acting Beckett's "piece for television," *Eh Joe*. He sums up the camera work indicated by Beckett's stage directions in the following way: "In effect, the camera moves its eye toward the interior of the character's brain to the point of entering the black mass of his skull" (67). The stage directions read: "After this opening pursuit, between first and final closeup of face, camera has nine slight moves in towards face, say four inches each time. Each move is stopped by voice resuming, never camera move and voice together" (*Collected Shorter Plays* 201). This telescoping effect of the camera accomplishes for television what Beckett usually produces primarily with lighting in the theatre; the camera mimics the spectator's progressive focus not so much on the "brain" or the "black mass of the skull"—as Fall would have it—as on the empty mind-space of the character.

48. Unless otherwise stated, references to *A Piece of Monologue, Ohio Impromptu, Catastrophe, Quad, What Where,* and *That Time* are from Beckett's *Collected Shorter Plays*.

49. Is this Beckett's way of admonishing would-be, misguided directors of his works?

50. Marie-Claude Hubert believes we should interpret "catastrophe" from a psychoanalytical angle, "in the Aristotelian sense of reversal. The catastrophe is the final uncovering of the face of the protagonist, which had been hidden during the entire day. Beckett also used film to define the meaning of this uncovering. The fear of being seen and of seeing oneself are two faces of the same anxiety" (*The Evolution of the Body in Beckett's Theater* 61).

51. These performances are included in *Peephole Art for Television*. Videocassette.

52. In his analysis of this performance piece, Gilles Deleuze suggested the "exhaustion" of space:

> The order, the course, and the ensemble render the movement all the more inexorable in that it is without purpose, like a moving walkway that would regulate the appearance and disappearance of moving bodies.
> Beckett's text is perfectly clear: it intends to exhaust space. (92)

(Deleuze's essay on *Quad* as reproduced in a condensed version titled "Il s'agit d'épuiser l'espace.")

53. In an essay titled "A Sublime Event: Gordon Craig's Über-marionette in Samuel Beckett's Late Drama," Jennifer M. Jeffers examines another kind of "tension" produced by Beckett's work, "the tension produced by the supposedly static image's capacity to come to life. . . . It is exactly this tension in Beckett's late drama which produces the effect of the sublime" (59). "Beckett achieves an image that is sublime because—paralogically—the actor is not a puppet" (63). I would add to this judgement that, paralogically, the hypersubject is still a social subject.

54. Note the concluding text of *That Time* (1976): "not a sound only the old breath. . . . something like that come and gone come and gone no one come and

gone in no time gone in no time." And the concluding stage direction: "Silence 10 seconds. Breath audible. After 3 seconds eyes open. After 5 seconds smile, toothless for preference. Hold 5 seconds till fade out and curtain" (235) (see figs. 14 and 15). In figure 14, the Beckett production, the protagonist's hair is teased into a nebulous corona, enhancing the effect of the head as an illuminated empty space within a dark empty space. In figure 15, the Paul Draper production, the protagonist's head literally protrudes from a mound of dark drapery.

4. Avatars of the Hypersubjective Dramatic Character

1. In this regard, hypersubjective theatre reminds us of the rise of surrealism. During and succeeding the postwar generation of existentialism, French culture was as fertile for nouveau théâtre in general and for hypersubjectivity in particular, as it was for surrealism in the 1920s. It took more than three decades for the hypersubjective mode of surrealism to mature into a polished metadramatic strategy (see chapter 2).

2. As early as 1966, Geneviève Serreau referred to the work of Beckett, Ionesco, et al. as a "nouveau réalisme" (*Histoire du «nouveau théâtre»* 11). See also the more recent study of W. B. Worthen, who develops a classification he calls "modern theatrical realism" that includes "the theater of the absurd" (*Modern Drama* 5)

3. In the late 1970s, David Grossvogel writes that "starting with Pirandello, there is a more deliberate attempt to turn the material stage into a part of the dramatist's statement, a more systematic reliance on the physical assertion of the boards rather than on words from which the metaphysical bashfulness of modern authors shies" (*Mystery and Its Fictions* 110). In chapter 2 we read Michel Corvin's remarks to the effect that, since the advent of nouveau théâtre, dramatists create human experiences that "act *with* space."

4. See also Monique Borie's *Le Fantôme ou le théâtre qui doute*, a study of the dramatic character as a statuesque or phantom-like image, from the Ancient Greeks to the present. Linking this image to sculpture, "the most archaic of the arts," Borie speaks, for instance of Tadeusz Kantor's characters as "sleeping volumes": "Like these sculptures, Kantor's body-objects are endowed with emptiness, with absence, but they are also charged with the power of a strange reminiscence" (264). Borie's thesis is tied to the monumentality of the character and to the suggestion of emptiness as ancient myth and ritual. Therefore, for her, the visual image of the characters acquires a religious quality.

5. Cited in Patrick McGuiness, "Ioneso and Symbolist Theatre: Revolution and Restitution in the Avant-Garde" 110.

6. Cited in Esslin, *Theatre of the Absurd* 152; author's emphasis.

7. Likewise, we encounter the reference to money in this work: "In order to prevent the exploitation of man by man, we need money, money, and still more money!" (145). Beckett never directly, openly broached the theme of money. In *Godot*, we remark the different manner in which Beckett broached the idea of "exploitation of man by man." The master-slave relation between Lucky and Pozo is presented quite primitively, and it is enacted, not explained. In *Endgame*, the "exploitation of man by man" is treated circumstantially, automatically. Increasingly in Beckett's drama it is treated imagistically.

8. When the orator finally makes his entrance as "a real person" (154), Ionesco's stage directions describe him as "something like an automaton" (155). In the next chapter I will deal with the question of the marionette-likeness of the characters of nouveau théâtre in a way that will place Ionesco's automaton here in context, comparing the idea of automaton with that of an empty form.

9. Likewise, among all the hypersubjective plays I treat in this chapter, plays which in one way or another deal with the theme of human mortality, no other work refers explicitly to suicide; yet scholars frequently discuss its inference. I return to this topic in my analysis of Vian's *Empire Builders*.

10. An inside which, because of the scarcity of referential decor and objects, denotes a more metaphysical than physical "inside."

11. It would be wrong to consider Marguerite in any equivalent or parallel relationship with the King. She exists only for and through the King.

12. Translation modified. The translation at hand reads, "fading into a kind of mist." The original French text reads, "sombrer dans une sorte de brume" (*Le Roi se meurt*, Paris: Hatier, 1985; 92). I believe that *"sombrer"* is more appropriately and effectively translated as "sinking," and the movement that this word implies.

13. Trans. Simon Watson Taylor (New York: Grove Press, 1967).

14. See chapter 2 for Jon Erikson's explanation of art as contradictory.

15. Michel Corvin has suggested a division of the categories of space, one resembling mimetic space that he calls "actual space" (*actuel*) and the other resembling diegetic space that he calls "virtual space" (*virtuel*). The former is that space that is—or that is destined by the text to be—visibly present on the stage, "within the visible reality of the stage." The other, the virtual space, is much more subtle, more difficult to identify, because it is generally characterized by Corvin as "absent space": "because of its virtual character, it is a matter of the evocation, by language as well as by gesture, of absent spaces" ("Contribution" 64). Needless to say, the virtual space of the text plays an important role in the determination of the actual space of any given mise-en-scène. The "pre–mise-en-scène" of hypersubjective theatre is, in fact, primarily constructed from virtual space.

16. The original French text specifies that the voices come *first:* "De l'escalier, montant d'en bas, viennent d'abord des voix" (*Bâtisseurs d'empire* 1).

17. Even on a less profound level this ascendancy within the apartment building is an evident movement toward increased isolation. The further one climbs in a building, the more one is distant from the earth or from society; and, conversely, the "closer" one becomes to "Self."

18. The more evident interpretation of this play would indeed accentuate the bourgeois desire for ascending the social classes. It would evoke the conflict between generations, where the daughter struggles against her parents' very bourgeois objectives. Within the context of my study, this interpretation becomes rather superficial. It is ultimately not so much the exterior materialist desire of a class that dominates this aesthetic structure of the work as it is the surreal interior psychic awareness of a very modern subject. It is moreover this latter desire that permits the radical manifestation of the former.

19. At the beginning of Act 3, the Father is the only member of the family to ascend to the last floor of the building: "There is no staircase leading up to the floor above. In fact, there is no floor above." Just as at the beginning of Act 1, we hear the

Father's voice as he ascends the staircase. Although he begins by addressing his wife who is still on the lower floor, she is not seen again:

> Father (*turning around as he calls out*): The yellow bag . . . For goodness' sake don't forget the yellow bag, Anna, the meat grinder's in it. . . .
>
> *He appears, dragging various packages behind him with all his strength, and pushing other packages along in front of him; he goes down a few steps again and repeats the performance.*
>
> Anna! Anna! Are you coming or not? Hurry up, for goodness' sake. . . . Pass me the yellow bag. (*Irritably.*) No, no, there's nothing to be afraid of! . . . Pass me the yellow bag, I say, we've got plenty of time. . . . (*He emerges, pushing a bag in front of him, and then goes down the stairs again.*) Now the small suitcase.
>
> *An indistinct murmur from the Mother.*
>
> . . .
>
> Father: For God's sake, of course you've got time. . . . Ah! what a lot of fuss for nothing!
>
> *He starts down the stairs again, when suddenly a bloodcurdling scream can be heard from the Mother.*
>
> Anna! Anna! What's going on? (*He beats a hasty retreat up the stairs.*) Yes, of course I'm here, my love. . . . Make an effort. . . . Come down and fetch you? Don't be childish, Anna, for goodness' sake; my arms are full of packages. . . . (61–62)

Finally, when the Mother no longer responds to his call, the Father's tone changes to "an anxious voice which is perhaps curious rather than anxious" (63). He begins his long monologue as he simultaneously considers the way his wife *has abandoned him* (!) and finishes blocking off the trap door leading to the lower floor (63).

20. For an alternative reading of the Father's ultimate "breakdown," a reading which is more representative of postmodern, "fragmentational" scholarship, see Charles J. Stivale's "Of Schmürz and Men: Boris Vian's *Les bâtisseurs d'empire.*" Stivale describes the final act in the following terms: "The emphasis of the final act continues to be on the disintegration of the subject through the disjointed monologue of *le Père* who first loses his capacity to impose any domination whatsoever over another person once he sacrifices his wife Anna to the encroaching forces of *le Bruit*" (107).

21. Translation modified. The translation at hand reads, "He slips and falls to the floor, screaming." However, a "translator's note" accompanying this text explains the ambiguity of the original French text that reads "Il glisse et tombe en hurlant" (77). The translator explains that Vian asserted he had envisioned the Father falling back onto the floor at this point. Yet many if not most French critics and theatre directors envision the Father's plunge through the window. In fact, dramaturgically it seems awkward to stage or to visualize the Father screaming in a fall to the floor. Accordingly, the translator takes note of a Royal Shakespeare Company production in which the Father "falls out of the window." He confides that "It seems perfectly legitimate for the reader to choose this alternative interpretation of the final action if he wishes" (77).

22. The articulation of *mise en abyme* in *Empire Builders* seems to neglect its metatheatrical dimension. Despite the clarity of the "abysmal" nature of the play's spatial structure, culminating in the consciousness of the protagonist, it is not readily

apparent that this "abyss" articulates or parallels a metatheatrical discourse. Yet I will maintain that this self-conscious aspect of the genre is nonetheless present in the sense that the theatrical space is so intimately tied to the subjective abyss of the subject. The theatrical space is involved in its own surrealist investigation of its inner space and the metaphor of theatrical (reflective) *mise en abyme* is simply less explicit.

23. Trans. Barbara Wright (London: Calder and Boyars, 1971).

24. The English translation of this work has omitted the introduction of the original version, in which Dubillard describes the setting ("The interior of a house") and provides instructions for the distribution of the roles (7–8).

25. Although this work has attracted enough interest to be included in many anthologies of French theatre, it has received less scholarly attention than any of the other works with which we have dealt thus far. Michel Corvin, however, has dealt with this work in his critical studies of theatrical space and *mise en abyme*. In one essay, Corvin comments on Dubillard's theatrical corpus with this conclusion: "Metaphysical theatre in the literal sense of the term, and all the more harrowing for its comicality in that it sets out to be an entirely physical theatre, limited to the *hic et nunc* of the body and the stage. Dubillard's theatre is totally monologic because it does its best to put together an I-subject; and it can be considered the impossible theatre of self-knowledge: a center of attraction like the black hole of astronomers, around which everything turns" ("Une écriture plurielle" 944).

Early on, the Master demonstrates his concern for the *image of* his own existence, one closely tied to that of the (interior of the) house ("I was brought up in this house. No, I grew up in it" [29]). Consequently, he evokes the self-conscious metatheatricality of the work even as he implies the existential relevance of the theatre: "I'm waiting for it. Still waiting. The image. A foil to this house. A theatre" (29). Is the (theatrical) function of the house supposed to shed light on the theatre/life— fiction/reality dialectic? Does the theatrical nature of the house determine the existential value of life within it? The house's *mise en abyme*–like relation to life is perfectly clear in *House*, since, in becoming the equivalent of a theatrical image, it also becomes the metaphorical image of the spatialized, interiorized, and verticalized psyche of the modern subject itself.

The metatheatricality of "the play *as* play" is further enhanced when, halfway through the work, a valet directly addresses the audience, reminding them that the play has not forgotten either them or the fictional structure of the work at hand: "The plan of this play?—Well now . . . the plan . . . you mean: 'What has happened?'—The plan—that's to say the order in which what has happened has happened?" (106). This momentarily extends the boundaries of the theatrical space, augmenting its theatricality.

One final preliminary word: The author has contributed only schematic stage directions and even seems to welcome a free interpretation of a "mise-en-scène." Yet the dialogue elaborately suggests the (implicit or virtual) space and, given the liberty of the *metteur en scène*, we could expect to see an enormous diversity in the material conception of the virtual production.

26. According to Gaston Bachelard's phenomenological theory: "A house is imagined as a vertical being. It rises" (cited in Georges Matoré, *L'espace humain* 55).

27. The original French reads "chambre-coffre-fort" (a "strongbox" bedroom) (34).

28. See Geneviève Serreau's *Histoire*: "The fact that this house is the very body—and the mind—of its owner is never expressed by way of a weighty allegory" (162).

29. The original text reads *"ce que je veux c'est me représenter le dedans de ma maison comme il est"* (28). A more literal translation would read: "what I want is to represent to myself the interior of my house as it is."

30. The original French reads, *"La Maison est ce par quoi l'espace se trouve divisé en un dehors et un dedans habitable par l'homme"* (64). A more literal translation would read, "The House is the means by which space is divided into an outside and an inside inhabitable by man."

31. See, for example, *Dyonisiac Poetics and Euripides' Bacchae*, where Charles Segal examines the theatrical importance of the interplay of these two spatial fields in Euripides' work. In the *Bacchae*, "The plot structure heightens the tension between the tangible theatrical space and the imagined but more vivid space behind the *skènè* where in fact the most exciting action occurs. . . . By making us particularly aware of the two spatial fields, seen and unseen, the play self-consciously delineates the symbolic and mimetic dimension of theatrical representation" (241–42).

32. "THE FIRST VALET. Holes. Holes. In the old days, men used to live in holes. THE SECOND. In what? THE FIRST. In nothing at all. In holes, just holes" (81). The "hole" (*trou*) is a vertical concept: it descends. The idea of inside as it relates to *trou* is naturally relevant: a hole, grotto, or cave within the earth is "naturally inside." The house, a *man*-made construction, a product of man's will, is not so much naturally as existentially "inside."

33. The windows of the house form a part of this discussion. The windows constitute a resistance to the interior frame. A window separates by its materiality (its material frame) but connects by its transparency. This rhetorical ambivalence of the window stems from its dual function of opening-closure. Thus, the windows constitute a resistance to the interior frame of the house. The Master craves a representation of the interior of his house for two reasons. First, to "manipulate the inside of my house. Get a proper grasp of it, something clear and definite" (25). But, ultimately, he envisions "throwing it out the window": "And then, when I have a proper grasp of the inside of my house, what shall I do with it? . . . I shall chuck it out the bloody window" (34). When anything or anyone goes through a window it subsequently falls. Why would anyone want to throw the "inside of a house" through a window? A comparison with the function of the window in *Empire Builders* is in order. The Father's hypersubjective leap through the window, representing the plunge into his psychic interior, is, as we have seen, a dramatically conclusive reversal to the dominant vertical ascendance of the play's spatial structure. In *House*, however, the obsession with the interior is so precipitously articulated and directly and concretely established that a very different conclusion results. That the window expresses depth in both plays is not really questionable. When the Father takes his leap and when the Master expresses his will to throw the inside of his house through the window, they both are at the vertical summit of the dramatic space. Can the window be a reflection of a social exterior, thus creating a dramatic, aesthetic tension between the hypersubject and the inevitable social space in which he must exist and through which he must pass? Or, is the window a metaphysical expression of a purely interior reality or space into which the Father takes a highly symbolic plunge and into which the Master would cast the inside of his house—which is no more than a

reflection of his own interior—thereby setting up a redoubled metaphorical echoing of interior *abyme?*

34. This idea of the hole above and below reminds us of the "abyss" of the kingdom in *Exit the King*, where, according to Marguerite, "We're poised over a gaping chasm. Nothing but a growing void all around us" (78). The original French text reads: *"L'abyme grandit. Au-dessous il y a le trou, au-dessus, il y a le trou."* A literal translation would read, "The abyss is getting larger. Below there is a hole, above there is a hole" (*Le Roi se meurt* 78). When the Guard reassures her that they continue to keep themselves at the surface, Marguerite replies that they are nevertheless doomed to the "abyss": "There's nothing but the crust left. We'll soon be adrift in space" (*Exit* 78). In the original French, this last sentence reads, *"[N]ous ne serons plus que l'abyme"* (*Le Roi* 61). A more literal translation would read, "We will wind up as an abyss" or "We will be no more than an abyss." The reader will have noticed how often I return to the original French for "hypersubjective accuracy" when dealing with all the "absurdist" texts of this study. This discrepancy in the translation, this need to rediscover the more literal sense of a hypersubjective idea or process suggested by the original text, demonstrates, once again, that contemporary translators (and scholars) are not sufficiently sensitive to the metaphysical properties of these texts.

35. "So I had a family. (*He reflects*) . . . Sometimes I feel as if I'm remembering things that happened to somebody else. (*He laughs.*) Somebody else! Whereas in fact I'm all alone" (66). "I always had the impression that I was alone, in any case" (*Empire Builders* 70).

36. In the original French, the last sentence is ambiguous: "Et puis ça revient" (*Maison* 170). This can mean "he comes back to life." But it can also be translated as "it starts over again."

37. No English version of play available. All references to this work are from the following edition: *Théâtre V* (Paris: Bernard Grasset, 1973), 169–216. Translations are mine.

38. E. Littré, *Dictionnaire de la langue française.*

39. Paul Robert, *Dictionnaire de la langue française.*

40. The bowler hat is, of course, the teacher's most essential accoutrement and the key to his identity. In addition, Annick, the first student to attack the teacher, is also the one who takes the initiative to retrieve the Cancre from his subterranean prison.

41. See chapter 2.

42. According to the student's account, when the teacher spoke of Don Juan, for example, he exalted him as an historical literary figure: "he exalted Don Juan, he went into ecstasy over Don Juan: eroticism, paneroticism, corporalism, neo-pornographism" (180). But when he sees a schoolgirl strip naked on his desk he is completely beside himself: "Put your clothes back on, Mademoiselle, put your clothes back on" (180). The students interpret this as his inability to *be* (or to truly understand or emulate) Don Juan, to interiorize his character: "There's what Don Juan said, and there's the response of Don Juan *en situation*" (180).

43. Ironically, the Cancre is the only individualized character in the play. The information revealed about his background, though rarefied, is more than we know about the other students. When the question arises as to why his parents did not complain of his missing during his seven years of imprisonment, one of the students mentions that he is an orphan, a circumstance which adds to his condition of social isolation.

44. Obaldia has evidently coined the verb "s'introvertir" in French to apply to his protagonist.

45. In this respect the Cancre embodies a powerful oxymoronic image of asocial "presence-absence" in the hypersubject. We remember that at the end of *House of Bones* the Master states "I'm not here," which I have interpreted to imply the hypersubject's antagonistic, contradictory relationship to social space. This is no less applicable to the Cancre: "Why are you acting like one who is not here?" asks the student Maryse (204).

46. See Vladimir Voloshinov's *Marxism and the Philosophy of Language,* esp. 9–41, where Voloshinov establishes the materialist argument that all human meaning is realized through signs, that all signs are social, and that "inner being" is actually nonmaterial in nature and therefore unembodied in signs.

47. We remember Vladimir's line near the conclusion of *Godot:* "Habit is a great deafener" (*sourdine*).

48. Trans. Neville and Stephen Plaice (London: Heinemann, 1976).

49. *La Force de l'habitude,* directed by Jacques Kraemer, Théâtre de la Tempête, Paris, 1986.

50. See also figure 18 for an interesting comparison between the empty stage space of the French production with the more furnished (less empty) space of the American production by Paul Draper.

51. Gruber distinguishes between repetition in Beckett and in Bernhard: "Because of the naturalistic subtext from which [mirrorings and echoes] originate, however, Bernhard's figures' repetitions suggest a palpable attempt to show the eerie theatricality on which human character ultimately rests. When words spread so infectiously from one individual to others, the separate characters from which they normally issue become alarmingly similar; a new identity is created, what one might call the mimetic subject" (*Missing Persons* 125).

52. On the topic of "The body in Beckett's theatre," Pierre Chabert points out that the body is not a "means" as it is in psychological theatre, but rather, "it is *worked*" ("The Body in Beckett's Theatre" 23; author's emphasis). The relatively immobile bodies of Beckett's characters "always exist in a state of lack or negativity: unable to be seen, or to move, or to see . . . or to hear. . . . And yet it is precisely this lack which gives the body its existence, its dramatic force and its reality as a working material for the stage." Chabert argues that Beckett's objective was "to affirm cruelly (as Artaud would have said) a space invested by the body" (24). I would expand this argument to include the following objective: a body invested by space, theatro-psychic space.

53. Not surprisingly, insomnia is a common affliction of Bernhard's characters. Stephen D. Dowden explains it in these terms: "Bernhard asks what it would be like if the mind were not able to forget the omnipresence of death. Among other things, the mind's unblinking vigilance would make it difficult to sleep" (*Understanding Thomas Bernhard* 25).

54. Referring to another of Bernhard's plays, *The President,* William Gruber makes the following observation: "The President's monologue differs qualitatively from a speech by, say, Volpone or Harpagon, mainly because its mode of expression and its peculiar mechanisms suggest a state of mind that is paralytic rather than intent upon action. Its attraction for an audience is therefore more mesmeric than comedic" (*Missing Persons* 129).

5. The Hypersubject Avatar Manqué

1. Cited in Esslin, *Theatre of the Absurd*, 325.

2. See Patrice Pavis's definition of "theatrical effect" (*effet théâtral*) and "reality effect" (*effet de réel*) in his *Dictionnaire du théâtre*. Referring to Roland Barthes's concept of *effet de réel*, he explains that the reality effect belongs primarily to the illusionist objectives of naturalistic theatre. The reality effect obscures the fictional nature of the stage image and transports the spectator into the "symbolized reality" of the stage. In effect, it tricks the spectator into interpreting the false truth as a real truth of which he/she is a part. The theatrical effect is an opposite process. According to Pavis, it is stage action that openly reveals its artificial, theatrical nature. Though he does not address the theatrical effect of the stage image itself, this too can produce such an effect. The *hyper*theatrical effect produced by the hypersubjective image is a combination of these two effects. Even as its metatheatrical quality reveals itself as theatre, it draws the spectator's consciousness into the suprareferential illusion of the empty psyche of the protagonist.

3. The process combining dramatic tableau with dramaturgical gesture to suggest the existence of a deeper consciousness is not without relation to the "absolute gesture" of Artaud's Balinese central dancer.

4. Andrew K. Kennedy examines Pinter's method of "shaping dialogue," which he sees in the "'word-painting' and 'sound-painting' patterns of *Landscape* and *Silence*" (*Six Dramatists* 178).

5. Bob Mayberry sees three spaces in this play, spaces marked by emptiness: "In a sense, *Landscape* includes three spaces: his, hers, and theirs. His and her places in the kitchen are visually separated by the long table that stands conspicuously empty between them" (*Theatre of Discord* 53).

6. Andrew K. Kennedy believes that Beth and Duff, i.e., their monologues, "are antithetical in every utterance; she is all inwardness, he a verbal Tarquin" (*Six Dramatists in Search of a Language* 189).

7. The despair, melancholy, and existential fear in Pinter's work is, to be sure, very different from that of the psychological theatre that precedes it and coexists with it. Pinter's "new realism" avoids enacting the psychological motivation we see in the theatre of Arthur Miller and Tennessee Williams, for example. It is a good deal more concentrated and "open" in the sense that it appeals to the personal consciousness and personal experience of the individual spectator.

8. Take the example of one of the first exchanges between the inseparable pair, in which they suggest they "better get on," painstakingly decide they must move "forward," and wind up recoiling at the sight of the audience (*Rosencrantz and Guildenstern* 20).

9. The *Times Literary Supplement* says this of Handke's *Sprechstücke*, the language plays, like *Offending the Audience* and *Self-Accusation:* "Man is depicted as the product of language and becomes a montage of linguistic banalities. . . . Handke created a special kind of verbal alienation, examining words on an empty stage, juggling with the same terms in various syntactical sequences and allowing the histrionics of presentation to make the familiar seem strange" (quoted in *Peter Handke. Plays: 1*, i).

10. In an introduction to this play, Tom Khun argues that "Perhaps Handke is not even just saying that language *can* be used to manipulate and indoctrinate. Rather, in a typically radical gesture, he seems to be saying that language has to be a trap,

that by language personality structures are necessarily deformed, if not destroyed" ("Introduction" xvii; author's emphasis).

11. There are, in fact, multiple sources of discourse in the play, including the language of the prompters who "speak from all sides . . . Over a good amplifying system" (60).

12. We see another hypersubjective rapprochement in Handke's *The Ride across Lake Constance* (1970). In a subtle reminder of the dramaturgy of space at the beginning of Beckett's *Endgame,* the action begins in a large room in which "Most of the furnishings . . . are covered with extremely white loose covers" (*The Ride* 167). Most of these are removed methodically by "A Woman" in blackface, apparently the maid. Whereas in *Endgame* Clov removes an old sheet covering Hamm, here the Woman "pulls the cover from under Emil Jannings," the only other character visible on the stage when the curtain rises. This technique of "whitening" the stage space and its contents is complemented by Handke's interest in motionlessness, which he uses to create a tableau. From curtain up, Jannings is frozen in his chair. After the Woman removes the covers and exits, Jannings continues to be immobile and "nothing moves on stage for a while except for the record" (169). Immobility also punctuates the end of the play. According to the stage directions, characters have bouts of motionlessness, and one character "tries a gesture that atrophies instantly" (232–33).

13. Bottoms also writes that *Action* is not "a celebration of immanent presence in the metaphysical, modernist sense of trying to capture something of the human essence of the artwork. Rather, the play explores presence in the postmodernist sense of blunt, three-dimensional physical fact" (*The Theatre of Sam Shepard* 120).

14. We see another contrast to the hypersubjective work in the explicit references to the state of crisis in which these characters are involved, such as this statement by Lupe: "It was smart thinking to raise our own [turkey]. To see ahead into the crisis" (131). Beckett's characters do not "name" their crisis, because they are not involved in one.

15. Yet Shepard did not completely reconcile himself to the safety of referentiality. He continued to work with the empty stage, one which continued to imply analogical connections to the mind of his characters. Ten years after *Action,* he produced *A Lie of the Mind* (1985), in which he clearly and directly deals with realistic, physical subject matter, such as food, sex, lies, the violence of human relationships, gender issues. He continues to experiment with metadramatic references in the dialogue of his characters, who refer to themselves as characters, articulating connections between the "real" world and the stage. Yet this realism plays out on a "Deep, wide, dark space" which creates the impression "of infinite space, going off to nowhere." Deeper still, Shepard creates the impression of a stage in the process of self-construction. In Act 1, there are no walls, "only furniture and props and light in the bare space." Walls with no ceilings make their appearance in the second and third acts (8). The architecture is not simply constructed *on* an empty stage; rather, it emerges within empty space and as a function of emptiness. Yet, the language of Shepard's characters does not fully co-operate with the "empty" dramaturgy of space.

6. The Hypersubjective Marionette-like Legacy of Pierrot

1. In *Theatre of the Absurd,* see Esslin's chapter "The Tradition of the Absurd," esp. 327–37, where he presents an illuminating survey of the evolution of the metaphysical properties of the mimus from Antiquity to the theatre of the absurd.

2. Robert F. Storey points to this complexity in his study of the history of the Pierrot mask: "Pierrot's theatrical and literary history is the record of vacillations between two dramatic and psychological 'types.' At one pole stands his Italian predecessor Pedrolino, who, like the Gallicized Harlequin, is a creature of insouciance and activity, a character of almost no psychological 'depth,' a symbol of comic irrepressibility and unselfconscious verve. He inhabits a dense social world, but, curiously, rarely suffers pangs of social conscience. At the other pole stands Hamlet—a figure of melancholy indolence, a character of inscrutable depth and complexity, a symbol of human vulnerability and mortality, a moralist tortured by conscience—but, just as curiously, an egoist who is profoundly asocial and solipsistic" (*Pierrot* xiv).

3. Bakhtin refers to "grotesque realism" and "renaissance realism" as aesthetic concepts (*Rabelais and His World* 18, 24).

4. Consider how the distorted human figures in the paintings of two important artists of the period, Jerome Bosch and Bruegel the Elder, seem to come together to form one giant socially organic mass.

5. See also David Madden (*Harlequin's Stick, Charlie's Cane* 88).

6. I prefer the term "anatomical" to "biological" because the latter of these terms was problematical for Bakhtin's Marxist-Formalist school of thought. See, for example, V. N. Voloshinov's charge of biological reductionism against the Freudian ahistorical approach to human psychology in *Freudiansism: A Critical Sketch*. Voloshinov not only accused Freud of what he described as "psychobiologism" (91), but he criticized most turn-of-the-century "modern" thinkers like Bergson for placing "life in the biological sense" at the center of their philosophical systems so that "Isolated organic unity is declared to be the highest value and criterion of philosophy" (12). For Voloshinov and others of the Bakhtin school, concepts promoting the "enclosed organic unity of individual life" or any kind of "self-sufficient unity" (13) aspired to "create a world beyond the social and the historical" (91).

7. The popular mask is the approximate plastic equivalent of Bakhtin's textual theory of "heteroglossia," which Michael Holquist explains as follows: "The base condition governing the operation of meaning in any utterance. It is that which insures the primacy of context over text . . . all utterances are heteroglot in that they are functions of a matrix of forces practically impossible to recoup, and therefore impossible to resolve" (*The Dialogic Imagination* 428).

8. Yet Bakhtin assures us that the romantic (subjectivist) mask can never become an entirely "asocial" motif cut off from the organic whole of popular culture: "Even in modern life it is enveloped in a peculiar atmosphere and is seen as a particle of some other world. The mask never becomes just another object among objects" (*Rabelais and His World* 40). For Bakhtin, the mask is like all other signs in the universe in that it can only communicate its metaphysical message in terms that are ultimately dialogic, and therefore, ultimately social. This Marxist theory of meaning, developed by the "Bakhtin Circle," is probably most clearly elaborated in V. N. Voloshinov, *Marxism and the Philosophy of Language*.

9. In her article "Masques, acteurs, marionnettes: objets «transitionnels»" Brunella Eruli discusses the connection between mask, actor, and marionette. She describes, for example, the Bread and Puppet Theatre's method of having the mask cover the entire body of the actor, thereby transforming the mask into what she calls an "inhabitable marionette" [*marionnette habitable*] (210–11).

10. In this respect, Jarry's Ubu provides a link, an intermediate stage in the evolution of the hyper-caricatural into the hypersubjective.

11. Bert States explains Artaud's resistance to referentiality, and consequently to the socialist basis of theatrical art, as follows: "The thing emphasized throughout Artaud's theory is its war against the tyranny of reference, or at least reference to the social world from which man, as dreamer, is automatically excluded." Consequently, the object of theatre "is to strip signs, to empty them of received content and to reconstitute them as a beginning or, in Rousseau's word, as a birth. It is what we might loosely call a phenomenological theater (as opposed to semiological) in that it seeks to retrieve a naive perception of the thing—its 'objective aspect'—before it was defined out of sight by language" (*Great Reckonings* 109).

12. See chapter 2 for a discussion of the con-fusion of mind with body in Artaud's writing.

13. See, for instance, Bakhtin's essay "The Spatial Form of the Hero." "Hence, any aesthetic existence, i.e., a whole, integral human being, is not founded and validated from within—from a possible self-consciousness" (91)

14. We must not view Artaud's subjectivist critical position as an endorsement of any individual essence, one which would contradict a priori an understanding of the profoundly social nature of human consciousness. See Franco Tonelli's *L'Esthétique de la cruauté*, where he explains that, in Artaud's writings, the practice of a bona fide organic theatre will lead to "the systematic disintegration of [the spectator's] individuality by a process of absorption into a universe of instinctive and primitive forces . . . becoming himself an integral part of this whole" (18–19). Simply put, Artaud's understanding of organic society is more holistic, and psychically universalist, than either Marxist or pragmatic theories would or could allow.

15. Cited in Nicoll, *The World of Harlequin* 73.

16. Nicoll explains the "appearance" of Pierrot as part of the occasional process of the substitution of one *commedia* character for another: "A typical example of this is the substitution of the French Pierrot for an original Pedrolino. In Scala's plays Pedrolino pushes himself forward as a gay-witted confident intriguer; Pierrot becomes the very image of sad-eyed simplicity. That the one took his name from the other is certain; yet the two are completely distinct" (*The World of Harlequin* 24). Curiously, this description of Pedrolino closely resembles that of Harlequin.

17. Nicoll supports this view: "Harlequin's personality depends partly on his suppleness; since he is masked, our eyes are intent upon him in his entirety, not merely upon his features . . . a gesture which might easily be missed when our attention is directed towards a comedian's features suddenly assumes an unwonted and even strange significance" (*The World of Harlequin* 41). Ferdinando Taviani offers a more extreme view of the strategy behind the mask, believing that the half-mask, the type worn by Harlequin, functioned to "efface" the face. For him, this mask produced "the negation of the face as locus of the body on which the interior manifested itself" ("Positions du masque dans la commédia dell'arte" 128). It was because of this erasure of interiority that the popular *commedia* character could only "live" through his actions (Baschera, *Théâtralité dans l'oeuvre de Molière* 18). See Baschera for an alternative view of the *commedia*'s link to popular culture. Contradicting Bakhtin, Baschera believes that many of the theatrical techniques associated with the *commedia* are not really "a spontaneous manifestation of a popular culture." Instead, we should study them as the expression of an artistic professionalism (141–42).

18. Note that in Watteau's eighteenth-century Pierrot portraits (figs. 2 and 3), instead of a black skullcap, which was more of a nineteenth-century development, Pierrot wears a headdress that, one might argue, still draws attention to the head by creating a corona that encircles or frames the face.

19. One might argue that Pantalone's nose too would surely draw attention to the head; but in this case, the emphasis is not on the particular location of the body part, but rather on its phallic form which, perhaps paradoxically, refers back to the lower body of the popular mode.

20. In Pierrot's white face, Robert F. Storey sees the metatheatrical fusion of "actor and type," a unity of "conception and interpretation" that contrasts with the role of Harlequin: "Harlequin seems always ready to pull off his mask and put his role aside to chat amiably with the Columbines of the *fêtes galantes;* but Pierrot's pathetic white face cannot be unmasked: creator and role are fused into a single character" (*Pierrot* 30–31).

21. This poem is included in *Antonin Artaud: Works on Paper,* edited by Margit Rowell. In this collection of Artaud's drawings, we remark the illustrations of his Pierrot-like portraits and self-portraits. We also remark his surrealist technique of representing figures suspended in empty space, i.e., the mind-space. See, for example, "The Hanged Woman," 64.

22. Somewhat surprisingly, in his book on the crisis of the dramatic character in modern theatre, Robert Abirached links the "gestural metamorphosis" of the *commedia* character to the theatrical and the social, nostalgically touching on the relationship among superhuman physical dexterity, inhuman nature, and the popular social objective of the *commedia:* "[One must imagine] in the gaily-colored daylight, Harlequin, Pantalone, Matamore, whining or muttering, executing high-flying arabesques, subjecting their bodies to gestural metamorphosis. To this extent they are different from the men they usually are since their theatrical names supplant their identity. Absent and present in their own right, they all have the primordial task of materially bringing to life an image of world, of society, and of men" (*La Crise du personnage dans le théâtre moderne* 20).

Linking the idea of farce with the "idea of an actor's art, the arte of *commedia* dell'arte," Eric Bentley too refers to the *commedia* as "the theatre of the human body but the body in a state as far from the natural as the voice of Chaliapin is from my voice or yours. It is a theatre in which, though the marionettes are men, the men are supermarionettes. It is the theatre of the surrealist body." Bentley believes that "the celebrated types of the *commedia* have deeper roots than social manners or even society itself" (*The Life of the Drama* 252).

23. The collective body relates to the idea of collective story in the *commedia* of Harlequin. The economy of story, despite its schematic scenario form, was still integral to the play's action. Though we could begin to describe the on-stage characters as marionette-like stereotypes, they were also interactive social symbols who maintained a symbiotic relationship with social—rather than psycho-metaphysical—reality. The story was a pretext to articulate the social *character* in the fullest sense of the term. The characters told their story through their individual bodies, which were part of a large social body in Bakhtin's sense of the concept. Patrice Pavis explains that in the *commedia* "the emphasis was on corporal skill, the art of replacing long text with gestural signs and of organizing the performance 'choreographically,' that is to say, according to the

group" (*Dictionnaire* 60). So the story was body as the body was story. In other words, the communion of the individual bodies produced and communicated the idea of a larger social body which, in effect, formed the essence of the story. With Pierrot, however, the character loses its "socio-narrative" function and becomes a pretext for metaphysical, psychic image.

24. Kleist's point of view, of course, is a romantic one. So, as Harold B. Segel points out, Kleist's essay on the marionette "evidences the Romantic belief in the cognitive and creative superiority of the unconscious over the conscious" ("On the Marionette Theater" 15).

25. In an attempt to explain the link between mask, posture, and pelvis, Lea Logie refers to the writings of the theatre anthropologist (and recent Nobel laureate in literature) Dario Fo: "Dario Fo, who has used masks extensively, writes that anyone wearing a *commedia*-style mask discovers that the entire performance hinges on movement emanating from the pelvis, describing how each *commedia* character has a distinct posture which is dependent on the position of the pelvis. . . . This is not surprising, as we have seen already that most of the pedagogues in this study find the pelvic area of the body to be the source of energy for movement and gesture" ("Developing a Physical Vocabulary for the Contemporary Actor" 240).

26. Louis Duchartre's description, cited in Martin Green and John Swann, *The Triumph of Pierrot* 6.

27. Describing Watteau's painting, the art historian Donald Posner writes: "he was given the characteristic pose of the Pierrot mask—frontal, stiff, arms-at-side . . . the development of the composition shows an effort to achieve grandeur and monumentality by means of clearly defined structure, massed forms and frontality of poses" (*Antoine Watteau* 265).

28. We recognize, of course, that one and the other is not without its social and cerebral dimensions, which are not, of course, mutually exclusive.

29. William E. Gruber asserts that "Broadly speaking, Beckett's late plays require 'Übermarionettes' to act them" (*Missing Persons* 10).

30. Mel Gordon describes the comic routines, or *lazzi*, of the *commedia* in the following manner: "*[L]azzi* allude to any discrete, or independent, comic and repeatable activity that guaranteed laughs for its participants" (*Lazzi* 5). The term "participants" is key, since it suggests that the characters (and the actors) themselves created a collective act as opposed to an individual role.

31. Louis Barrault, the great twentieth-century French director, called the *commedia* "the true art of the theatre" which "denounces the absurdity of life and endeavours to restore its equilibrium. The Commedia dell' Arte, which I cannot claim to know fully, seems to me just as an old man. How many 'doctors' do we not meet in life, and is the second Zanni with the white mask not the modern lamplighter? Don't we meet everywhere these extraordinary characters which Callot had already fixed on copper?" (cited in James Fisher, *The Theatre of Yesterday and Tomorrow* 236–37)

32. One often reads of the "dehumanization" of the dramatic character. Modern theorists perceive the characters of both traditions, the stock characters of the *commedia* and the "absurd" beings of nouveau théâtre, to have one particularly outstanding trait in common: they are both dehumanized. As Giacomo Oreglia puts it, the *commedia* was famous for having produced some bizarre, if not entirely absurd,

stage images: "Like comic strip characters, they seemed unreal and ageless, masks without souls or nerves" (*The Commedia dell'arte* xi). In speaking of the nouveau théâtre characters, on the other hand, Emmanuel Jacquart says they are "'abnormal' beings, or more precisely, '*limited beings*'" (*Le théâtre de la dérision* 146; Jacquart's emphasis). To explain the abnormality, Jacquart cites the Spanish philosopher Ortega y Gasset's famous formula for contemporary art, an art whose primary tendency is to resolutely deform reality, "to destroy its human aspect, to dehumanize it" (146). So both the *commedia* and the nouveau théâtre have dehumanized the dramatic character calling into question the role of a "naturalized" human nature within the aesthetic frame of theatre art. But "dehumanized" has as many meanings as there are humans.

33. This is my translation from the French translation.

34. Recently, during a discussion of Artaud's theatrical theory in a graduate seminar, I experimented informally with the reception of the mask by comparing my students' reaction to two types of mask. Having set the ambience for the experiment by lowering the lights in the seminar room, I placed a wooden Mayan mask in front of my face. They reacted by acknowledging its "strangeness." Then I placed a very different type of mask on my face, a more contemporary, rubberized, completely expressionless, white face. They were visibly, audibly moved, saying that they were more "frightened" by this image than by the former. We agreed that their intensified reaction to the "empty" mask was probably related to Artaud's poetic expression of the potential of the human face to function as "an empty force."

35. James Fisher, for example, links the creation of today's theatrical tragic doll directly to Arlecchino instead of to the Arlecchino mutant, Pierrot: "Particularly in the character of Arlecchino, the leading *zanni* of *commedia*, modern theatre found a model in which to embody an absurdly lyrical vision of contemporary humanity, leading to such creations as Chaplin's 'Little Tramp' and Beckett's and Ionesco's existential clowns" (*The Theatre of Yesterday and Tomorrow* 11).

36. The annual journal *PUCK* provides evidence for the extraordinary interest of the French in the marionette. This journal, produced by the Institut International de la Marionnette and dedicated entirely to scholarly and artistic research on the marionette, has provided an excellent barometer for contemporary sensibility toward the marionette since the late 1980s.

37. As early as the mid-nineteenth century, Charles Magnin referred to the marionette as a "theatrical microcosm"(9); and more recently, Roger D. Bensky has elaborated on the innate theatricality of the marionette, writing that, unlike the human actor,

> Offstage, the marionette is inert and inexpressive. It is an object and not a being.
> Therefore, the only expressive power of the marionette must come from theatrical animation. (*Recherches sur les structures et la symbolique de la marionnette* 26)

38. See Craig on masks and marionettes, esp. *The Theatre Advancing* 107–42.

39. See Patrice Pavis's analysis of the actor's work and the spectator's perception of this work in the following essays: "Acting" (*Encyclopedia of Languages and Linguistics*) and "Le Jeu de l'acteur." Pavis points out that the actor has a new role in

contemporary culture: "Thus, in contemporary theater practice, the actor does not refer to a real person, an individual that forms a whole. . . . The contemporary actor is no longer responsible for imitating an inalienable individual; rather, he performs his insufficiencies, his absences, his multiplicity" ("Acting" 18).

40. See also Monique Borie, *Le Fantôme ou le théâtre qui doute,* where she discusses Craig's idea of the *Übermarionette* [*surmarionnette*] as a return to the revelatory visual force of the ancient idol. She writes of the "in-between of the live body and the statue, this in-between that the Übermarionette comes to signify" (229).

41. The distinguished producer-director of marionette theatre Enno Podehl writes that he "experiments and constructs space with marionettes" and that the most critical quality of his stage is its emptiness: "Wherever there is no uncertainty, no empty space, no performance space, there is no theatre either—and we can't expect anything from it. That is why I'm for 'empty' space (and for the 'empty' marionette), for space that is violently formulated, but that is also a creator of space, an opener of space. I'm for a space that is formed, but only formed through performance" ("Ceux qui touchent le ciel" 31–32).

42. In the 1920s the Dutch scenic designer Hendricus Wijdeveld, Gordon Craig's contemporary, wrote that marionettes "are strong because they are all mind, and they mercilessly surpass the human actor" (cited in Plassard, *Les Mains de lumière* 236).

43. Michèle Foucré, for example, maintains that the marionette-like status of Beckett's characters derives from the mechanical gesturing indicated by the written text. She observes that in Beckett's theatre, "There is a tendency toward the reabsorption of the character into a marionette, an automaton who mechanically executes gestures from which all thought, and consequently all utterance, are erased" (*Le Geste et la parole dans le théâtre de Samuel Beckett* 21). Though she suggests the erasure of thought and utterance—i.e., the disengagement of intentionality from gesturing—she does not address the question of the character's body or its mind as an empty space, and she certainly does not discuss the metatheatrical relevance of the erasure (see also 17–33). We remember too what Jean Claude said of the connection between death, space, and the individual in Ionesco's *Exit the King:* "[the] shrinking of the kingdom . . . suggests the shrinking of the individual's consciousness, or the progressive capitulation of thought" (247–48). Yet Claude, too, neglected to elaborate on this emptiness of mind and its relation to theatrical space.

44. Monique Borie refers to the "force of immobile expression" of the mask (*Le Fantôme* 211), which resembles, of course, the fixed head.

Conclusion

1. See, for example, Ronald Vince's "The Aristotelian Theatrical Paradigm as Cultural-Historical Construct." Investigating the "historical-historiographical process that provided the basis for the Aristotelian paradigm," Vince affirms that Athenian theatre "was historically embedded in the ideology of the Athenian polis. In the class struggle that marked Athens' internal politics, and in the struggle to preserve and elevate her status over that of her rivals, it was necessary to select details from the common mythology of Mycenean Greece that would support the ideology of Athenian political, cultural and religious superiority" (38).

WORKS CITED

Abirached, Robert. *La Crise du personnage dans le théâtre moderne.* Paris: Gallimard, 1994.

Adorno, Theodor. *Aesthetic theory.* Trans. C. Lenhardt. Ed. Gretel Adorno and Rolf Tiedemann. New York: Routledge and Kegan Paul, 1986.

———. "Trying to Understand *Endgame*." *Samuel Beckett's Endgame.* Ed. Harold Bloom. New York: Chelsea House, 1988. 9–40.

Alter, Jean. *A Sociosemiotic Theory of Theatre.* Philadelphia: University of Pennsylvania Press, 1990.

Aristotle. *La Poétique.* Trans. and annotated by Roselyne Dupont-Roc and Jean Lallot. Paris: Seuil, 1980.

Arnheim, Rudolph. "From Chaos to Wholeness." *Journal of Aesthetics and Art Criticism.* 54.2 (Spring 1996). 117–20.

Artaud, Antonin. "From *The Nerve Meter.*" *Antonin Artaud: Selected Writings.* Ed. Susan Sontag. Trans. Helen Weaver. Berkeley: University of California Press, 1988. 79–88.

———. "L'Homme contre le destin." *Oeuvres complètes.* Vol 8. Paris: Gallimard, 1971. 184–95.

———. "Les nouvelles révélations de l'être." *Oeuvres complètes.* Vol. 7. Paris: Gallimard, 1967. 145–76.

———. *The Theater and Its Double.* Trans. Mary Caroline Richards. New York: Grove Press, 1958.

———. "Le Théâtre et les dieux." *Oeuvres complètes.* Vol. 8. Paris: Gallimard, 1971. 196–206.

———. "Van Gogh le suicide de la société." *Oeuvres complètes.* Vol. 13. Paris: Gallimard, 1974. 13–20.

————. "Le Visage humain . . ." *Antonin Artaud: Works on Paper.* Ed. Margit Rowell. New York: The Museum of Modern Art, 1996.

Bablet, Denis. "D'Edward Gordon Craig au Bauhaus." *Le Masque: du rite au théâtre.* Paris: Editions du CNRS, 1985. 137–46.

————. *The Revolution of Stage Design in the Twentieth Century.* Paris: Léon Amiel, 1977.

Bachelard, Gaston. *La Poétique de l'espace.* Paris: PUF, 1958.

————. *Psychanalyse du feu.* Paris: Gallimard (Folio), 1949.

Bakhtin, Mikhail. *Rabelais and His World.* Trans. Helene Iswolsky. Cambridge, Mass.: MIT Press, 1965.

————. "The Spatial Form of the Hero." *Art and Answerability: Early Philosophical Essays by M. M. Bakhtin.* Ed. Michael Holquist and Vadim Liapunov. Trans. Vadim Liapunov. Austin: University of Texas Press, 1990. 22–99.

Bal, Mieke. "Mise en abyme et iconicité." *Littérature* 29 (1978). 116–28.

Barthes, Roland. *Camera Lucida: Reflections on Photography.* Trans. Richard Howard. New York: Hille and Wang, 1981.

————. "The Structuralist Activity." *Critical Essays.* Trans. Richard Howard. Evanston, Illinois: Northwestern University Press, 1972.

————. "Le Théâtre de Baudelaire." *Essais critiques.* Paris: Seuil, 1964. 41–47.

Baschera, Marco. *Théâtralité dans l'oeuvre de Molière.* Tübingen, Germany: Gunter Narr Verlag, 1998.

Baty, Gaston, and René Chavance. *Histoire des marionnettes.* Paris: PUF, 1972.

Beckett, Samuel. *Collected Shorter Plays.* New York: Grove Press, 1984.

————. *Disjecta: Miscellaneous Writings and a Dramatic Fragment.* Ed. Ruby Cohn. New York: Grove Press, 1984.

————. *Endgame.* Trans. Samuel Beckett. New York: Grove Press, 1958.

————. *Fin de partie.* Paris: Minuit, 1957.

————. *Ill Seen Ill Said.* New York: Grove, 1981.

————. *Malone Dies.* London: John Calder, 1958.

————. *Not I: First Love and Other Shorts.* New York: Grove Press, 1974.

————. *Peephole Art for Television.* Videocassette. Dir. John L. Reilly. Prod. Global Village for the Beckett Project, 1988–1989.

————. *Rockaby. Rockaby and Other Short Pieces by Samuel Beckett.* New York: Grove Press, 1981.

Benedikt, Michael. Introduction. *The Avant-Garde, Dada, and Surrealism: Modern French Theatre.* Ed and trans. Michael Benedikt and George E. Wellwarth. New York: Dutton, 1966. ix–xxxv.

Bensky, Roger D. *Recherches sur les structures et la symbolique de la marionnette.* Paris: Nizet, 1971.

Bentley, Eric. *The Life of the Drama.* New York: Applause, 1991.

Bergson, Henri. *Creative Evolution.* Trans. Arthur Mitchell. New York: Random House, 1944.

————. *L'Evolution créatrice.* Paris: Félix Alcan, 1937.

Bernhard, Thomas. *The Force of Habit.* Trans. Neville and Stephen Plaice. London: Heinemann, 1976.

————. *Ténèbres: textes, discours, entretiens.* Paris: Maurice Nadeau, 1986.

Boal, Agusto. *Jeux pour acteurs et non-acteurs.* Paris: La Découverte, 1991.

————. *The Rainbow of Desire: The Boal Method of Theatre and Therapy.* Trans. Adrian Jackson. New York: Routledge, 1995.

———. *Theater of the Oppressed.* Trans. Charles A. and Maria-Odilia Leal McBride. New York: Urizen Books, 1979.

Borie, Monique. *Antonin Artaud: Le théâtre et le retour aux sources.* Paris: Gallimard, 1989.

———. *Le Fantôme ou le théâtre qui doute.* Avignon, France: Actes Sud, 1997.

———. *Mythe et théâtre aujourd'hui: une quête impossible?* Paris: Nizet, 1981.

Bottoms, Stephen J. *The Theatre of Sam Shepard: States of Crisis.* Cambridge: Cambridge University Press, 1998.

Bourdieu, Pierre, and Loic J. D. Wacquant. *An Invitation To Reflexive Sociology.* Chicago: University of Chicago Press, 1992.

Bowie, Malcolm. *Lacan.* Cambridge, Mass.: Harvard University Press, 1991.

Brater, Enoch. *Beyond Minimalism: Beckett's Late Style in the Theater.* New York: Oxford University Press, 1987.

Brecht, Bertoldt. *Brecht on Theatre: The Development of an Aesthetic.* Trans. John Willett. New York: Hill and Wang, 1964.

Brecht, Stephan. *The Bread and Puppet Theatre.* London: Methuen, 1988. Article (Chapter 5, Part 3) Rpt. as "The Puppet and the Mask: The Power of the Mask, the Dependency of the Puppet." *Bread and Puppet Museum.* Ed. Peter Schumann. Glover, Vt.: Bread and Puppet Theater, 1989. 16–24.

Brée, Germaine and Edouard Morot-Sir. *Littérature française: 9. Du surréalisme à l'empire de la critique.* Nouvelle édition révisée. Paris: Arthaud, 1990.

Breton, André. *Manifestes du surréalisme.* Paris: Gallimard, 1985.

———. *Manifestoes of Surrealism.* Trans. Richard Seaver and Helen R. Lane. Ann Arbor: University of Michigan Press, 1977.

Burns, Elizabeth. *Theatricality: A Study of Convention in the Theatre and in Social Life.* London: Langman Group, 1972.

Caillois, Roger. *Obliques.* Paris: Editions Stock, 1975.

Camus, Albert. *Le mythe de Sisyphe: essai sur l'absurde.* Paris: Gallimard, 1942.

Capra, Fritjof. *The Tao of Physics: An Exploration of the Parallels between Modern Physics and Eastern Mysticism.* 3rd ed., updated. Boston: Shambala, 1991.

Capusan, Maria Voda. "Theatre and Reflexivity." *Poetics* 13 (1984): 101–109.

Certeau, Michel de. "Practices of Space." *On Signs.* Ed. Marshall Blonsky. Baltimore: Johns Hopkins University Press, 1985. 122–45.

Chabert, Pierre. "The Body in Beckett's Theatre." *Journal of Beckett Studies* 8 (Autumn 1982): 23–28.

———. "Genèse d'une transposition scénique d'un texte de Samuel Beckett." *Théâtre et création.* Ed. Emmanuel Jacquart. Paris: Honoré Champion, 1994. 123–33.

———. "Samuel Beckett: lieu physique, théâtre du corps." *Cahiers Renaud Barrault.* 106 (1983). 80–98.

Claude, Jean. "La mort au théâtre: l'exemple du *Roi se meurt* de Ionesco." *La Mort en toutes lettres.* Ed. G. Ernst. Nancy, France: Presses Universitaires de Nancy, 1983. 239–52.

Cohn, Ruby. *Samuel Beckett: The Comic Gamut.* New Brunswick, N.J.: Rutgers University Press, 1962.

———. "Surrealism and Today's French Theatre." *Yale French Studies* 31 (May 1964). 159–65.

Copeau, Jacques. "Registres 1." *Esthétique théâtral: textes de Platon à Brecht.* Ed. Monique Borie. Paris: SEDES, 1982. 256–59.

———. "La Scène et l'acteur." Unpublished essay. *Le théâtre en France du Moyen Age à nos jours.* Ed. Jacqueline de Jomaron. Paris: Armand Colin, 1992. 734–36.

Corvin, Michel. "Contribution à l'analyse de l'espace scénique dans le théâtre contemporain." *Travail théâtral* 22 (1976): 62–80.

———. "Une écriture plurielle." *Le théâtre en France 2.* Ed. Jacqueline de Jomaron. Paris: Armand Colin, 1992. 912–58.

———. "Espace, temps, mise en abyme: le jeu du même ou de l'autre." *Mélanges pour Jacques Schérer: Dramaturgies: langages dramatiques.* Paris: Nizet, 1986.

Craig, Gordon. *The Theater Advancing.* 1947. New York: Benjamin Blom, 1963.

Dällenbach, Lucien. *Le Récit spéculaire: essai sur la mise en abyme.* Paris: Seuil, 1977.

Découflé, Philippe. "Le Mouvement impossible." *PUCK* 4 ("La marionnette et les autres arts"). Charleville-Mezières, France: Institut International de la Marionnette, 1991. 61–63.

Delbee, Anne. "Entretien avec Anne Delbee." With Philippe Foulquié and Alain Recoing. *Les Théâtres de marionnettes en France.* Ed. Philippe Foulquié. Lyon, France: La Manufacture, 1985. 45–52.

Deleuze, Gilles. "Il s'agit d'épuiser l'espace." *Théâtre Aujourd'hui. 3: L'univers scénique de Beckett.* Ed. Jean-Claude Lallias and Jean-Jacques Arnault. Paris: CND Press, 1994. 92–93.

Deleuze, Gilles and Félix Guattari. *Anti-Oedipus: Capitalism and Schizophrenia.* Trans. Robert Hurley, Mark Seem, and Helen R. Lane. New York: Viking Press, 1977.

Derrida, Jacques. "Freud and the Scene of Writing." *Writing and Difference.* Trans. Alan Bass. Chicago: University of Chicago Press, 1978.

———. "La parole soufflée." *Writing and Difference.* Trans. Alan Bass. Chicago: University of Chicago Press, 1978. 169–95.

———. "The Theater of Cruelty and the Closure of Representation." *Writing and Difference.* Trans. Alan Bass. Chicago: University of Chicago Press, 1978. 232–50.

Dort, Bernard. *La Représentation émancipée.* Arles, France: Actes Sud, 1988.

Dowden, Stephen D. *Understanding Thomas Bernhard.* Columbia: University of South Carolina Press, 1991.

Dubillard, Roland. *The House of Bones.* Trans. Barbara Wright. London: Calder and Boyars, 1971.

———. *La Maison d'os.* Paris: Gallimard, 1966.

Duckworth, Colin. *Angels of Darkness: Dramatic Effect in Samuel Beckett with Special Reference to Eugène Ionesco.* New York: Barnes and Noble, 1972.

Ducrot, Oswald and Tzvetan Todorov. *Encyclopedic Dictionary of the Science of Language.* Trans. Catherine Porter. Baltimore: Johns Hopkins University Press, 1983.

Duvignaud, Jean. *Sociologie du théâtre.* Paris: PUF, 1965.

———. *Le théâtre contemporain.* Paris: Larousse, 1974.

Eco, Umberto. "Interpreting Drama." *The Limits of Interpretation.* Bloomington: Indiana University Press, 1990. 101–10.

Elam, Keir. *The Semiotics of Theatre and Drama.* London: Methuen, 1980.

En attendant Godot. By Samuel Beckett. Dir. Philippe Adrien. Théâtre de la Tempête, Paris. 1993.

———. By Samuel Beckett. Dir. Joël Jouanneau. Théâtre des Amandiers, Nanterre, France. 1991.

Erikson, Jon. *The Fate of the Object: From Modern Object to Postmodern Sign in Performance, Art, and Poetry.* Ann Arbor: University of Michigan Press, 1995.

Eruli, Brunela. "Masques, acteurs, marionnettes: objets «transitionnels»." *Le Masque: Du rite au théâtre*. Ed. Odette Aslan and Denis Bablet. Paris: Editions du CNRS, 1985. 209–17.

———. "Ruptures d'échelle." *PUCK* 4 ("La marionnette et les autres arts"). Charleville-Mezières, France: Institut International de la Marionnette, 1991. 7–12.

Essif, Les. "Beyond the Structuralist Language-Space of the Mind: French Theorists Detecting *Signals* from the Psychic Underworld." *Arachne* 5.1 (1998). 140–74.

———. "Introducing the 'Hyper' Theatrical Subject: The *Mise en Abyme* of Empty Space." *Journal of Dramatic Theory and Criticism* 9 (Fall 1994): 67–86.

———. "Teaching Literary-Dramatic Texts as Culture-in-Process in the Foreign Language Theater Practicum: The Strategy of Combining Texts." *ADFL Bulletin* 29.3 (Spring 1998). 24–33.

———. "Twentieth-Century Surrealism and the Theatrical Psychic Space of French Nouveau Théâtre." *Essays in Theatre* 12.2 (May 1994). 157–68.

Esslin, Martin. *Theatre of the Absurd*. 3rd ed. New York: Penguin, 1983.

———. "A Drama of Disease and Derision: The Plays of Thomas Bernhard." *Modern Drama* 23:4 (Jan. 1981). 367–84.

Fall, Jean-Claude. "Voyage à l'intérieur de l'être humain." *Théâtre Aujourd'hui. 3: L'univers scénique de Beckett*. Ed. Jean-Claude Lallias and Jean-Jacques Arnault. Paris: CND Press, 1994. 64–67.

Fisher, James. *The Theatre of Yesterday and Tomorrow: Commedia Dell'Arte on the Modern Stage*. New York: Edwin Mellon Press, 1992.

Foucault, Michel. "Of Other Spaces." *Diacritics* 16.1 (Spring 1986). 22–27.

Foucré, Michèle. *Le Geste et la parole dans le théâtre de Samuel Beckett*. Paris: Nizet, 1970.

Freud, Sigmund. *An Outline of Psychoanalysis*. Trans. J. Strachey. New York: W. W. Norton, 1949.

Fuchs, Elinor. *The Death of Character: Perspectives on Theater after Modernism*. Bloomington: Indiana University Press, 1996.

Garner, Stanton B., Jr. *Bodied Spaces: Phenomenology and Performance in Contemporary Drama*. Ithaca, N.Y.: Cornell University Press, 1994.

Gilles, Annie. *Images de la marionnette dans la littérature*. Nancy, France: Presses Universitaires de Nancy, 1993.

Gontarski, S. E. *The Intent of Undoing in Samuel Beckett's Dramatic Texts*. Bloomington: Indiana University Press, 1985.

Gordon, Mel. *Lazzi: The Comic Routines of the Commedia dell'Arte*. New York: Performing Arts Journal Publications, 1983.

Green, Martin, and John Swann. *The Triumph of Pierrot*. 1986. Revised ed., University Park: Pennsylvania State University Press, 1993.

Greimas, A. J. "Pour une sémiotique topologique." *Sémiotique de l'espace*. Ed. Jean Zeitoun. Paris: Denoël/Gonthier, 1979. 11–43.

Grossvogel, David. *Four Playwrights and a Postscript*. Ithaca, N.Y.: Cornell University Press, 1962.

———. *Mystery and Its Fictions: From Oedipus to Agatha Christie*. Baltimore: Johns Hopkins University Press, 1979.

Gruber, William E. *Missing Persons: Character and Characterization in Modern Drama*. Athens: University of Georgia Press, 1994.

Hale, Jane Alison. *The Broken Window: Beckett's Dramatic Perspective*. West Lafayette, Ind.: Purdue University Press, 1987.

Handke, Peter. *Kaspar. Peter Handke. Plays: 1.* Trans. Michael Roloff. London: Methuen, 1997. 51–141.

———. *Peter Handke. Plays: 1.* Trans. Michael Roloff. London: Methuen, 1997.

———. *The Ride across Lake Constance. Peter Handke. Plays: 1.* Trans. Michael Roloff. London: Methuen, 1997. 163–233.

Hauck, Gerhard. *Reductionism in Drama and the Theatre: The Case of Samuel Beckett.* Potomac, Md.: Scripta Humanistica, 1992.

Heidegger, Martin. *Basic Writings.* Ed. David Farrell Krell. New York: Harper and Row, 1977.

Holman, C. Hugh and William Harmon. *A Handbook to Literature.* 6th ed. New York: Macmillan, 1992.

Holquist, Michael, ed.. *The Dialogic Imagination.* By M. M. Bakhtin. Trans. Caryl Emerson and Michael Holquist. Austin: Texas University Press, 1981.

Homan, Sidney. "*Endgame:* The Playwright Completes Himself." *Samuel Beckett's Endgame.* Ed. Harold Bloom. New Haven: Chelsea House, 1988. 123–46.

Hubert, Marie-Claude. "The Evolution of the Body in Beckett's Theatre." *Journal of Beckett Studies* 4.1 (1994). 55–65.

———. *Histoire de la scène occidentale: de l'Antiquité à nos jours.* Paris: Armand Colin, 1992.

———. *Langage et corps fantasmé dans le théâtre des années cinquante (Ionesco-Beckett-Adamov).* Paris: Librairie José Corti, 1987.

Hugo, Victor. Preface. *Oliver Cromwell.* By Hugo. *Dramas.* Vol. 9. Trans. I. G. Burnham. Philadelphia: George Barrie and Son, 1896.

Husserl, Edmund. *Ideas: General Introduction to Pure Phenomenology.* Trans. R. W. Boyce Gibson. New York: Macmillan, 1962.

Ionesco, Eugene. *Amédée ou Comment s'en débarrasser. Théâtre complet.* Paris: Gallimard, 1991. 261–343.

———. *The Chairs. Four Plays by Eugène Ionesco.* Trans. Donald M. Allen. 1958. New York: Grove Weidenfeld, 1982. 111–60.

———. *Exit the King.* Trans. Donald Watson. New York: John Calder, 1963.

———. *Le Roi se meurt.* Paris: Hatier, 1985.

Issacharoff, Michael. "Répétition et création." *Théâtre et création.* Ed. Emmanuel Jacquart. Paris: Honoré Champion, 1994.

———. "Space in Drama." *Discourse of Performance.* Stanford, Calif.: Stanford University Press, 1989. 55–67.

———. "Space and Reference in Drama." *Poetics Today* 2.3 (Spring 1981). 211–24.

Jacquart, Emmanuel. *Le théâtre de la dérision: Beckett, Ionesco, Adamov.* Paris: Gallimard, 1974.

Jameson, Fredric. "The Cultural Logic of Late Capitalism." *Postmodernism, or, the Cultural Logic of Late Capitalism.* Durham, N.C.: Duke University Press, 1991. 1–55.

Jarry, Alfred. "Discours d'Alfred Jarry." *Tout Ubu.* Paris: Librairie Générale Française, 1985. 19–21.

———. "De l'inutilité du théâtre au théâtre." *Tout Ubu.* Paris: Librairie Générale Française, 1985. 139–45.

Jeffers, Jennifer M. "The Image of Thought: Achromatics in O'Keeffe and Beckett." *Mosaic.* 29.4. (Dec. 1996). 59–78.

———. "A Sublime Event: Gordon Craig's Über-marionette in Samuel Beckett's Late Drama." *Text & Presentation: Journal of the Comparative Drama Conference* 18 (1997). 58–63.

Johnson, Mark. *The Body in the Mind: The Bodily Basis of Meaning, Imagination, and Reason.* Chicago: University of Chicago Press, 1987.

Jones, Louisa E. *Sad Clowns and Pale Pierrots: Literature and the Popular Comic Arts in 19th-Century France.* Lexington, Ky.: French Forum, 1984.

Kadivar, Pedro. "Poétique de l'immobilité." *Théâtre Public* 129 (May–June 1996). 12–16.

Kalb, Jonathan. *Beckett in Performance.* London: Cambridge University Press, 1989.

Kennard, Joseph Spencer. *Masks and Marionettes.* New York: Kennikat Press, 1967.

Kennedy, Andrew K. *Six Dramatists in Search of a Language.* Cambridge: Cambridge University Press, 1975.

Kenner, Hugh. "Life in the Box." *Samuel Beckett's Endgame.* Ed. Harold Bloom. New Haven: Chelsea House, 1988. 41–48.

Kirby, Michael. *A Formalist Theatre.* Philadelphia: University of Pennsylvania Press, 1987.

Klaver, Elizabeth. "Ionesco and Textual Madness." *Themes in Drama: Madness in Drama.* Ed. James Redmond. Cambridge: Cambridge University Press, 1993. 183–90.

Kleist, Heinrich von. "On the Marionette Theater." Trans. Christian-Albrecht Gollub. *German Romantic Criticism.* Ed. A. Leslie Willson. New York: Continuum, 1982.

Knowlson, James, and John Pilling. *Frescoes of the Skull: The Later Prose and Drama of Samuel Beckett.* London: John Calder, 1979.

Kuhn, Tom. "Introduction." *Peter Handke. Plays 1.* London: Methuen, 1997. ix–xxiv.

La Force de l'habitude. By Thomas Bernhard. Dir. Jacques Kraemer. Théâtre de la Tempête, Paris, France, 1986.

Lacan, Jacques. "L'Instance de la lettre dans l'inconscient." *Ecrits 1.* Paris: Seuil, 1966.

Lallias, Jean-Claude, and Jean-Jacques Arnault. *"En attendant Godot." Théâtre Aujourd'hui. 3: L'univers scénique de Beckett.* Paris: CND Press, 1994. 36–51.

Langbaum, Robert. *The Mysteries of Identity: A Theme in Modern Literature.* Chicago: University of Chicago Press, 1982.

Lawley, Paul. "Counterpoint, Absence and the Medium in Beckett's *Not I.*" *Modern Drama* 26 (December 1983). 407–14.

Lepinois, Gérard. *L'Action de l'espace.* Paris: Deyrolle, 1992.

Levy, Shimon. *Samuel Beckett's Self-Referential Drama.* New York: St. Martin's Press, 1990.

Littré, E. *Dictionnaire de la langue française.* Paris: Librairie Hachette, 1889.

Logie, Lea. "Developing a Physical Vocabulary for the Contemporary Actor." *New Theater Quarterly* 11.43 (1995). 230–40.

Lyons, Charles. "Character and Theatrical Space." *The Theatrical Space.* Ed. James Redmond. Cambridge: Cambridge University Press, 1987. 27–44.

MacDonald, Erik. *Theater at the Margins: Text and the Post-Structural Stage.* Ann Arbor: University of Michigan Press, 1993.

Madden, David. *Harlequin's Stick, Charlie's Cane.* Bowling Green, Ohio: Bowling Green University Popular Press, 1975.

Maeterlinck, Maurice. "Menus propos: Le Théâtre." *La Jeune Belgique* (September 1890). 331–36.

———. "Un Théâtre d'Androïdes." *Annales—Fondation Maurice Maeterlinck.* Vol. 23 (1977). 7–21.

Magnin, Charles. *Histoire des marionnettes en Europe.* Paris: Editions Michel Lévy Frères, 1852.

Malachy, Thérèse. *La mort en situation dans le théâtre contemporain.* Paris: Nizet, 1982.

Matoré, Georges. *L'espace humain.* Paris: Editions du Vieux Colombier, 1966.

Matthews, J. H. *Theatre in Dada and Surrealism.* Syracuse: Syracuse University Press, 1974.

Mayberry, Bob. *Theatre of Discord: Dissonance in Beckett, Albee, and Pinter.* Cranbury, N.J.: Associated University Presses, 1989.

McGuinness, Patrick. "From Page to Stage and Back: Mallarmé and Symbolist Theatre." *Romance Studies* 26 (Autumn 1995). 23–39.

———. "Ioneso and Symbolist Theatre: Revolution and Restitution in the Avant-Garde." *Nottingham French Studies.* 35.1 (Spring 1996). 108–19.

Merleau-Ponty, Maurice. *Phenomenology of Perception.* Trans. Colin Smith. New York: Humanities, 1962.

Nicoll, Allardyce. *The World of Harlequin: A Critical Study of the Commedia dell'Arte.* Cambridge: Cambridge University Press, 1963.

Nietzsche, Friedrich. *The Birth of Tragedy.* New York: Vintage Books, 1967.

Nodier, Charles. "Les Marionnettes." *Les Mains de lumière: Anthologie des écrits sur l'art de la marionnette.* Ed. Didier Plassard. Charleville-Mézières, France: Editions Institut International de la Marionnette, 1996. 71–78.

Obaldia, René de. *Classe terminale. Théâtre V.* Paris: Bernard Grasset, 1973. 169–216.

Oppenheim, Lois. "Female Subjectivity in *Not I* and *Rockaby.*" *Women in Beckett: Performance and Critical Perspectives.* Ed. Linda Ben-Zvi. Urbana: University of Illinois Press, 1990. 217–27.

Oreglia, Giacomo. *The Commedia dell'arte.* Trans. Lovett F. Edwards. New York: Hill and Wang, 1968.

Pavis, Patrice. "Acting." *Encyclopedia of Languages and Linguistics.* Edinburgh: Pergamon Press, 1993. 16–20.

———. *L'Analyse des spectacles.* Paris: Nathan, 1996.

———. "The Classical Heritage of Modern Drama: The Case of Postmodern Theatre." *Theatre at the Crossroads of Culture.* Trans. Loren Kruger. London: Routledge, 1992. 48–74.

———. *Dictionnaire du théâtre.* Paris: Dunod, 1996.

———. "L'Héritage classique du théâtre post-moderne." *Journal of Dramatic Theory and Criticism.* 3.1 (Fall 1988). 217–32.

———. "Le Jeu de l'acteur." *Protée: théories et pratiques sémiotiques.* 21:3 (Fall 1993). 56–68.

———. "Parcours au bout du sens." *Voix et images de la scène: pour une sémiologie de la réception.* Lille, France: Presses Universitaires de Lille, 1985. 221–30.

———. "Du texte à la scène: un enfantement difficile." *Théâtre/Public* 79 (1988): 27–35.

Pinget, Robert. *Abel et Bela.* Arles, France: Actes Sud (Répliques), 1992.

Pinter, Harold. *Landscape. Complete Works.* Vol. 3. New York: Grove Weidenfeld, 1978. 173–98.

———. *Monologue. Complete Works.* Vol. 4. New York: Grove Weidenfeld, 1981. 269–77.

———. *The Room. The Birthday Party and The Room: Two Plays by Harold Pinter.* Revised ed. New York: Grove Press, 1968.

———. *Silence. Complete Works.* Vol. 3. New York: Grove Weidenfeld, 1978. 199–219.

Plassard, Didier, Ed. *Les Mains de lumière: anthologie des écrits sur l'art de la marionnette.* Charleville-Mézières, France: Editions Institut International de la Marionnette, 1996.

Podehl, Enno. "Ceux qui touchent le ciel: la perception spatiale du manipulateur." *PUCK* 4 ("La marionnette et les autres arts"). Charleville-Mezières, France: Institut International de la Marionnette, 1991. 31–38.

Posner, Donald. *Antoine Watteau*. Ithaca, N.Y.: Cornell University Press, 1984.

Robert, Paul. *Dictionnaire de la langue française*. Paris: Nouveau Littré, 1965.

Rockaby. By Samuel Beckett. Dir. Alan Schneider. Film by D. A. Pennebaker and Chris Hegedus, 1981.

Rowell, Margrit, ed. *Antonin Artaud: Works on Paper*. New York: The Museum of Modern Art, 1996.

Salino, Brigitte. Rev. of *The Force of Habit* (*La Force de l'habitude*), by Thomas Bernhard. Dir. André Engel. Scenic designer Nicky Rieti. Maison de la Culture de Bobigny, Paris, France. *Le Monde* 1 March 1997. 29.

Sarrazac, Jean Pierre. *Théâtres intimes*. Arles, France: Actes Sud, 1989.

Schechner, Richard. *Environmental Theatre*. New York: Hawthorne, 1973.

Schmitt, Olivier. "Un entretien avec Giorgio Strehler." *Le Monde*, Dimanche–lundi, 10 July, 1995. 8.

Schneider, Pierre. *The World of Watteau: 1684–1721*. New York: Time Inc., 1967.

Segal, Charles. *Dionysiac Poetics and Euripides' Bacchae*. Princeton, N.J.: Princeton University Press, 1982.

Segel, Harold B. *Pinocchio's Progeny: Puppets, Marionettes, Automatons, and Robots in Modernist and Avant-Garde Drama*. Baltimore: Johns Hopkins University Press, 1995.

Serreau, Geneviève. *Histoire du «nouveau théâtre»*. Paris: Gallimard, 1966.

Shepard, Sam. *Action. Angel City and Other Plays. Sam Shepard*. New York: Urizen Books, 1976. 123–45.

———. *A Lie of the Mind*. New York: Dramatists Play Service, 1986.

Sollers, Philippe. *L'écriture et l'expérience des limites*. Paris: Editions du Seuil, 1968.

Sontag, Susan. "Artaud." *Antonin Artaud: Selected Writings*. Ed. Susan Sontag. Trans. Helen Weaver. Berkeley: University of California Press, 1988. xvii–lix.

States, Bert O. *Great Reckonings in Little Rooms: On the Phenomenology of Theater*. Berkeley: University of California Press, 1985.

———. "Performance as Metaphor." *Theatre Journal*. Vol. 48:1 (March 1996). 1–26.

Stivale, Charles J. "Of Schmürz and Men: Boris Vian's *Les bâtisseurs d'empire*." *Cincinnati Romance Review* 7 (1988). 97–112.

Stoppard, Tom. *Jumpers*. London: Faber and Faber, 1972.

———. *Rosencrantz and Guildenstern Are Dead*. New York: Grove Press, 1967.

Storey, Robert F. *Pierrot: A Critical History of a Mask*. Princeton, N.J.: Princeton University Press, 1978.

Strehler, Giorgio. "Un entretien avec Giorgio Strehler." With Olivier Schmitt. *Le Monde*, Dimanche–lundi, 10 July 1995. 8.

Styan, J. L. *Modern Drama in Theory and Practice*. Vol. 2: *Symbolism, Surrealism and the Absurd*. Vol. 3: *Expressionism and Epic Theatre*. Cambridge: Cambridge University Press, 1981.

Surel-Tupin, Monique. "L'Espace théâtral chez Copeau." *Théâtre et cinéma. Années vingt. Une quête de la modernité*. Ed. Claudine Amiard-Chevrel. Lausanne: L'Age d'Homme, 1990. 73–86.

Suvin, Darko. "Approach to Topoanalysis and to the Paradigmatics of Dramaturgic Space." *Poetics Today* 8.2 (1987). 311–34.

Szondi, Peter. *Theory of the Modern Drama*. Ed. and Trans. Michael Hays. Minneapolis: University of Minnesota Press, 1987.

Taviani, Ferdinando. "Positions du masque dans la commédia dell'arte." *Le Masque: Du rite au théâtre.* Ed. Odette Aslan and Denis Bablet. Paris: Editions du CNRS, 1985. 119–36.

Todorov, Tzvetan. *Théorie du symbole.* Paris: Seuil, 1977.

Tonelli, Franco. *L'Esthétique de la cruauté.* Paris: Nizet, 1972.

Turner, Victor. *From Ritual to Theatre: The Human Seriousness of Play.* New York: PAJ, 1982.

Ubersfeld, Anne. *L'Ecole du spectateur: Lire le théâtre 2.* Paris: Editions Sociales, 1982.

———. *Lire le théâtre 1.* Paris: Editions Sociales, 1982.

———. "Pedagogics of Theatre." *Approaching Theatre.* Ed. André Helbo. Bloomington: Indiana University Press, 1991. 135–64.

Valency, Maurice. *The End of the World: An Introduction to Contemporary Drama.* New York: Oxford University Press, 1980.

Vian, Boris. *Les Bâtisseurs d'empire.* Paris: J.-J. Pauvert, 1965.

———. *Empire Builders.* Trans. Simon Watson Taylor. New York: Grove Press, 1967.

Vidal, Mary. *Watteau's Painted Conversations: Art, Literature, and Talk in Seventeenth- and Eighteenth-Century France.* New Haven, Conn.: Yale University Press, 1992.

Vince, Ronald. "The Aristotelian Theatrical Paradigm as Cultural-Historical Construct." *Theatre Research International.* 22.1 (Spring 1997 Supplement). 38–47.

Voda Capusan, Maria. "Theatre and Reflexivity." *Poetics* 13 (1984).

Voloshinov, V. N. *Freudianism: A Critical Sketch.* Trans. I. R. Titunik. Bloomington: Indiana University Press, 1987.

———. *Marxism and the Philosophy of Language.* Trans. Ladislav Matejka and I. R. Titunik. Cambridge, Mass.: Harvard University Press, 1986.

Waiting for Godot. By Samuel Beckett. Dir. J. R. Tompkins. Scenic Designer Brynna C. Bloomfield. University of Louisville's Belknap Theatre. Louisville, Kentucky. March 6, 1992.

Walker, Craig Stewart. "Reckoning with States on the Phenomenology of Theatre." *Journal of Dramatic Theory and Criticism* 11.2. 65–83.

Wiles, Timothy J. *The Theater Event: Modern Theories of Performance.* Chicago: University of Chicago Press, 1980.

Wittig, Susan. "Toward a Semiotic Theory of Drama." *Educational Theatre Journal* (Dec. 1974). 441–54.

Worthen, W. B. "Disciplines of the Text/Sites of Performance" *The Drama Review.* 39.1 (Spring 1995). 13–28.

———. "Of Actors and Automata: Hieroglyphics and Modernism." *Journal of Dramatic Theory and Criticism* 9.1 (Fall 1994). 3–19.

———. *Modern Drama and the Rhetoric of Theater.* Berkeley: University of California Press, 1992.

Zinder, David G. *The Surrealist Connection: An Approach to a Surrealist Aesthetic of Theatre.* Ann Arbor: University of Michigan Press, 1980.

Page numbers in *italics* indicate illustrations.

LES ESSIF
is Associate Professor of Modern Languages and Literatures
at the University of Tennessee, Knoxville.